MW00357115

printer handbook

second edition

printer handbook

second edition

mark l. chambers

IDG Books Worldwide, Inc.
An International Data Group Company

Foster City, CA ■ Chicago, IL ■ Indianapolis, IN ■ New York, NY

Printer Handbook, 2nd Edition

Published by
IDG Books Worldwide, Inc.
An International Data Group Company
919 E. Hillsdale Blvd., Suite 400
Foster City, CA 94404
www.idgbooks.com (IDG Books Worldwide Web site)

Copyright © 2000 IDG Books Worldwide, Inc. All rights reserved. No part of this book, including interior design, cover design, and icons, may be reproduced or transmitted in any form, by any means (electronic, photocopying, recording, or otherwise) without the prior written permission of the publisher.

ISBN: 0-7645-3530-7

Printed in the United States of America

10 9 8 7 6 5 4 3 2 1

1O/RW/RQ/QQ/FC

Distributed in the United States by IDG Books Worldwide, Inc.

Distributed by CDG Books Canada Inc. for Canada; by Transworld Publishers Limited in the United Kingdom; by IDG Norge Books for Norway; by IDG Sweden Books for Sweden; by IDG Books Australia Publishing Corporation Pty. Ltd. for Australia and New Zealand; by TransQuest Publishers Pte Ltd. for Singapore, Malaysia, Thailand, Indonesia, and Hong Kong; by Gotop Information Inc. for Taiwan; by ICG Muse, Inc. for Japan; by Intersoft for South Africa; by Eyrolles for France; by International Thomson Publishing for Germany, Austria, and Switzerland; by Distribuidora Cuspide for Argentina; by LR International for Brazil; by Galileo Libros for Chile; by Ediciones ZETA S.C.R. Ltda. for Peru; by WS Computer Publishing Corporation, Inc., for the Philippines; by Contemporanea de Ediciones for Venezuela; by Express Computer Distributors for the Caribbean and West Indies; by Micronesia Media Distributor, Inc. for Micronesia; by Chips Computadoras S.A. de C.V. for Mexico; by Editorial Norma de Panama S.A. for Panama; by American Bookshops for Finland.

For general information on IDG Books Worldwide's books in the U.S., please call our Consumer Customer Service department at 800-762-2974. For reseller information, including discounts and premium sales, please call our Reseller Customer Service department at 800-434-3422.

For information on where to purchase IDG Books Worldwide's books outside the U.S., please contact our International Sales department at 317-572-3993 or fax 317-572-4002.

For consumer information on foreign language translations, please contact our Customer Service department at 800-434-3422, fax 317-572-4002, or e-mail rights@ idgbooks.com.

For information on licensing foreign or domestic rights, please phone +1-650-653-7098.

For sales inquiries and special prices for bulk quantities, please contact our Order Services department at 800-434-3422 or write to the address above.

For information on using IDG Books Worldwide's books in the classroom or for ordering examination copies, please contact our Educational Sales department at 800-434-2086 or fax 317-572-4005.

For press review copies, author interviews, or other publicity information, please contact our Public Relations department at 650-653-7000 or fax 650-653-7500.

For authorization to photocopy items for corporate, personal, or educational use, please contact Copyright Clearance Center, 222 Rosewood Drive, Danvers, MA 01923, or fax 978-750-4470.

Library of Congress Cataloging-in-Publication Data

Chambers, Mark.
    Hewlett-Packard official printer handbook /
Mark L. Chambers.–2nd ed.
        p.   cm.
    ISBN 0-7645-3530-7 (alk. paper)
    1. Computer printers–Handbooks, manuals, etc.
I. Title.
TK7887.7.C48   2000
004.7'7–dc21   00-063364

LIMIT OF LIABILITY/DISCLAIMER OF WARRANTY: THE PUBLISHER AND AUTHOR HAVE USED THEIR BEST EFFORTS IN PREPARING THIS BOOK. THE PUBLISHER AND AUTHOR MAKE NO REPRESENTATIONS OR WARRANTIES WITH RESPECT TO THE ACCURACY OR COMPLETENESS OF THE CONTENTS OF THIS BOOK AND SPECIFICALLY DISCLAIM ANY IMPLIED WARRANTIES OF MERCHANTABILITY OR FITNESS FOR A PARTICULAR PURPOSE. THERE ARE NO WARRANTIES WHICH EXTEND BEYOND THE DESCRIPTIONS CONTAINED IN THIS PARAGRAPH. NO WARRANTY MAY BE CREATED OR EXTENDED BY SALES REPRESENTATIVES OR WRITTEN SALES MATERIALS. THE ACCURACY AND COMPLETENESS OF THE INFORMATION PROVIDED HEREIN AND THE OPINIONS STATED HEREIN ARE NOT GUARANTEED OR WARRANTED TO PRODUCE ANY PARTICULAR RESULTS, AND THE ADVICE AND STRATEGIES CONTAINED HEREIN MAY NOT BE SUITABLE FOR EVERY INDIVIDUAL. NEITHER THE PUBLISHER NOR AUTHOR SHALL BE LIABLE FOR ANY LOSS OF PROFIT OR ANY OTHER COMMERCIAL DAMAGES, INCLUDING BUT NOT LIMITED TO SPECIAL, INCIDENTAL, CONSEQUENTIAL, OR OTHER DAMAGES. FULFILLMENT OF EACH COUPON OFFER IS THE RESPONSIBILITY OF THE OFFEROR.

Trademarks: All brand names and product names used in this book are trade names, service marks, trademarks, or registered trademarks of their respective owners. IDG Books Worldwide is not associated with any product or vendor mentioned in this book.

 is a registered trademark or trademark under exclusive license to IDG Books Worldwide, Inc. from International Data Group, Inc. in the United States and/or other countries.

 HP and the HP logo are registered trademarks of Hewlett-Packard Company.

ABOUT IDG BOOKS WORLDWIDE

Welcome to the world of IDG Books Worldwide.

IDG Books Worldwide, Inc., is a subsidiary of International Data Group, the world's largest publisher of computer-related information and the leading global provider of information services on information technology. IDG was founded more than 30 years ago by Patrick J. McGovern and now employs more than 9,000 people worldwide. IDG publishes more than 290 computer publications in over 75 countries. More than 90 million people read one or more IDG publications each month.

Launched in 1990, IDG Books Worldwide is today the #1 publisher of best-selling computer books in the United States. We are proud to have received eight awards from the Computer Press Association in recognition of editorial excellence and three from Computer Currents' First Annual Readers' Choice Awards. Our best-selling ...For Dummies® series has more than 50 million copies in print with translations in 31 languages. IDG Books Worldwide, through a joint venture with IDG's Hi-Tech Beijing, became the first U.S. publisher to publish a computer book in the People's Republic of China. In record time, IDG Books Worldwide has become the first choice for millions of readers around the world who want to learn how to better manage their businesses.

Our mission is simple: Every one of our books is designed to bring extra value and skill-building instructions to the reader. Our books are written by experts who understand and care about our readers. The knowledge base of our editorial staff comes from years of experience in publishing, education, and journalism — experience we use to produce books to carry us into the new millennium. In short, we care about books, so we attract the best people. We devote special attention to details such as audience, interior design, use of icons, and illustrations. And because we use an efficient process of authoring, editing, and desktop publishing our books electronically, we can spend more time ensuring superior content and less time on the technicalities of making books.

You can count on our commitment to deliver high-quality books at competitive prices on topics you want to read about. At IDG Books Worldwide, we continue in the IDG tradition of delivering quality for more than 30 years. You'll find no better book on a subject than one from IDG Books Worldwide.

John J. Kilcullen
John Kilcullen
Chairman and CEO
IDG Books Worldwide, Inc.

Eighth Annual Computer Press Awards ≥ 1992

Ninth Annual Computer Press Awards ≥ 1993

Tenth Annual Computer Press Awards ≥ 1994

Eleventh Annual Computer Press Awards ≥ 1995

IDG is the world's leading IT media, research and exposition company. Founded in 1964, IDG had 1997 revenues of $2.05 billion and has more than 9,000 employees worldwide. IDG offers the widest range of media options that reach IT buyers in 75 countries representing 95% of worldwide IT spending. IDG's diverse product and services portfolio spans six key areas including print publishing, online publishing, expositions and conferences, market research, education and training, and global marketing services. More than 90 million people read one or more of IDG's 290 magazines and newspapers, including IDG's leading global brands — Computerworld, PC World, Network World, Macworld and the Channel World family of publications. IDG Books Worldwide is one of the fastest-growing computer book publishers in the world, with more than 700 titles in 36 languages. The "...For Dummies®" series alone has more than 50 million copies in print. IDG offers online users the largest network of technology-specific Web sites around the world through IDG.net (http://www.idg.net), which comprises more than 225 targeted Web sites in 55 countries worldwide. International Data Corporation (IDC) is the world's largest provider of information technology data, analysis and consulting, with research centers in over 41 countries and more than 400 research analysts worldwide. IDG World Expo is a leading producer of more than 168 globally branded conferences and expositions in 35 countries including E3 (Electronic Entertainment Expo), Macworld Expo, ComNet, Windows World Expo, ICE (Internet Commerce Expo), Agenda, DEMO, and Spotlight. IDG's training subsidiary, ExecuTrain, is the world's largest computer training company, with more than 230 locations worldwide and 785 training courses. IDG Marketing Services helps industry-leading IT companies build international brand recognition by developing global integrated marketing programs via IDG's print, online and exposition products worldwide. Further information about the company can be found at www.idg.com. 1/26/00

Credits

Acquisitions Editors
Kathy Yankton
John Gravener

Project Editor
Marti Paul

Technical Editor
Susan Glinert

Copy Editor
Cindy Lai

Proof Editor
Patsy Owens

Project Coordinator
Marcos Vergara
Danette Nurse

Graphics and Production Specialists
Bob Bihlmayer
Jude Levinson
Michael Lewis
Victor Pérez-Varela
Ramses Ramirez

Quality Control Technician
Dina F Quan

Book Designer
Kurt Krames

Illustrator
Clint Lahnen
Gabriele McCann

Proofreading and Indexing
York Production Services

Cover Image
© Noma/Images.com

About the Author

Mark L Chambers has been a computer consultant, technical writer, and hardware technician for more than fifteen years. His first book, *Running a Perfect BBS*, was published in 1994. Mark is now a full-time author, writing several books a year and spending entirely too much time on the Internet. His other books include *Computer Gamer's Bible*, *Teach Yourself the iMac Visually*, *The Hewlett-Packard Official Recordable CD Handbook*, *Building a PC for Dummies*, *Recordable CD Bible*, *Official Netscape Guide to Web Animation*, and *The Windows 98 Optimizing and Troubleshooting Little Black Book*. You can reach Mark at http://www.geocities.com/SiliconValley/Bay/4373/.

To Mike Danna, Steve Stewart, and Mark Case . . .
three friends for a lifetime.

You can always depend on me.

Foreword

For over twenty years, a collaboration of inspired minds from the HP labs, research and development, and engineering teams has been consistently reinventing popular thinking of what a printer can do. In the last couple of years alone, we have taken the printer out of the office, untethered it from the PC, and transformed it into a Web appliance.

With the Internet coming into the homes of everyone, the world is a smaller place. Pictures, images, and files can now be sent from almost anywhere to be printed in dens, home offices, and bedrooms around the world. To harness this Internet revolution and make it work for you, HP has pushed the boundaries of printing with technological advancements in print quality and speed, lower ownership costs, and wireless, Internet, and photo-quality printing.

From color inkjet and photo printers that create picture quality to rival traditional film processing, to LaserJet and all-in-one multifunction printers that are perfect small-business productivity tools, HP provides the world's favorite printers.

This book is an outstanding read for those looking for help in choosing a printer or for advice on what they can do with their printer. It takes the reader on an outstanding "under the hood" journey of the remarkable technology that makes up an HP printer. It is also a veritable feast of advice, tips, and instructions on how to get the most out of your printing experience.

Enjoy!

Pradeep Jotwani
Vice *President, Hewlett-Packard Company*
President, Consumer Business Organization

Preface

In the early days of personal computing, a printer was a very expensive peripheral that was usually reserved for a home office. If you could afford one, your choice was limited, which generally made the selection process very easy. The printers were limited, as well; they produced black text (or very simple graphics) at the speed of a fast touch typist, and some could print labels and envelopes. Case closed.

Within 15 years, everything has changed for the better. Printers are no longer just clunky home office peripherals that only professionals can afford: no personal computer system sold today is considered complete without a printer that can produce dazzling color or high-quality black text. With a huge assortment of different printing materials — including greeting cards, T-shirts, business cards, buttons, and banners, just to name a few — printers have suddenly become a focus of hobbyists, kids, parents, and educators as well.

However, there is one downside to all these enhancements and the popularity of the modern computer printer — confusion! If you're a newcomer to the world of printers, prepare to be swamped by all of the technobabble that surrounds them today, including a wealth of strange acronyms and confusing standards. I can tell you from personal experience, it's practically a full-time job just keeping tabs on the latest "cutting edge" hardware and software.

If you're in the market for a computer printer or if you'd simply like to learn more about them, you'll be faced with dozens of competing brands using several different methods to produce documents, including inkjet, laser, thermal, and dot-matrix printing technology. Each model offers specifications to compare, but which of those figures are important? How fast a printer do you need? Color or monochrome? Parallel port or USB? And that's just the beginning: once you've bought your printer, how do you configure it, and what can you create?

This book was designed and written especially to answer those questions, and many more. You'll find complete information you need about personal computer printers here, including how to shop for a printer, how to set it up and maintain it, and how to produce all sorts of printed items with professional results.

Who Should Read This Book?

Printer Handbook, 2nd Edition was designed for any owner of a PC or Macintosh who needs information about today's personal computer printers. It is especially valuable for readers who are

- Computer novices or have a basic knowledge of personal computers; no prior experience with any program or operating system is required

- Currently shopping for a printer or who have just bought one

- Interested in the technical details of inkjet or laser printing

- Buying or using an "all-in-one" multifunction unit

- Experiencing problems with installing, configuring, or using a computer printer

Although this book uses various Hewlett-Packard printers as examples for step-by-step projects, it is not specifically geared toward owners of Hewlett-Packard printers — so no matter what brand or model of personal computer printer you own, you'll benefit from the information you'll find here.

Helpful Icons

In this book you find four icons that alert you to information that supplements the text.

Tip

A tip icon signifies useful information that can save you time, money, or aggravation.

Note

A note icon highlights extra information about the subject.

Cross-Reference

A cross-reference icon points you to a related discussion elsewhere in the book.

Warning

A warning icon alerts you to a potential problem associated with the topic being discussed.

How This Book Is Organized

As you scan the contents, you'll notice that separate chapters are devoted to inkjet, laser, and all-in-one units. If you've decided to buy a specific type of printer (or you've already bought a printer and you'd like to learn all about it), this organization makes it easy for you to focus on the features, configuration, and maintenance for that type.

The chapters are organized into the following four parts:

- **Part I, "Printer Basics,"** begins with an overview of the printers available on the market today (inkjet printers, laser printers, and all-in-one units) and discusses the parallel, serial, and USB ports that you use to connect printers to your computer. I show you how you can determine your needs and select the right printer. Finally, I discuss in detail the three major types of printing hardware: inkjet, laser, and all-in-one units.

- **Part II, "Printer Connections,"** discusses the details of connecting your printing hardware to your computer, including unpacking your unit, cabling, testing, installing a driver, and configuring your printer. You'll find tips and tricks for optimizing the performance of your printer under Windows 98 and Me, Windows NT and 2000, Linux, and Mac OS. Printer networking, printer sharing, and switching systems are also covered in this part.

- **Part III, "Having Fun with Your Printer,"** introduces you to the world of fonts: where to find them, how to install them, and how to use them in your printing projects. You'll read about the wide range of creative print materials you can use, including T-shirts, greeting cards, and much more. You'll learn how to print images from Web pages and how to use color effectively. Finally, I review some representative software packages to help you put your ideas to work.

- **Part IV, "Printer Projects,"** offers a variety of projects that lead you step-by-step through the procedures mentioned in earlier chapters. The "hands-on" chapters in this part show you how to install, configure, maintain, and use your printer, as well as guide you through a number of fun, creative projects.

The book also features two helpful appendixes with information on

- Troubleshooting your Hewlett-Packard printer (with tips, suggestions, and answers to frequently asked questions directly from the Hewlett-Packard Technical Support department)

- Printer manufacturers, printing software, and accessories

At the back of the book you'll find a glossary to help you keep track of printing standards, terms, and even those pesky acronyms that computer folks like so much.

Where to Go from Here

Are you ready to dive into the world of the computer printer? I recommend that you follow one of these four "paths" through the book:

- *If you're considering buying a printer or you're interested in what makes them tick,* start with Chapter 1.

- *If you've already purchased a printer and you're ready to install it,* jump to Chapter 6. Once you've successfully installed it, you can read the rest of the book to learn how to use and optimize your printer.

- *If you're familiar with your printer,* begin with Chapter 9. Once you've learned about all the printing possibilities, you can read the rest of the book at your leisure.

- *If you'd like detailed instructions on how to accomplish a certain task or procedure,* go to the appropriate chapter in Part IV.

Acknowledgments

When you've finished a book of this size, it's not hard at all to find people who you need to thank; the only problem is finding the remaining energy to type these important paragraphs.

First, a heartfelt vote of thanks to everyone at Hewlett-Packard who provided me with specifications, driver software, product images, test units, and troubleshooting suggestions for the printing hardware I've mentioned in this book — and often for printer models that hadn't even passed the beta test stage. In particular, I'd like to thank Cheri Gavin, who provided me with an invaluable collection of FAQ (Frequently Asked Questions) and technical support material for the hands-on chapters (Part IV) and the troubleshooting guide (Appendix A). Thanks also to the Hewlett-Packard reviewers whose valuable assistance helped improve the manuscript.

Thanks are also due to Jody Cooper, Bryan Chilcutt, Erik Jorgensen, and Mike McGuirk, a group of technically-savvy PC salesmen, programmers, and hardware technicians who practically buried me in tips and warnings from real-world printing encounters.

Next, my sincere appreciation to the hard-working people who helped me polish the rough edges of the manuscript, including Susan Glinert for her technical review of the manuscript. As always, the folks in the Production department at IDG Books Worldwide did a terrific job with the design, layout, and coordination of this book.

And last (but certainly not least), I'd like to thank four editors at IDG Books Worldwide who guided and supported my writing every step of the way: Kathy Yankton and John Gravener, my acquisitions editors; Marti Paul, my project editor; and Cindy Lai, my copy editor. Thanks to their professional help, this luxury liner of a book avoided icebergs and made it safely to home port.

Contents at a Glance

Contents

Part I: Printer Basics   1

Chapter 1: Understanding Printer Technology 3

Part IV: Printer Projects   237

Chapter 12: Font and Fun Projects. 271

Appendix A: Hewlett-Packard Technical Support's Frequently Asked Questions 301

Appendix B: List of Manufacturers. 367

→ Printer Basics

Understanding Printer Technology

IN THIS CHAPTER • Explaining impact printers

  • Using inkjet printers

  • Understanding how laser printers work

  • Evaluating an all-in-one (multifunction) unit

  • Packing up with a portable printer

  • Using thermal and dye-sublimation printers

  • Using large-format printers

  • Understanding the parallel port

  • Using the Universal Serial Bus

  • Explaining bidirectional printing

  • Determining your cable needs

  • Understanding EPP and ECP

Walk into any computer store, or thumb through any computer-related catalog, and you'll probably be struck by the plethora of peripherals (a fancy technoword for external devices) that you can add to your computer. You can attach scanners that copy photographs and documents to electronic files, expensive speaker systems that rival your home stereo, drawing tablets, microphones, video cameras, projectors, trackballs, removable disk drives, 3-D glasses, and even joysticks that actually transmit the jolt of laser blasts and missiles in your favorite games.

No matter what peripherals appear on the scene, however, one particular piece of hardware reigns supreme. Only the computer printer can claim to be the most popular and most useful device you can attach to your computer, as it has been from the early days. In fact, many PC and Macintosh owners don't consider their computer and monitor to be a full "system" until they've added a printer, and a large percentage of new owners buy a printer at the same time they buy their computer and monitor.

You're not just limited to a simple peripheral that only prints: You can also buy one of the new all-in-one units. These *all-in-one* (sometimes called "multifunction") peripherals print, copy, and scan. In addition, some all-in-ones include the functionality of a fax machine. To make things simpler, it's important to remember that the term "printer" may refer either to a simple printer or the printing function of an all-in-one unit.

Today's printers and all-in-one units are inexpensive, reliable, relatively easy to install, and useful for an ever-growing number of activities. They produce stunning color photographs, text, and graphics suitable for the most elegant and formal documents, greeting cards, stickers, signs, brochures, T-shirt transfers . . . the list goes on. You find a computer printer in most schools, libraries, offices, and businesses around the world, as well as most homes with a computer.

Great, so printers are neat machines: but *how do they work?*

That's one question that most computer owners can't answer, no matter how long they've been using their printer. Like the computer itself, most of us see the printer as a "black box" — it uses its own brand of magic to produce words and pictures on paper, and it has to be fed more paper and ink from time to time. However, if you're shopping for a new printer or trying to properly maintain an old printer (or if you're just curious to know what's going on inside that sleek plastic case), it's important to understand how different types of printers work.

In this first chapter, I explain the basics of printer technology: how type and graphics are applied to paper by each type of printer, how the parallel printer port works (and what other devices can use it besides your printer), and why it's so important to select the right printer cable. By the time you're finished, you'll probably know more about printers and printing technology than anyone else in your neighborhood. And if you're considering buying a printer, you'll be armed with the basic knowledge of how these amazing devices work, which you can use in the next chapter. (Plus, you'll have some high-tech information that will amaze your guests at your next technowizard dinner party!)

Impact Printers: Daisywheel and Dot-Matrix

A long time ago, the two types of computer printers, daisywheel and dot-matrix, functioned by impact (like Gutenberg's original printing press). In this section, I discuss daisywheel, print ball, and dot-matrix printers, all of which fall into the *impact printer* class.

The Early Years of Computer Printing

In order to introduce impact printers (which are now largely considered antiques and inferior technology), I should review the early history of the computer. If you're an old-timer like me, you probably remember these events, and perhaps you have one of those antiques sitting in a corner of your garage. The rest of you just have to imagine the noise and fury of a daisywheel impact printer, and wonder why anyone would ever be satisfied with the quality of a dot-matrix printer. As I discuss later, the dot-matrix printer is still around but not much in the home. You still find — and hear — such printers in your supermarket's cash registers, in automatic teller machines, and in some businesses.

The earliest printers were used exclusively on mainframe computers during the late 1960s and early 1970s; in the days before video terminals with monitors, huge printers called *teletype machines* actually provided *all* of the output from the computer, including program output and error messages. Dedicated mainframe printers produced payroll checks, code listings, reports, and the occasional text-only game of Star Trek .

Then it was 1981 and the arrival of the first personal computer from IBM (complete with an honest-to-goodness standard connector called a *parallel* port), and a more compact computer printer made it possible for some lucky human beings to finally retire their typewriters (and even better, their typing erasers and white-out). Because of the incredibly high price of these first word processing and billing systems, owners of the IBM PC tended to be small businesspeople, doctors, lawyers, and other professionals.

As the '80s progressed and less-expensive eight-bit computers such as the Atari and Commodore 64 became more popular, the prices of the original printers dropped as well, and suddenly the average computer hobbyist could afford a personal printer. It's no coincidence that during this time many common applications that you may take for granted today, such as the word processor, the spreadsheet, the paint program, and the personal finance program, also arrived on the scene. These programs required (or benefited greatly) from hard copy output and the printer immediately became the computer add-on of choice — a position it has occupied ever since.

What happened to the impact printer? Like the disappearance of the dinosaurs, a combination of events took their toll on the first personal printers:

- **Superior competitors arrived.** Inkjet and laser printers offered vastly superior print quality, improved reliability, and unheard-of speed.

■ **A cataclysm occurred.** The Macintosh and PCs running Windows provided applications with high-resolution graphics and high-resolution printing, and impact printers just couldn't keep up.

The daisywheel and print ball impact printers are essentially dead and gone, but the dot-matrix printer lives on in many forms (most of them not related to personal computers, though). This section covers the rise and fall of the impact printer, and explains the mechanics of daisywheel, print ball, and dot-matrix printers.

How Do Impact Printers Work?

As you can probably guess from the name, impact printers create characters on paper by striking the paper, much as a typewriter strikes the paper through an ink ribbon each time you press a key. The difference between the different types of impact printers is the method they use to strike the paper.

Daisywheel and print ball printers explained

In fact, the daisywheel printer was practically an electronic typewriter with a parallel port connector. *Daisywheel* printers used a rotating print head shaped like a wheel (complete with spokes) to strike the paper through an ink ribbon, exactly like a typewriter; other impact printers used *print balls*, as shown in Figure 1.1. Each character was fully formed on the print head, and the printer could accept different print balls or daisywheels that included alternate fonts and international and scientific characters.

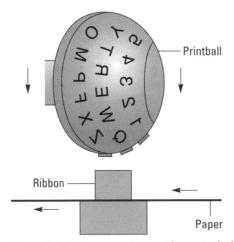

Figure 1.1 An impact printer with a print ball operates almost exactly like a ball typewriter.

Because of this similarity to typewriters, daisywheel and print ball machines became the first *letter-quality* printers (meaning that their output could not be distinguished from a typewriter). Unfortunately, daisywheel printers also suffered from these disadvantages of the typewriter:

■ **Limited graphics capability.** An impact printer was only capable of printing text, with little or no capability of printing graphics or changing fonts. In the days of DOS applications, this wasn't a problem, but as graphics improved on the monitor, people wanted that improvement reflected in their printed output as well.

■ **Large size.** The earliest daisywheel printers were often as large as a family-sized barbecue grill. Although later models eventually shrunk to a little larger than a modern home laser printer, they were still much bigger than the average inkjet sold today.

■ **Slow speed.** Of course, the print ball printer was faster than a human typist, but the top speed for most of these massive printers never surpassed two or three pages per minute. Now we have modern inkjet and laser printers, the fastest of which can print nearly 30 pages per minute!

■ **High noise level.** Much like a typewriter, a daisywheel printer is far too loud for the home or small office environment. In fact, they were often housed in an insulated case — or even another room — to dampen the noise they produced.

Dot-matrix and near–letter quality

The dot-matrix printer also forms characters by impact, but the method it uses is quite different from the typewriter or the daisywheel printer, and it's much more complicated — which explains why dot-matrix printers were the first computer printers to contain their own on-board microprocessors.

Unlike the preformed characters on a daisywheel (and print ball) print head, the dot-matrix print head uses a number of small, vertically aligned pins, each of which fire separately and produce a single dot on the paper. Older dot-matrix printers had 9 of these pins, and moving the head horizontally a fraction of an inch at a time, the printer formed a rectangular *matrix* of dots (hence the name). The improved dot-matrix printers available today have 24 pins, and some models have 48 pins. Figure 1.2 illustrates the rectangular matrix formed by these two print heads — as you've probably guessed, the more pins in the print head, the faster the print speed and the more detailed the graphics the printer can produce.

As paper is fed past the dot-matrix print head, the print head moves back and forth, firing pins against the ribbon and paper. The printer tracks the movement of the print head and fires only those pins necessary to create the proper image on the paper, forming characters and graphics. Figure 1.3 illustrates the dot-matrix process.

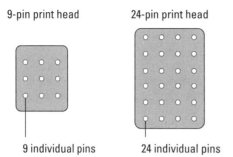

Figure 1.2 A comparison between 9- and 24-pin dot-matrix print heads

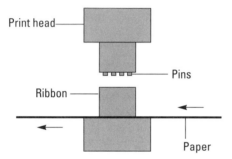

Figure 1.3 The components of a dot-matrix printer

Early dot-matrix printers couldn't produce type at anywhere near letter–quality and were thus considered inferior to daisywheel printers. You may remember these older printers, especially how they formed letters, such as the *p* and the *g*, that were supposed to have true descenders; instead of dropping below the letter, the tails on these characters lined up with the other characters in the word. Nine-pin printers were suitable only for producing programming code listings, draft copies of documents, printing labels, and checks.

I should point out, however, that these dot-matrix printers were much "smarter" machines than daisywheel printers. Dot-matrix printers were the first to require an extensive command language, which enabled them to print graphics and special formats such as bold and strikethrough characters, superscripts, subscripts, and international character sets (all without changing a print head).

Cross-Reference

See Chapter 2 for a discussion of printer control languages.

Eventually, some printers supported what was called *near-letter quality* on nine-pin dot-matrix printers: in this mode, the print head would make two full trips across each line of the page, firing its pins on the second pass *between* the horizontal dots made on its first pass. Although a page took twice as long to print, it looked much better, producing documents that could be submitted as schoolwork and personal letters. Dot-matrix printers took a leap forward with near-letter quality, and the daisywheel printer began its slide to oblivion . . . suddenly you had to examine a document closely to tell if it had been printed on a computer or typed on a typewriter.

The dot-matrix printer reached the pinnacle of its development with the introduction of actual letter-quality models that used a 24-pin print head. These models also marked the final demise of the daisywheel impact printer, because they produced similar results at a much faster speed, and they were also capable of printing grainy, monochrome photographs and graphs. However, even the 24-pin models had problems. They

- **Were prone to failure.** Dot-matrix print heads required cleaning on a regular schedule, and ink ribbons could tangle or smudge. Also, most dot-matrix printers used tractor-fed paper, which was notorious for jamming. (Some of the most troublesome peripherals I've ever attached to a computer were dot-matrix printers.)

- **Had high noise level.** Dot-matrix printers are just as loud as the older daisywheel printers; most homes and offices that use a dot-matrix printer put it in a soundproof enclosure that reduces this din to a low buzz.

- **Produced monochrome print.** Although dot-matrix printers were well suited to producing *monochrome* (that is, black-and-white) text and graphics, very few color dot-matrix printers were ever produced.

Why Use an Impact Printer Today?

"Okay, Mark, if impact printers are so bad, why do people still use dot-matrix printers these days?" Good question! The answer is very simple. Only an impact printer can transfer a character through a printer ribbon *and* all the sections of a multipart form. Inkjet and laser printers are superior to impact printers in almost every way, but neither an inkjet nor a laser can use forms based upon carbon paper. This is why you see dot-matrix printers at banks, supermarkets, warehouses, and small businesses: in order to produce multiple copies of the same form using multipart paper, you need an impact printer.

Today's dot-matrix printers are workhorses: they're not particularly glamorous, they don't print 16 million color images, and they still sound like a miniature cotton gin, but dot-matrix printers will still be available in the near future. As time goes by, it becomes harder and harder to locate printer ribbons and replacement print heads for older dot-matrix printers, so if you're still using one for multipart forms, I recommend that you stock up on these supplies.

Inkjet Printers

Dot-matrix printers were a giant step in the right direction, but they were still too slow, too loud, and too expensive to maintain. Plus, the average computer owner craved quiet operation and better print quality. There was also a call for inexpensive color printing without the hassle of changing ribbons, and the dot-matrix printer simply couldn't provide quality color.

Then came the inspiration that again changed the direction of computer printing: "Who needs the pins, anyway? Why not simply shoot the ink itself against the paper?" The inkjet printer was born, and it reigns today as the most popular type of computer printer — and with good reason, for the inkjet is so versatile that it can handle just about anything from monochrome text to high-quality color photo printing, on a variety of media.

At this point I should take a moment to define the term *resolution.* The resolution of any printer is a measurement of the number of dots that fit in an inch, both horizontally and vertically (hence the abbreviation *dpi*, which is short for *dots per inch*). Figure 1.4 illustrates the difference in resolution between 300 × 300 and 600 × 600 dpi. For example, a printer that advertises a monochrome resolution of 600 × 300 can print 600 dots horizontally and 300 dots vertically within a square inch. A higher resolution generally results in better print quality, but the higher the resolution, the longer a printer typically takes to complete a document. Also, some printers can't actually print all of the dots simultaneously in the maximum resolution that they advertise.

Cross-Reference

Other methods of improving print quality without slowing printing speed to a crawl have evolved, as is discussed in Chapter 3.

Figure 1.4 Higher resolution is one method of delivering better print quality. (Courtesy Hewlett-Packard Co.)

In this section, I discuss the inkjet printer in detail, and you'll be able to trace its lineage directly back to the dot-matrix printer.

How Do Inkjet Printers Work?

Like a dot-matrix printer, an inkjet printer applies dots of ink in groups to form type and graphics, but the ink is not transferred from a ribbon; instead, the ink is kept in liquid form in a tank connected to the print head. Instead of a vertical column of tiny pins, an inkjet printer uses columns of tiny ink nozzles, each of which can dispense a single microscopic drop of ink to the paper. (To give you some idea of the scale, each nozzle is smaller than the diameter of a human hair, and you can fit several million of those microscopic drops in a single raindrop!) As you might expect, the ink used in these devices is specially formulated to adhere to the paper, flow reliably in the print head, provide good quality print, and dry very quickly to avoid smearing. Figure 1.5 displays a cross-section of a typical inkjet cartridge.

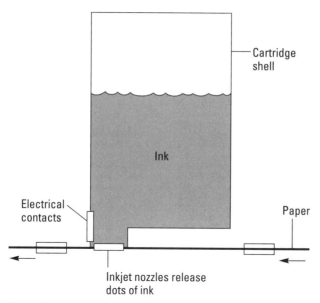

Figure 1.5 A cross-sectional view of an inkjet cartridge

As I mentioned earlier, one of the big advantages of the inkjet printer is its capability to print high-quality color graphics and photographic images at a low price. This makes you ask: How does an inkjet produce color as well as black output? Actually, the process is the same as it is for monochrome documents; however, the printer must use more than one group of nozzles and separate tanks for black, cyan, magenta, and yellow inks, as illustrated in Figure 1.6.

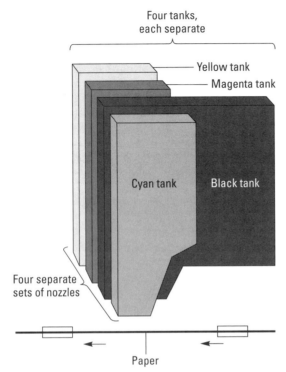

Four tanks,
each separate

Yellow tank

Magenta tank

Cyan tank

Black tank

Four separate
sets of nozzles

Paper

Figure 1.6 A color inkjet uses multiple print heads.

If you remember your art and science classes in school, you'll recall that cyan (blue), magenta (red), and yellow act as base colors for reflected or transmitted light; they can be mixed together to form every color in the rainbow. The base colors red, green, and blue (hence the abbreviation *RGB*), on the other hand, are mixed together for emitted light, like the light from your television or your computer monitor. The printer's on-board microprocessor keeps track of which color to apply at what interval to form more than 16 million colors, and your eyes help complete the image by merging the colors between neighboring dots.

Because the print head and ink nozzles are very complex (they're actually integrated into the cartridge itself), cartridges are considerably more expensive than a simple dot-matrix printer ribbon. Most black and color inkjet cartridges average from $20 to $40 each. However, this extra expense has a silver lining: because you're actually replacing the print head each time you replace the print cartridge, your inkjet's print head never wears out. Also, an inkjet printer requires much less maintenance, and the printer's output remains as good as the day you bought it.

The Home Solution

Inkjet printers have met every requirement that most of us have set for a home or small office printer. They

- **Are inexpensive to buy and maintain.** Many inkjet printers start at about $50. Full-featured printers with the latest technology can cost a few hundred dollars and usually the only maintenance required is replacing the print cartridge when the old one runs out of ink.

- **Are easy to use.** Inkjet printers set up in minutes. Plug in the cable and the power cord, load your printer driver software and you're ready to go. There are no messy ribbons to thread, no printwheels to change for different fonts

- **Are relatively quiet.** Compared to older impact printers, most inkjet printers are practically silent. The noise level created by an inkjet printer is minimal (it's certainly within the comfort zone of an average home or office).

- **Produce spectacular color.** Most inkjet printers can match the black text quality of an inexpensive laser printer, meaning that the human eye cannot tell the difference between a sentence printed by a laser printer and a sentence printed by an inkjet. The same inkjet printers can also print a full-color, full-page photograph — and versatility such as that is perfect for a home or office PC.

- **Print fast.** Although inkjet printers aren't the fastest printers under the sun, they are still well suited for home use; a typical printer selling for $200 can print up to eight pages per minute in color and 11 pages per minute in monochrome mode.

Figure 1.7 illustrates one of the most popular inkjet printers made these days, the HP DeskJet 842C. The 842C is the perfect low-cost fit for just about any home PC system.

Laser Printers

Although inkjet printers are fast, the less expensive inkjet models on the market today are not speedy enough to keep up with the demands of a busy office, where performance and reliable paper handling are a must — you need a more expensive, high-end inkjet printer for office use. Also, some inkjet printers tend to suffer from *banding* on large areas of black or a single color. If you've ever tried to print a large illustration using solid black on an inkjet printer, you may have seen this effect: visible bands running horizontally across the image. If you're using an inkjet that suffers from banding, it's a good idea to use a slower, better quality print mode for final copies.

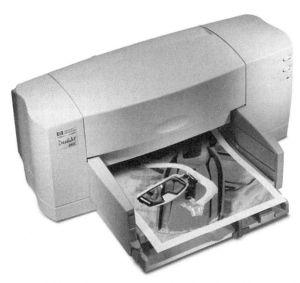

Figure 1.7 The HP DeskJet 842C inkjet printer (Courtesy Hewlett-Packard Co.)

Cross-Reference

See Chapter 10 for more information on adjusting print quality.

These disadvantages may not be tremendously important to the owner of a home PC, but office workers need the best possible print quality, and they needed those pages yesterday. For this reason, either a high-end inkjet printer or a laser printer is better suited for a networked office environment.

Laser printers have been around for years now — Hewlett-Packard introduced the LaserJet Classic, the first affordable desktop laser printer, in May 1984 — but most of us remember why they weren't popular for home or small office use. Ten years ago, the least expensive laser printer available would set you back nearly $1,000. Prices have dropped to the point where that same $1,000 buys you an office-quality laser printer that delivers 16 pages per minute at 1,200 dpi. In fact, prices for many "personal" laser printers have dropped to less than $400, making them affordable for the home user who wants the best black and gray-scale documents.

In this section, I discuss the inner workings of monochrome and color laser printers, as well as other features you find on most laser printers that make them the right choice for an office setting.

How Do Laser Printers Work?

Is a laser printer the same as a laser copier? Not really . . . instead of scanning input from a hard copy document, a laser printer accepts its input of the original image as a series of codes from your computer. Your laser printer's microprocessor uses these codes to build an image of the page in the printer's internal memory, which the microprocessor then transfers to the printed page. (This is why you often see the RAM or buffer memory listed in advertisements for laser printers.)

Your laser printer uses *toner* instead of ink. Toner is a very fine black powder that is very sensitive to electric charges. Luckily, you usually don't have to pour toner into your printer; as with an inkjet, you simply replace a cartridge to add more toner to virtually all laser printers. Laser toner cartridges use a roller to spread a wide, continuous layer of toner over the length of the cartridge.

But how does that toner stay on the paper, and what arranges it to form text and graphics? Let's follow the laser printing process step by step:

1. A roller moves across the face of a turning cylinder inside your laser printer; the charging roller transfers an electrical charge to the cylinder, which is called the photoconductor. As I mentioned earlier, toner powder is very sensitive to electrical charges, and this charge repels the toner powder away from the photoconductor.

2. The photoconductor cylinder keeps turning, which next brings it into contact with a laser beam. (It had to be called a "laser printer" for some reason.) The laser beam is controlled by the printer's microprocessor, or "brain," which turns the beam on and off as it sweeps back and forth across the surface of the photoconductor. Areas struck by the laser beam reverse the electrical charge, so the toner sticks to just the imaged areas of the photoconductor cylinder.

3. The next stop for the photoconductor cylinder is another roller — this one is the *toner* roller, which dispenses an even line of toner across the face of the photoconductor. Those areas of the cylinder that have been hit by the laser beam attract toner, while the rest of the roller still repels it. In effect, the cylinder now carries an image of the page, but it hasn't yet been transferred to the paper.

4. As the photoconductor cylinder continues to turn, it comes into contact with the *transfer* roller — paper from the paper tray is simultaneously fed between the two surfaces. The transfer roller applies a slight electrical charge to the paper, so the toner that remains on the photoconductor cylinder now sticks to the paper. (At this point, however, the toner is not actually affixed to the page; it would fall off if you shook the page.)

5. Now our attention turns to the paper — it passes through another two rollers. The top roller, which is on the same side of the paper as the toner, is called the *fuser* roller; it's heated by the printer, so the toner partially melts and sticks to the page for a permanent bond. To provide pressure, another roller simultaneously presses the paper against the fuser roller.

Warning

The fuser roller is exposed on many laser printers when you open the cover, and if the printer has been running, this roller is often hot. It's important not to touch the fuser roller, and to pay close attention to any warning labels or stickers inside your laser printer when you're replacing toner cartridges or cleaning the interior mechanism.

6. As the two rollers turn, the paper is drawn through them and moves outside the machine to the paper collection tray.

7. Now that the photoconductor cylinder has transferred the image to the page, it must be cleaned before the process can repeat. As the cylinder continues to turn, it passes under a cleaning brush or a scraper blade that removes any stray particles of toner.

8. Finally the photoconductor cylinder completes the cycle by returning to the charging roller. If another page has to be printed, the entire process is repeated.

Figure 1.8 gives you an overall picture of what goes on inside your laser printer during this process.

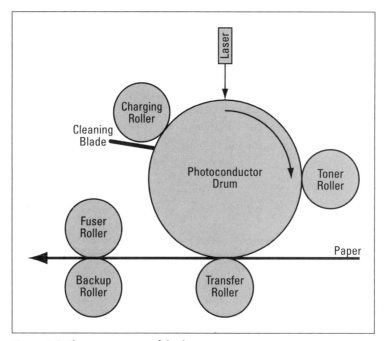

Figure 1.8 The components of the laser printing process

Color laser printers follow this general process, but they use four toner colors instead of one. (Sometimes these colors are added as individual cartridges or poured individually into the unit, while other printers combine all of the separate colors into a separate color toner cartridge.) The photoconductor cylinder in a color printer makes four complete passes to transfer each of the four base colors to the page before the paper passes to the fuser roller. As you can imagine, these printers are far more complex and require more internal memory to hold four separate images of the same page, so even with the drop in laser prices, a color laser printer is still quite expensive.

The Office Choice

Traditionally, laser printers have been the top sellers for office environments, although inkjet printers are rapidly becoming more popular around the office as technology improves. Besides the advantages listed earlier, laser printers also have other features that make them especially attractive for heavy printing traffic:

- **High printing speed.** Although inkjet technology is improving in speed, high-performance laser printers can still double the output speed of even the best inkjet printer in monochrome printing, making laser printers the favorite in any office that requires a high volume of printing.

- **Network connection capability.** Most laser printers have an option for a network connection, which simplifies their use as a network printer. (Some high-end inkjet printers also offer built-in network support, or the option to add it later.)

- **Improved paper handling.** Laser printers can usually hold more paper than an average inkjet printer, meaning the paper supply lasts longer and requires less user intervention. Many models also come with accessory trays that enable you to use legal and European paper sizes.

- **Resident fonts and font cartridges.** Many older models of laser printers can be upgraded with additional on-board fonts through font cartridges, whereas today's models are upgraded with internal font memory cards. Because Windows doesn't have to download these fonts to your printer each time you print a document, on-board fonts can save you anywhere from 15 to 30 seconds of printing time. The more you use a specific font in your documents, the more you benefit if you add that font cartridge to your laser printer. (Inkjet printers don't need font cartridges.)

Cross-Reference

Okay, you know you want to add a font cartridge, but you're not sure how to go about it. Check out Chapter 10, which includes a set of general instructions for installing a font cartridge.

Figure 1.9 shows the HP LaserJet 5000, a best-selling laser printer suitable for an office, while Figure 1.10 shows the HP LaserJet 1100se, a popular model in the HP line of personal laser printers (selling for under $400).

Figure 1.9 The HP LaserJet 5000 is a popular office printer. (Courtesy Hewlett-Packard Co.)

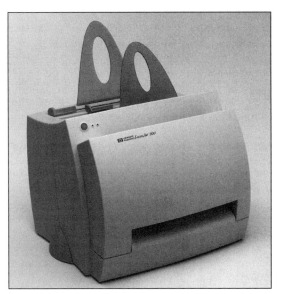

Figure 1.10 The HP LaserJet 1100se is a good example
of a personal laser printer. (Courtesy Hewlett-Packard Co.)

All-in-One Peripherals

In 1994, the first *all-in-one* (sometimes called a "multifunction" device) appeared
on the market. An all-in-one unit can perform three or four functions — depending
on the model, these functions may include printing, faxing, scanning, and copying. These units are ideal for the small office or home where space is a premium.

All-in-one machines are based on either inkjet or laser technology. Some have
a flatbed like a copier, while others are sheetfed like a fax machine; some have
both of these features. Newer inkjet all-in-ones print, scan, and fax in color, while
laser all-in-one units print, scan, and fax only in black.

How Does an All-in-One Work?

An all-in-one unit relies on the fact that each of the four PC applications —
printing, scanning, copying, and faxing — shares something in common with
at least one other application. For example, the fax application requires the scanner and the printer, as well as the copier. Each of the all-in-one unit's subsystems
can be accessed separately as well; for instance, you can scan a page and include
a portion of the image in an e-mail, or you can print out a hard copy of a document created on your PC.

Note

Although your PC probably came equipped with a fax modem, an all-in-one with fax functions doesn't require an additional modem (it has a fax modem built in); it can act as a stand-alone fax machine.

Most all-in-one units use an inkjet printer engine, so most of these devices can produce color output. They can also produce laser-quality black (monochrome) text.

In sheetfed devices, a standard sheetfed scanner engine, which operates much like a fax machine, does the scanning. The paper is drawn inside and past the scanning head, which remains motionless. This method of scanning is inexpensive, and it makes it possible for an all-in-one machine to occupy much less space on your desk than a dedicated flatbed scanner; unfortunately, most of these scanners have a limited resolution of 300×300 or 600×300 dpi. The dedicated scanner provides much better results. Flatbed devices look like copy machines; they can scan (and copy) books and other materials that the sheetfed products cannot. The resolution of flatbed scanners is similar to that of dedicated scanners.

Unlike a standard personal printer, an all-in-one has a control panel that enables users to send faxes and make copies without using the computer. Some units have buttons that launch software in your computer, such as a button that lets you scan directly to a program or an e-mail attachment. Most all-in-ones also have alphanumeric displays that display menus and information. One tray feeds paper, another tray receives original documents that you wish to scan or copy, and a third tray holds the output.

Figure 1.11 shows the interrelationships between the different subsystems of a multifunction unit; some of the specifications may change from manufacturer to manufacturer, but virtually all of these devices operate this way.

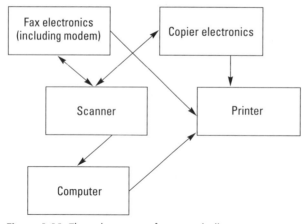

Figure 1.11 The subsystems of a typical all-in-one unit

The Home Office in a Box

All-in-one peripherals seem almost magical — in one small box, they fulfill almost all of the computer hardware requirements for a complete small home office (or a busy family). Besides the versatility of all-in-one units, other features have added to their popularity:

- **Complete solution.** Many computer owners would rather make one hardware purchase and install and configure one box. With a multifunction unit, you're not stuck buying four separate machines (with all of their accompanying software drivers and cables), and you can avoid the hassle of connecting all those separate components.

- **Inexpensive.** An all-in-one can save you money. Compared to the cost of a separate printer, scanner, copy machine, and fax machine, the $300–800 you spend on an all-in-one unit is a real bargain!

- **Small size.** If you run a small home business on a shoestring budget and a closet's worth of space, you'll appreciate the small size of an all-in-one. Like the Swiss army knife, this machine can pack a tremendous amount of functionality into a very small space.

However, owning a multifunction peripheral is not all milk and cookies. These units have their downside as well:

- **Repair concerns.** Although an all-in-one is just as reliable as a traditional stand-alone printer, you're essentially putting all of your eggs into one basket. If a subsystem fails — for example, the scanner — you've lost the ability to fax or scan anything until it's repaired. If your all-in-one has to be sent away for repairs, you've suddenly lost all of your office functionality. If you use separate components, you lose only the functionality of the missing piece. (Luckily, many manufacturers offer "overnight exchange" for these products just to solve these worries for customers.) Finally, multifunction printers are much more complex than the average printer, and they're typically more expensive to repair than a simple printer, so you'll pay more if your all-in-one printer needs repairs.

Warning

If you consider that an all-in-one with faxing functions has both an AC connection and a telephone connection — two prime routes for a power surge — you can see why I always recommend that clients connect their multifunction printers to surge protectors. Most good-quality surge protectors available these days have both AC and telephone sockets, so they provide complete protection.

In Figure 1.12, you see the HP OfficeJet K80, one of the best all-in-one units on the market. It can fax and scan as well as print color documents, and it can produce laser-quality black text as well.

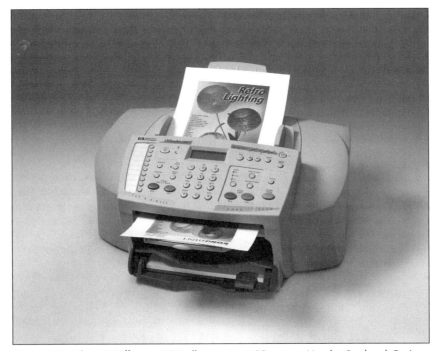

Figure 1.12 The HP OfficeJet K80 all-in-one unit (Courtesy Hewlett-Packard Co.)

Portable Printers

Just what makes a printer portable? I consider three criteria important:

- **Size.** The maximum size you'll accept for a portable printer is based on your own preference; most of the models I've seen or used that advertise themselves as being portable are somewhere near the size of a hardback book. For example, the HP DeskJet 350CBi portable printer pictured in Figure 1.13 weighs a mere 4.3 pounds, and measures a stout 5.9 inches high by 12.2 inches wide by 2.6 inches deep.

- **Noise.** A true portable printer must be quiet enough for use in a library, a meeting, or even a lecture.

■ **Power supply.** In order for me to consider a printer as truly portable, it must operate without AC power . . . and that means batteries. Of course, you can carry a desktop printer along with you, and several models that I know can fit into a large notebook computer case, but you're still saddled with an AC adapter unless you can use battery power. Again, using the HP DeskJet 350CBi as an example, you can use the built-in recharger to power up your NiMh battery whenever you're near an AC outlet.

Figure 1.13 The HP DeskJet 350CBi is a petite powerhouse of a portable printer. (Courtesy Hewlett-Packard Co.)

How Do Portable Printers Work?

Almost all portable printers use inkjet technology to produce laser-quality black print, and most are also capable of printing color. These printers use either a specially fitted rechargeable battery or accept standard C or D alkaline batteries. If you happen to be close to an AC socket, you can use an external AC adapter as well.

In operation, these portable units work like any other inkjet printer — only quieter. Because of their size, they take up less space (a good choice for that studio apartment you rented in New York City) and are light enough to share a carrying case with your notebook computer. They connect to your computer with a standard parallel printer cable.

But wait: some portable printers don't even need a cable. For example, the DeskJet 350CBi offers both the standard parallel port and a wireless infrared adapter. Naturally, the computer you're using must have an infrared port as well, but that's becoming standard equipment on most laptops these days.

The downside of portable printers is that they usually lack the advanced paper-handling features of a larger desktop unit (although the DeskJet 350CBi does come equipped with a portable 30-page sheet feeder). On the upside, you can produce specialized documents with the same media that you would commonly use on a desktop printer, such as transparencies and labels.

The Road Warrior

Are you considering a portable printer? If so, remember that you pay extra for that convenience. Does your application demand immediate hard copy? Some applications do indeed require hard copy on the spot, but many laptop owners seem to think their only printing option is a portable printer.

A number of methods of printing from a laptop or notebook eliminate the need for a portable printer; as an alternative, you may print later from your desktop system or bring a smaller desktop printer with you instead of a dedicated portable unit.

Cross-Reference

If you're asking yourself "Do I really need the road warrior," look at Chapter 2, which discusses portability.

Thermal and Dye-Sublimation Printers

The color graphics provided by the average inkjet printer are well suited for a home PC or a home office, and most offices that need color output connect a color laser printer to the office network. Why spend anywhere from $500 to a whopping $6,000 on a photo-quality dye-sublimation color printer like the types professionals use?

The answer, as any graphic artist or desktop publishing expert would tell you, is because the output from one of those less expensive personal inkjet printers simply doesn't measure up. Professionals use a photo-quality color printer to prepare prepress examples, create photo-quality prints, and — in some cases — actually print the final product. These printers must accurately match the color shading of a book illustration or magazine advertisement, or create a color plot for an architect or designer. (As inkjet technology improves, however, the line between inkjet and wax or dye printers grows less distinct; some high-end inkjet printers can now produce similar — and sometimes better — results.)

Most high-end graphics printers share these characteristics (both good and bad):

- **Slow printing speed.** Dye-sublimation printers typically produce a maximum of five pages per minute, while thermal wax printers move at a blinding three pages per minute.

- **Photographic quality.** Unlike a color laser printer, a high-resolution graphics printer can produce 16-million-color pictures with blended, continuous tones, so they can actually pass for 35mm film photographs to the naked eye. Many inkjet printers have reached this level of quality as well.

■ **Expensive maintenance.** Dye cartridges and thermal wax ribbons are more expensive than a standard inkjet ink cartridge, and they're typically harder to find at your local computer store or office supply warehouse — typically, you save both time and money if you order them over the Internet or through a mail-order catalog.

■ **PC and Macintosh connections.** Because many graphics professionals use the Macintosh, some high-end graphics printers are available with both PC and Macintosh printer ports (or in two separate models). Most inkjets and laser printers, however, have standardized on the PC platform. Luckily, the flexibility of USB (and the addition of USB support to the Macintosh computers a few years ago) makes it easier to buy a Macintosh printer today.

How Do Graphics Printers Work?

Practically all high-end graphics printers fall into one of two categories:

■ **Thermal wax.** Imagine a dot-matrix printer, but one that uses super-hot pins. A thermal wax printer uses a special multicolored ribbon impregnated with a solid wax dye instead of ink. Unlike a dot-matrix printer, the impact pressure of these pins isn't enough to transfer the wax; instead, the heat from the pin melts the wax and transfers it permanently to the paper. Figure 1.14 illustrates how a thermal printer works.

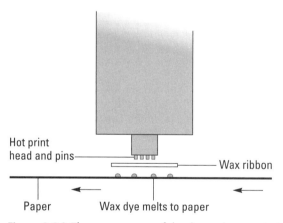

Figure 1.14 The components of the thermal wax printing process

■ **Dye-sublimation.** These printers also use heat, but they transfer dye (similar to a child's crayon) to the paper. Although the dpi of a dye-sublimation printer is often lower than the dpi of an inkjet printer, dye-sublimation output produces beautiful, high-quality images that are favorites of graphic artists. Figure 1.15 shows a dye-sublimation printer at work.

I should also mention engineering plotters in this section; although they're not technically printers, they can produce architectural plans and engineering blueprints that stretch several feet. These plotters use a set of special ink pens in different colors to precisely draw the image delivered by a drafting or landscape-drawing application. Here, too, inkjet technology is supplanting older technology — the HP DesignJet line of printers uses a roll-fed inkjet engine to print many types of oversize documents (for example, life-size copies of artwork for client review).

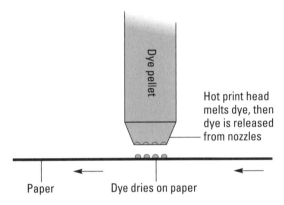

Figure 1.15 The components of the dye-sublimation process

The Artist's Friend

Because thermal wax and dye-sublimation printers are expensive to buy and maintain, a typical professional desktop publishing or graphics design computer system typically has two printers. One is a standard inkjet or laser printer to handle the majority of the printing chores, and the other is a thermal wax or dye-sublimation printer used only to produce the best quality output.

If one of these advanced dye or wax printers is beyond your budget, you can choose to spend extra cash instead on a high-end inkjet that can produce good-quality color. For example, the HP 2500CM, shown in Figure 1.16, is a great example of an inkjet color printer with built-in 10Base-T and 100Base-T network connectivity. Naturally, it produces laser-quality black-and-white text, but the real attraction is that it enables you to print color at a blazing nine pages per minute, making it one of the fastest photo-quality office inkjet color printers around. Moreover, you can expect near–photo quality results on plain paper, without special paper or cartridges. Each ink color can be changed individually, making this printer more cost-efficient than most other printers of this type. The 2500CM holds up to 400 sheets of paper, too, which cuts down on the number of visits you have to make to refill the paper tray.

Figure 1.16 The HP 2500CM is a good example of a high-end inkjet printer suitable for a workgroup. (Courtesy Hewlett-Packard Co.)

Large-Format Printers

So far in this chapter I've discussed printers that use standard 8.5×11-inch paper, but not every printing job fits on standard business letterhead. Imagine a printer that's designed to handle 13×19 inch sheets of paper . . . or even continuous rolls of paper 24, 36, or even an unbelievable 54 inches across! Now you've entered the realm of the *large-format* printer, which is specifically designed for producing photo-quality posters, blueprints, maps, and signs (perhaps even the occasional reproduction of a Rembrandt or da Vinci).

As a rule, large-format printer designs fall into one of two categories:

■ **Wide-format inkjets.** A printer such as the HP DesignJet ColorPro GA looks very much like a typical inkjet printer that's been working out at the gym. It's oversized and features a huge paper tray, but most people would still recognize it as an inkjet printer. The ColorPro GA can produce a photo-quality 600×600 dpi, 11×17-inch image in about 2 minutes. As you might expect for a printer with a street price of around $1500, the ColorPro GA has top-of-the-line features such as a 400-sheet paper capacity, a four-cartridge print system, a maximum of 68MB of memory (that's more than the amount found in many older computers), computer-monitored ink levels, and built-in support for an Ethernet office network.

■ **Roll-feed inkjets.** Like a traditional plotter you'd find in a drafting studio, these printers don't use sheets of paper at all; instead, you load them with huge rolls, so you can print continuously. The HP DesignJet 3800CP shown in Figure 1.17 can handle paper rolls with widths up to 54 inches — imagine a banner that size at your next birthday party! Professional graphic artists use these large-format units to print posters on the spot using a variety of special papers (including signs meant for outdoor use that are specially treated to withstand the sun's ultraviolet light without fading). You can even create "paintings" by printing photo-quality on certain types of fabrics! Naturally, roller-based inkjets don't use the typical "pages per minute" benchmark to advertise printing speeds; instead, these printers advertise specifications of square feet (or meters) per hour. For example, the DesignJet 3800CP delivers up to 92 square feet per hour in economy mode, and up to 32 square feet per hour in high-speed photo-quality mode. If you're considering a top-of-the-line large-format printer like the DesignJet 3800CP, be prepared: this model will set you back over $14,000.

Figure 1.17 Forget sheets of paper — the HP DesignJet 3800CP takes rolls of paper. (Courtesy Hewlett-Packard Co.)

How Do Large-Format Printers Work?

As you might expect, a large-format inkjet uses the same technology as a standard inkjet printer, but the cartridges are naturally much larger. On the other hand, a roller-based inkjet really doesn't have a paper tray; the printer head simply moves back and forth across the entire width of the roll, which advances through the machine much like a traditional offset printing press. When I watch one of these behemoths at work, it's fascinating to see them literally "painting" the image slowly, line-by-line.

Large-format printers usually include top-of-the-line features demanded by professional graphic artists and drafting shops and publishers. These features include

■ **Support for different computers and operating systems.** A typical large-format printer recognizes several different printer languages, so they're compatible with both the PC and Macintosh versions of the professional desktop publishing and prepress printing software used by graphic artists.

Cross-Reference

Chapter 2 discusses printer control languages.

■ **Tremendous amounts of on-board memory.** As I mentioned earlier, anywhere from 32 to a whopping 160MB of memory is not an uncommon amount of RAM for a large-format printer — remember, a digital image or desktop publishing document the size of a movie poster is going to need elbow room! A few models will even supplant that on-board RAM with an on-board hard drive like the one in your computer, allowing faster processing for 20GB of data.

■ **Color matching.** Most large-format printers include sophisticated support for *color matching* within Windows and Macintosh. This makes sure the colors produced from the printer are as close as possible to the colors displayed on your monitor.

Cross-Reference

Jump to Chapter 9 for more details on color matching.

■ **Network connections.** Since a large-format printer is such an expensive investment, it's likely to have on-board support for your office Ethernet network so that everyone can share it.

The Printer That Thinks It's a Press

Most home computer owners will never need the oversized printing capabilities of a large-format printer. Also, the expense of buying, maintaining, and replacing cartridges for one of these units is simply far too high for a typical computer owner to even consider.

However, if you do find that you need poster-sized output from time-to-time, keep in mind that your local copy center may have a large-format printer that can print your document (plus, it's already hooked up and ready to go)!

The Parallel Port

Congratulations, you're a printer expert! That introduction covers the various types of printing hardware available today. I provide more information on how to select, buy, install, and maintain most of these printers and all-in-one units throughout the rest of the book, including discussions of hobby projects and business applications.

Are we done? Is that all you need to know about printer technology? As you can tell, plenty of pages are still left in this chapter, so the answer is definitely "No!" So far, you've learned details about printers themselves, but I haven't discussed the other two important parts of a successful printing system: the *parallel port* and the *parallel printer cable*.

A few printers, such as the wireless infrared portable printer I mentioned earlier in this chapter, actually don't require a cable. But every printing device needs some sort of a port to transfer data back and forth with your PC. Almost all printers use a parallel port. The parallel port is one of the three primary gateways between your PC, your printer, and a number of different external devices.

Let's turn our attention to the parallel port.

Serial versus Parallel Communications

Along with ports for the keyboard and monitor, the original IBM PC specification called for two different types of ports for general-purpose external devices: the serial port and the parallel port. From the beginning, the majority of printers used the parallel port; however, serial printers did exist, and you may hear older hardware hackers mention them at a PC user group meeting.

In the end, though, the serial port took a back seat to the parallel port. Today — to add insult to injury — the parallel port is fast becoming the port of choice for connecting other devices as well. (You'll read more about these other devices in a page or two.) Why has the serial port fallen from favor?

If you compare the two ports, shown side-by-side in Figure 1.18, you can see that the serial port only has 9 pins, and the parallel port has 25 pins. That's part of the key to unlocking the mystery: the parallel port can obviously transfer more data. In fact, a parallel communications circuit can send data bits across several of those pins simultaneously. (In case you haven't heard the term in your computer travels, a *bit* refers to the smallest unit of information recognized by your computer; like a light switch, a bit can have a value of "on" or "off," represented by 1 or 0, respectively. Groups of bits form all of the data stored in your PC, such as numbers, words, and images, and data flows from your PC to your printer as groups of bits.)

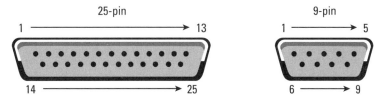

Figure 1.18 The two ports that started it all

A serial communications circuit, on the other hand, sends data bits down a single wire, one after another (hence the name "serial"), so the data pathway is much smaller. Figure 1.19 illustrates the difference in transfer methods. The top diagram shows parallel communications, in which all wires send data simultaneously. The bottom diagram shows serial communications, in which one wire carries data in sequence.

This is the reason why serial printers are antiques; the parallel port can send more data faster than the serial port. Imagine sending water from a fire hydrant through a straw, and you can imagine the bottleneck that can occur when you send a large 10MB PostScript document to a serial printer.

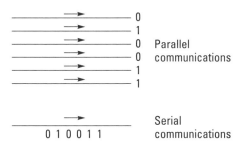

Figure 1.19 A comparison between parallel and serial data transfer

Feeling sorry for the archaic serial port? Don't lose any sleep; the serial port is still the *interface* (a way of connecting and communicating data between devices) of choice for external modems, which makes sense because a modem transfers data bits across a telephone line one after another, in serial fashion. Serial pointing devices such as mice and trackballs are still in use as well, and some of the fancy, high-tech joysticks available these days actually connect to the serial port.

Other Parallel Port Peripherals

As I mentioned earlier, the parallel port has offered the fastest data transfer rates of any standard port on your computer. In fact, it has been the king since the first IBM PCs rolled off the assembly line. (Recently, the parallel port lost this distinction with the arrival of the USB port, but I talk more about that in the next section.) Because practically every PC on the planet has a parallel connector, that capability to move bits has made the parallel port a natural choice for connecting all kinds of external peripherals. This list includes:

■ **Scanners.** In years past, scanners have traditionally used the SCSI interface (Small Computer System Interface) on both the PC and the Macintosh. This is no big deal on the Mac, which has always supported SCSI — for most PC owners; however, SCSI is quite a headache. Rather than add a SCSI adapter card and spend time debugging a SCSI device chain (technical tasks that often entail hours of frustration), the parallel-port scanner is a natural choice. SCSI scanners may be faster, but most PC owners are happy to wait a bit longer for their images. There's no adapter card to install, and Windows 98 and Windows 2000 automatically recognize a parallel-port scanner. Figure 1.20 illustrates one of the most popular parallel-port scanners available these days, the HP ScanJet 5300C. The 5300C is a single-pass flatbed scanner that can deliver 9600 dpi resolution in 36-bit color (that's true photographic quality) with a single-button copy utility that automatically sends an image to your system printer.

Figure 1.20 The HP ScanJet 5300C is one of the most popular parallel-port scanners. (Courtesy Hewlett-Packard Co.)

■ **Removable-media drives.** You may be already using an Iomega Zip drive, which stores a tidy 100MB of data on a single 3.5-inch format disk. The parallel-port connection on the Zip drive makes it a natural for sharing between PCs in an office or school. Simply hook up the cable to the PC's parallel port, run a single program under Windows 95/98 or Windows 2000, and you suddenly have enough space to swap digital video or entire subdirectories.

- **Video capture devices.** Parallel-port video capture devices enable your PC to capture still images from a VCR or DVD player in over 16 million colors, and they're much cheaper than a dedicated video capture adapter card.

- **Video cameras.** Before the arrival of the USB port, computer video conferencing cameras used the parallel port to deliver digital video to the PC — and if your PC doesn't have USB ports, you can still do the same thing.

- **CD recorders.** A number of parallel-port CD recorders are now available. Using one of these portable external drives, you can record your own data CD-ROMs or your own custom audio CDs.

For most of us, the parallel port will continue to provide the connection between printer and PC for the near future; however, a PC port has appeared on the scene within the last couple of years that offers more features and a much faster data transfer rate. This PC port is sure to capture at least a small portion of the printer market (especially for high-speed laser and graphics printers that connect to a single PC rather than through a network). This new port has been christened the *Universal Serial Bus*, or USB for short, and it's time we examine it in detail.

The USB Port

The parallel port can transfer signals to multiple devices, such as a Zip drive and an inkjet printer (a process called *daisy chaining*), but it wasn't designed for this purpose. Some parallel port devices do not work well when connected to another device, but no alternative was available for several years. You installed a second parallel port or simply hung what hardware you could off of your parallel port, or you bought an "A/B" switching device that would enable you to choose which device was connected to the port.

Another solution to peripheral overpopulation is to install a SCSI adapter card, which can accept the SCSI version of scanners and removable media drives. Unfortunately, you have to open your PC and install the card, and the configuration of a SCSI card for a novice is often akin to building a medieval catapult with an ice cream scoop. (Okay, perhaps SCSI is no longer that hard to handle, and it's easier under Windows 98 and Windows 2000 — but even though I'm a hardware hacker, I'll tell anyone that SCSI isn't "plug-and-play" by any means.)

Never fear, the truly easy answer is here. Although a long time coming, the Universal Serial Bus promises to finally deliver plug-and-play installation of PC hardware under Windows 98/2000 and Windows NT, and that will apply to many printers in the future as well.

Inside the Universal Serial Bus

Although the USB port on your new computer may look small, it's really a titan of connectivity. With the USB standard, you enjoy these advantages:

- **Speedy data transfer.** Standard USB ports transfer data at 12 megabits per second (as compared to about 1500 kilobytes per second for a parallel connection), which makes them perfect for connecting peripherals such as video cameras, modems, joysticks, scanners and, of course, printers.

- **Almost unlimited connectivity.** I don't know about your computer, but I think the maximum of 127 devices on a single USB connection is fine for my system.

- **No configuration required.** USB is fully supported within Windows 98/2000, Windows NT, and the OSR2 version of Windows 95 (version 4.00950B or later). Plug in a device, and Windows automatically detects it. Apple has also enthusiastically embraced the USB standard, as any owner of an iMac or Macintosh G4 can attest.

- **Windows and Mac OS do not need rebooting.** USB devices can be "hot-swapped" while your computer is running, without requiring you to shut down and restart your system.

- **On-board power supply.** Your USB port can even provide power to many peripherals so they don't require an AC adapter.

The new port is already standard equipment on almost all new computers, and if your PC's BIOS supports USB you can easily "retrofit" your older Pentium computer with USB ports.

USB as a Printer Connection

Even with all the features it offers, the USB port will not totally replace the good old parallel port for many years to come; the parallel standard is too widespread, and it can handle almost any printer made today, so there's really no need to discard it.

However, most printing devices benefit from USB connections (especially portable printers, high-end graphics printers, and all-in-one units, which can make use of the speed and convenience of USB). For example, a portable printer can be powered by the USB port, which would eliminate the need for an AC adapter. Moreover, because scanned image files in over 16 million colors are often over 30 or 40MB, a photo-quality graphics printer can receive an image much faster through a USB connection. USB cables are smaller and more flexible, making them a good connection for portable computer peripherals like digital cameras.

As the USB market grows and matures, you may find you have another connection choice for your next piece of printing hardware — and if your PC supports the USB standard, I certainly recommend that you invest in the USB version.

Printer Cables

Okay, so the world of computer printers may actually be more complex than you had imagined . . . you have many more choices (and many more decisions) than you may have originally thought. At least there's only one type of printer cable, right? You can't go wrong buying a standard IBM parallel printer cable from your local discount store, right?

Sorry. Unfortunately, not even the standard Centronics IBM parallel printer cable is truly standard. Without a special type of cable, today's inkjet and laser printers may refuse to perform certain functions, or they may refuse to work altogether.

In this section, I discuss the differences in parallel printer cables, and I help you pick the right cable for your printer.

Attack of the Bidirectional Monster

In days of old — in this case, at the time of the original impact printers I discussed at the beginning of this chapter — communications between a computer and a printer were usually one way. The computer sent specific printer commands and simple text through the parallel port and the attached cable, and the printer processed them (although the printer could pause the stream of data it was receiving, sending signals called *flow control* signals through the printer cable). Therefore, the computer typically never heard a squeak from the printer.

The original parallel port specification (usually called the *original Centronics standard* by folks who talk about such things all the time) had no provision for a simultaneous two-way flow of data. The IEEE-1284 parallel-port specification changed that, enabling printers and other parallel-port devices to send and receive data to and from your PC at the same time.

With the arrival of Windows and more powerful inkjet and laser printers, things changed dramatically. Now the enhanced microprocessors inside printers are required to hold "conversations" with your computer. These communications from printer to computer include messages such as, "Hey, my ink cartridge is running low," and "You need to flip the pages if you're printing on both sides." The data flow also provided identifying characteristics that enabled Windows to determine what type of printer was connected to the system. Some of these messages from the printer to the computer result in the computer pausing the printing process, while others simply update your computer with the latest information on the current print job. (Two-way communication also enables you to use a scanner through your parallel port.)

This simultaneous two-way communication between computer and printer is called *bidirectional* communication (illustrated in Figure 1.21), meaning that data now flows regularly in both directions between computer and printer. Many printers no longer work correctly (or at all) without a bidirectional computer cable. Luckily, computer and printer manufacturers have created a standard international specification for a bidirectional parallel cable, IEEE-1284, which helps guarantee that your printer will work with a standard bidirectional cable.

Figure 1.21 An illustration of bidirectional computer communication

Do You Need an IEEE-1284 Cable?

Here's a quick checklist to help you determine whether you need an IEEE-1284 cable:

- **Age.** If your printer is an inkjet or laser printer built within the last two or three years, you very likely need an IEEE-1284 cable.

- **Written requirements.** Check your printer's user guide to see if it requires an IEEE-1284 cable.

- **Test results.** The installation software that comes with many printers now tests to see whether you're using a bidirectional printer cable. If you receive a message during the installation of a new printer telling you that your printer's communications link has failed — and the cable is correctly connected at both ends — it's probably time to go cable shopping. (Oh, boy! Talk about exciting . . . pack up the kids and make a day of it.)

- **Recurring errors.** Some printers may not report a communications error, but if you use the wrong cable many of the more advanced features offered by your printer won't work properly. For example, you may not be able to print on both sides of a page, or the printer will not report that the ink cartridges need replacing.

Tip

It's generally a good idea to check your cable connections and verify that you have an IEEE-1284 cable *before* you call the manufacturer's technical support. You may save yourself the cost and hassle of ten minutes on a long-distance support call.

The Acronym Invasion

I should also mention two rather confusing abbreviations that have a lot to do with today's parallel-port printers and external hardware: EPP (short for *Enhanced Parallel Port*) and ECP (short for *Enhanced Capability Port*). These two standards have completely changed the way you and I use parallel ports today.

Both standards are typically mentioned together, as EPP/ECP, because they're both part of the IEEE-1284 standard; however, ECP documents bidirectional communications for printers and scanners, whereas EPP handles all other bidirectional parallel-port connections for other devices.

The older Centronics standard could provide a data transfer speed of up to 100K per second, but EPP/ECP connections can move data as fast as 1MB per second. As you might expect, many parallel-port devices wouldn't be possible without the EPP/ECP standard (especially portable external hard drives and Zip drives).

Thanks to Microsoft, all 32-bit versions of Windows support IEEE-1284, so both bidirectional printers and other parallel-port devices are automatically detected during the startup sequence.

Note

Although you may be currently running Windows 95, 98, or 2000, your PC may not automatically support EPP/ECP transfers. It doesn't matter whether your motherboard has on-board printer ports or you have an older serial/parallel I/O adapter card — your parallel ports must support EPP/ECP in hardware, or you won't be able to use a printer or other device that requires IEEE-1284 support. To determine if your PC can support the standard, check your motherboard or I/O adapter card manual.

Summary

This chapter introduced you to the wide, wonderful, slightly wacky world of modern printing hardware — what method each type uses to put characters and text on the page, what applications each type can handle, and what environment fits each type the best. You also learned about the printer cable and the parallel port, the other two important pieces of hardware that control your printer. Finally, you encountered a nest of abbreviations and technical terms as I discussed the IEEE-1284 standard for the PC parallel port (and why it's so important for other external peripherals as well as your printer).

Coming up in Chapter 2, you'll find everything you need to know to research printers and all-in-one units, compare features, and buy one . . . either at a local store or by mail.

Buying a Printer

IN THIS CHAPTER
- Determining what printing device is right for you
- Comparing features
- Evaluating warranty and support
- Buying locally versus buying online
- Favorite online stores

Some computer owners love to shop — they're the people you see at your local computer store holding clipboards and making detailed notes. They ask the salesperson those embarrassing technical questions that are so hard to answer. They surf the Internet and bop back and forth between online shopping sites. They post hardware comparison questions and request advice on Internet newsgroups and read every reply. (I have to admit that I fall in this group.)

Then you have the other group: computer owners who would rather visit the dentist than spend even a couple of hours shopping for a new PC peripheral. Folks from this group are likely to grudgingly visit that local computer store, walk up to the first salesperson they see and announce, "I just want a good solid printer that will last . . . I don't need all the bells and whistles." Unfortunately, the same shopper will likely want those very same "bells and whistles" in a year or two.

Here's a pop quiz: which type of computer shopper gets the better deal on a printer, with the right set of features? If you guessed the first group, you're right — reward yourself with a cup of coffee or a soda. Keep in mind, however, that you don't have to be a dedicated computer wizard or plan for several weeks to find the right piece of printing hardware. Preparation is indeed important, but you shouldn't set aside more than an afternoon or two. It takes a simple evaluation of your needs, a little bit of research, and a series of comparisons before you can choose the printer you really need. If you've never bought a peripheral, you may even find you enjoy researching the best deal.

If you fall into the second group, you'll find that this chapter is a complete tutorial on how to select the right printer for your needs — including a discussion of how you can buy that unit for the least amount of money. However, if you're already a dedicated computer comparison shopper, don't skip to the next chapter. You can still find plenty of tips and tricks in this chapter that help you improve your shopping.

The First Step: Evaluating Your Needs

As a computer consultant, I often hear people say, "I just don't know where to start. What do I need?" Talk about a common feeling! Many people — including parents, medical and legal professionals, business owners, teachers, department managers — feel lost when faced with buying computer hardware.

Why is selecting computer hardware such a hassle? Here's a list of the observations I've made over the last few years:

■ Many people still consider a computer to be somewhat of a "black box"; it runs the programs they use, but they don't know what goes on inside. Therefore, they don't feel qualified to evaluate their hardware needs.

■ Although most computer hardware is no longer exorbitantly expensive, it certainly used to be. For example, a laser printer that now costs $400 would have set you back three times that amount just five years ago. Some folks remember those prices, and they haven't heard that technology is now cheaper.

■ Some people feel a little overwhelmed by the number of features available with today's hardware. The explosion of numbers and acronyms can give you a headache while you're shopping.

If you're feeling a little lost when it comes to buying a computer printer, here's some welcome news: the process of evaluating your needs is really quite simple. Although you may not know all the features of a typical printer, you *do* know what you want it to do; therefore, you're ready to determine the functions it has to perform, which is half the battle. This section helps you evaluate your printing needs.

Grab a pencil and a notepad so that you can make notes along the way. (If you're really a perfectionist, add a title at the top — something like "My Printing Specifications" should do nicely.)

Color or Monochrome?

Let's start the evaluation process with the most important printer feature question you can ask: do you need color printing, or are your printing requirements limited to monochrome (black and white)?

Before you answer, make sure you consider your future needs. If you buy an inexpensive laser printer, for example, you've committed yourself to monochrome unless you buy a color printer later. Of course, all color printers also print straight black and white, but they may not produce the superior print quality of a dedicated monochrome printer. Also, it typically costs less to print a page of black text on a laser printer than it does to print the same page on an inkjet printer.

Even if you print only simple black-and-white documents now, will you need to print color documents or color materials in a year or two? Such color materials may include any of the following:

■ **Schoolwork.** Banners, posters, and children's artwork all benefit from color printing.

■ **Business materials.** Brochures, transparencies, presentation charts and graphs, certificates, and even the traditional business card can be accented with spot color.

■ **Hobby and community service projects.** Specialized materials such as T-shirt transfers, photo scrapbooks and albums, greeting cards, and CD-ROM labels are prime candidates for color printing.

I know, it seems that I'm heavily biased in favor of recommending a color printer. Don't get me wrong — I'm certainly not saying that black-and-white printing has gone the way of the dinosaur. Most businesses use a standard monochrome laser printer more than they use an office copier. Most professionals demand the speed, lower operation costs, longer life and quality document appearance of a laser printer, and some niche markets (for instance, architects and designers) still rely on monochrome printing or plotting. If you print a high volume of black text, a laser is usually the best choice.

However, I *strongly* recommend a color printer or all-in-one unit for typical home or school use. As proof, consider the success of the color inkjet printer as the printer of choice in homes and schools everywhere. It has become the top seller because it is versatile and capable of printing vibrant color at a low cost.

Tip

Have you been given a "legacy" monochrome printer (one that's been replaced) from your office, or have you bought one for practically pennies at a garage sale? If you can use it, by all means, add it to your system. However, if it's more than five years old, make sure you buy a good stock of printer ribbons or toner cartridges. Check your local office supply store — if you can't find supplies there, consult Computer Shopper magazine, which always carries advertisements from mail-order companies that specialize in stocking hard-to-find ribbons and cartridges. You can also search for supplies on the Web; addresses for these online companies are at the end of this chapter.

Take a moment to consider both your present needs and any possibilities the future may hold, and then jot down either "monochrome only" or "color" on your specification sheet.

A Good Picture Is Worth $10,000

Well, maybe not in *every* case, but you definitely pay more for photo-quality color! If you've decided that you need a monochrome printer, skip this section, and jump to the next one. On the other hand, if you've decided that you need color printing, it's time to determine the quality of that printing.

As you learned in Chapter 1, an inkjet printer is capable of printing excellent color graphics, but thermal wax or dye-sublimation printers (both of which are considered high-end hardware) are still a mainstay with graphics professionals. Continuous tone color quality and Pantone matching (which I get into later in Chapter 9) are especially important to graphics artists, desktop publishers, and publishing houses. Because these professionals create and edit artwork and lay-outs for commercial printing, they demand the best printing technology available. These printers typically cost several thousand dollars, they're usually as slow as drying paint, and the quality of their black-and-white print is usually pretty dismal. However, with color output quality that rivals a 35mm photo-graph, they're the royal family of graphics printing.

The prices of color laser printers are rapidly falling, but you still pay around $1,000 for a low-end model. Although pricey for a single PC owner, color laser printers are always a popular choice for office networks.

As I discuss later, dpi resolution isn't a reliable indicator of image quality, so that ratio is not really the best specification to use when shopping (however, these guidelines help put you in the right ballpark). For home use, a personal color printer should be capable of at least 600×600 dpi; most inkjet printers fall squarely into this category. You can find inkjet printers with even better print quality for only about $100 to $150 more, and they make a good pick for the home or office user who often prints 24-bit color graphics from a scanner, a digital camera, or Web sites.

An example of a quality printer at a very low price is the APOLLO P-2200 color inkjet printer shown in Figure 2.1, which features Hewlett-Packard inkjet technology. This inkjet produces 600×600 dpi black-and-white text and 300×300 dpi color — yet it costs only about $80! The P-2200 prints up to six pages per minute in monochrome and up to three pages per minute in color, making it the perfect choice for a student's computer system, or a first-time computer owner who wants to add a color printer for less than $100. Like more expensive inkjets, the P-2200 produces envelopes, labels, greeting cards, and other projects such as those discussed in Chapter 12. Other printers in the APOLLO line, such as the Barbie P-1220 inkjet printer, are designed especially for kids. This printer carries the Barbie logo and pink accents and includes stickers that kids can use to personalize their printer, as well as Barbie CD-ROM software.

Figure 2.1 The APOLLO P-2200 inkjet printer is a great example of low-cost inkjet technology.

If you're buying a color printer for home or an office (including a network), jot down "standard-quality color" on your specification sheet. If you're shopping for a high-resolution graphics printer (or you'll be using an expensive high-resolution digital camera or scanner), write down "photo-quality color" instead.

Desktop Printer Meets the Road Warrior

Our next criteria to examine in evaluating your needs is portability: do you need a portable printer, and if so what size? This may seem an easy question to answer at first, but consider these points:

■ Just because you have a notebook or laptop computer, you may not necessarily need a portable printer. Do you absolutely require that printer when you're traveling? Remember, Windows 98 and Windows 2000 enable you to create print jobs that you can process later, after you've returned home.

I often send documents from my laptop as e-mail attachments without ever actually printing them! Some travelers don't even need hard copy when they fax documents. You can simply save your documents and send them electronically with your faxmodem. If you only print at home, buy a standard desktop printer, and connect your laptop whenever you need to print a document.

■ On the other hand, I know at least two friends who maintain large networks of desktop computers and carry portable printers with them. These printers can be easily connected to a network workstation to produce a quick hard copy on the spot, without the trouble of marching to a network printer (which is usually busy anyway and may be located three doors farther down the hall). Because just about every existing PC has a parallel printer port, a single portable printer can move around an office just like a portable tape backup unit (it also saves valuable space on a crowded desktop).

■ Although portable inkjet printers are typically somewhat more expensive than their desktop cousins, they certainly produce good results. A handful of portable printers are available today that can match the 600×600 dpi resolution of a low-end personal laser printer.

If you do, in fact, need a portable printer, does it have to fit in a briefcase? If you carry a larger soft bag with you and space-saving isn't of prime importance, you may find that many desktop inkjets can also do double duty as portables. For most of us, a desktop printer is the right choice. If you need to print documents on battery power, however, or if you need to transport your printer with your laptop in as small a space as possible, then the portable printer is the way to travel. Add either the word "desktop" or "portable" to your specification sheet.

Speed Is Important

The last question to ask during your self-evaluation is, "How fast a printer do I need?" Do you work in an office environment, where minutes are money? In fact, speed translates almost directly to the relative expense of a new printer; some printers in the same product line from the same manufacturer are almost identical except where speed is concerned (and, as you may expect, the faster the printer, the more expensive it is). Two such printers may offer the same print quality, hold the same number of pages, and understand the same printer control language — but one is simply one or two pages per minute faster.

A typical office printer averages between 10 to 20 pages per minute in monochrome, but speed demons can range up to 70 or 80 pages per minute. If you're buying a printer for an office network, it pays to ask the system administrator how many pages generally get printed in a typical day, and then select a printer with a speed rating that can accommodate that usage.

Of course, most home systems don't need such blazing output. A suitable printer can churn out anywhere from four to eight pages per minute in monochrome and at least three pages per minute in color.

Tip

Unfortunately, you may find that the speed figures for many printers actually reflect their lowest print quality, which is often suitable only for draft documents. I recommend that you see for yourself. Ask for a demonstration of how fast a particular model can print at the quality level you plan to use the most. Remember, your printer should be judged on its ability to deliver high speed and high quality at the same time!

Add the maximum number of pages you need printed per minute to your specifications.

What Type of Printer Do You Need?

You now have a basic idea of what you need in a printer, and you're ready to advance to the next step: selecting a specific type of printer that best meets the requirements you've set.

Cross-Reference

If you like, you can refer to the overview of printer technology in Chapter 1 while following the steps in this section.

Matching a Printer to Your Purpose

Now that you've built a simple specification list, let's examine the various combinations of requirements you could have selected in the previous section. Each of these combinations points toward a different type of printer.

- **Color/standard quality color/desktop/8–15 pages per minute (or less).** This combination is the most popular and common, and it again underlines why inkjet printers are so popular today. If this matches your specification list, you should concentrate on a good quality *inkjet unit*.

- **Color/standard quality color/desktop/over 15 pages per minute.** This description points to a *color laser* or *high-end inkjet*, suitable for use by a workgroup, on an office network, or by a single PC that requires a faster printer. You spend more, but your printer has probably been designed with an office in mind, so it is probably more rugged and reliable than a personal inkjet printer.

- **Color/standard quality color/portable/any speed.** Although *portable printers* are slow, they're designed to run off of batteries, and they're typically quieter than a regular desktop inkjet. As I mentioned earlier in this chapter, many so-called "desktop" printers are actually small enough to bring with you. However, you are saddled with an AC adapter, so you'll need a wall socket. Portable printers also have limited paper-handling features.

- **Color/high-quality photo color/desktop/any speed.** If you're looking for photo-quality color with accurate color matching and continuous tones, consider a *dye-sublimation* or *high-end inkjet printer*. Most color laser printers can't provide the quality of output that you're looking for. However, the latest high-end inkjet printer may meet your needs (and it's certainly cheaper and more versatile than a dye-sublimation unit).

- **Monochrome/desktop/eight pages per minute (or less).** This combination guides you to a low-end *personal laser printer* or an all-in-one unit. Of course, an inkjet printer can also fill these requirements, but it won't offer the detail or reproduce grayscale as accurately as the laser printer. Plus, documents printed with a laser printer won't smear like those printed with inkjets.

- **Monochrome/desktop/over eight pages per minute.** You've entered the domain of the *office laser printer*. Although they're more expensive, these printers are unmatched at delivering black-and-white documents under high-load network conditions.

As you can see, it's really not hard to evaluate your own needs for a printer. (So much for my consulting job.) You've just eliminated the "middleman" from your buying process — say goodbye to that computer salesperson — because you know which type of printer you need. By narrowing your range of comparison to one specific type of printing hardware that matches your needs, you can ignore all other types of printers and make your shopping easier.

Wait, you're not quite done yet. Before I discuss the individual features that help you with your comparison, I suggest you consider any accessories you may need.

Accessorize

As any supermodel can tell you, accessories make the outfit. The same is true for many printing products: you can add features by adding things such as scanning cartridges, larger paper trays, or sheet-feeding attachments. It pays to check if these kinds of extras are available when you compare the features of specific printers in the next section. Some manufacturers offer accessories for every model they make, while others sell accessories only for their higher-priced printers.

Note

In case you hadn't already guessed, a scanning cartridge replaces the ink cartridge in some inkjet printers; however, the scanning resolution is usually not very high, and an inexpensive flatbed scanner does a much better job. (Plus, you won't have to tear pages out of a book or magazine to scan them.) A scanning cartridge is well suited for faxes and text documents, but you lose quite a bit of detail on images and complex line drawings. Unless you need to conserve space on your computer desk and you're not picky about the scan quality (or you're simply mesmerized by the very convenience of the idea), I definitely recommend that you avoid this particular accessory.

I generally check the manufacturer's Web site to see what accessories I can order for a new printer. Some manufacturers allow direct accessory purchases online with your credit card. Never take the word of your local computer salesperson that "you can't get that add-on with that particular printer"; even the best retail computer stores may not carry the full line of parts for the hardware they sell. Online stores are a little better — they're certainly easier to visit. Look for links on the printer's specifications page that may lead to accessory items.

Note

Don't worry about searching for software when evaluating accessories. I tend to think of bundled software as a feature rather than an accessory, because you should receive some sort of creative software with any inkjet or personal laser printer you buy these days. You shouldn't have to buy this software separately, unless you need more sophisticated software for a particular task.

Don't forget the "required accessory": a printer cable. I'm not familiar with a single printer manufacturer that still includes a PC-to-printer cable as standard equipment with a new printer. Naturally, this helps the company cut costs and reduce the price of the product — but before you get upset, keep in mind that it's impossible for the company to know whether you're buying your first printer or upgrading from an older printer. On the other hand, most all-in-one units come with the required IEEE-1284 or USB cable — check before you buy.

Comparing Features

At this point in the chapter, you know which type of printer you need, and you're ready to compare specific models within the printer type you've chosen. In this section, I discuss the features that you should consider (no matter which type of printer you've chosen). I also do a little comparison of my own — between window-shopping locally and researching features online.

Resolution

I touched lightly on *resolution* (expressed as dots per inch) earlier in Chapter 1 — as a rule, the higher the dpi resolution, the more detailed and realistic the appearance of monochrome text on the printed page. However, it's important to note that resolution can differ widely between manufacturers of the same type of printer — or, for that matter, widely between two printers that look identical in the same product line. For example, one well-known printer manufacturer has two printers that retail for about $150 and $200, and their appearance and specifications are almost the same. However, that extra $50 means the difference between 720×720 dpi and 1440×720 dpi, respectively.

As a standard, remember that most monochrome personal laser printers offer 600×600 dpi output; therefore, if a printer is advertised as providing "laser-quality black text," it should be at least 600×600. Some printers advertise laser-quality text at 720×360 dpi, but I've always been able to detect the difference just by examining a page of text printed at 720×360.

Is resolution the only specification that impacts the quality of a printer's output? That's a common myth I've encountered from both computer novices and experts alike, and the answer is *definitely not*. Resolution is only *one* criteria, and it has less impact on print quality than other factors.

For example, the appearance of the final printed page also depends on the type of paper you're using — just print the same photograph on regular paper and high-gloss photo paper, and you'll see the difference — as well as the print quality mode you've selected, and any special print technology built into your hardware. While shopping locally, ask the salesperson to print a sample on the type of paper you'll be using.

Cross-Reference

In Chapters 3 and 9, I discuss special papers and printing technology that can greatly improve printing quality, no matter what resolution your printer uses.

Speed

Ah, the attraction of high speed! Like a sports car among a herd of station wagons, any printer — no matter what type — costs more if it delivers pages significantly faster than the average printer in the same class. For home use, home offices, and small businesses, speed is less of an issue. For example, printing the kids' homework doesn't require 20 pages per minute. All inkjets (and many color lasers as well) print color output significantly slower than black-and-white output, so make sure that you compare the color and black-and-white printing speeds when choosing your printer.

Currently, inkjets range in black-and-white speed from a low of 3 pages per minute (or, if you love computer abbreviations, *ppm* for short) to a high of about 11–14 ppm. Because of their low cost and laser-quality text in black and white, most inkjets can do double duty as an inexpensive monochrome office printer for a single workstation or a workgroup of four people. However, I don't recommend an inexpensive personal inkjet printer for a busy office, especially on a network. Color printing speeds for inkjet printers range from 1.5 ppm to 9 or 10 ppm for the fastest models, so if you're looking for an inkjet printer for a workgroup of eight people or more, shop for a high-end office unit with built-in network support.

Most personal laser printers (those costing less than $500) are quite happy to churn out pages at between 6 to 8 ppm. Again, this speed is fine for a workstation or a typical home system, and considering that the same printer would have cost twice that much three or four years ago makes these printers "feel" like a real bargain. Again, however, the traffic on a typical large office network can leave a personal laser printer gasping for breath.

Color lasers tend to range from 4–6 ppm in color and 10–24 ppm in black and white, depending on the money you're willing to spend. Because you're spending the extra money for color, I strongly recommend you spend a little more for a faster machine. A color laser printer with faster output can also perform quite well as a regular office network monochrome printer, eliminating the need for two machines.

Finally, the fastest dedicated monochrome office laser printers can service an entire floor of a building with ease; average speeds for these top-of-the-line machines range from 16–32 ppm (or even higher). Again, take care in balancing the cost of the printer against its speed (and the average number of pages printed per day on your network): a difference of 4 to 5 ppm between two printers may mean an increase of $300 or $400. For example, why buy the fastest network printer in town if your entire office only prints 5 or 6 documents a day?

Size

Will you station your printer in a separate room, with plenty of space? If so, you can afford to buy a printer the size of a deep freezer. Most of us, though, are limited on desk space, and the dimensions of a printer can make a real difference when comparing different models. Figure 2.2 illustrates two popular styles of inkjet printer engines, each of which has a significant effect on the overall size of the printer:

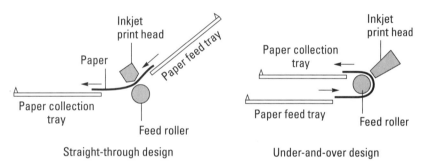

Figure 2.2 Comparison between the straight-through and under-and-over printer designs

■ **Straight-through design.** An inkjet printer with a straight-through design feeds paper in a single direction, straight past the printing head, without folding or curving the paper as it moves. This design requires the printer to have a large tray in back and a large tray in front to feed and catch the sheets of paper. These trays tend to take up a lot of space — especially if you're using legal size paper — and straight-through inkjet printers have the largest dimensions in their class. (However, many of them can fold up to a very small size for storage.)

■ **Under-and-over design.** This printer engine pulls paper from a tray, curls it around a roller, and then guides it past the printing head. The printed sheets are actually deposited right back on top of the paper tray. With no requirement for a paper tray at both the back and the front of the machine, under-and-over inkjet printers can fit in a very small space. Many popular inkjet printers around today use this technique. Figure 2.3 is a picture of the top-selling Hewlett-Packard 935C color inkjet printer, a classic under-and-over model. You can see how the single-tray design saves space on the average desk.

Figure 2.3 The HP 935C is a perfect example of a space-saving under-and-over design. (Courtesy Hewlett-Packard Co.)

By the very nature of the laser printing method, virtually all laser printers are under-and-over designs; the drum makes an ideal roller, and the toner is applied to the page after it has curled around. Some printers also enable you to select a straight paper path, so that you can use heavier media such as card stock without curling it.

Number of Cartridges

This feature applies only to inkjet printers. Some of the least expensive inkjets use a single cartridge (which can be either color or black, and must be manually switched if necessary), while most inkjets that retail for more than $100 or so use a double-cartridge system (where both cartridges are installed at once, and either can be used). A single-cartridge printer can use its color cartridge to also print black by mixing the colors together, although it probably won't be a pure black.

If your printing needs are limited to only black or only color, a single-cartridge printer really isn't a disadvantage at all, and you can save money by choosing one instead of a dual-cartridge system. On the other hand, if you've picked an inkjet printer because you print a mixture of black and color, it's worth every penny to buy a dual-cartridge system. Why?

■ **Convenience.** To achieve the best output with a single-cartridge printer and mixed black and color documents, you must pause the printer and switch cartridges. In most cases, the manufacturer's printer driver automatically pauses the printer, but it's still a hassle to have to "baby-sit" your printer whenever you need to print color text or graphics in a document.

- **Speed.** As you can imagine, a dual-cartridge printer saves you time as well as trouble when printing documents with both black and color material. It takes several seconds to pop the cover on a single-cartridge printer, remove the existing cartridge, and replace it. With a dual-cartridge printer, you can leave your printer unattended and take care of really important business (such as acquiring another soda or answering the door for a pizza delivery).

- **Reliability.** Switching the cartridge on a printer involves a fair number of moving parts, from the cover to the motor and the carriage, as well as the lock that holds the cartridge in place. The more you have to juggle black and color cartridges, the more wear and tear you inflict upon your innocent single-cartridge printer. For this reason, a single-cartridge printer that's heavily used to print a mixture of black and color is more likely to experience mechanical failures than a dual-cartridge printer.

Warning

Are you considering a single-cartridge inkjet printer for printing pages of laser-quality black text? If so, I strongly recommend that you use a black cartridge rather than using the color cartridge to print black text. Most printers of the latter variety mix a black with a definite purple or brown tinge to it.

Memory

With the improved efficiency of 32-bit processing and better use of system RAM, Windows 98 and Windows 2000 have rendered onboard laser printer memory much less important than it was in the days of DOS and Windows 3.1. In the medieval days of the PC (meaning five or six years ago), a laser printer needed 8 or 16MB of on-board RAM to process complex graphics or high-level printer languages such as PostScript. Today, most personal laser printers need only about 2 or 4MB of RAM if you're running under Windows 98, Windows 2000, or Windows NT — your PC actually devotes part of its RAM to simulate the function of built-in printer memory.

If you do decide on a laser printer, make sure that additional printer RAM is available and as inexpensive as possible. The prices of printer memory modules can vary widely. With extra printer memory, print jobs take less time, enabling you to get back to work faster (especially with a slower PC).

Software

Sure, all printers come with software drivers — at least for Windows 98, Windows 2000, and sometimes still for Windows 3.1. (Some printers work only under Windows, so they don't come with DOS drivers.) Many USB printers also include Mac OS drivers as well. But those drivers are only the tip of the iceberg; make sure you compare the software bundled with each printer or all-in-one unit you're considering.

Depending upon the manufacturer, a standard inkjet typically comes with at least some of the following software:

■ **Printer driver.** This is the only software actually required to run your printer. Make sure that your printer comes with the correct driver to match your operating system (this is especially important if you're running a more exotic operating system such as Windows NT or OS/2). An all-in-one has scanning and, if necessary, faxing software included in the driver.

Tip

Always check the manufacturer's Web site or BBS (bulletin board system) for the latest driver for your printer — even *immediately* after you buy it! Because it may take a month or two for a printer to make the journey from the factory's warehouse to your computer table, you may find an updated driver that's more recent than the driver that shipped with your printer.

■ **Printer configuration utility.** Most printers also ship with a useful setup and configuration program. You can use this program to clean or align the heads on your inkjet printer or print a test page (as illustrated in Figure 2.4, which shows a window from one of the utility programs that shipped with my Hewlett-Packard DeskJet printer). A printer utility may also enable you to set advanced parallel-port options or adjust the print quality for different documents. Many recent models have these utilities incorporated into their drivers, and you can locate these functions through the driver help system.

Figure 2.4 An example of a screen from a printer utility program

- **Creative printing program.** If you don't already have a program such as PrintMaster or Print Shop, by all means get one. These creative programs can really entertain your whole family by printing greeting cards, T-shirt transfers, signs, banners, certificates, placemats, calendars, and much more. If you have an all-in-one unit with a scanner, a digital camera, or a stand-alone scanner handy, you can even use pictures of yourself or your family as clip art. I talk about these different hobby and craft materials in Chapter 9.

- **Simple desktop-publishing program.** A program such as Publisher 2000 can help you design your own brochures, pamphlets, and even book-length works — all with professional features such as footnotes, superscripts and subscripts, and text wrap.

- **Image editing program.** An image editor enables you to add special effects to an image, change color depth and size, or add your own text to a picture before you save it to disk or print it. Adobe PhotoDeluxe is an excellent commercial image editor that's shipped with many inkjets. If you don't receive an image-editing program, don't panic — you can buy one separately or register a shareware editor. For example, Figure 2.5 illustrates my favorite shareware image editor, Paint Shop Pro, in action; of course, you can also print your graphic from inside the editor. You can download the shareware evaluation version of Paint Shop Pro from the manufacturer's Web site at `www.jasc.com`.

Figure 2.5 Resizing an image with Paint Shop Pro

Printer Languages and Emulations

What are printer languages and emulations? They are sets of standards that ensure that your printer can cooperate and communicate with your applications software and that different printers can print the same document the same way — however, they provide these functions in different ways.

- A printer *language* is a common computer "dialect" recognized by many different models and software applications. This generic language contains instructions on how to form fonts, graphics, and formatted text, no matter what specific printer and software you're using. As long as both the printer and the application support the same language, you can design and create a document on one computer system, transfer that document to another computer with a different printer, and successfully print the document. The two most common printer languages are PostScript, which was originally designed for use on Macintosh computers, and PCL (Printer Control Language), which was developed by Hewlett-Packard and is supported by almost all of their printer lines. PostScript is generally supported only on laser and high-end photo-quality graphics printers, but programs are available to "translate" a PostScript document for printing on a printer that doesn't support the PostScript language.

- A printer *emulation* enables a printer to "act like" another printer so it can recognize and print documents formatted for that other model. Common emulations are based on drivers and printer commands originally created for older, popular printers that were widely used. For example, many laser printers can emulate the HP LaserJet III (probably one of the most popular printers ever built). Most dot-matrix printers can emulate the Epson LQ or MX series of dot-matrix printers. Emulations enable your older software applications to work with newer printers, even though the software doesn't directly support the new hardware or its language.

Luckily, it's no longer as important to select a printer with the proper list of recognized emulations; if you're using Windows 95, 98, 2000, or NT, the manufacturer's printer driver ensures that your PC can talk to your printer. PostScript is a different matter, though — if you need a printer with PostScript support, expect to pay more. PostScript is still widely used in publishing and graphic design work, so it is a feature on most high-end laser and color laser printers.

Cost per Page

Although you may not have heard of the term, *cost per page* is a great comparison feature. The idea is very similar to the power consumption stickers on major appliances. The cost-per-page figure is an estimate of how much an individual page costs when you factor in the price of the toner or ink (and, for laser printers, the cost of the electricity used to create the page as well).

Unfortunately, most printer manufacturers provide a cost-per-page figure only for office-class monochrome and color laser printers, while other manufacturers don't calculate the figure at all. If you spend more than $1,000 for your printer, it pays to check the manufacturer's Web site for specifications on the model you're interested in — it may include a cost-per-page estimate.

Photo Printing

If you're shopping for an inkjet printer, it's a good idea to check and see whether each model you're considering requires a special photo cartridge to print its best photo-quality images. Typically, these photo cartridges are used with older printers, and only in conjunction with special glossy paper especially designed for printing high-resolution color graphics. For instance, if you're going to print a 16-million-color image and you want the absolute best results your printer can provide, you would swap the standard color cartridge for the photo cartridge, and the standard inkjet paper you usually use for glossy photo paper. After you've printed the image, you replace the expensive cartridge and paper with the standard color cartridge and plain paper.

As you might imagine, installing and removing a photo cartridge can become quite a hassle, especially if you print many 24-bit color images. Most newer printers don't require a special photo cartridge, but I still recommend that you use that glossy photo paper I mentioned earlier for the best results.

Digital Camera Support

One of the latest innovations to appear on an inkjet printer is a port that accepts the digital "film" used by digital cameras. If you're one of the millions of people hopelessly addicted to digital photography or you'll be buying a digital camera in the near future, I'll bet you'll be interested in this feature! After all, why spend all that time downloading those images to your computer when they can go straight to your printer?

For example, the HP PhotoSmart P1000 series of printers can print directly from the industry-standard CompactFlash and SmartMedia memory cards used in a wide range of cameras . . . you don't even need a computer, unless you want to view or edit your digital photographs before you print them. The process is about as simple as it can be: plug the memory card into the slot on the side of the printer, select which images you want to print (and the size you want the finished images to be) using the buttons on the front panel, and press the Print button. The PhotoSmart P1100 even comes with two paper trays; one holds standard $8^{1}/_{2} \times 11$-inch paper, and the other can hold up to 20 sheets of high-resolution glossy photo paper. With 8MB of RAM and a top printing speed of up to 12 pages per minute, this printer is perfectly suited for the digital shutter crowd.

As digital photography becomes more and more popular, I predict you'll continue to see new features like these that are designed to turn your printer into a self-contained "photo lab."

Banner Paper Support

Of the popular inkjet projects that I've already mentioned in this chapter, only one requires a special printer feature. If you print banners with your new inkjet, make sure the paper tray can be raised to an incline to properly feed the banner paper. Without this feature, the banner paper, which is perforated so that it can fold, may feed incorrectly and tear.

Macintosh Support

The Macintosh may have fallen somewhat behind the PC in popularity, but many graphics and publishing professionals still prefer Mac systems, and the popularity of the iMac computer has made it a favorite among first-time computer owners. Printers that offer connectors for both PC and Mac computers tend to be capable of high-resolution graphics — these printers come in very handy for those of us who have one of each type of computer, enabling both PC and Macintosh to remain connected to the same device.

If you use PCs exclusively, then you can ignore this feature, but if you need to print from an older Macintosh, this feature is worth its weight in gold. It saves you the money you would otherwise have to spend on a dedicated Macintosh printer. (By the way, the latest Macintosh computers use USB connections for printing, so they don't need a special connector.)

Online Comparisons versus the Local Touch

Should you perform your comparison shopping on the Internet, or should you compare printers available locally? I've heard opinions both ways, and I personally think the answer lies somewhere between . . . but I'll get to my recommendations in a moment.

Here's a quick rundown of the advantages of online comparison shopping:

- **Wide variety.** If you compare features online, I can guarantee that you have a greater selection of printers from which to choose. In this regard, no local retail store can compete with a larger online computer store.

- **Automated comparisons**. Many sites make it very easy to compare features on the models you select. My two favorite comparison sites are the Computer Shopper NetBuyer site at www.zdnet.com/computershopper and the NECX online store at necxdirect.necx.com. I check these sites when shopping for any kind of computer hardware because generating comparison charts on both sites is easy and very fast. For example, if you select the product comparison feature on NetBuyer, you can choose printers from the list of hardware. Select the general features for the device — for a laser printer, for instance, choose monochrome/any speed/any manufacturer/any price range/any laser printer — and start the search.

Within seconds, NetBuyer displays a list of printers that meet those criteria. Once you've highlighted the printers you're interested in, NetBuyer displays a side-by-side comparison for each feature.

■ **Saves time and gas.** You avoid running all over town by shopping from your PC.

Tip

Note that most of the largest computer magazine publishers also maintain electronic versions of their magazines on their Web sites. You can search these online magazines for printer reviews and printer comparisons. Also, the number of magazine awards won by a specific printer helps ensure its value. For example, if I see that a printer was named in the *PC World* Top Ten last year, I know that it performed well during their tests and offers all of the basic features that it should.

Many computer owners do all of their feature comparisons online, but I've found that local comparison shopping has its advantages as well:

■ **Help from salespeople.** Of course, not every local store has a printer expert, but a local salesperson can probably demonstrate the different printers and answer questions about them.

■ **Hands-on printer comparison.** Believe me, a simple dpi rating is not enough to indicate which model is right for you. Only a copy of the same document printed on several printers can help you determine which printer or all-in-one unit has the best monochrome and color output. It's certainly easier to judge dimensions and how simple the printer is to operate with the real McCoy in front of you, rather than with a picture on a Web site.

■ **Local prices for cartridges.** Most of us don't buy our toner or inkjet cartridges on the Internet (although you can save a few dollars that way). Instead, we wait until a cartridge runs out and buy a replacement at a local store. While shopping locally, check on the prices for replacement cartridges for each printer you're evaluating. There often is a surprising difference in the prices and capacity between cartridges from different manufacturers.

Personally, I start my comparison shopping for any computer peripheral online. That way, I can weed out those products that definitely don't meet my needs before I spend time looking at them locally, and I also end up with a base mail-order price. Once I'm done with my online comparison shopping, I've reduced the field of possible contenders down to three or four models, and I'm ready to make the trip to one or two of my local computer stores.

If you use this technique, you arrive at the store focused and ready to compare two or three specific models. You can evaluate the size and ease-of-use of each candidate and ask the salesperson any specific questions that you couldn't get answered online. (Of course, you may have to visit more than one store to try out all of the models you're considering.)

Tip

Ask the salesperson to demonstrate the models you're evaluating. During the demonstration, listen to how loud the printer is, and ask the salesperson to show you how difficult it is to change cartridges, print envelopes, and add paper. This is also a good time to check on the actual printing speed and quality you get using both plain paper and other types of media you may use.

This method of mixing online and hands-on comparisons has always worked for me — and although you may not enjoy your hardware shopping experience as much as a dedicated technowizard, at least you'll be confident that you've selected just the right computer printing hardware for your needs. (If you are a computer technotype as I am, hardware shopping is much, much more fun than grocery shopping . . . but we all have to eat *sometime*.)

I discuss the actual purchase process in a page or two, but first, let's cover the importance of comparing warranty and support for the printers you're evaluating.

Comparing Warranty and Support

I've met many shoppers intent on buying the perfect printer who have spent hours on the Internet researching their possible choices. They've checked every computer magazine available, and they're thoroughly familiar with every feature of the printer they've selected. That's good work, but very often those same shoppers forget to evaluate the warranty and support they'll receive from the company *after* they've made their purchase.

Why is it important to compare warranty and support? Of course, you can certainly cross your fingers and hope that you never need warranty service or technical support, but you still need updated printer drivers (and possibly an answer to a sticky question or two). It's possible that your new printer will work like a Swiss watch for as long as you own it, but I strongly recommend that you consider what will happen if it doesn't.

Warranties 101

As you may guess, not all warranties for computer printers offer the same coverage or last for the same amount of time; however, these general guidelines cover most of the printers sold today:

- **Inkjet printers.** Look for at least a standard one-year warranty for both parts and labor; this is usually all you need for home or workstation use.

- **Multifunction devices.** Like inkjet printers, most all-in-one units have a one-year parts and labor warranty; however, these printers have more features than a simple inkjet printer. Plus, an all-in-one is usually very important to a small home office or business, and that same office or business may not have a bundle of spare cash lying around for computer hardware repairs.

Therefore, I recommend that you purchase a warranty extension of two extra years or more when you buy a multifunction unit. I also recommend that you check on the possibility of an "exchange" warranty, where the manufacturer offers a warranty or a service upgrade with overnight exchange of another unit while your multifunction printer is repaired.

- **Personal laser printers.** Personal laser printers under $500 typically feature a one-year parts and labor warranty. Depending on the number of pages you print, you may want to consider an extended warranty that adds on an extra year or two.

- **Office laser printers.** More expensive monochrome and color laser printers intended for office use may offer as much as three years' coverage on parts and labor. They're also usually covered for preventive maintenance and repairs by an office computer maintenance agreement with the manufacturer (or a local computer shop).

- **High-end graphics printers.** Expensive dye-sublimation and thermal wax printers are usually covered for at least three years' parts and labor, and they may also be protected by an office computer maintenance agreement.

Warning

Manufacturer's standard warranties *do not* cover damage from lightning strikes and power surges. At the very least, it's important to connect your printer's AC power cord to a surge suppressor instead of the wall socket; a surge suppressor can stop many power surges that would otherwise fry your printer like a burger at your favorite fast food joint. However, even the best surge suppressor can't hold back a lightning strike on your home or office wiring. More expensive printers should be covered by your homeowner's or office insurance. (Some extended warranty plans offered by local computer retailers may include coverage for lightning strikes and power surges, so check with the salesperson at the store.)

The Advantage of an On-Site Warranty

Some standard warranties (and many extended warranties) for high-end laser and inkjet printers offer *on-site repair* — a technician comes to your home or office, diagnoses the problem, and fixes your printer. On-site repair is neat, but remember that these technicians make house calls only within a certain distance from the store, so if you live in a rural area you may have to ship your printer via UPS or FedEx anyway. Also, it generally takes at least 24 hours before an on-site repairman can schedule a visit to your house. If you need repairs immediately, it's a better idea to pack up your printer and visit your local computer repair shop as quickly as possible.

But what if you've got a research paper to print or a business document due tomorrow? If you desperately need a printer while yours is being repaired, ask the technician if you can borrow a "loaner." Once your printer is working properly again, you can return the loaner machine. You can also go to a place such as Kinko's, which has computers and printers to rent on-site.

Tip

I always use my credit card when buying computer hardware. Not only is it more convenient, but I don't have to wait for a personal check to clear before my merchandise is shipped. Also, some credit cards automatically extend the standard warranty on hardware that you purchase with the card, and provide other protections as well.

Even Technotypes Need Support Sometimes

What is "good" support, anyway? It's rather hard to quantify just what everyone needs in the way of technical support. For example, consider two types of printer owners: one is a computer hardware novice with no previous printing experience who has no idea what a parallel port looks like, while the other is a computer guru with years of experience installing and using (and perhaps even repairing) printers. The novice computer owner is much more likely to need voice technical support, while the experienced computer owner is more interested in obtaining the newest printer drivers and solving hardware and software incompatibilities.

Here's a checklist of common technical support functions — you decide which is more important to you and compare the manufacturers according to those criteria.

- **Voice technical support.** Virtually all manufacturers now charge for any voice support past a certain time limit. As I've already mentioned, first-time printer owners are likely to need more voice technical support than those who have owned PCs for years. Other forms of direct technical support include fax and e-mail support.

- **Access to updated drivers.** As I mentioned earlier, a well-written, bug-free printer driver is essential to proper operation of your printer under Windows 98 and Windows 2000. The manufacturer should provide printer drivers on its BBS and Web site and update them from time to time to correct any problems. The manufacturer's driver library should include older models that have been discontinued, so you'll be able to download and reinstall the proper driver in the future (even if your printer is no longer being manufactured).

- **Technical specifications and FAQs.** You should be able to access technical information and *FAQs* (Frequently Asked Questions) concerning your printer on the manufacturer's Web site. The answers to the most commonly asked technical support questions appear in the FAQs, and that's always the first file I download from the manufacturer's site after I buy a piece of hardware.

- **Example templates, projects, and documents.** Some manufacturers provide example documents, formatted word-processing templates, and professionally designed graphics for use in your printing projects. This example material makes a great starting point for your own work. Check the manufacturer's Web site for any free "goodies" they may offer for the model (or models) you're considering.

Again, online magazines come in handy when comparing the technical support offered by different manufacturers. Check the magazine's Web site for printing hardware reviews that rate the quality of technical support as well as features offered by the hardware. Another resource is word-of-mouth; if you have a friend who's owned the same printer, ask their opinion of the support they received. Other possible sources of information include computer user groups, Internet hardware mailing lists, and Internet newsgroups devoted to PC hardware. You'll find that members of these forums are very eager to tell you what they think of a manufacturer's products.

Should You Buy a Refurbished Printer?

In case you're scratching your head, here's a quick definition: "refurbished" merchandise was returned by the original owner to the manufacturer for some reason (usually because it arrived broken, or broke sometime during the first few days of use). The manufacturer repairs the item and sells it at a greatly reduced price to one of several discount chains or online Internet stores; it's then resold. There's nothing illegal about this, as long as the merchandise is clearly indicated as "refurbished" or "remanufactured" (of course, the definition of the word *clearly* is open to interpretation). For example, I recently went to a Web site called Surplus Direct (`www.surplusdirect.com`) and found a great deal on a Canon LBP-465 laser printer for only $159.88. Sounds like a great deal, doesn't it? However, I had to scroll down through three screens' worth of description in order to find out that it was refurbished.

I can't deny that refurbished hardware is becoming a big business on the Internet, and even some retail stores are starting to feature refurbished products. Some stores also offer demo and returned products at lower prices. Some people consider refurbished hardware to be as good as new. "After all," they argue, "refurbished hardware is tested by the factory before it's shipped, so any potential problems would be found and corrected." Plus, you generally receive a short warranty, and the prices are outstanding. It seems like a winning proposition.

My personal opinion of refurbished hardware, on the other hand, is a little different: I would rather dig a hole in my backyard, drop in that "remanufactured" printer, mix up some concrete, and give it a decent burial. Although you may be perfectly satisfied with a refurbished printer, keep these guidelines in mind while shopping, and get straight answers from the salesperson or the company:

- **What was wrong with it?** Although you won't know specifically why the original owner returned the printer to the manufacturer, it obviously needed repair or was unsatisfactory in some way.

- **How thoroughly was the printer tested?** Again, you're in the dark. Did the manufacturer retest every component or just what broke the first time? Because you have no idea how the original owner treated the printer, this question is a very important one.

- **Can you return this printer?** Read the advertisement (and perhaps the company's return policy) closely before you buy a refurbished printer. Sales are often final, and you have no recourse if the printer breaks again.

- **The Incredible Shrinking Warranty.** I've never seen a refurbished piece of hardware that had the same length of warranty coverage as a brand-new product. For example, most of the refurbished inkjet printers that I've seen have a mere 90 days of warranty instead of the full one year you would receive with a new printer. If you do buy refurbished hardware, make sure you get the same warranty as you would with a new model.

- **It sure doesn't look like a bargain.** Remanufactured and refurbished hardware sometimes arrives at your doorstep with assorted bumps, scratches, and nicks picked up during its travels. Sure, it's only cosmetic damage, but it's another reason why I avoid refurbished computer peripherals like the plague.

Of course, the decision on whether to save money by purchasing a refurbished printer is up to you, but let me remind you of that famous phrase (usually spoken with the benefit of hindsight): If it seems too good to be true, then it probably is.

Oh, and here's another well-worn cliché that's perfect to end this section: Let the buyer beware!

Time to Buy a Printer

Okay, you've arrived at the end of the comparison process, and you've chosen the model that has all the features you're looking for. It can handle the workload at the right speed, and you're satisfied with the print quality and graphics resolution. Now comes the easy part: you just walk in to your local store and buy one, right?

I hope your answer was, "Wrong!" Although you're nearing your destination, you still have decisions to make, and perhaps some time to spend online and at one or two of your local computer stores. In this section, I discuss the pros and cons of buying locally and buying online, and I provide the addresses of a number of well-known online stores.

Like the feature comparison you performed earlier in this chapter, you have two choices for purchasing your new printer: you can buy your printer from a local store, or you can buy it from a catalog (either online or printed). Which method is better? Which is more expensive in the long run? There is no one "right" buying source for everyone, and the route you take depends upon you. Next, I walk you through the advantages of each method.

The Local Method: The Value of Local Service and Support

For those buying their first printer, it's important to have direct eye contact with another person — even if that person is not a printer expert. Only a local discount or computer store can provide personal service (although most discount stores don't hire knowledgeable computer technicians, most computer store salespeople are familiar with the printers they offer).

Also, buying your computer from a local company usually entitles you to local service in case you run into problems; instead of mailing your printer halfway across the country, you can bring it to the store and drop it off for service. (Of course, it's a good idea to ask about service before you buy.)

In this section, I list the reasons why millions of computer owners buy printers from a local store rather than order them from a mail-order company. I also include several tips that help you steer clear of problems when you buy locally.

You can take your time

If you buy locally, you don't have to rush. Formulate questions about the features that matter the most to you, ask the salesperson's opinion, verify the store's warranty, and just generally make a nuisance of yourself (bring this book tucked under your arm, and let 'em know you mean business). Even though you've done your research and you know which printer or all-in-one unit you want, don't allow yourself to be rushed into buying. Many times I've found something that's changed my mind about a purchase in a computer store at the last minute. If you need a technical term explained, don't be embarrassed to ask the salesperson.

You can haggle

Should you haggle over the price of your new printer? That depends on three things: the type of store you're visiting, the sticker price of the printer, and your own personality. Most discount stores don't deviate from the sticker price, and for a good reason: usually the price you pay is already very competitive. Haggling does no good in this situation.

However, if you're visiting a privately owned computer store or an electronics megaplex that sells everything from CD-ROMs to speaker wire, the price is probably high enough to allow the salesperson a little leeway. For example, if you spend $500 on a new personal laser printer, five or ten dollars off buys you a box of paper. I've sold computers in an electronics chain store, and I can tell you from personal experience that the confident customers who ask for a deal have a chance of getting one (unless, of course, you ask for an outrageous discount). If haggling doesn't work, try haggling at other stores first before you pay the sticker price.

You can get support

Once you've bought your printer, make sure you note some important pieces of information in case you need support while installing and configuring your printer: the salesperson's name, the manufacturer's voice technical support telephone number, and the store's return policy.

Avoid the fee

Some stores are now charging a restocking fee if you return your printer without a specific complaint, just like mail-order stores have been doing for years. This fee is a 10 or 15 percent charge for boxing the printer up and putting it back on the shelf (or tagging it "refurbished" or "used," and charging a lower price for it). I understand the reasoning behind a restocking fee, but I still don't want to pay it; generally, the best way to avoid paying this fee is to choose your printer carefully, so you buy the right model. If you return the printer because of an honest-to-goodness mechanical error (rather than, "I just didn't like it"), you won't have to pay the restocking fee, and the store will probably give you a replacement printer.

Save that box

Many novice computer owners throw away the printer box as soon as they get home — and that's a mistake. If your particular printer turns out to be a lemon and you have to return it, many stores charge you a fee if you don't return the unit with all the original packaging and the box. (See the previous pointer.) The box and packaging also come in handy if you have to send the printer back to the manufacturer for service work within the warranty period.

Remember to register

It's important to register your new printer as soon as possible. Many manufacturers send notices of driver upgrades and special offers for accessories and software to the registered owners of their products. Registration may also be required to obtain voice technical support for your new printer.

Get the right software

If you're running Windows 3.1, OS/2, DOS, or Windows NT, you're leading an "alternative" computer lifestyle — there's nothing wrong with such strange behavior, but remember that most of the world is running either Windows 95/98/Me or Windows 2000. Make sure that your printer comes with the right drivers — and if they're not in the box, have the salesperson connect to the manufacturer's Web site and download the drivers you need.

Grab a cable and spare cartridges

As mentioned earlier in this chapter, you need a printer cable if you don't already have one (unless you're buying a multifunction printer, which probably includes the cable). Your salesperson should know if you need a bidirectional cable; if you do, look for a printer cable that complies with the IEEE-1284 standard. Whenever I buy a printer, I always buy a spare cartridge (or two, for a dual-cartridge color inkjet). That way, I'm covered if I'm printing long documents and I run out of ink.

A final word

I rarely buy anything but software from local computer stores in my area; I'd rather save money and buy directly from one of my favorite mail-order catalog stores.

However, if this printer is the first one you've owned, or if you feel more secure with repairs and service performed by a local company, I encourage you to pay the extra money and avoid buying that printer through a mail-order company. The feeling of security is worth it.

The Mail-Order Method: Saving Money, Time, and Gas

What's that you say? "I can take an inkjet printer apart in 60 seconds flat with a paperclip. And put it back together in total darkness!" Okay, you've owned a printer before, you hate computer salespeople, and you want to save money. You're the perfect candidate for buying a printer from a mail-order company.

Once you're familiar with your favorite mail-order companies, you can order everything from a mousepad to a complete state-of-the-art PC system with all the bells and whistles — and with confidence that you're buying from a reputable company that stands behind the products it sells.

In this section, I discuss the advantages of spending your money on a printer over the Internet or a toll-free telephone call, as well as give a few tricks of the trade that you may find useful.

Order anytime, anywhere

Most mail-order companies allow online ordering from a Web site, complete with a secure connection to safeguard your credit card number — but what if you don't have access to the Internet? Fear not . . . any mail-order company worth its salt also provides a toll-free order line, and many are open 24 hours a day. Call and order your printer during your lunch break, after the kids are asleep, or before you leave for work; there's nothing quite like the convenience of mail-order shopping.

Buy any printer you can name

Sure, you've decided on the Ultravox 9000 Combination Laser Printer and Lawn Sprinkler . . . but can you find it *locally*? It's often very hard to track down more expensive color lasers or high-resolution graphics printers at your local computer store — they're not popular with the general public, and they're typically too expensive for the average computer owner. Therefore, most local computer stores carry several of the best-selling inkjet printers, one or two personal monochrome laser printers, and a multifunction printer or two.

No such problem on the Internet. The powerful search utilities on sites such as NetBuyer or CDW (Computer Discount Warehouse) make it easy to locate that specific printer you've chosen, no matter how expensive. The selection is always better than any local store, no matter where you live. Most mail-order houses can also order models that they don't have on hand.

Consider the tax break

In the old days of mail-order shopping — you know, five or six years ago — mail-order companies usually didn't charge any taxes on your purchase. It felt somewhat like "duty-free" shopping on a cruise ship. Sure, you paid a charge for shipping and handling, but your bottom line was still much lower than it would have been if you had bought the same printer at a local store and paid state taxes as part of the price. Unfortunately, that's no longer the case for many mail-order companies. Now they must charge you state tax (and they still tack on the shipping and handling fee). If your mail-order company of choice doesn't add in state taxes, consider yourself lucky.

Find the best prices

There's no question: if you purchase your new printer from a mail-order catalog or online through the company's Web site, you're almost guaranteed to receive a better price than any local store. However, this doesn't mean you can't shop around between different online storefronts. I always spend a few minutes doing a little "virtual window shopping" among my favorite companies to make sure I'm getting the lowest possible price. You can't haggle over a modem, but you can exercise your right to locate the best deal on the printer you've selected.

Where is it now?

Many online stores also provide an order-tracking system: you can tell whether your printer has left the company (and if so, where it is). This is another feature I like to use when buying a peripheral online, especially if I paid extra for faster shipment. If the mail-order company has an online storefront on the Web, you may set up a user account. Such an account enables you to display information about past purchases as well.

The incredible $50 shipping and handling fee

As I said earlier, mail-order stores are notorious for charging a restocking fee if you return your printer for any reason other than a hardware failure. You can avoid the restocking fee by choosing the right printer, but you may never escape those evil *shipping and handling charges* tacked on to your total by all mail-order companies. It's a good idea to ask how much a company charges for shipping before you buy. Unless you really need second-day air delivery, *why pay for it?*

Just in case . . .

If you order your printer through the mail or the Web, it's especially important for you to keep the box and packaging material. You need the original box in case you have to return the printer to the mail-order company or ship the printer back to the manufacturer for service work. (By the way, the box also comes in handy if you're planning on a major move in the near future.)

Choose a secure site

Are you planning to buy your printer from an online store's Web site? If so, it's a good idea to place credit card orders over secure Internet connections, where your credit card is encrypted — both Netscape Navigator and Microsoft Internet Explorer support secure sessions (if you're using at least version 3.x of either browser). Although the possibility that your credit card information may be intercepted on a regular connection is very slim, a secure connection is usually a sign that you're buying from a reputable company that wants to safeguard your privacy. You can tell that your session is encrypted and secure when you see a "locked" padlock icon appear on the status line at the bottom of the browser window.

Make sure everything's included

I always check (and double-check) to make sure that hardware I'm buying from a mail-order company arrives with everything. Do you need a printer cable? (Luckily, you can probably buy a cable locally, unless you live in the Sahara desert.) Did you specify software for the right operating system? It's a real hassle to return a printer to a mail-order company because the salesperson thought you wanted the Macintosh model — and you probably pay to ship the printer back, too. While you're at it, consider buying a replacement toner cartridge or replacement inkjet cartridges along with your printer; you probably end up saving money on those, too.

Bargain hunt through e-mail

Do you often buy computer hardware and software from a specific mail-order company? If so, check to see if that company offers an Internet e-mail list or newsletter for its customers. These e-mail lists typically alert you to special deals, including rebates, exclusive sale prices, and new product arrivals. Be careful, however: joining too many of these mailing lists clogs your e-mail with advertisements, so I recommend that you join lists offered by only your top two or three favorite mail-order companies.

A final word

If you're confident of your installation abilities and printer knowledge, you can save a bundle on your new printer or all-in-one by purchasing it online or over the phone. As long as you choose reputable mail-order companies and you verify your order, you're likely to end up with a good deal. I always have, and as I said earlier, I haven't bought a printer from a retail store in many years.

As you buy hardware, you're likely to find companies on the Web you can trust — make sure you bookmark those sites (as well as the software and driver page on the manufacturer's Web site). To get you started, I list and describe a few of my favorite online companies at the end of this chapter.

What Was That Clunk?

It's Murphy's Law . . . well, at least some of the time. Here's the scenario you don't want to consider: you get your new printer home, you open the box, and something's missing. Or perhaps you can't read the CD-ROM that came with your printer. Or maybe your PC locks up while you're installing the printer's software. No matter what the cause, you're stuck with a very expensive paperweight until you can reach the manufacturer's technical support. I've been in that situation a few times, and I can tell you from experience that it's the definition of the word "frustrating."

Before you make the call, do yourself a favor, and prepare the answers to the questions the support technician will ask you. The call will go faster, and the technician will be able to concentrate on the problem at hand rather than trying to figure out which model of printer you bought. In this section, I discuss what information you need and who you should call in case you need technical support immediately after buying your printer.

Note

I discuss the installation process in Chapter 6, so I won't discuss all the steps here — but because many novice printer owners encounter problems before the installation begins, this section explains what to do if a piece is missing or the installation software simply doesn't load.

Before You Call . . .

Have you read the installation guide that accompanied your printer? If not, take the time to read through it before you make the call — it may contain the answer to your problem, or at least offer a clue to the cause of the problem. Unfortunately, reading a user manual is probably not your idea of a good time (I can't think of anything less entertaining at this moment), but the information it contains may save you half an hour of telephone time.

Another important source of troubleshooting information is the README file, which usually contains last-minute tips and instructions that were compiled after the manual was sent to the printer. You typically find the README file in the root directory of the CD-ROM or driver diskette that accompanied your printer. In Windows 98 and 2000, you can open this file using either Notepad or WordPad.

Who Gets the Call?

Okay, you've determined that the problem isn't explained in the printer's documentation, so you have to make a call to someone. Now you need to determine who to call: will it be the store or company that sold you the printer or the printer manufacturer?

If your problem fits in one of these categories, you should call the local store or mail-order company that sold you the printer:

■ **Obvious impact damage.** The printer's cover or case was damaged or shattered.

■ **Missing parts.** Printers are complex peripherals, and there's usually something detachable — the printer's installation guide should include a listing of what you were supposed to receive. As I mentioned earlier in this chapter, your printer very likely does not come with a parallel printer cable. Also, don't be surprised if your printer comes with a single CD-ROM and no floppy diskettes. Floppies can no longer hold the drivers, setup utility, and the various bundled applications that ship with a printer these days.

 Tip

If your computer doesn't have a CD-ROM, you should call the manufacturer and request a disk set. Usually this set includes only the required drivers and utilities necessary to get your printer running, so you'll probably miss out on the bundled application software.

■ **The wrong software.** Occasionally a Macintosh CD-ROM gets accidentally substituted for the Windows 95 CD-ROM that's indicated on the box.

On the other hand, if you encounter one of these problems during the initial setup of your printer, call the manufacturer for help:

■ **Installation program won't run or locks up.** If you're using the correct version of the installation software for your operating system and it won't run, you should contact technical support.

■ **No printer activity.** Check to make sure that your printer's AC power cord is correctly connected and plugged into the wall, and make sure that you've turned the printer's master power switch on. If the printer's power light doesn't glow, you may have a defective unit — a technician can tell you for certain.

■ **No PC-printer/printer-PC communications.** Today's inkjet and laser printers require true bidirectional communications. If your PC's parallel port is not correctly set for bidirectional operation, or you don't have an IEEE-1284 cable, you won't be able to successfully install your printer. For example, Figure 2.6 shows the bidirectional printer test that occurs during the installation of a typical HP printer.

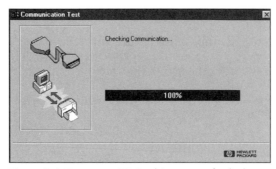

Figure 2.6 Testing an HP DeskJet printer for bidirectional communication

Data You Need to Know

Next, grab a pen and a notepad, and write down the following important data:

- **The printer's model and serial numbers.** These numbers should appear on the bottom or back of your unit. If you received a shipping invoice for your unit, keep it handy.

- **The operating system and version number of the included software.** Copy down the operating system requirements and the version number of the software included by the manufacturer.

- **Your system details.** If you're running Windows 98, Windows NT, or the new Windows 2000, it's easy to find out how much RAM your system has, what specific Windows version you're using, and the type of processor installed in your machine. From your Windows desktop, right-click the icon labeled "My Computer," and select Properties from the menu. Windows displays a screen similar to Figure 2.7 that lists these details.

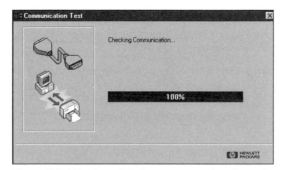

Figure 2.7 Windows 98 shows system details on this dialog box.

- **Other system peripherals.** Take a moment to note the other peripherals attached to your PC (especially any parallel-port devices such as an Iomega Zip drive or a parallel-port scanner).

■ **Error messages displayed by your system.** If your PC displays any error messages before you experience problems, it's *very* important to write down the full text of the error message for your technician.

With this information in hand, you are prepared to answer the questions asked by the salesperson or technical support representative. Because you obviously haven't had time to register your printer yet, you may also be required to provide personal information.

Recommended Internet Online Stores

In this final section, I introduce you to a few of my favorite online sites for purchasing printers, all-in-one models, and cartridges (as well as all the other computer hardware you could possibly imagine). Each of these companies has proven itself to me in the past, and they offer a solid discount over local retail prices.

CDW

Computer Discount Warehouse (or CDW for short) is probably the best-known online discount store for computer systems, peripherals, and supplies. This company advertised long before the arrival of the Internet, however, and you'll see the familiar red-bordered pages in every major computer magazine (including *Computer Shopper*). CDW salespeople are very knowledgeable and well trained. The online store offers more than 30,000 products, with descriptions and updated prices, which makes the CDW site a natural for your comparison shopping. You can connect to CDW at `www.cdw.com`.

Egghead

If you remember the Egghead retail chain, you'll be right at home with the Egghead online computer discount store. Besides sales of the latest printer models, Egghead is well known for its surplus and liquidation sales, and it has one of the most successful online auction sites on the Internet. Egghead also offers great prices on software, and you can download many titles . . . you can even "try before you buy." The Egghead store is at `www.egghead.com`.

MicroWarehouse

MicroWarehouse has been offering great deals through print catalogs for many years now, and you can find all the best manufacturers on the Web site as well. As with Egghead, it pays to check the site once every couple of days for liquidation and surplus merchandise. Or if you like, you can join its e-mail list, and the deals are delivered right to your desktop. The site address is `www.microwarehouse.com`.

MidWest Micro

MidWest Micro is another print catalog favorite that has hit the Web, but it has a long history as a computer peripheral store. The company's site is one of the best around, complete with a searchable knowledge base of technical documents and online manuals in Acrobat .PDF format. You can find MidWest Micro at www.mwmicro.com.

Toner Cartridge Depot

Looking for hard-to-find laser toner cartridges, dot-matrix printer ribbons, or inkjet cartridges? The Depot is a great online store, with a huge selection of cartridges . . . if a device supplies ink or toner to any type of printer, you're likely to find it at the Depot. Plus, the site features secure ordering and a powerful search utility to help you locate the printer supplies you need. The company's Web address is www.tonercartridgedepot.com.

Summary

In this chapter, you learned the fine art of selecting the right printing hardware for your needs, and then you found out how to buy that hardware at a local store or from an online store. Finally, this chapter covered the importance of a good warranty, how to spot quality service, and how to fully utilize a company's technical support.

In the next chapter, we'll explore the world of inkjet printers in detail.

Up Close: Inkjet Printers

IN THIS CHAPTER
- Using an inkjet for high-resolution printing
- Understanding dpi (dots per inch)
- Understanding Hewlett-Packard's PhotoREt II and III
- Understanding Hewlett-Packard's MIDS system
- Selecting a print quality
- Selecting duplex (two-sided) mode
- Printing multiple copies
- Printing collated copies
- Selecting landscape mode
- Choosing a paper size and type
- Feeding and caring for your inkjet printer
- Using a surge suppressor or UPS

Inkjet printing has closed the gap between high-quality output and low cost — instead of the daisywheel impact printers and the laser printers that used to be associated with letter-quality output, the arrival of the inkjet changed the "balance of power" forever in the PC world. In fact, it fills the requirements of most home computer owners so well, PC owners never look at another type of printer while they're shopping.

Additionally, only the inkjet can produce low-cost color; many of the school projects, business applications, and PC hobby projects I cover later in the book were unheard-of until the inkjet printer appeared on the market. For example, can you imagine having as much fun printing T-shirt transfers, audio CD labels, and even paper doll outfits if you were limited to monochrome black?

But the inkjet printer isn't popular only because of its print quality or its low price: inkjets are also practically maintenance-free. (That's one of the big reasons why I own one.) Change the cartridges from time to time, feed it another load of paper, and these modern marvels keep churning out documents.

In this chapter I focus on the inkjet printer, including the features and capabilities that make it so appealing.

Printing High-Quality Graphics

As I mentioned in earlier chapters, today's inkjet printers can produce stunning color graphics and laser-quality black print. The ability to print high-quality graphics at a low cost makes the inkjet printer an ideal choice for demanding digital applications, such as:

- **Printing graphics from the World Wide Web.** What better way to complete a virtual tour of the Louvre over the Web than to capture the Mona Lisa in 24-bit color? The Web offers a practically unlimited source of material for printing on your inkjet.

Warning

Just because you downloaded an image from a Web page does not give you the right to reproduce it in a publication of your own. Copyright infringement is no laughing matter, and an image doesn't have to have a visible copyright line in order to be protected. Because I'm no lawyer, I recommend that you consult your lawyer for advice if you want to distribute an image that you found on the Web. (This also includes images you've scanned from books, magazines, and even video still images.) On the other hand, you can consider copyrighting the original images you've taken yourself with a digital camera.

- **Printing scanned graphics.** In the years before inkjets, there was no inexpensive way to print a high-quality color copy of an image that you had scanned. Scanner technology at the time was far ahead of the dot-matrix crowd, boasting better dpi resolution and up to 24-bit color. Today's inkjet printers, however, easily surpass the image quality of most low-end scanners, and reproducing 24-bit color is a cinch.

■ **Printing images from a digital camera.** Figure 3.1 illustrates a goofy image I took for this book with my Nikon digital camera, which offers a resolution of 640×480 in 24-bit color. (Yes, it's Godzilla and me. He's the one on the right.) An inkjet printer is the perfect companion for your digital camera — especially if you use glossy photo paper and print your image at full size. Instant glossy photograph!

Figure 3.1 Two old friends get together — a moment captured by a digital camera

Cross-Reference

In Chapter 10 I demonstrate how a new generation of inkjet printers from Hewlett-Packard enables you to print your photos directly from the camera's "digital film" — you don't even need to download the images to your computer!

■ **Printing color transparencies for projectors.** If you're a dedicated user of business presentation graphics packages such as PowerPoint and Visio, an inkjet printer can produce the color transparencies and hard copies you need for your next dog and pony show.

■ **Printing artwork from CD-ROMs and PhotoCDs.** If you've committed your 35mm film photographs to a CD-ROM, a color inkjet can create a print for you in less than a minute. Or, you can print an image from a CD-ROM containing stock photographs and photo clip art.

In this section, I discuss the photo print quality offered by inkjet printers and how you can select the right print quality for your printing needs.

Discussing Dots per Inch

As I mentioned in Chapter 2, the dots-per-inch resolution of a printer has always been a specification that people use while shopping for printing hardware. In fact, many shoppers simply compare dpi figures, cost, and speed and choose a printer based solely on those characteristics. (I don't recommend this method, by the way.) What are the benefits of a high dpi resolution?

- **Higher detail.** Typically, the more dots that make up an image, the better the detail. In Chapter 1 you saw an example of the same image at two different resolutions, one at 300×300 and the other at 600×600.

- **Sharper edges.** In Figure 3.2 you see a corner of an enlargement of the two images shown in Chapter 1. This is the same edge of the apple image displayed at two different resolutions. Note how the higher-resolution edge looks cleaner than the lower-resolution version. (The same is true for boundaries between colors in an image. However, higher resolution doesn't directly translate into more realistic color.)

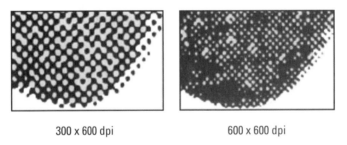

300 x 600 dpi   600 x 600 dpi

Figure 3.2 It's the same edge, but it sure looks better at 600×600 dpi.

I chose 600×600 dpi for these examples because that resolution is generally considered the standard for a good inkjet printer. But, as you may expect, the results from a 1200×1200 dpi inkjet are better still. Keep in mind that this comparison only applies to conventional inkjet printers, which dispense only one drop of each primary color per pixel.

Unfortunately, increasing the resolution of a printer also *dramatically* increases the amount of time it takes to print a document (as well as over-saturating the paper with ink in many cases), so high resolution is not a blanket answer to high-quality print. Let's explore another solution.

Understanding PhotoREt Technology

Although resolution is a factor in the appearance of the finished hard copy, a few years ago Hewlett-Packard introduced a feature that enables its inkjet printers to produce outstanding print and image quality without relying on sky-high dpi ratings (which greatly reduces the importance of simple dpi comparisons). This revolutionary technology, called *Photo Resolution Enhancement technology*, or more commonly, PhotoREt, improves the quality of color graphics, photos, and images on any type of paper. Currently, most of the inkjet printers offered by Hewlett-Packard use PhotoREt II, but a new line of inkjet printers offering the enhanced PhotoREt III have begun to appear as well.

The Standard: PhotoREt II

How does PhotoREt II work? The secret is in the printer's microprocessor brain and the cartridge. The enhanced microprocessor is capable of much finer control over the application of ink, so the nozzles in a PhotoREt II cartridge can apply smaller and more dots of ink to the paper. In fact, the cartridge in an HP DeskJet 895C color printer using PhotoREt II can produce dots up to 70 percent smaller than older inkjet printers made a couple of years ago. Plus, PhotoREt II technology doesn't affect printer speed, so your color printing won't slow to a crawl when you send it a high-resolution, photo-quality image.

With smaller dots, the printer can combine more drops of ink into each pixel of an image. A cartridge using PhotoREt II technology can apply 16 individual dots of color into a single pixel. Mixing more primary inks per pixel means a greater choice of pixel colors. With three basic ink colors (and black), the PhotoREt II printer can produce over 250 hues, giving it a palette 30 to 80 times greater than most inkjets, which can apply only one or two colors per pixel.

Because of the color-layering feature of PhotoREt II, you find that any printer with this technology provides smoother blending and more realistic color tones and shades than a standard inkjet printer. In addition, PhotoREt II also greatly reduces the characteristic "banding" displayed by most inkjet printers when printing large areas of black or a single color. Figure 3.3 illustrates the difference that PhotoREt II technology makes at any resolution.

The Improvement: PhotoREt III

Recently, Hewlett-Packard introduced PhotoREt III, which improves the technology even further! PhotoREt III features:

- Drops that are 20 percent smaller than PhotoREt II

- A phenomenal 29 dots of color per pixel (instead of the 16 dots applied by PhotoREt II)

- Over 3,500 colors per pixel

- Twice as many ink nozzles per cartridge, applying ink 50 percent faster than a PhotoREt II cartridge

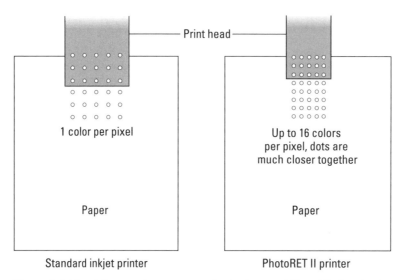

Figure 3.3 The difference between standard inkjet and PhotoREt II technology

The enhancements of the PhotoREt III printers truly blur the traditional dividing line between inkjet and those expensive dye-sublimation printers that I mentioned earlier in the book, offering virtually the same image quality as a 35mm photograph on glossy photo paper.

Understanding MIDS

Many of the latest HP inkjet printers feature a new *Modular Ink Delivery System* (MIDS). To understand the next-generation performance of the new printers, you have to focus on the cartridge. Unlike a traditional inkjet cartridge, which contains both the ink reservoir and the print head, Hewlett-Packard's new MIDS printers separate the ink supply from the print heads. The ink is stored in single-color, stationary tanks inside the body of the printer. This separation results in:

- **Increased print head size.** The print head on a MIDS printer has a lower mass but a much larger printing area, producing faster printing speeds.

- **Increased ink capacity over standard ink cartridges.** Always a plus!

- **Lower ink cost.** Because you're not changing the print head each time you change ink cartridges, MIDS printers also save you money and reduce your cost per page.

The Hewlett-Packard MIDS design also uses four individual print heads, rather than a single print head, which provides:

- **Increased print head life.** Multiple print heads reduce the typical printing wear and tear, and a print head may even last for the life of the printer. Each print head can be individually replaced as well.

- **Improved print quality.** The new print heads developed by Hewlett-Packard deliver ink at a faster rate and with better control. They also use the PhotoREt II technology I mentioned earlier.

- **Increased printing area.** Each print head can print a full ½-inch path across the paper; the print head in an older integrated cartridge can print only ⅕ or ⅓-inch across the page in one pass. This increased printing path increases the speed of the printing product.

Each print head in an HP MIDS device is equipped with a special read/write memory chip and sensor. This new hardware:

- **Alerts you when the ink or print head needs changing.** No more discovering that your printer has already run out of ink.

- **Retains information.** The chip records the total number of drops and pages printed by the print head, enabling the unit to track print head life and provide information on the amount of ink left in a cartridge.

- **Automatically calibrates the print head.** The chip automatically adjusts the characteristics for a new print head (for example, the proper drop volume and velocity) when you install it.

The MIDS system also makes a number of improvements to both the ink and the ink delivery system:

- **Pressurized ink delivery.** The printer receives a constant flow of ink.

- **Faster drying ink.** New ink formulas require less drying time, which helps prevent smudges.

- **Automatic nozzle cleaning.** The printer regularly cleans the print head's nozzles automatically to prevent clogging.

The first HP color inkjet series to debut with MIDS were the HP 2000C Professional Series, but look for these improvements in many more inkjet models in the future. As the technology continues to evolve, these features will be applied to future color inkjet designs in every price range.

Selecting a Print Quality

Most inkjet printers (and all-in-one units that use an inkjet-printing engine) enable you to select from three or four different levels of *print quality*: the higher the quality level, the more ink your printer uses and the longer it takes to print your document. For example, the HP 722C offers three different print quality settings, as shown in Figure 3.4.

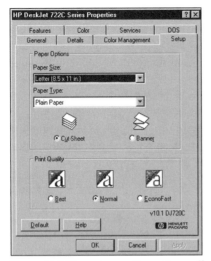

Figure 3.4 The print quality settings offered by the HP DeskJet 722C inkjet printer

- **EconoFast.** This is the best print quality for draft work — printing first copies of a document, dumping a quick copy of a Web page as a hard copy, or printing any job where quality is less important. By reducing the number of dots in each pixel (or, for some printers, even the number of pixels in the image), EconoFast significantly reduces the amount of ink used and the time it takes to print your document.

- **Normal.** This is the best compromise between quality and speed, and the default setting that I use. Most of my documents look their best at this setting, but printing doesn't take as long or use as much ink as it would at the Best mode.

- **Best.** Best mode produces the highest detail and most accurate color in your documents, so choose it when the quality of the output is all-important. Naturally, it takes your printer longer to produce the document, so don't use Best mode if you're in a big hurry.

Cross-Reference

Turn to the section, "Adjusting Print Quality," in Chapter 10 for a quick step-by-step procedure for selecting a print quality before printing from a Windows 98 application.

Using Duplex and Advanced Inkjet Printing

Earlier in the book, you learned about the basic features available with an impact printer: a dot-matrix or daisywheel printer produces text and simple monochrome graphics, but that's about it . . . no advanced features with these printers. Laser printers offer more advanced features (some even included sorting and stapling accessories), but typically at a price that the home PC owner couldn't touch. For many years the home PC user was limited to printing on a single side of a single sheet of paper.

Today's inkjet printers solve that problem. They offer the advanced printing capabilities of most office laser printers, including duplex mode, multiple copies, and collation. Now the average home PC owner can produce the same documents, and it usually takes very close examination to tell the difference between hard copy produced on an inkjet and documents printed on a laser printer.

In this section, I discuss the advanced printing features offered by one of the most popular inkjet printers offered today: the HP DeskJet 722C.

Cross-Reference

Go to Chapter 10 for quick and easy procedures for using the printing features discussed in this section — duplex mode, multiple copies, collating, landscape mode, and paper size and type.

Printing in Duplex Mode

The typical inkjet printer isn't versatile only because it is able to print crisp, laser-quality monochrome text and lifelike color graphics. Unlike most older impact printers, inkjet technology enables you to print on both sides of the paper, in what is called *duplex* mode.

The HP DeskJet 722C offers three choices for the way you print pages, each of which comes in handy for a different application. (Of course, duplex mode is handled differently on printers from different manufacturers — some new models even handle it automatically — so check your printer's documentation before trying duplex printing.)

- **Book mode.** The most common duplex mode for printing large text documents. The printer prints the front side of each page, then displays the message shown in Figure 3.5; the paper is manually removed from the printer and turned 180 percent, and then it's fed back into the printer paper feed tray. This mode saves paper, and it creates a typical double-sided document that's perfect for binding into book form along a long side of the pages. Figure 3.6 illustrates the entire duplex process.

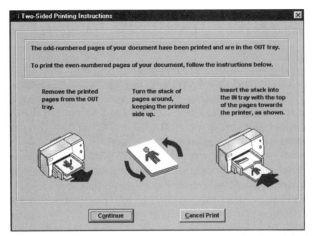

Figure 3.5 The paper handling message box displayed by the HP DeskJet 722C in duplex mode

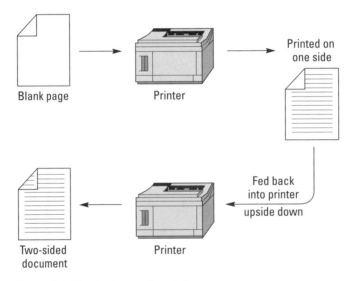

Figure 3.6 The duplex mode printing process

- **Tablet mode.** In Tablet mode, the pages are printed so that they can be read like a flip-top tablet, with a short side of each page bound together.

- **None.** This mode prints single-sided pages.

Figure 3.7 illustrates the HP printer driver dialog box where you set the duplex characteristics.

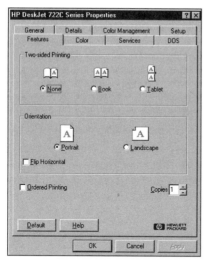

Figure 3.7 You control the duplex setting for the HP DeskJet 722C from this printer driver dialog box.

Options like those mentioned above enable your home inkjet to perform the same printing chores as a dedicated office printer. Duplex printing on an office printer does have its advantages, however. These more expensive models usually print in duplex mode without any intervention from you (unless, of course, the printer runs out of paper or toner).

Since you must manually remove and refeed duplex document pages to the printer, printing in duplex mode on an inkjet is not truly automatic. However, if you have to leave the printer unattended, the paper handling dialog box pauses printing until you return.

Tip

If you are using duplex mode with your inkjet printer, it's important to choose your paper carefully. Remember that most glossy paper made for high-resolution color graphics is intended for one-sided printing and not for duplex printing. Also, make sure your paper is opaque; for example, some expensive brands of onionskin paper are too thin for duplex printing.

Printing Multiple Copies

Do you need multiple copies of a single document? In the days of impact printers, I can remember producing one master copy of a document, hopping in my car, and driving to my local copy center to create the rest of the copies on a photocopying machine. The dot-matrix printer I had at home was too expensive to reproduce multiple copies of the same work, and it took far too long to print them.

With a good-quality inkjet printer, those days are behind me. A printer like the HP DeskJet 722C is perfect for printing multiple copies:

■ This type of printer is more reliable and quieter than a dot matrix.

■ Inkjet printers offer a much less expensive cost per page than a color copy machine, so printing multiple copies of long documents or printing a number of copies of the same color image now makes economic sense.

■ It takes far less time to produce multiple copies, so you won't fall asleep waiting for the printer to finish the job.

■ Most inkjets can hold 50 to 100 pages in their output trays, making them better suited for printing multiple copies of long documents than older dot-matrix printers. The HP DeskJet 722C produces a maximum of 50 copies of a single document, which easily fits the needs of most home PC owners.

Collating Copies

Another feature that impact printer owners once yearned for, in vain, was *collation.* Most copy machines can be set to collate, where the pages in a multiple-page document are automatically sorted in the correct order. For example, instead of picking up a four-page document from your printer with the pages ordered 4-3-2-1, you pick up the document with the pages ordered 1-2-3-4.

Collation doesn't sound like an earth-shattering feature, but if you print several copies of a 20-page document at one time, you'll see what I mean. The longer the documents you print, and the more copies you need, the more time collation saves you. No laborious manual sorting — just pick up your copies and go.

Like other printers that offer this feature, the HP DeskJet 722C doesn't violate any rules of physics to collate your documents — the printer driver software that controls your printer simply arranges the pages in the proper order before sending the data. This feature works with both single- and two-sided documents.

Taking Advantage of Landscape Mode

So you've just finished the family budget or a spreadsheet outlining the company's expenses, and you need a printed copy. Don't try to print your average spreadsheet or financial report on a piece of paper $8\frac{1}{2}$ inches wide . . . I can tell you from experience, it won't fit. You'll end up with half a document printed, and the other half will likely have disappeared into thin air.

Some older DOS programs used to print two pages, each with half the data. If you had one of these applications, you could grab your tape dispenser and tape the two pieces of paper together to form a semblance of a complete hard copy.

These days, Windows 98 and Windows Me make it easier to print smaller fonts and fit more characters on a page than older impact printers. By using a smaller font, you may just be able to fit your entire report on a page in portrait mode. However, the solution I like to use is to print odd-shaped or extended documents in landscape format. In *landscape* mode, the length of the page runs from side to side rather than top to bottom. This mode can create double-sided hard copy for spreadsheets and reports that won't fit within the 8½ × 11-inch portrait format.

The HP DeskJet 722C takes landscape printing even further. You can select landscape format for either Book mode or Tablet mode, enabling you to save paper and create smaller documents in landscape mode.

Choosing Paper Size and Type

Inkjet printers use a variety of paper sizes, and the HP DeskJet 722C is no exception. Of course, the selection includes familiar standard business sizessuch as U.S. letter, legal, and envelope, but you can also choose from international standards such as the A4 size. Like the HP DeskJet 722C, most inkjet printers have paper feed trays equipped with sliding guides that adjust to different paper sizes.

As I've mentioned in previous chapters, inkjets can use several types of paper to achieve different results:

■ **Plain paper.** Most inkjet printers are perfectly happy with standard 20-lb. copier paper — even recycled paper usually provides good results. I use recycled plain paper for draft documents and quick hardcopies . . . when I use such paper with EconoFast print quality, I achieve the least expense per page.

■ **Inkjet paper.** This is an improved grade of bond paper with a higher brightness and smoother finish. Ink doesn't spread as much on a sheet of inkjet paper, so the print quality and definition of the image is slightly improved over plain paper. The downside, as you may have guessed, is that inkjet paper is a bit more expensive per sheet than standard copier paper. Premium inkjet paper is also available — this is a coated paper that produces even better image quality. I use inkjet paper for all final copies of text documents.

■ **Photo paper.** This is a single-sided glossy paper especially designed for printing high-resolution color graphics. If you've never seen a 24-bit color image printed on photo paper, I guarantee you'll be surprised by the results. Many people mistake a print on photo paper for an enlargement of a standard film camera photograph. Photo paper is somewhat more expensive than plain or inkjet paper, so use it only when you need spectacular color reproduction.

- **Envelopes.** I haven't put a pen to an envelope in years now. Every Christmas, I remember what a hassle addressing 50 envelopes used to be — but now my inkjet printer breezes through the work in a couple of minutes. An inkjet printer is perfect for adding a touch of color or your company logo to your return address on your outgoing mail. Most inkjet printers are already configured to handle standard No. 10 and business envelopes, but with office software suites such as Microsoft Office and Corel WordPerfect, you can create your own envelope-printing format for odd sizes.

- **Transparencies.** The arrival of the inkjet printer has made a big difference for presentation graphics software such as PowerPoint. Instead of simple monochrome, an inkjet can print color transparencies for use with over-head projectors. This clear plastic film is generally priced about the same as photo paper.

- **Business cards.** You can create your own business cards from special stock that uses fine perforation lines, leaving a smooth edge similar to the edge of an expensive custom-printed business card.

- **Transfer paper.** You can use this specialized paper to print iron-on transfers for fabrics. The most popular item is, of course, the custom-made T-shirt!

- **Stickers and labels.** Last (but certainly not least) on the list is *label stock*: peel-off or perforated labels arranged in a regular pattern on a backing sheet. Of all the common paper types that I've mentioned, label stock can be the most troublesome. Most label manufacturers use standard arrangements and formats (often based on label dimensions from Avery, a leading label manufacturer), but these standard formats come in a bewildering variety of names, sheet sizes, label dimensions, and alignments. Therefore, it may take some experimentation and a bit of manual configuration to match the label stock with the software dimensions.

Tip

When I shop for labels, I always pick the same brand and standard format, and I've always saved to disk any label templates or document files that I've created. This guarantees that I won't spend 30 minutes experimenting and adjusting the spacing and label dimensions all over again for a sheet of labels from another manufacturer. Don't be lured into buying a different brand of labels because they're on sale, or you're asking for trouble. Label printing is the perfect example of the old adage: "If it works, don't fix it!"

Cross-Reference

Those paper sizes and types cover about 99 percent of printer applications, but I cover other types and sizes of specialized paper in Chapter 9, including banner paper and precut greeting cards.

Care and Feeding of Your Inkjet Printer

Today's inkjet printers are sturdy and practically maintenance-free, but you can follow some basic rules and simple actions to help your printer produce the best documents possible. These tips also help you avoid accidents that can damage your inkjet, help you avoid paper jams, and lengthen the life of your inkjet cartridges.

Liquids Are Forbidden, Period

Just in case that wasn't clear enough: sodas, mineral water, juice, or anything else that exists in liquid form is a deadly enemy of your printer. In fact, rule number one for your entire computer system should be "No Drinks of Any Kind!" A keyboard or a mouse can be rescued after a spill, but any exposed electrical components will likely be ruined by contact with water or other liquids.

Loading Paper

As I mentioned in Chapter 1, some printers are somewhat more susceptible to paper jams than others. However, the following general rules for loading paper apply to any inkjet printer and any type of paper you may use:

- **Adjust the paper guides.** I've observed many printer owners who switch paper often, first loading legal paper, then envelopes, then standard paper — all without adjusting the paper guides in the paper feed and paper output trays. Coincidentally, these are also the printer owners who complain about how much their printer jams or how it feeds paper incorrectly. Remember to adjust the paper guides to the correct position so they'll fit the paper you've loaded, and you'll avoid misfeeds and paper jams . . . after all, that's why those paper guides are there.

- **Align the paper correctly.** Along with adjusting the paper guides, you should also take the time to align all the sheets of paper as indicated by your printer's manual. Never push paper farther into the machine than indicated, and straighten the paper to make certain that it feeds evenly.

- **Remove staples and paper clips.** Your inkjet printer is prepared to accept pages, but nothing extra. To avoid paper jams and punctures, make sure that you check each sheet of paper for stray staples and paper clips.

- **Check for torn or creased edges.** All edges of your paper should be straight, without tears or creases that can cause a paper misfeed within the bowels of your inkjet printer. This is especially important if you're using thicker paper like construction paper, labels, or business card stock.

Tip

Do the pages produced from your inkjet printer seem slightly askew — in other words, does the text or graphic content seem to be slightly out of alignment with the paper? If so, check your paper guides and be sure that the paper is correctly aligned. If the paper is misaligned as it feeds into the printer, your finished document will reflect the problem.

Cleaning the Exterior

Unfortunately, computers don't often receive the best treatment or the best possible operating environments — and it doesn't take long before that new printer you took out of the box has developed its own unique patina of dust, stains, smudged ink, and (worst of all) glue from countless sticky notes. What's the best way to restore your printer's good looks and keep it clean in the future?

Many PC owners recommend one product or another for cleaning and protecting the plastic case on most inkjet printers; I use a cleaning product that's usually associated with cars. A car interior cleaner/protector not only helps to remove dust and stains, it also contains an antistatic ingredient that helps keep dust from collecting again on your printer's case. However, don't spray any fluids directly on your printer — remember my rule number one? Instead, spray fluids on a soft cloth, and then wipe down the exterior. Also, keep any fluids away from the interior of the printer.

Between yearly applications of a cleaner/protector, wipe the printer's case with a soft cloth; that will be enough to remove dust before it becomes a problem.

Tip

Never set any heavy objects on your inkjet printer's cover, paper feed tray, or paper output tray — your printer was not designed for use as a table.

Cleaning the Interior

Your printer's case keeps out much of the dust and other contaminants from your workspace, as well as protects your printer from liquid spills. Eventually, however, dust will find its way into your printer. It's even more important to properly maintain the interior of your printer than the outside, since the condition of the printer's mechanism directly affects the quality of the output. I've seen many an inkjet printer returned for repair that actually needed only a simple cleaning and lubrication to eliminate streaks and gaps in printed documents.

Naturally, the interior mechanism of your inkjet printer should be treated with care while you remove dust, and the best way to do this is with a can of compressed air (also known as "the computer nerd's best friend"), which blasts dust and dirt out of your printer. The compressed air does not hurt any of your hardware's chips or circuitry, so you can use it without worrying. Plus, these cans come with a nifty plastic hose that helps you clean the nooks and crannies of your printer — no more poking around with a cotton swab.

You'll find compressed air at any well-stocked computer supply store, office supply store, or camera store. Figure 3.8 illustrates the method for dusting your printer's interior with one of these compressed air cans: set your printer on its side, open the cartridge access door or the printer's cover, and blast dust and dirt down and outwards. Your printer will thank you with better performance.

Compressed air

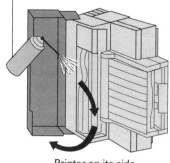

Printer on its side

Figure 3.8 Dusting the interior of an inkjet printer is easy with a can of compressed air.

As you clean the interior of your printer, check the guide rollers for tiny scraps of paper that may lead to misfeeds and paper jams. Your printer's interior cabling to the print head should be free of kinks and bends, and it should be free to move along with the print head. Make sure that your cartridges are firmly seated.

Cross-Reference

If you have an HP DeskJet 722C or a similar model, you'll find step-by-step directions for changing printer cartridges in Chapter 10. While you're there, why not brush up on a couple of other tasks — cleaning the print head and aligning the print cartridge.

I should also mention that some inkjet printer manufacturers recommend applying a light coat of oil on the print head rail (the metal rod which supports the print head as it moves back and forth across the paper). This procedure is required only if it's mentioned in your printer's manual, and be careful: it's very easy to add too much oil, and an extra drop falling on the electrical circuitry inside your printer is about as beneficial as a handful of sand inside your car's gas tank. Use a cotton swab or a medicine dropper to dispense single drops.

Refilling Ink Cartridges

It is possible to refill black inkjet cartridges; most office supply stores sell refill kits for popular inkjet cartridges from Hewlett-Packard and other manufacturers. I don't refill cartridges for a number of good reasons:

- **Varying ink quality.** The quality of the ink used in these refill kits is almost never as good as the ink in a cartridge made by the manufacturer, which has been especially formulated to work with your print cartridge. Refills often result in uneven ink coverage across large areas of black, or a purple tinge to text that is supposed to be solid black. The ink used in refill kits may also take longer to dry.

- **Reusing nozzles.** One of the reasons inkjet printers continue to offer excellent print quality over the life of the machine is that each time you replace an ink cartridge you also replace the print head (essentially restoring ink delivery to factory-new condition). When you refill cartridges, the inkjet nozzles are used far longer than intended, and they're more prone to clog or release an incorrect amount of ink.

- **Getting messy.** Unless you know what you're doing, refilling an ink cartridge can be a very dirty operation; we're talking gloves to wear and newspapers to protect your table.

Here's the official stance of Hewlett-Packard on refilling cartridges:

Hewlett-Packard does not recommend the use of refilled inkjet print cartridges in its inkjet printers. HP print cartridges are designed as part of an entire printing system, which is tested extensively to ensure exceptional performance across a range of conditions. The quality of all components of the cartridge is guaranteed for a certain product lifetime. HP patented ink formulations are optimized to provide excellent print quality, water resistance, and compatibility with the cartridge and printer components. We believe the highest quality output and most reliable operation of the printer will be obtained when genuine HP inkjet cartridges are used with HP inkjet printers. Refilling processes and the use of incompatible inks may disrupt the print system, potentially resulting in printer damage, reduced print quality and customer dissatisfaction. HP cannot predict the long-term effect that using different ink may have on printer reliability.

Well, I've made my recommendation and you've read the warnings from Hewlett-Packard, so now you know the pitfalls of refilling printer cartridges.

Using a Surge Suppressor

We've all heard the horror story before . . . a PC owner wakes up one morning after a bad thunderstorm to find that a massive power surge or a lightning strike has hit the family PC and all its peripherals during the night. Nothing works when they flip the switch (or their PC displays the computer equivalent of permanent amnesia). Virtually everything in the system has to be replaced, and all the applications and data stored on the PC have vanished to Byte Heaven. But are stories like these really true? Does this really happen?

Believe me, tragedies like these really do happen — after working for several years as a PC consultant and technician, I can tell you of dozens of computer owners who have been hit hard by a power surge. It doesn't matter whether your PC and printer are turned on at the time the strike occurs, or whether the surge trips your home fuse box — all that matters is that each component in your computer system is plugged directly into an AC wall socket.

Unfortunately, that AC cord also provides a wire connection that the power surge can use to flow from your house wiring into your computer system. A massive electrical surge can literally burn to a crisp the solid-state chips and integrated circuitry inside your PC and peripherals, complete with a black, charred residue that signals the end of a perfectly good piece of hardware.

"How can I prevent my equipment from being destroyed by a lightning strike or power surge?" There are only two methods of protection:

- **Unplug your system.** The only absolute protection against a power surge or lightning strike is to remove that wire connection between your PC and printer and the AC wall socket . . . in other words, pull the plug. Unfortunately, this isn't the most convenient solution to the problem, since most PC systems have at least three power cables — the PC itself, the monitor, and the printer. Crawling underneath your computer desk and plugging in or unplugging all three cables each time you use your PC is too much of a hassle.

- **Use a surge protector or UPS.** The other method of protecting your PC and printer against power surges is to add a surge protector or *uninterruptible power supply* (UPS) to your system. On the outside, a surge protector looks like a simple power strip with multiple AC sockets. Inside, however, the surge protector includes a circuit that automatically disconnects the AC sockets if it detects a power surge of sufficient voltage. In fact, this circuit resembles a fuse, and it simply melts or vaporizes if it's hit by enough electricity, as illustrated in Figure 3.9. Of course, this means you'll have to replace the entire surge suppressor, but if it performed correctly your PC should still work. Look for a protector specifically designed for computer hardware; it's worth paying a few dollars more for better protection. (Your computer modem can also be hit with a power surge through the telephone wall socket — many surge protectors sold today also have a socket for your telephone wire to prevent damage from a phone-line surge.)

Tip

A UPS is a surge suppressor that also carries a built-in battery. It can provide electricity to your entire PC system for a few minutes, even during a total power blackout, which should enable you to finish saving any critical files (or even print any critical documents) and shut your PC down normally. UPS units are now common for under $100, and I recommend one to any PC owner who regularly experiences power outages. UPS units also "condition" your AC power, preventing problems caused by power brownouts and AC interference.

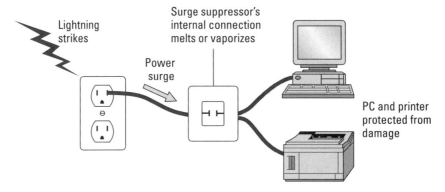

Figure 3.9 The surge suppressor sacrifices itself to save your computer and printer.

Warning

Although many manufacturers of surge suppressors offer "insurance" in case your system is hit by a power surge, remember that even the best surge suppressor is no match for a direct lightning hit on your home's electrical system (that's why the only absolute prevention for a power surge is to unplug your system completely). If you're shopping for a surge suppressor, be sure to read the manufacturer's policy to see what it covers (and how much you can receive if your system is damaged).

Summary

In this chapter, I covered how to use some of the advanced features available on today's inkjet printers, including duplex printing, collation, and printing multiple copies. You learned the importance of print quality, and how you can select the right print quality for each document. I explained an important measure of high-resolution print capability — dots per inch — and the advantages of Hewlett-Packard's PhotoREt II, PhotoREt III, and MIDS technologies for high-resolution color printing. You also explored the features of a modern inkjet printer, the HP DeskJet 722C. Finally, you learned the details of maintaining your inkjet printer, both inside and out.

In Chapter 4, I discuss laser printers in depth.

In Chapter 10, you'll find a number of step-by-step projects that help illustrate some convenient printer features, such as adjusting the print quality and paper size, using duplex mode, choosing landscape or portrait orientation, printing multiple copies, and collating copies. You'll also learn how to perform the simple maintenance tasks that keep your inkjet printer running smoothly, such as cleaning your inkjet print head, aligning cartridges, testing printer communications, and changing inkjet cartridges.

CHAPTER 4

Up Close: Laser Printers

IN THIS CHAPTER

- Comparing page description languages
- Adding printer memory to improve performance
- Using font memory cards and cartridges
- Printing full-page graphics on a laser printer
- Using manual feed for special tasks
- Adding the Copy/Scan Accessory to an HP LaserJet 1100
- Handling toner and cartridges
- Cleaning and maintaining your laser printer

In the past, a laser printer was considered strictly as a piece of commercial office hardware. A highly paid doctor, lawyer, or graphics professional may have had one in a home office, perhaps, but laser printers were so expensive that most of us couldn't even afford a used model.

Those days are definitely over. Today's personal laser printer is no more expensive than a business inkjet printer, and in most cases the modern laser printer offers better resolution and faster delivery than its more expensive ancestors. For instance, the HP LaserJet 1100xi shown in Figure 4.1, which I use as an example throughout this chapter, is much faster and quieter and offers better print quality than the HP LaserJet IIISi that I used just five years ago, yet you can find it at your local computer store for under $400.

Figure 4.1 The HP LaserJet 1100xi printer is much faster and quieter than the printer I used just five years ago. (Courtesy Hewlett-Packard Co.)

This chapter focuses on today's laser printers: the page description "language" they speak when communicating with your computer, the available hardware upgrades and how you can install them, the importance of fonts, some laser printing tips, and how to maintain your new laser printer.

Understanding PostScript and PCL

Of course, your computer and printer don't really speak to each other, but they do communicate. And, just like people, they use a specific language to get their messages across.

Adobe's PostScript and Hewlett-Packard's PCL are *page description languages*. In effect, a page description language is a technical dialect that describes the entire structure of a printed page. PCL is understood by printers, printer drivers, and application software. When you consider the complexity, printing speed, and the resolution of today's laser printers, you understand that an entire language of text and graphics commands is required to deliver the printed goods.

The description of a page to be printed with either PostScript or PCL contains both the characteristics of the page and the actual text and graphics that appear on that page — in effect, a complete architectural plan for a printed page. For example, the page description includes:

- Margins and spacing
- Fonts and text effects, as well as the text itself
- Placement of graphics and the graphics themselves
- Color and shading
- Printer features such as duplex selection and collation

In this section, you learn about the similarities and the differences between PostScript and PCL — the two most popular and widely recognized page description languages.

The Whole PostScript Thing Explained

PostScript is probably the single most widely used page description language in the publishing industry today, and it's tightly integrated into the Apple line of printers and the Macintosh operating system (another reason why the Macintosh is still the computer of choice for publishers and graphic designers). PostScript first appeared in the mid-1980s, and today it's so popular that just about every operating system has a program that enables it to display and print PostScript documents.

The importance of device independence

The fact that PostScript is available for just about every type of computer and operating system points to one of the reasons why it has become a worldwide standard — *device independence*. This is a fancy technoterm that boils down to a simple idea: a PostScript file can be transported to any PostScript-compatible device and printed, and you end up with the same page.

That files can so easily be transported is pretty neat, especially when you consider that the brand of hardware is irrelevant. In fact, many computer monitors, plotters, printing presses, and even laser etching machines use PostScript files as input, so the target device doesn't even have to be a laser printer. As long as your printer supports PostScript, you can print PostScript pages created under Windows 95/98, Windows 2000, Windows NT, Mac OS, OS/2, UNIX or Linux, and even professional typesetting equipment.

No wonder PostScript has so completely captured the publishing industry. The page you're reading now was prepared on a Macintosh or a PC, exported as a PostScript file, proofread on a PostScript display terminal, and eventually loaded directly into an offset printing press, all without any conversion required, regardless of the device.

PostScript command structure

Unlike a computer program, which is based on binary code, PostScript is based on alphanumeric characters, like the written language you're reading now; however, it would be practically impossible for a person to actually read a PostScript document. (I've met programmers who can "translate" a few sentences, but they don't enjoy it.) Because all computers share at least the same alphanumeric characters you see on a typewriter, this character-based structure helps PostScript remain device-independent.

To illustrate, Figure 4.2 shows a sample of the beginning of a document prepared for PostScript printing, as shown in a text editor. Pretty cryptic, isn't it? If you look closely, though, you can see fragments of words interspersed throughout the PostScript commands. In fact, all of the various PostScript printer commands are embedded within the text and graphics of the document itself, so a PostScript file is actually a long, continuous stream of document data interspersed with formatting and printer control commands. Since everything is based on alphanumeric characters, PostScript files can grow huge, and a printer can take from 30 to up to 120 seconds to process an entire page before it starts to print anything.

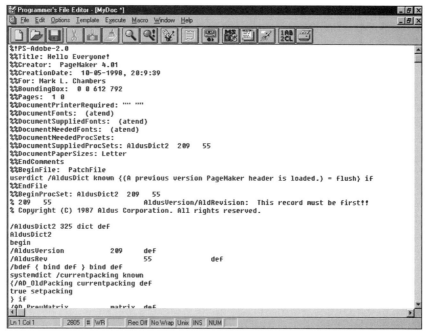

Figure 4.2 The inner workings of a PostScript document

Using fonts in PostScript

If you ever see a reference to PostScript *dictionaries* in a computer magazine, don't get the wrong idea — the author isn't talking about a list of word meanings. In PostScript terminology, a *dictionary* file is a storehouse for the fonts your printer can use — for example, Geneva or Times, two popular font *families* often used in typesetting. The dictionary contains a description of how each character in a font family is constructed, including bold and italic versions. Because the description is independent of the size of a font, characters in that font can be scaled up or down (most PostScript fonts default to a range from 8 to 72 points).

Many companies sell PostScript font families — they're usually called "ATM" or "Type 1" fonts — and these fonts can be downloaded directly to your PostScript printer as part of a page description. Downloading fonts adds to the printing time, though, so the more fonts your printer recognizes internally, the better. Because your printer already knows how to form the characters, they don't have to be downloaded. It's worth paying extra for a printer that has more internal fonts. Older printers enabled you to add internal fonts by plugging in cartridges, while current laser printers can usually accept internal font memory cards.

Using encapsulated PostScript graphics

If you're familiar with high-end desktop publishing and graphic design applications such as PageMaker, Illustrator, and Photoshop from Adobe, you've probably already run into an image stored in the rather cryptic-sounding *encapsulated PostScript format*. Or perhaps someone has sent you a logo or a piece of company line art in a Windows document that ends with the extension .eps. What are these documents?

Encapsulated PostScript (thankfully, almost always called EPS) graphics are actually self-contained PostScript documents that completely describe the contents of an image, and you can *import* (or include) them in another PostScript document within your application — in effect, "pasting" the image into another PostScript file, so that they appear to be a single, combined document. What's really neat about most EPS graphics is that they can be easily resized to fit specific dimensions. Popular graphic formats you find on the Web such as Windows bitmap (.bmp), .gif, and .jpg look "jagged" around the edges if you resize them larger, but a vector-based EPS file is easily scalable to other sizes within your application. EPS images can be black and white or color.

Many of the more expensive commercial clip-art packages include images in EPS format, so you're likely to encounter them if you're a clip-art aficionado. You can probably also create your own EPS graphics within your graphics editor. For example, Figure 4.3 shows an EPS graphic created and saved in Paint Shop Pro.

Figure 4.3 Creating an EPS graphic with Paint Shop Pro

The Advantages of PCL

Hewlett-Packard's PCL (*Printer Command Language*) appeared in 1984, and it has constantly been improved and expanded since then. In fact, PCL was originally developed by HP for use with dot-matrix printers. Of course, these days PCL is now primarily an inkjet and laser printer command language, but almost all HP printing hardware still recognize and support it.

Unlike PostScript, PCL (at least in its early versions) focused more on controlling printer features than precise control of page layout or formatting output, so it's not as widely used as PostScript in the publishing industry. PCL is also not device-independent — a PCL software driver creates a PCL printing job especially for a particular piece of hardware.

Because PCL is capable of far more control over all the different features and functions, you immediately notice how many extra settings and configuration options are available within the Windows 98 Printer Options dialog box for a typical HP inkjet or laser printer. In contrast, a typical PostScript laser printer running under the Mac OS offers fewer options for directly controlling the operation of your printer through the software driver.

This is not to say, however, that PCL version 6 (the most recent version) falls short of being a full-page description language like PostScript — the two produce the same quality output on today's personal laser printers. In fact, PCL does handle complex text formatting — margins, spacing, and font characteristics were part of the language from the beginning. Today's enhanced PCL 6 includes support for color printing, fast network communications, several graphics formats, and downloaded fonts. PCL 6 has other advantages over PostScript as well:

- **PCL is optimized for the Windows environment.** It's more efficient and generally prints documents faster than a PostScript system.

- **PCL is a common standard that's used by default on virtually all home and office laser printers.** If PostScript is available for a laser printer, it's often an optional upgrade.

- **Larger PCL documents do not require a printer to be upgraded with additional memory.** However, a printer will often have to be upgraded with more memory to handle larger PostScript documents.

PCL command structure

Like PostScript, PCL is entirely character-based, so it can be easily transmitted over a standard parallel connection or any network. Also, like PostScript, PCL commands are embedded in the data sent to your printer by the printer's driver software — the commands are prefaced by escape codes that identify the commands to your printer.

However, because PCL originated with the older technology of dot-matrix printers, it's more akin to the control character codes that were used to send commands to impact printers. In fact, many of those original codes still exist in PCL (like the character CR to indicate a carriage return).

Some of the latest Hewlett-Packard LaserJet printers using PCL can automatically switch back and forth between page description languages, so you can send a document over a local area network using PCL, and then you can immediately follow it with a document formatted for a PostScript printing device.

Developments and changes in PCL

As I mentioned earlier, Hewlett-Packard has constantly enhanced PCL to keep up with the new features that have been added to computer printers over the years. As you might imagine, the simple controls needed to print and format text on a dot-matrix printer are a far cry from the complex text and graphics you can produce under Windows or Mac OS. There are a number of different levels of PCL, each of which was developed separately and addressed a specific printing need:

- **PCL 1.** The first level of PCL provides the basic text printing functions, including spacing and margins.

- **PCL 2.** An enhancement to PCL 1 that adds support for text-only network and multiuser printing.

- **PCL 3.** The first widely recognized version of PCL supported by non-HP printers, PCL 3 is often emulated by other printer manufacturers as "LaserJet Plus" or "HP LaserJet." This level appeared in 1984, adding basic support for font downloading and simple transfer and placement of graphics.

- **PCL 4.** An enhancement to PCL 3 introduced in late 1985 that adds embedded macro commands, larger and more complex fonts, and more control over graphics.

- **PCL 5.** This level of PCL was introduced in 1990, and it includes support for *scaling* (changing the size of) the dimensions of downloaded fonts. PCL 5 also includes support for additional graphic formats. A number of revisions have been made to PCL 5, including PCL 5C (which was the first version of PCL to support color printing) and PCL 5E (which added bidirectional communication between computer and printer and enhanced printing of Windows TrueType fonts).

- **PCL 6.** Appearing first on the HP LaserJet 4000 and LaserJet 2100 in 1996, PCL 6 is an improvement in almost every respect. This latest version of the Printer Command Language provides faster printing for Windows users (especially for documents with complex graphics), more efficient operation over a network, and *font synthesis*, which allows the printer driver to "create" a font to match the font on your screen, instead of substituting another font like previous versions of PCL did.

Advanced Laser Printing

Now that you understand the page description language (or languages) that your printing application, operating system, and laser printer use to print the content of a page, let's discuss some of the advanced features and functions of laser printers in general. As an example, I use the HP LaserJet 1100xi, a popular personal laser printer; however, the material and the tips you find in this section apply to all laser printers and all-in-one units, no matter which model you're using.

You Need More Printer Memory (and Why)

When most computer owners think of the memory used on their system, they think of the system RAM (*random access memory*) first. System RAM provides the working space for your computer's CPU to control peripherals, run programs, and perform serious number-crunching. Most PCs running Windows 95/98 or Macs running Mac OS 8.*x* or 9 require a minimum of 32MB of RAM. You probably know that the more RAM you add to your system, the faster and more efficiently it operates.

Another place for memory on your computer is your video card. With the demands of today's video cards, high-resolution Web surfing in 24-bit color, and even onscreen TV and digital video, your computer needs a minimum of 4MB of video RAM; graphics professionals and game players usually need advanced 3D video cards with 16MB or more of video RAM. Adding more video memory on your computer increases the number of colors it can display, and you'll be able to increase the video resolution of your monitor as well.

"Okay, so my computer and my video graphics card use memory to perform calculations and display graphics. What does my printer need memory for?" Actually, your laser printer needs memory for two similar reasons:

■ **Storage space for printing jobs.** As I said before, print jobs sent from your computer to your printer can reach many megabytes in size, and if your printer can't store the entire contents of a printer job, it must be spooled by your computer. In effect, your computer sends part of the data, waits until your laser printer has processed that portion, and then sends another portion of the job. While the job is spooled, you can continue to use your computer; this feature is often called *background printing*. Both Windows and Mac OS have sophisticated printer spooling features (which use space on your hard drive as virtual printer memory), enabling you to print documents with a huge page count — but spooling a huge print job can slow down your computer. The more memory your printer has, the larger the print job it can accept without slowing down your computer.

Tip

If you can't add extra memory to your laser printer and you regularly print large documents or documents with a large number of graphics, you may consider investing in more system RAM and dedicating more memory to your print spooler. Windows and Mac OS both make use of as much free system memory as possible to spool print jobs. Alternately, you can buy a hardware-based print buffer, which is essentially a stand-alone printer spooler with its own built-in memory that connects between your computer and your laser printer. A print buffer performs the same spooling job that your computer would normally have to perform. Graphics professionals who generate large PostScript documents often use print buffers to help print their jobs faster and more efficiently.

■ **Working area to process pages.** Like your computer, your laser printer also has a built-in processor (often called a CPU, for *central processing unit*) that follows the page description commands sent to it by your computer — and, like the CPU in your computer, that processor needs RAM to provide working space. For example, a PostScript printer needs RAM to hold the image of the page that's built by your printer's processor as it executes the commands embedded in a PostScript print job. The more printer memory reserved for this processing, the faster your printer prepares a print job. In fact, the pages-per-minute printing speed of your laser printer usually has a lot to do with the amount of onboard RAM it carries (which is another reason why the most expensive and fastest network laser printers usually come stuffed with 8 or 16MB of dedicated printer memory).

All laser printers come with at least some printer RAM, but usually the manufacturer has provided some method to add more printer RAM if you need it. Some printers can accept special RAM cartridges; however, this is an older proprietary solution that has been dropped by most laser printer manufacturers. These cartridges are often discontinued and hard to find, but owners of older laser printers can still find them on the Internet (contact the manufacturer of your printer for possible leads on companies that sell printer RAM cartridges, or search the Web for companies that sell printer RAM).

Most of today's printers accept RAM modules that act much like the memory used in your computer — most printers still use proprietary memory, but some use the same standard SIMM (*Single Inline Memory Module*) or DIMM (*Dual Inline Memory Module*) memory modules used in your computer.

Cross-Reference

Depending on the age of your printer, additional printer memory can be added either externally (older models) or internally (newer models). See the section "Adding Printer Memory" in Chapter 10 for a step-by-step guide to each of these methods.

If your printer uses a proprietary RAM upgrade, search the Web for a company that stocks the specific type you need.

If your printer uses standard RAM, you should be able to buy it at your local computer store or order it directly through the mail; check your printer's manual for details, because memory comes in many speeds and configurations.

Tip

Because memory prices have come down so dramatically in the last two or three years, it's now much easier for the owner of a personal laser printer to upgrade memory. Therefore, if you find yourself printing at least one document of several pages in length per day (or if your documents contain a large number of graphics), I recommend that you consider adding additional printer memory to speed up both your computer and your printer.

Adding Fonts

Fonts are the tools of today's graphic designers and desktop publishers, and most professionals have literally hundreds of fonts loaded on their computers — but, as you might imagine, your average laser printer does not include all of those fonts as standard equipment. Instead, fonts that are not built in to your laser printer must be added if needed, and there are two methods of doing this:

■ **Downloading the fonts as part of the print job.** Earlier, I mentioned that both the PCL and PostScript page description languages enable your computer to literally download the characteristics of an entire font family as a part of a print job. This enables your laser printer to print practically any font in your collection — but the process is not without its performance penalties. First, downloading an entire font family adds a considerable amount of time to the print job's transfer and processing time, and many documents you create probably have more than one unique font. Thus, the procedure must be repeated for every font in the document that is not built in to your printer. (By the way, these built-in fonts are usually called *resident* fonts, because they reside in your printer's hardware, and most laser printers have at least three or four resident fonts.) Second, the font description takes up much of that valuable printer memory I discussed in the previous section, leaving less for your document data. Finally, not all fonts appear the same when printed as they do on your computer monitor — in fact, some Windows fonts are "screen-only" fonts, meaning that they do not print correctly if sent to your laser printer.

Tip

If you must download fonts to your laser printer, make a note of which fonts are already resident, and use those fonts whenever possible within your documents — you save time when you print the smallest number of downloaded font families in a document.

■ **Adding resident fonts in hardware.** The other method of printing fonts is much more expensive than downloading them each time you use them, but if you can afford the cost of adding hardware-based fonts to your laser printer, you'll greatly reduce the time needed to print that font in a document. On older laser printers, you can probably add a font by plugging in a font cartridge; current models accept fonts stored on memory cards that you install internally. However, the effect is the same — suddenly that font is a resident font and your laser printer no longer needs to download it, saving both time and printer memory.

Tip

If your budget is tight and you can afford only one- or two-font memory cards for your laser printer, take a moment and consider which font(s) you use most often when you're printing your work. Choose the font(s) which you use the most, and you'll experience a bigger increase in printer speed.

Make It a Scanner and Copier Too

We've talked about adding memory and fonts to improve the performance of your laser printer, but you may be asking, "What's the ultimate upgrade?" If you're the owner of an HP LaserJet 1100xi, here's the answer: with a Copy/Scan Accessory upgrade module, you can literally add the functionality of a scanner and a copier to your existing laser printer and turn it into an all-in-one unit.

The LaserJet 1100 is actually available in two models: the 1100 series (which performs as a stand-alone laser printer that can be upgraded) and the 1100A series (the all-in-one with the upgrade already installed). Both printers come with software, of course, but the 1100A models include the extra drivers and application software for the scanning and copying features.

Figure 4.4 shows how the upgrade works. The Copy/Scan Accessory module (the 1100se), which holds a sheetfed scanner and all of the additional hardware needed to scan and copy, snaps onto the front of the 1100xi, additional software installs on your PC, and you're ready to begin scanning and copying.

Like any other multifunction printer, the Copy/Scan Accessory enables your LaserJet 1100xi to copy as a stand-alone unit, so you don't need to connect it to a computer to make copies. You have no cables to connect, no jumpers to set, no drivers to install. As I said, you attach the module onto the front of the LaserJet 1100xi, and it's automatically recognized by your printer software — you don't have to reconfigure anything.

The Copy/Scan Accessory is so easy to install because of an HP technology called *JetPath*, which HP developed specifically to make upgrading the LaserJet quick and effortless. The JetPath expansion technology also enhances performance. Most scanners available today use a parallel port connector, which can transfer data no faster than 1 megabyte per second. The JetPath method provides a direct connection from printer to scanner without the bottleneck of traveling across your computer's parallel port. Data can be transferred twice as fast and save you considerable time.

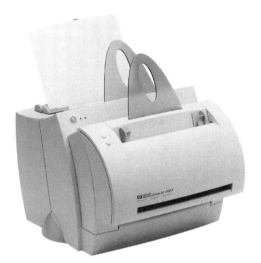

Figure 4.4 Upgrading an HP LaserJet 1100xi to a LaserJet 1100Axi is a simple operation.

The Hewlett-Packard Copy/Scan Accessory is a great idea — you can start out with a simple laser printer today, and add the capability to scan and copy later when you find yourself needing an all-in-one unit. I predict you'll see more of these upgradable printers in the future from Hewlett-Packard and other printer manufacturers.

Printing Full-Page Graphics

As you might imagine, a complex, full-page, line-art graphic is probably the most demanding document you can print on your laser printer. It has no resident fonts or simple blocks of text, and your printer's processor must calculate shading and position for every section of the graphic. I've seen a PostScript laser printer spend 4 to 5 minutes printing the most complex engineering drawings, which are often printed in landscape mode. Almost all of that time is actually spent calculating, and only 10 or 15 seconds is actually required to put the toner on the page in the right place.

You can, however, follow a few guidelines to help reduce the amount of time it takes to print a full-page graphic, especially in landscape mode:

■ **Reduce the number of textures and patterns.** Typically, you can't reduce the number of actual lines that make up your drawing or blueprint, but you may be able to remove some of the grayscale detail, or complex shading, texture, or patterns in your graphic.

- **Dedicate extra spooler memory.** If you're going to send a particularly large or complex image to your printer, add several megabytes of hard drive space to the size of your operating system's print spooler (if possible — Windows 95/98, Windows Me and Mac OS don't allow you to directly modify the size of your spooler file). After you've printed your complex drawing, you can reduce your print spooler back to its previous size and regain that hard drive territory.

- **Delete unnecessary files from your hard drive.** If your operating system provides a printer spooler but you can't modify the size directly, simply delete as many unnecessary files as possible from your hard drive. This step frees up additional hard drive space so that your operating system can automatically use it as virtual printer memory.

As I mentioned earlier, if you use your laser printer often during the day, your computer system benefits from additional printer memory or a dedicated printer buffer, and this is especially true if your work involves full-page graphics. Remember, the "virtual" printer memory provided by your operating system (either Windows 98 or Mac OS) is actually space being used on your hard drive, and your hard drive is nowhere near as fast as dedicated printer RAM; therefore, you'll see a significant increase in printing speed if you add printer memory.

Using Manual Feed

All laser printers have a manual feed system — on most machines, this is an adjustable slot that can accept paper from 8½ inches down to 3×5 index cards, and it's used for everything from envelopes to labels and special laser transfer paper. A manual feed is a convenient way of loading paper without removing the main paper tray, which comes in handy for situations like these:

- **Printing a different first page.** If you need to print the first page of a document on letterhead and the rest on plain paper, you can manually feed the first page and the rest can be loaded from the printer's paper feed bin.

- **Loading envelopes or odd-sized paper.** Generally, manual feed is the only way you can print odd-sized documents.

- **Loading two sheets.** Many paper companies stock special metallic, textured, and patterned transfer paper that can add all sorts of exotic highlights to documents printed on a standard laser printer. These transfer pages are sometimes manually fed into the laser printer on top of a sheet of paper, where the heat from the fuser roller bonds the material to the paper.

- **Cleaning your printer.** If you're using a special laser printer cleaning sheet (see "Cleaning Internal Parts" later in this chapter), you should use your printer's manual feed to load it into the machine.

Care and Feeding of Your Laser Printer

Like an inkjet printer, a laser printer requires little preventative maintenance to ensure that things run smoothly — but the maintenance you do need to perform is important, and it varies depending upon the age and model of your laser printer. In this section, I provide general tips and suggestions that help you maintain any type of laser printer.

Toner Can Be Messy

Some of the required maintenance for a laser printer involves opening the printer and removing the toner cartridge, so I think it's a good time to pause here to talk about that black toner — and warn you about it. Believe me, if you've ever spilled toner inside a laser printer, you'll agree that this stuff has a mind of its own. The good news is that modern laser printers have almost eliminated any chance for you to encounter toner. Today's toner cartridges are especially designed to eliminate toner spills.

On the other hand, if you have an older laser printer, it pays to be careful. Here are a few tips about toner:

- **Older cartridges can leak toner.** Older laser printer cartridges may leak toner if they're turned to a certain angle. For example, the cartridge used in an Apple LaserWriter II printer can spill toner into the printer body if it's not handled correctly. Most of the laser printer cartridges manufactured for today's printers don't have this problem, but take a few moments to read the instructions for your particular printer before you install your first cartridge. Although you can tilt a toner cartridge back and forth — more on this method later in this chapter — it's never a good idea to shake or drop a cartridge.

- **Toner is hard to clean up.** Toner is a fine powder that is sensitive to static charges — and that should give you a good idea of just how hard it is to clean tiny nooks and crannies inside your printer.

 Tip

Just had an accident with a toner cartridge (or even toner from your office copy machine)? Your local office supply store probably stocks toner clean-up cloths, which are treated with a special chemical that helps attract toner and keep it on the cloth.

- **Toner can permanently stain clothing.** If you accidentally get toner on your clothing, it's very difficult to remove — if you'll be opening your laser printer or handling a toner cartridge, wear casual clothing.

- **Toner is harmful to children and pets**. If you work in a home office with pets or children, make sure you immediately clean up any spilled toner.

In case you're wondering, the toner you use in your laser printer is similar to the toner powder used in office copy machines (which are actually very similar to laser printers, since the two types of machines use the same method of putting toner on paper). Although many of the latest copy machines use cartridges, most require that you pour toner into a tank of some kind (which, as you can imagine, is a great invitation for spills) — at least you won't have that worry with a laser printer cartridge.

What Should You Clean?

In this section, I cover some of the basic cleaning procedures for the interior and exterior of your printer. These procedures apply to almost any laser printer.

Warning

Before opening your laser printer and beginning any maintenance on the internal parts, or before beginning any maintenance on the exterior of the unit, read your printer's manual from cover to cover and follow any specific procedures and warnings. Your printer's manual may contain additional information about what you can and cannot clean.

Cleaning internal parts

Rule number one when cleaning the interior of your printer: *most of the internal parts that you can access should not be cleaned or touched!* Even wiping or oiling these internal parts adversely affects the quality of your printing — at worst, however, you can quickly disable your printer completely.

Warning

Laser printers use intense heat to bond toner to the paper. *Never* try to clean the interior of your laser printer right after using it to print a document, and avoid any portions of the interior that bear temperature warning labels!

With these warnings and cautions in mind, here's a general list of the interior parts that can be cleaned on many laser printers:

- **Corona wires.** These wires help transfer the static charge that attracts the toner to the paper, but dust can interfere with this process (especially on older laser printers). You can usually clean the dust off with a cotton swab, but don't add alcohol or other solvents — just gently wipe the wires. If the corona wires are exposed within your printer — and they often are in older laser printers — your printer's manual should indicate their location.

- **Paper feed rollers.** These rollers pull the paper from the paper cassette into the interior of your laser printer, but they can pick up oil and dirt from that same paper, causing paper jams and misfeeds. I use a cotton swab soaked in alcohol to remove this buildup. Some office supply stores carry roller cleaner.

Cross-Reference

Check out "Cleaning Corona Wires" and "Cleaning Paper Feed Rollers" in Chapter 10 for instructions on the best way to handle laser printer cleaning chores.

- **Toner guard.** Many printers have felt pads that capture excess toner from the system of rollers that move the paper through the machine. A new cartridge may include a new pad, or you may be able to remove this pad from the machine and clean it by hand by rubbing it on a clean cloth to remove the toner build-up.

- **Fan vent.** Many laser printers have internal fans, similar to the internal fan within every PC — these fans can become clogged with dust and dirt. If your printer has one of these fans, make sure that you clean the vent and the fan blades on a regular basis to keep the airflow clear.

Tip

Your local office supply store may stock laser printer *cleaning sheets*, which are coated papers that attract dust and excess toner from your printer's paper path. At the same time, because it passes through the entire paper path, a cleaning sheet may help to clean the many rubber rollers within your printer. For example, the KleenLaser cleaning sheet from AudioSource, Inc. is fed into your printer using the manual feed, just like a regular sheet of paper. Laser sheets can really help maintain your printer, especially in a smoky or dirty environment.

Cleaning the exterior

Although the exterior of your printer is generally easier and safer to clean than the interior, your printer may have cooling slots or pushbutton controls that would be damaged by using the wrong cleaning agent.

On the exterior of computer hardware, I generally use a cleaner/protector spray designed for automobile interiors. Such a product helps cut down on static electricity and is typically safe for plastic surfaces. Spray fluids onto a soft cloth first, and then wipe down the outside of the unit (making sure that you don't accidentally get any fluids inside the case). While you're cleaning the outside of your printer, you can also use a can of compressed air to blow dust and dirt from air vents, fan openings, and the inside of paper cassettes.

Rock That Toner Cartridge

Here's another preventive maintenance trick that helps prolong the life of your toner cartridge: remove it from the printer and rock it along its axis, keeping the cartridge level, as shown in Figure 4.5. (A few manufacturers may also advise rocking forward and backward, but I wouldn't do this unless it's specifically mentioned in your printer's manual or the instructions that accompany the cartridge.) Rocking helps the cartridge to distribute toner evenly — if the toner cakes or settles within the cartridge, your printed pages may suffer from spots or streaks. Plus, it's a great aerobic workout for you!

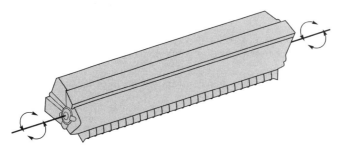

Figure 4.5 Rocking your cartridge is good for both your printer and your health.

Rocking the cartridge is also a good idea if it is running low on toner. By rocking the cartridge as described, I've often been able to print several more pages after my laser printer has reported that it's out of toner.

Tip

Most manufacturers of toner cartridges provide some method of returning a used cartridge for recycling; check the instructions for the cartridge and look for a mailing envelope or cardboard box. Many manufacturers send you a rebate coupon toward the price of a new cartridge if you send in your old one.

Summary

In this chapter, you learned the details on laser printers, including the language they use to communicate with your computer, some of the upgrades you can add to them to improve performance, how to add cartridge fonts to your printer, and how to maintain your printer. Laser printers no longer carry the high prices of five or ten years ago, and today's personal laser printers are as easy to use and easy to maintain as their inkjet cousins. If you need to print the best possible monochrome text, graphics, and grayscale shading at eight pages per minute, one of these printers is your best choice.

In Chapter 5, I discuss all the features available on today's multifunction devices, many of which can fax as well as copy and scan. You can easily build a home office around one of these units. Some of them do everything but make coffee.

In Chapter 10, you can follow a number of step-by-step projects that illustrate how to perform the simple maintenance tasks that keep your inkjet printer running smoothly — such as adding printer memory (both external RAM and internal RAM modules), installing font cartridges, changing toner cartridges, and cleaning corona wires and paper feed rollers.

Up Close: All-in-One Units

IN THIS CHAPTER • Connecting and configuring your multifunction device

• Using your all-in-one's scanning features

• Sending and receiving faxes

• Using advanced fax features

• Copying documents

• Creating a phone chain

• Understanding autoanswer and distinctive ring

• Adding a telephone line surge suppressor

• Using different multifunction features simultaneously

• Feeding and caring for your all-in-one

Today's all-in-one unit (also called a *multifunction* device) is truly a marvel: it can fulfill three or more of the functions required by an entire small office, all within the desktop space of a simple laser printer. Along with printing, a multi-function unit can perform at least two other office chores, including scanning, copying, or faxing. Many machines of this type can perform all of these functions. The multifunction peripheral doesn't even need a computer to perform many of its tasks, and those all-in-ones that send and receive faxes typically carry a full set of control buttons for fax and copy functions.

If you've never used an all-in-one before, here's a good example of its versatility. You can leave the unit on by itself to receive incoming faxes late at night and then load and view those faxes in the morning after you've turned on your computer; or you can simply specify that they be printed immediately, like a traditional fax machine.

In the past, all-in-one units were exclusively based on inkjet printers. With in the last few years, however, a new generation of compact laser multifunction peripherals has appeared that carry very competitive prices compared to standard laser printers. Would you pay a little more for the extra functionality of an all-in-one device? It seems that many printer owners would, because the sales of multifunction units have been steadily rising for the last few years.

This chapter covers the current generation of multifunction peripherals in detail, including their features — so if you're currently shopping for a printer and you're not familiar with the extra functionality of an all-in-one unit, this is the chapter for you.

Configuration and Setup

Because of the nature of an all-in-one unit, configuration and setup are some-what different than a traditional inkjet or laser printer. Most all-in-ones can still operate solely as a system printer with only a simple parallel port connection. You also may have guessed that you have to connect an additional telephone cable to your wall telephone jack to take advantage of your all-in-one's fax functionality.

Things can get more complex than that, however. Depending upon your computer's configuration, you may have to add peripherals like an external modem, an answering machine, or a telephone to your system's telephone connection. Surprisingly enough, they can all work together in harmony, if you set them up correctly.

Warning

Do you have an external parallel port device such as a Zip or Jaz drive, an external hard drive or tape backup, or a parallel port CD recorder? Most all-in-ones do not work with these devices — check with the printer manufacturer's technical support to determine if your unit works as a "passthrough" device on the parallel port.

If your multifunction peripheral can't share the parallel port, consider connecting those devices to your second parallel port (if your computer has one), or buy an I/O card to add another parallel port to your computer. (Make sure you get an IEEE-1284 compliant adapter card if you add a parallel port.)

In this section, I outline some common rules to follow in configuring and setting up an all-in-one within an existing computer system.

Creating a Phone Chain

If your all-in-one has a built-in telephone handset, you won't need to connect a telephone to it — but you can add other telephony devices to your machine's *phone chain* (a term I use to describe a line of devices all connected to the same telephone wall socket). These devices may include:

- Telephone line surge protector
- Internal computer faxmodem
- External computer faxmodem
- Answering machine
- Standard telephone

All of these devices have one connector in common: a standard phone jack (usually marked as *Phone*) that must connect to the wall socket. All of these devices, except the telephone, have a second jack as well, typically called the *Line* connector.

Creating a basic phone chain is easy and logical if you follow these important rules:

- **Your machine always comes first.** Your multifunction unit must always be the device connecting to the wall socket (or, even better, the telephone line surge protector). For example, the Line connector on the HP LaserJet 3100 should run to the wall socket/surge protector.

- **The telephone always comes last.** If you add a telephone to your phone chain, it must be the last device in the chain (which makes sense, since your telephone usually only has one connector).

- **Phone jacks always lead to Line jacks.** The Phone jack from the preceding telephony device should be connected to the Line jack of the following telephony device.

- **Unplug all devices before adding them to the chain.** This is always a good idea when connecting electrical devices (even through the telephone jacks).

Figure 5.1 shows how a phone chain is connected.

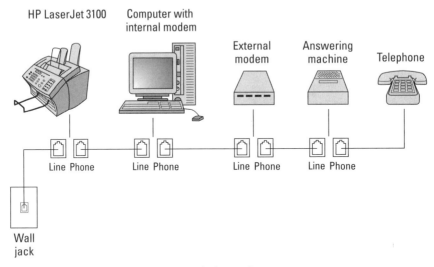

Figure 5.1 The connections in a typical phone chain

Warning

Why do I keep harping away about surge protectors? Weren't protectors designed for AC current? Actually, that's only part of the story — electrical surges can pass through your telephone line as well as your AC electrical system. I've seen countless telephone modems and fax machines ruined by a telephone line surge. If you've invested several hundred dollars in your all-in-one unit, computer modem, and a fax machine, *buy an inexpensive telephone line surge protector* (many standard AC current surge protectors now include a modem/telephone line surge protector as well, so you may already have one). The protector is connected directly to the wall jack, and all telephony devices plug into it. A telephone line surge protector can shield your entire phone chain from surge damage.

Understanding Autoanswer and Distinctive Ring

If you've ever used a computer faxmodem, run a dial-up host program on your computer, or run a computer BBS (short for *bulletin board system*), you're probably familiar with the idea of *autoanswer*: your all-in-one unit automatically picks up incoming fax calls after a specified number of rings, just like a dedicated fax machine. If you're sharing a voice line with your all-in-one, you can set the number of rings to five or six, which should give you time to pick up the phone before the machine picks up the line.

Autoanswer can occasionally be a hassle, however, because at least one or two of your callers are almost guaranteed to hear those wonderful fax carrier signal tones that everybody hates with a vengeance. You'll be outside, for example, or opening the door to your home, and you won't be able to reach the telephone in time. On the other hand, if you have an answering machine hooked into your phone chain, you can set the answering machine to answer a call on three or four rings, and the all-in-one can answer the phone on the fifth or sixth ring. This feature enables the answering machine to take a voice message. If your multifunction peripheral detects fax tones at the beginning of the call, it can automatically take the call instead. Note that telephone company voice mail does not work with your fax machine; a separate answering machine is required.

Naturally, most all-in-ones enable you to turn autoanswer off as well — this ensures that your human callers never receive those fax carrier signals, but it also forces you to manually initiate fax receive mode on your machine whenever you receive a fax call.

Distinctive ring is another species of telephone connection entirely — it's a service that's available only through some telephone companies, and it provides more than one individual telephone number for one incoming physical telephone line. If the voice number is dialed, one unique ring pattern is used; if the fax number is dialed, another unique pattern is used. If your all-in-one supports distinctive ring, it can detect that unique pattern and answers only those calls made to that number.

Tip

If you do decide to use distinctive ring, check with the manufacturer of your all-in-one device to determine if your model needs a specific ring pattern. For example, the HP LaserJet 3100 can only recognize a double-ring pattern, so your fax number must be assigned to the double-ring pattern.

Finally, you can always choose to do what most home and small office owners do if they want foolproof voice and fax answering: have a second physical telephone line with a separate number installed. It may cost you a little extra each month, but you can forget once and for all about your multifunction peripheral accidentally picking up your voice telephone calls.

Another advantage of separate telephone lines is their convenience. Separate lines can be in use at the same time. But if you're using a single line for both your voice and fax calls, an incoming call of one type busies the line and prevents all calls of the other type from connecting. (This is also true of a distinctive ring setup — although you have two separate telephone numbers, you still only have one physical telephone line, so if it's busy on one number, the other number is busy as well.)

Creating a Fax Header

It may seem strange to you that I mention the header information used on your outgoing faxes in a chapter devoted to all-in-one units, but there's a good reason. In many countries (including the United States), you are legally required to provide truthful and complete information within the header of *every* single outgoing fax you send. This requirement is to help identify those who send faxes with questionable content. It is common courtesy to fully identify yourself and your company in your fax header.

With these requirements in mind, here's a quick list of the information you should provide in the fax header:

■ Full name

■ Company name (if applicable)

■ Fax telephone number

■ Voice telephone number

■ Station ID (the abbreviated name displayed on the fax machine while it's connected)

Many all-in-one units enable you to change the fax header information through software, but you can also change it from the fax numeric keypad (and, in case you're currently using your device as a stand-alone fax machine, without connecting it to your computer). Remember, *do not* send a fax without entering this information!

Scanning Documents

Scanning is one of the most important functions performed by your all-in-one unit. After all, the copying features depend on it, and if you're faxing something from a hard copy original, it has to be scanned into electronic format first.

A number of other possible uses for the built-in scanning feature may not be immediately obvious, however. For example, with your scanner you can:

■ Archive important hard copy documents by scanning them into electronic format and storing them on your computer's hard drive (or, if you need true archival backup, record those electronic documents on a CD-ROM using a CD-RW drive).

■ Scan logos, clip art, and images into electronic format for use in all sorts of documents — everything from greeting cards to your Internet and intranet Web pages.

■ Use OCR (*optical character recognition*) to scan text directly from a page into your word processor where it can be edited.

■ Attach scanned material to an Internet e-mail message — the recipient can use any graphics viewer or graphics editor to display the scanned image. Some programs can even create image "packages" that include a viewer, so the receiver doesn't need any other program to view the image.

■ Recreate your family photo albums in electronic format; once recorded onto a CD-ROM, your photos last for years without curling or fading.

In this section, you learn more about the scanning process and how to improve the quality of your scans, no matter what model you use.

How Does a Scanner in an All-in-One Work?

A scanner works much like a dot-matrix or inkjet print engine. However, instead of moving a print head across paper, a scanner moves a light-sensitive pickup over the surface of the paper or moves the paper past a fixed pickup. This sensor can detect and signal the changes in color within the source document as it moves (or, for a monochrome scanner, the shades of gray or black), and those signals are converted into corresponding monochrome or color patterns within an electronic image. Figure 5.2 illustrates the components of the scanning process.

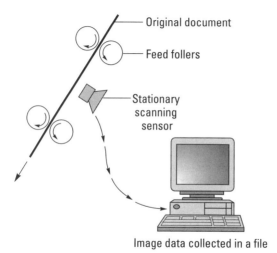

Figure 5.2 The components of the document scanning process

Every digital scanner uses this same process; however, that does not mean that all scanners are created equal. Different methods of moving the sensor across the paper result in two different types of scanners:

- **Flatbed scanners.** These scanners move the sensor itself across the face of your document, so the original document remains stationary. This is the same technique used by larger copy machines. Flatbed scanners are the most accurate, and they can scan odd shapes and sizes (like pages from a bound book). However, they do take up more space than a typical sheetfed all-in-one. If you're looking for a stand-alone scanner, an inexpensive flatbed scanner with a parallel port or USB connection is probably your best choice.

■ **Sheetfed scanners.** Many all-in-ones use this type of scanners in which a system of rollers moves the paper past the stationary scanning sensor. Sheetfed scanners take up little room, they're relatively fast, and they offer adequate resolution. If, however, your original document isn't $8^1/_2 \times 11$ inches or $8^1/_2 \times 14$ inches — a driver's license or a business card for example — you may need to put it in a special clear plastic sleeve to make sure that the document passes correctly through the rollers. (Some new all-in-one units feature advanced document handling for smaller items and photographs, so they don't need a sleeve.) Also, you can't scan pages from a book or magazine unless you tear the pages out.

Tip

If you're interested in producing the best scan quality with your all-in-one, it's important to remember that a sheetfed scanner uses rollers to move the document past the scanning sensor. That means that most sheetfed all-in-ones won't scan thicker material as accurately as a standard sheet of paper, especially if the material you're scanning varies in thickness within a single page. (As an example, consider a page of construction paper decorated with stickers.) Whenever possible, don't mix document pages printed on paper of different thickness in the same scanning session. Your final scanned images maintain the same quality from page to page if you follow that advice.

All-in-one units like the HP LaserJet 3150xi shown in Figure 5.3 use the sheetfed scanning system. Although it is often mistaken for a simple fax machine, a sheetfed scanner is valuable equipment for any size office. Like a standard fax machine, your sheetfed scanner can also scan more than one page automatically; for example, the HP LaserJet 3150xi can scan up to 30 sheets of standard thickness paper unattended.

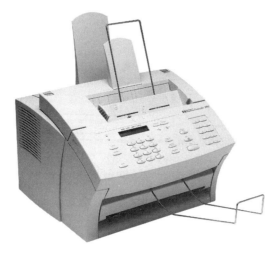

Figure 5.3 The HP LaserJet 3150xi all-in-one unit (Courtesy Hewlett-Packard Co.)

Monochrome (Black-Only) versus Color Scanning

With the arrival of inexpensive parallel-port color flatbed scanners, black-and-white monochrome scanners have all but disappeared from store shelves; however, this is not the case with laser-based multifunction peripherals. Many multifunction units still offer only monochrome scanning.

Keep in mind that color scanning on an all-in-one unit is significantly slower than the same scan on a printer with monochrome scanning, because your color scanner must differentiate between red, green, and blue at the same time. Why those colors? Because they are the colors used in the RGB color model (short for Red/Green/Blue, the three colors of light that are mixed to produce other colors). These colors must be individually scanned and, using software, the results are combined to achieve colors that match the original document.

Selecting a Scan Mode

As you may have guessed, you won't find a "perfect" setting configuration for scanning the different types of documents you're likely to run across. For example, simple printed text doesn't require the same level of scanning detail and resolution as a screen snapshot. The same is true of text and a clip art cartoon or a line drawing. Generally, the more detailed the images that appear within a document, the harder your scanner has to work (and the longer it takes to finish the scanning process). For this reason, high-resolution photographs tend to take the longest scanning time of any document.

Much like other printers, the scanning software used with your all-in-one unit may enable you to choose from more than one print quality mode. For example, the LaserJet 3150 offers these scan modes:

- **Text.** This print quality is perfect for typewritten or simple printed material that contains an occasional line drawing or chart; the final scanned image takes up less disk space, and the entire scanning process requires the least amount of time to complete.

- **Standard Photo mode.** This print quality offers a midpoint between the lowest and highest-quality scanning, so it's the best choice for documents with logos, more complicated and detailed line drawings, or photographs that don't need to be scanned at the highest quality.

Tip

As a rule, I recommend Standard Photo mode for OCR scanning on a laser-based all-in-one — it's a good compromise. The additional resolution and detail result in a higher character recognition accuracy rate, but the entire scanning procedure doesn't take nearly as long to complete as it does if you use High-quality Photo mode.

■ **High-quality Photo mode.** Setting your scanner to this print quality delivers the best image possible, with the highest level of detail and the closest possible reproduction of grayscale shading. Unfortunately, it also results in the slowest possible scanning rate, and the image file can easily grow to 20 or 30MB (or even larger). I use High-quality Photo mode only for scanning photographs or high-resolution images from books and magazines.

Figure 5.4 illustrates the Scan Settings dialog box that enables you to select a print quality mode with an HP LaserJet all-in-one unit.

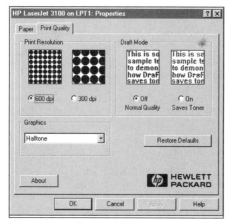

Figure 5.4 Selecting a print quality mode for an HP LaserJet all-in-one unit

Many inkjet-based all-in-ones automatically choose the most appropriate scanning mode setting for the original document. You can usually override the setting made by your all-in-one, but I've found it almost always makes the right choice.

Scanning Software: Viewing and Editing

Once your multifunction peripheral has completed the scanning process, you may think that's all there is to it — the image is saved to disk, and you can print it, fax it, or create multiple copies. But what if you simply want to view the image file, or edit and change the scanned image?

As an example, I usually have to *crop* a photograph or a block of text. (Cropping is an old graphic design term — it means removing any extraneous material from the background, such as removing surrounding text from a picture you want to scan.)

Most multifunction units come with their own image viewing software (and sometimes even a simple image editor). For example, the built-in image viewer shown in Figure 5.5 can display or print a scanned image.

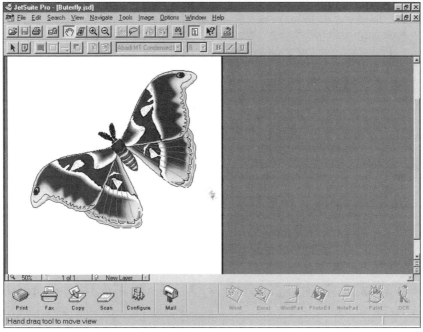

Figure 5.5 Viewing a scanned image

That doesn't mean, however, that you're limited only to the viewing software that accompanied your machine. As long as your multifunction peripheral can produce a scanned image in a standard image format like Windows bitmap (.bmp), JPEG (.jpg), or TIFF (.tif), you can use any one of the hundreds of image editing applications available today for the PC and Macintosh. Using an image editor, you can display your scanned image, reduce or enlarge it, change the brightness or contrast, draw on the image, or even add a part of another image to it. My favorite image editors are Photoshop and PhotoDeluxe (both from Adobe), Picture It! from Microsoft, and Paint Shop Pro from Jasc.

Cross-Reference

You can find a discussion of Paint Shop Pro and its many features in the section "Your Image Editor" in Chapter 9.

Faxing Documents

You may have already noticed that many all-in-one units have a numeric keypad, as well as other buttons with descriptions that sound suspiciously like fax functions (for example, "broadcast send," "speed dial," and "manual dial"). No matter which manufacturer you selected and which multifunction unit you bought, you'll be happy to know that the unit is very likely to offer the same functions as a standard stand-alone fax machine. (In fact, some all-in-ones are designed around an existing fax machine . . . the manufacturer can save money by duplicating the case, parts, and even some of the internal circuitry.)

In this section, I discuss the fax capabilities common to most multifunction peripherals, using the HP LaserJet 3150xi as an example.

Selecting a Fax Resolution

As I mentioned earlier in this chapter, the scanning quality you select determines how long it takes to scan a document, how detailed the scan is, and how much space the scanned image takes up on your hard drive. The fax resolution you select for your outgoing and incoming fax documents is a similar value: it determines the detail level of the faxes you send and receive, as well as the time it takes to transfer the document.

For example, the HP LaserJet 3150xi all-in-one offers four increasingly detailed levels of fax resolution, each of which is the best choice for a particular type of document:

■ **Standard.** This mode delivers a standard resolution of 203×98 dpi; it's the fastest transfer mode, and all fax machines and faxmodems can send and receive documents in this mode. Standard mode is good for text documents with either no graphics or simple line drawings.

■ **Fine.** Fine mode offers a maximum resolution of 203×196 dpi. All faxmodems and almost all fax machines can receive documents in this mode. Fine mode is the default setting on my fax machine, as it's a good compromise between speed and detail level. Fine mode is suitable for text and line drawings, but it still falls short of the resolution needed for a photograph.

■ **Superfine.** With a maximum resolution of 300×300 dpi, superfine mode is suitable for documents with complex, detailed graphics and photographs. Unfortunately, most fax machines and faxmodems don't support superfine mode, and this mode takes far more time to transfer a document than standard or fine mode.

■ **Photo.** Although photo mode offers the same 300×300 dpi resolution as superfine mode, it's the best mode for transferring high-resolution graphics — that's because photo mode is the only fax resolution that can reproduce halftone shading within a photograph. Like superfine mode, photo mode is available only on a select few fax machines and faxmodems. A document sent in photo mode typically takes at least twice as long to transfer as the same document sent in fine mode.

Warning

Don't select Superfine or Photo resolution if you're planning on sending a fax to multiple recipients or if you're setting up faxes for polling — these two high-resolution fax modes do not support these special features.

You may be wondering how you can choose a resolution mode when you're sending a fax to another machine. After all, you don't know if the receiving machine supports superfine or photo mode. Thankfully, resolution selection is done automatically as a part of the fax negotiation process that goes on each time your machine connects to another fax machine (much like the negotiation between two computer modems that determines the speed of the connection). If the receiving fax doesn't support the mode you've specified, the two machines negotiate to the next lowest mode until they reach a resolution mode supported by both fax machines.

Faxing in Color

Although the traditional fax has been black-and-white, color faxing (which has actually been around since 1996) is becoming more popular. Prices for color fax machines have dropped to the same level as black-and-white units, and all-in-one units have followed this trend, providing color scanning, photo-quality inkjet printing, and color faxing features.

You may be asking yourself, "How can a fax machine send all the data required to reproduce a color image without taking an entire afternoon?" If you've scanned a typical 35mm photograph, you have some idea of the size that a digital image can reach — but instead of sending 10 or 20MB of data across the telephone connection, a color fax machine (or all-in-one unit) uses the same JPEG (Joint Photographic Experts Group) compression standard used to reduce the size of images on the Web. In effect, many of the dots in the image are discarded; however, the human eye can't tell this. Therefore, the actual data sent is far less than the original image, and the quality of the received image is still quite good at 100, 200, or 300 dpi.

Of course, a color fax machine can also send and receive fax documents with a black-and-white fax machine, so if you're shopping for an all-in-one and you're considering a color unit, compatibility with existing fax machines is a given.

Look, Ma, No Computer!

Most of us are familiar with the operation of a fax machine, but a multifunction unit has all those extra features, and it connects to your computer: How hard is it to send a simple fax?

Good news: Since your all-in-one unit has the same functionality as a fax machine, you can use it to send and receive faxes on paper just like any standard fax machine. To send a fax, you load paper, enter the destination telephone number, and press Start. To receive faxes, set the machine for autoanswer and load it with paper. (If you expect to receive a large number of faxes during the night, make sure you fill the paper tray before leaving.)

Of course, that's the simple way to go, and it may suffice for the majority of your faxing needs. However, your multifunction peripheral can perform magic on your fax documents — if you're not familiar with today's fax software you'll be amazed at the options you have.

Faxing from Applications

First, you can buy software for the PC that enables you to send a fax directly from within an application. For example, if you're using the software that ships with the HP LaserJet 3150xi, you can send a resume or an invoice you've created with Windows Microsoft Word from within Word itself. Microsoft also includes a fax driver within Windows that can perform this same job — select the Microsoft Fax driver as your printer and print your document as usual.

How does a word-processing program send a fax? Actually, your word processor doesn't know that it's sending a fax; it thinks that it's just printing a document to your printer. However, the all-in-one software automatically intercepts that document before it's sent to the printing engine and reroutes it to the fax engine, so it's faxed instead of printed. (Not every application supports this internal fax send function, so you may have to experiment with each program.)

Tip

If you've used popular fax applications such as Procomm Plus or WinFax Pro, you may be familiar with this process; however, these programs are designed to send faxes with a computer faxmodem, so they may not work with a multifunction device. You can, however, use your all-in-one to print faxes from one of these applications.

To fax a document from within an application, choose Print from the File menu and select the fax software driver as the printer, then print your document as usual. The software driver displays additional dialog boxes where you can create a cover sheet, enter the receiver's telephone number (or select a machine from a dialing directory), and enter a note or memo.

Broadcast Faxing

Have you ever wanted to send the same message to a number of different people? That's easy to do with e-mail — you can use your e-mail program's carbon copy feature. But in the early days of fax machines, one had to laboriously enter a number, wait until the transmission completed, and then repeat the process with a new number.

Luckily, your all-in-one unit can perform these tasks for you automatically, using a feature called *broadcast faxing* (the same fax is sent to multiple recipients). Most all-in-one units enable you to assign multiple recipients in three ways:

■ **Assign a group-dial code.** If all of the intended recipients are assigned the same dialing code to identify them, you can fax the entire group by entering the code as the recipient. (A computer does not need to be attached to your all-in-one for this method to work.)

■ **Select numbers from a list.** If your faxing software includes a dialing directory list, you can select entries from this list (much like an address list within an e-mail program).

■ **Select numbers from the speed-dial keypad.** If you've created speed-dialing entries for the fax machines that should receive the transmission, you can simply choose them from your speed-dial menu or control panel and create a quick dialing queue. (This method works without a computer.) HP OfficeJets make this chore even easier by allowing you to enter your preset choices from the computer's keyboard, rather than reach for the keypad on the all-in-one.

Scheduling Your Faxes

Naturally, an all-in-one unit can also schedule faxes by sending them at a specified date and time. Scheduling faxes is especially important when you're sending a fax document to another country; you can hold the transmission until telephone rates are the lowest, and the document arrives during the recipient's business day rather than during the middle of the night (their time). Many fax applications have this same feature built in for use with faxmodems. For example, Figure 5.6 shows the Fax Scheduling dialog box from Procomm Plus, one of the most popular data and fax transfer applications available for the PC under Windows 98 and Windows 2000.

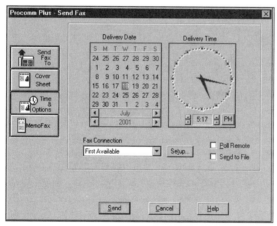

Figure 5.6 Scheduling a fax using a Windows 98 fax application

Of course, many all-in-one units can send scheduled faxes, but some advanced models can store a scheduled fax in internal memory, which frees up other functions for immediate duties. For example, the HP LaserJet 3150xi can read a document for later transmission, and then you can schedule that fax to be sent to one or more recipients at the time you specify. (A connection to your computer isn't even necessary because you can program a schedule from the numeric keypad on your multifunction peripheral.)

Once you've completed this procedure, your all-in-one is ready to send an immediate fax or receive faxes as usual. It automatically dials and transfers the documents at the set time, and it even redials one or more numbers if they are busy during the first attempt.

Although fax scheduling is still a popular feature, a growing number of PC owners are turning to fax-to-e-mail instead. Rather than faxed in the traditional manner over a telephone connection, the document is automatically attached to an e-mail message. Naturally, this saves you money on your long-distance telephone bill for those faxes you send outside your local area, and it eliminates the need for scheduling. The recipient opens the e-mail message and prints the fax document directly from it. Fax-to-e-mail is especially good for sending color fax documents because these documents take considerably more time to send than a simple black-and-white fax. Also, most older fax machines can't receive color faxes.

Configuring Fax Polling

Most owners of fax machines, faxmodems, and all-in-ones with fax features have no idea what *fax polling* means, and they've never used this feature. I think it's time that fax polling receives the recognition it deserves. If you've set up fax polling correctly on your multifunction unit, it can automatically send one or more documents stored within its internal memory whenever requested by the other fax machine. In the meantime, however, your fax machine can continue to send and receive other fax documents.

I have found some nifty applications for this feature. For example, I've used fax polling from my home office for:

- **Providing a fax catalog.** By connecting to your fax machine and polling it, your customers can receive your latest product catalog, newsletter, or order form via your fax machine.

- **Distributing a schedule or sales data.** If you have salespeople or representatives on the road, they can use their laptop faxmodem to connect to your multifunction peripheral and request an updated schedule or work order list.

- **Transferring a single document without using Internet e-mail.** Normally, I send documents via e-mail as attachments, but some clients may not have access to Internet e-mail. As a workaround, I set my multifunction unit for fax polling, and the document can be retrieved by using any standard fax machine with a polling function.

Note that some fax machines and all-in-one units automatically erase the document after it has been polled once, whereas most commercial fax applications enable automatic unlimited polling of one or even multiple documents. If your fax equipment falls into the first category, you have to reload the document and restart the fax polling function if you want another caller to retrieve it.

Using Fax Forwarding

If you're on the road often, faxes sent to your office in your absence may sit unanswered until you return — and that can often result in an angry client or a missed opportunity. If you stay at a motel with a fax machine, or if you can retrieve your faxes from another location while you're away, you may want to use your all-in-one's *fax forwarding* feature.

With your machine set to fax forward, it accepts all incoming faxes in the normal fashion, but instead of printing them locally, your device dials the number you've specified and sends them automatically to another fax machine, where you can retrieve them.

Warning

Before you use fax forwarding, carefully consider the possibility of a private document being sent by accident to a hotel or remote office. Remember, your all-in-one sends all received faxes to the number you enter. If you're worried about the security of your documents, and your model is capable of remote retrieval with a secure password, use that feature instead.

Using Remote Retrieval

Remote retrieval is an advanced feature that has recently appeared on the latest fax machines, computer faxmodems, and multifunction units such as the HP LaserJet 3150xi. This feature functions in the same manner as fax forwarding, enabling you to retrieve your faxes from another location; however, remote retrieval isn't automatic. Retrieving faxes remotely requires a little more work on your part, but enables you to password-protect access to your fax documents, so it's much more secure than simple fax forwarding. If you really need to stay on top of your fax traffic, you'll find that some multifunction machines beep your pager to notify you that you've received a fax.

The specific steps you follow to retrieve faxes remotely varies with the manu-facturer of your multifunction unit, but you initiate the process by calling your fax number from any touchtone telephone (much like retrieving calls from your answering machine). After you enter your password correctly, you enter the number of the fax machine that will receive your documents, and you hang up.

Copying Documents

Another function that is built-in to an all-in-one unit is the simple copying of hard copy documents. After all, the all-in-one probably has all the features of both a sheetfed scanner and a printer, so it should have everything it needs to simply copy your documents.

However, the advanced processor inside your all-in-one unit may be advanced enough to hold a few surprise features that you may have expected to find only on a full-size stand-alone copier. For instance, the HP LaserJet 3150xi can collate, reduce or enlarge copies, and even perform duplex copying — I've also seen other all-in-one units that can copy in "mirror image" for T-shirt transfers, clone multiple images on one sheet from one original, and enlarge to poster size. You can even shift the margins when copying a document to make room for binder holes!

I cover the copy functions generally found on most all-in-one units in this section.

Selecting Copy Contrast and Resolution

Sheetfed all-in-one units use their *fax engine* (the circuitry and processor that controls the fax functions) to create copies, so often that your multifunction peripheral offers the same copy resolutions as the fax resolutions it supports. For example, the HP LaserJet 3150xi uses Superfine mode by default for copying documents. You can switch resolutions to Photo mode for the best possible copy; however, this change significantly increases the time required to copy a page (just as it increases the time required to transfer a fax).

Contrast, however, is another matter entirely. You can use the contrast setting on your multifunction peripheral to lighten or darken the entire copy. Darkening contrast often comes in handy if the original document is faded or too light to be easily read; on the other hand, lightening contrast helps if the document has a heavy black background or text that you want to tone down. Some all-in-one units (like many HP OfficeJets) have both a black and a color copy button, making it easier to choose the right setting.

Reducing and Enlarging Copy

Have you ever wished you could reduce that entire page of figures or that daily calendar to a more manageable size to fit in your wallet or purse? Or perhaps you need to keep a good, legible copy of a driver's license on file for future reference, and you'd like it to be larger so that you can read it more easily? If so, you've probably made a quick trip to the office copy machine and created a reduced or enlarged copy — most all-in-ones can perform this same trick. For example, the HP LaserJet 3150xi can reduce an original document by a maximum of 50 percent, and it can enlarge an original document by a maximum of 200 percent. As a comparison, a flatbed HP OfficeJet all-in-one can usually reduce and enlarge from 25 percent to a whopping 400 percent!

Consider other factors, however, when changing the size of a document, especially if it contains complex artwork or grayscale shades. If you enlarge the document by a big percentage, you may find that you have to darken the contrast to achieve the right appearance for the final copy. The same is true of lightening the contrast if you're reducing a document by a large percentage.

Using Ordered Printing and Collation

Depending upon the software that's included with your all-in-one unit, you may be able to print the pages of a single copy in order. Instead of arranging pages as 3-2-1 when they're ejected, the pages are ordered correctly as 1-2-3. This function is called *ordered printing*. Some units also *collate*, which means they can print multiple copies of the same document in sorted order, as in 1-2-3-1-2-3. You can use both of these features together, too, making it much easier to print multiple copies of a document with multiple pages. You don't have to manually sort pages after they've been printed; this saves you several minutes of work.

Tip

If you're shopping for an all-in-one unit and you intend to do a lot of copying with it — for example, if you need five or six copies of a multiple-page document several times a day — look for a model that's equipped with as much on-board memory as possible. That extra RAM helps hold large documents in ordered or collated format while they're being printed. The background printing function in Windows 98 and Windows 2000 works more efficiently if the printing device has more on-board memory and can accept a larger print job.

Most multifunction units can't collate duplex copies, so if you're printing a double-sided document or you'd like to print 2-up or 4-up documents (that's copying two or four pages of a document on a single sheet of paper), you have to sort the finished copies by hand.

Copying Duplex Documents

Most multifunction peripherals handle duplex copying in the same manner as a standard inkjet or laser printer. For most inkjet and laser all-in-one units, that means you have to remove the document pages after the first side has been printed and turn them around manually to print the second side. If your all-in-one unit features an advanced document sorter or an automated paper feed system for printed documents, they should also work while copying duplex documents, so your device should be able to copy duplex pages without your intervention.

Cross-Reference

For more information on printing duplex pages on an inkjet or laser printer, refer to Chapter 3.

Using Multiple Functions Simultaneously

An all-in-one may be able to take the place of a complete set of stand-alone machines, but it is limited in one very important way. Because your multifunction peripheral shares the printing and scanning engines between functions and it only has one paper feed and output tray, it cannot handle many tasks simultaneously (also known as *multitasking*).

As an example of this limitation, consider a common multifunction unit chore — scanning a paper document, which uses only the scanning engine. Here's a rundown of what the HP LaserJet 3150xi can do simultaneously as it scans:

■ Print a document

■ Receive a fax

Not a big list (especially when you consider all of the functions this machine can perform). So why can't the all-in-one simultaneously copy a document while scanning? Because copying also uses the scanning engine, and in sheetfed products, both scanning and copying require the paper feed tray.

Tip

Multitasking is another reason why it's important to have the largest amount of on-board RAM for your all-in-one unit. Models like the HP LaserJet 3150xi can scan that fax and load its contents directly into memory, which frees up the scanning engine and enables you to perform additional copying and scanning. (Meanwhile, the fax is transmitted from the all-in-one's memory.)

Now, if you have a small home office or if your all-in-one is reserved exclusively for your own use, you probably won't have a problem, After all, most of us perform only one task at a time, requiring a computer printer, fax machine, copier, or scanner. However, the picture is entirely different if your machine must serve the document needs of an entire office. A bottleneck may form at an all-in-one, as you wait for someone else's scanning, copying, or printing job to complete before you can load your document. (Some all-in-one units, such as the HP OfficeJet G95, have networking features that solve this bottleneck problem because they let you print and scan at the same time.)

For this reason, it's generally a better idea for a larger company to invest a little more in separate components for a busy office with many employees. Separate components have other advantages, too — keeping a separate scanner, fax machine, and printer helps you safeguard your office against a complete breakdown in printing functions, graphics work, and communications if your multifunction unit breaks and needs to be sent away for repair work.

If you do use a multifunction peripheral for simultaneous tasks, look for a chart or a quick-reference table in the user manual that tells you which functions can be performed together at the same time.

Care and Feeding of Your All-in-One Unit

Except for cleaning the scanning engine, maintaining your multifunction unit is basically the same as the maintenance I discussed in detail in Chapters 3 and 4. Refer to your manual's procedure for cleaning the scanning sensor on your all-in-one unit. Remember, most manufacturers recommend that you use isopropyl alcohol (rather than ammonia-based solvents) and a lint-free cloth or cotton swab to clean the interior.

Cross-Reference

If you have an inkjet all-in-one, refer to the section titled "Care and Feeding of Your Inkjet Printer" in Chapter 3. If you have a laser all-in-one, refer to the section titled "Care and Feeding of Your Laser Printer" in Chapter 4.

Summary

In this chapter you discovered the amazing functionality — including scanning, copying, faxing, and printing — of today's all-in-one machines. You learned about configuring multiple devices on a single telephone line and the importance of properly configuring autoanswer and distinctive ring.

Your tour of scanner options covered resolution, color versus monochrome scanning, and various utility programs that you can use to view and edit the images you've scanned. You explored the fax applications available on most multifunction machines, including scheduling, broadcast send, polling, and remote access.

In Chapter 6, you follow the general installation and configuration steps that apply to all printing devices.

In Chapter 10 you find step-by-step projects for common all-in-one tasks, including sending and receiving faxes, scanning a document, using the copy function, changing the toner (or ink) cartridge, and recalibrating the scanner.

→ Printer Connections

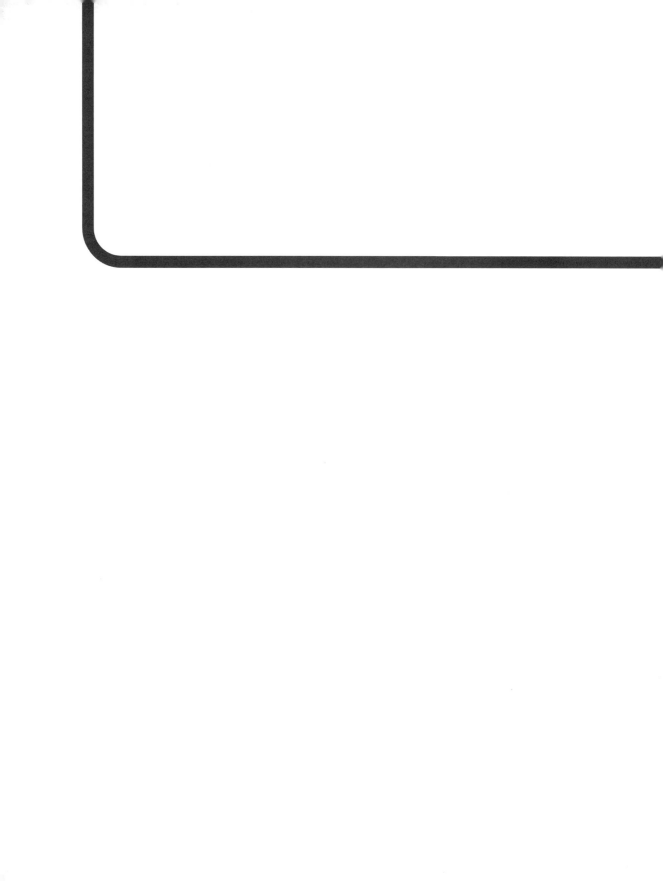

CHAPTER 6

Installing and Configuring Your Printer

IN THIS CHAPTER
- Locating ports and such
- Configuring and optimizing printing under Windows 98
- Configuring and optimizing printing under Windows 2000 Professional
- Configuring and optimizing printing under Windows NT
- Configuring and optimizing printing under Mac OS
- Configuring and optimizing printing under Linux
- Updating your printer driver
- Handling installation problems
- Testing printer-to-computer communications

In earlier chapters, I compared impact, inkjet, laser, and multifunction printing devices and discussed the details unique to each species of printer. In this chapter, however, the type of printer you've selected won't matter. I discuss installing and configuring just about any printing hardware under the two favorite personal computer operating systems in use today: Windows 98 and Mac OS 9. I also provide tips and information about Windows NT, Windows 2000 Professional, and Linux.

"Do I need any exotic tools to install a printer on my PC or Macintosh?" The answer is most definitely, "No!" A screwdriver is the only tool possibly required for the job (and that's only for the PC). And you won't need much time, either. As long as your initial cable connections and software configuration go without a hitch, you can expect to finish in 15 to 30 minutes.

Without further ado, then, let's get your new printer or all-in-one unit out of the box, connected, and running.

Unpacking Your New Hardware

This may seem like a self-explanatory topic — after all, you cut through the tape on the box, pull out the printer, and toss the box in the trash, right? In theory, that's all you need to do, but in fact, there's definitely a wrong way to unpack. I've talked to many computer owners who have paid the price for not following a few common sense rules in their excitement and haste to get that cool piece of the latest printing hardware out of the box. Yes, you *can* damage your new printer by unpacking it incorrectly, and you *can* throw away a loose part by mistake if you're in a hurry . . . and those are only two of the common mishaps you may encounter.

To avoid problems while you're unpacking, remember the first rule: *take your time.* If you rush, you're more likely to make a mistake.

Here are a few additional guidelines you should follow as well:

■ **Look for damage to the box.** If the box has a huge rip or puncture, the printer may have survived without a scratch, but the possibility of damage to the unit is naturally multiplied. If I have a choice, I ask for another unit without a damaged box. If that's not possible, make sure you check for any damage as soon as you unpack it, and return the unit if you find something.

■ **Look for unpacking instructions.** Your box may carry printed instructions on which end of the box to open and how to lift the unit from the box, so check each side before you choose an end of the box to open.

■ **Pull — do not dump!** Set the box down flat on the floor and pull the unit out from one end; never open one end of a box containing computer hardware and turn it upside-down to "dump" the contents onto the floor. If you turn the box upside-down, there's a good chance your brand-new printer may take a quick uncontrolled slide and a nasty bounce.

- **Always check for small parts**. Many manufacturers tape small parts to the Styrofoam packing material, including ink cartridges, cables, wire paper guides, and software CDs. Before you put any packing materials back in the empty box, check them thoroughly to make sure parts aren't stowed away in the packing material.

Tip

Your new printer's manual probably comes with a packing list that details each part that you should have received with your printer. Always consult that list to make sure you have everything. Because printers don't have many external parts, this is usually a quick process — but if your printer was accidentally shipped without a necessary part, you'll know immediately.

- **Hold on to that box!** This is especially important for those who order computer hardware from a mail-order store or from an Internet Web site, but many local stores also refuse to accept the return of a printer without all of the original packaging and the original box. Returning a unit for warranty service also requires the original box and packaging. Additionally, it's great to have the box and the original packaging if you'll be moving in the future. For these reasons, I always keep my hardware boxes for at least a year after the purchase (or until I run out of storage space).

Tip

Storing your printer's empty box is also a good idea if you usually sell your secondhand computer hardware after a few years of use. Of course, the device's manual is a requirement when selling a piece of hardware, but your used item can often command a higher price if you can sell it in the original box.

- **Recycle whenever possible.** Naturally, your printer's box is recyclable when you finally do decide to get rid of it, but other packing materials can be reused for Christmas packages or moving. If your printer was cradled by molded Styrofoam, cut the foam into smaller pieces to use later as packing material.

Although I specifically talk about printers in this book, these common sense rules work with any large piece of computer hardware, including monitors and the computer case itself.

Selecting a Location

"How much is your time worth?" That's the first question that a business consultant asks you when designing the layout of a new office, and that's also the question you should ask yourself when selecting the location for your new printer or all-in-one unit. You can save yourself time and energy by choosing the right spot. Of course, the proper location is even more important if the new printer will be used by more than one person.

I think the best spot for printing hardware is right next to your computer, but there may be problems with this arrangement. You may not have the necessary space, your model may make too much noise and interfere with your work environment, or there may not be enough ventilation next to your computer.

Keep these general rules in mind while picking a location:

- **Performance is limited by cable length.** Most parallel printer cables reach a maximum of six or ten feet — the longer the cable over ten feet, the more the signal weakens and the more likely you'll encounter printer errors. Therefore, your location must fall somewhere within a six- to ten-foot radius around your computer (and if that cable has to snake its way behind desks or around furniture, your cable length decreases even more).

- **Proper ventilation is important.** Like your computer, your printer gives off heat. This is typically more of a problem with a laser printer, which generates heat to bond the toner onto the paper, than it is with an inkjet or impact printer. (Many thermal wax printers also generate a significant amount of heat.) Your printer should always have sufficient space around it for proper ventilation — I recommend at least two inches of open airspace.

 Tip

Does your laser printer have its own fan? If so, make sure that this fan isn't blocked — it must have access to room air. It's always a good idea to use a compressed air can to blow any dust or dirt from the fan vent during your regular printer maintenance.

- **Your printer can go mobile.** If your printer must travel from computer to computer in an office environment, you can buy a printer cart from your local office supply store or mail-order office catalog. These wheeled carts hold the printer and a supply of paper; it also usually has a number of shelves to hold supplies. A printer cart is a great way to share a printer across a wide space if the computers aren't connected by an office network.

 Tip

If your printer travels on a cart like this from office workstation to workstation, I recommend that you buy a USB printer (if all the computers that will use the printer have USB ports, that is). A USB printer is much easier to share because it can be connected or removed without rebooting the computer.

- **A central location is best.** If an entire office shares your new printer, consider a desk or printer cart positioned roughly in the center of the room, perhaps surrounded by a cubicle to help shield everyone from the noise. If a central location isn't feasible, I usually recommend placing the printer by the office door, allowing you to print a document and take it with you as you leave the room.

■ **Printer protection is available.** Do you work in an industrial area where dust, dirt, and liquids can damage an unprotected printer? Does your printer make so much noise that you have to leave the room while it's printing? If so, you may want to invest in a printer booth — these boxes are usually made of fiberglass or Plexiglas, and they're insulated to reduce noise. You can run cables through holes cut in the back of the booth. You can open the hood on a booth to collect your printed documents and add paper.

Connecting Cables and Such

Just about every computer printer is guaranteed to need at least two cable connections, but some multifunction models need at least one more additional connection. Most printers also have a number of plastic or wire supports that hold the paper as it enters or leaves the printer.

The general instructions in this section help you with a variety of connections and attachments that you may have to make, but consult your printer's manual for any specific switch settings that you'll need to adjust or any additional steps you may need to perform.

Connecting the Printer Cable

The first cable connection you should make is the printer cable that runs from your computer to your new printer. You still have to make this connection even if you're installing a network printer. The computer acting as a printer server is connected to the printer with a printer cable, while the other computers on the network send print jobs over the network to the printer server. As I mentioned earlier in the book, the printer cable probably isn't included with your printer (although most all-in-one devices do include the cable), so you may have to buy one separately. They're generally available at most discount and department stores.

You may have noticed that I didn't say "parallel cable." There are two reasons for this:

■ The Macintosh typically uses a different type of printer cable with a completely different connector. Figure 6.1 illustrates the two connectors on both ends of a standard PC Centronics parallel printer cable, while Figure 6.2 illustrates the connector on both ends of a typical Macintosh printer cable.

■ Today's printers may use a USB connection instead of the traditional parallel cable. As the owner of a USB printer, I can tell you that installation and configuration is about as hassle-free as it can get . . . I highly recommend a USB printer if your computer has USB ports!

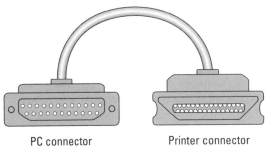

PC connector   Printer connector

Figure 6.1 The connectors on a PC parallel cable

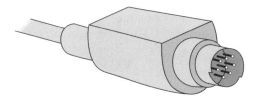

Mac printer connector

Figure 6.2 The connector on a Mac printer cable (both ends are identical)

Locating a PC parallel port

Generally, it's pretty easy to locate the proper parallel port on the back of your PC; look for a female port with 25-pin holes, generally marked with a stylized printer icon. Things may get a little confusing if your printer has a 25-pin serial port because they look alike. However, serial ports are male (and most PCs today use 9-pin serial connectors for external modems), so generally only one port will work with your parallel printer cable.

Some I/O (short for *input/output*) adapter cards may provide not one, but two printer ports. These cards are especially useful if you have a device that won't work well with a parallel-port device such as a Zip drive or a scanner, which can use the second port instead of trying to share a single parallel port with your printer. However, if your PC has a second parallel port and it's not properly marked, you have to experiment to determine which port is the primary parallel port (I cover this later in the section "Testing Printer Communications").

Locating a USB port

Because a USB connection can transfer data much faster than a standard parallel port, automatically configures itself, can provide AC power for a peripheral, and can be "hot-swapped" without rebooting your computer, a USB interface is a good choice for just about any printer (especially portable printers and high-resolution color printers).

With the hot-swap and auto-configuration features of USB, connecting a USB peripheral is as simple as plugging in the connector — you can immediately print to a USB printer without fear of locking up your applications because of a hardware conflict or a parallel port without bidirectional support.

Locating a Mac printer port

On a Macintosh, your printer cable simply plugs into the port marked with a printer icon, and either end fits. Most older Macs can also use a printer over a LocalTalk or AppleTalk network. If you need to connect a PC printer to a Macintosh, converters are available. My favorite is the PowerPrint system from Infowave (www.infowave. com), which includes both a special cable and the software you need to print from your Mac to one of those "foreign" printers.

The new generation of Mac computers represented by the iMac is a little different. The iMac offers USB ports and an Ethernet connector instead of the traditional Mac serial printer connector — you need a USB printer, or you have to connect your iMac to an Ethernet network that has access to a printer. If you want to use an older Mac printer that doesn't support the USB standard, you have to shell out the cash for a *USB-to-serial converter* box, which typically connects to one of your USB ports and provides two or three of the older standard Mac connectors.

Making the PC connection

Okay, you've got the proper cable for your PC printer, and you've located the ports on the back of your computer and the printer. There are two methods of connecting a cable, depending on the connector itself:

- **Screws or knobs.** This is the method used on the PC side. Align the connector with the port (due to the angled edges, it goes on only one way), and push it in firmly. Tighten the connector by turning the knobs or screws clockwise until they're snug.

- **Clips.** This is the method used to connect a parallel cable to your printer or multifunction device. Align the cable connector with the port on the unit (again, the connectors are designed to work only one way), and push it in firmly. To hold the cable connector in place, snap the clips on the edge of the connector toward the cable, and they should lock in place. To remove the cable, pull the clips away from the connector.

Here are a few guidelines you should follow when connecting cables:

- **Keep cables straight.** Never crimp or bend a cable. Some people wrap cabling around a piece of furniture or between a door and a frame, which can lead to printer communication errors.

- **Never force a connector.** If a cable connector doesn't seem to fit properly and resists pressure, don't force it! Instead, check the connectors on the cable and the port: are the pins bent, or is one of the holes plugged? You can generally use a pair of needle-nose pliers to bend a pin back into alignment, but if you break a pin you're out of luck.

■ **Mark the connections**. If the ports on your PC aren't plainly marked, take a moment to identify them with a fine point permanent marker, or create labels for each port. You'll be happy that you did the next time you have to reattach those cables. Also, label the cables — with many peripherals creating a rat's nest of cables, labeling makes identifying them easier.

Connecting a Fax Cable

If you're installing an all-in-one with fax capability, you connect a telephone cable to the wall socket. This is the connection for your unit's fax engine.

First, unplug any telephone or telephony device that's currently connected to the wall socket (you can reattach these devices to your all-in-one once it has been installed). Next, align the cable connector with the wall jack (make sure the friction catch on the top of the connector is facing the right way), and push it in firmly until it snaps into place.

Cross-Reference

You can find more information about the proper way to set up a phone chain in the section, "Creating a Phone Chain" in Chapter 5.

The multifunction-unit end of the telephone cable connection may be a little more complicated because most have both a line jack and a phone jack. Consult your manual for information on which jack should connect to the wall. In most cases, this is the line jack, which is either marked "Line," or marked with a wall jack icon (for example, the HP LaserJet 3150 marks the line jack with an *L*). Align the connector with the line jack, and push it in firmly until it snaps into place.

Tip

Now is also a good time to add a telephone line surge suppressor to your phone chain cabling. Such a device can help protect your expensive multifunction device and any other telephony devices in your phone chain from being damaged by an electrical surge carried through your telephone line.

Attaching Supports

Most printers have some sort of wire, metal, or plastic supports that need to be attached to hold blank paper or printed pages. If you're like me, you have a strong temptation to add these minor parts later, but they're included for a reason, and your printer probably will not work correctly until they've been installed. Therefore, make it a point to install them now, before you use your printer for the first time.

Wire tray supports are generally installed by squeezing the sides of the wire and inserting the ends into matching holes in the printer's case. Plastic supports are generally pushed firmly into the matching slots in the case until they snap into a locked position.

Even if you don't attach supports manually, they're probably there. Many new printers use supports that retract into the body somewhere. A number of the printers that I've seen lately look like porcupines when you pull out all their built-in paper guides and supports.

Tip

Be sure to avoid another temptation — throwing that instruction manual in a drawer! Read it from cover to cover before you turn on your new printer.

Connecting the Power Cable

First, check to make sure your printer is "currently" (pardon the pun) turned off at the switch. Next, align the power cord's female connector with the power socket on the back or side of your printer (once again, most manufacturers create power cables that can only be connected the right way, or they use the standard PC/Macintosh power cable connector design). Push the power cord connector firmly until it's snug in the socket. Finally, plug the male end of the power cord into your AC wall socket.

Tip

You've probably already invested in an AC power surge suppressor or a UPS (short for *uninterruptible power supply*) for your computer system; if you haven't, run to your nearby discount or hardware store and buy one. Without a surge suppressor, the only way you can feel *absolutely* safe about your entire computer system is if you unplug your computer and all of its peripherals from the wall, and that's not practical for most of us. A typical surge strip costs only about $15, and it can save you thousands of dollars in case of a lightning strike on your neighborhood power lines. Plus, connecting everything to a surge strip or UPS makes it easy to conveniently turn your entire system on and off from a single switch, so you know that your monitor and peripherals are always ready when your computer is on.

Installing a Printer under Windows

There are two methods you can use to install a standard parallel-port printer under Windows 95, Windows 98, and Windows Me:

- **Automatically.** Because it requires very little intervention, this is the preferred method for adding a system printer; Windows uses automatic device detection to recognize that you've added a new printer to your parallel port and refers to a printer database to determine what drivers should be loaded. (In fact, the drivers for your printer may be included on the Windows CD-ROM, so you may not even need the driver disks that accompanied your printer.) Automatic installation should be used only for printers. All-in-one peripherals must use the installation software that comes with them unless the documentation says to use this automatic process. Multifunction devices require more software than the Windows printer driver in order to work properly.

■ **Manually.** If Windows doesn't automatically recognize your printer after you've checked the parallel-port connection, you can still install it manually — this can happen with older impact printers.

Tip

It's always a good idea to check the manufacturer's instructions for your printer before you start the installation process. Some printers should be installed using a software setup program provided by the manufacturer (instead of the automatic or manual methods I cover in the next sections).

Automatic installation with a parallel connection

Follow these steps for automatic installation under Windows 95, Windows 98, or Windows Me with a parallel printer:

1. Shut down Windows, and turn off your PC.

2. Attach the printer cable to your printer and to the printer port on the back of your PC (usually marked with a printer icon or labeled "LPT1" or "Printer"). Connect the AC cord from your printer to the wall socket or surge suppressor, load the feed tray with paper, and turn your printer on. (Your printer must be on for Windows to successfully poll it. After installation, it should always be connected and turned on before you boot your PC so that Windows can access it during the operating system boot process.)

3. Turn on your PC. Windows should boot as usual.

4. Windows should recognize that you've added a printer, and a dialog box like the one displayed in Figure 6.3 should appear. If your printer is included in the printer database and a driver exists on the Windows CD-ROM, the system loads the driver and automatically configures your printer. (If necessary, you are prompted to load the Windows CD-ROM.) Skip to Step 6.

Figure 6.3 Windows 98 automatically detects that you've connected a new printer.

5. If Windows can't identify your printer, it displays a scrolling listbox of all the different printer models in its database, grouped by manufacturer (shown in Figure 6.4). If you have a driver disk, click the Have Disk button and browse for the floppy disk or CD-ROM that contains the driver. If you don't have a driver disk for the printer, find the manufacturer, and choose the closest model to yours.

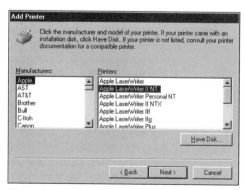

Figure 6.4 Selecting a printer from the Windows driver database

Tip

If you don't have a driver for Windows 98/Me but you do have a driver for Windows 95, you can always try the older software instead. You may be able to download the correct driver from the manufacturer's Web site as well.

6. The icon for your new printer should now appear in your Printers folder. To check, click the My Computer icon on your desktop, and click the Printers folder to open it.

Automatic installation with a USB connection

If you're using a USB printer under Windows 95 (with USB support), Windows 98, or Windows Me, follow these steps for automatic installation:

1. Connect the USB cable to your printer. Connect the AC cord from the printer to the wall socket or surge suppressor and load the feed tray with paper.

2. Turn on your printer.

3. Plug the USB connector into a USB port on your computer.

4. Windows should recognize that you've added a USB device. In almost every case, Windows prompts you to load the manufacturer's CD-ROM that came with your printer so that it can install the correct drivers (this only happens the first time you connect your USB printer). You may also be prompted to load your Windows CD-ROM if necessary.

5. The icon for your new printer should now appear in your Printers folder. To check, click the My Computer icon on your desktop, and click the Printers folder to open it.

To remove your USB printer from your system, simply disconnect the USB cable. You can plug your printer back in at any time.

Manual installation

Follow these steps for manual installation:

1. Shut down Windows, and turn off your PC.

2. Next, connect the printer cable to your printer, and connect it to the printer port on the back of your PC (usually marked with a printer icon or labeled "LPT1" or "Printer"). Connect the AC cord from the printer to the wall socket or surge suppressor, load the feed tray with paper, and turn your printer on. (Even though your computer can't recognize the manufacturer and model of your printer at this time, it's still necessary for you to connect the printer and turn it on before you boot your PC so that Windows can access it.)

3. Turn on your PC, allowing Windows to boot normally.

4. Click Start, and select Printers from the Settings menu, which displays the Printers folder shown in Figure 6.5.

5. Click the Add Printer icon, which runs the Add Printer wizard, and click Next in the opening wizard screen.

Figure 6.5 The Printers folder in Windows

6. The wizard displays a scrolling listbox of all the different printer models in the Windows database, grouped by manufacturer. If you have a driver disk, click the Have Disk button, and browse for the floppy disk or CD-ROM that contains the driver. If you don't have a driver disk for the printer you're installing, find the manufacturer, and choose the closest model to yours. Click Next to continue to the next wizard screen.

7. Because Windows can't automatically detect the printer, the wizard displays the dialog box shown in Figure 6.6 requesting that you identify the parallel port your printer will use. If you're not sure which port to choose, pick LPT1 (which is usually the right port). If you're using a serial printer (practically a museum piece on the PC these days), pick either COM1 or COM2, depending upon which serial port you use to connect the printer. Click Next to continue to the next wizard screen.

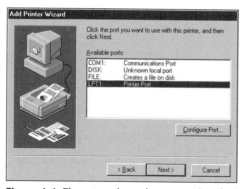

Figure 6.6 The wizard needs you to identify the correct port for your printer.

Tip

If Windows instructs you to run Setup from the manufacturer's CD-ROM, you may not be able to follow Steps 7–9. The device installation program may take over and do these things for you. In that case, follow the instructions on your screen.

8. The wizard now prompts you for a printer name to identify your new connection and a default control (which enables you to select this printer as the default system printer in all of your Windows applications). Type a name for your new printer, and click Yes if you would like it to be the default printer on your system. Then click Next to continue to the final Add Printer Wizard screen.

9. Before closing, the wizard asks if you would like to print a test page to check things out. It's a good way to test if your PC and your printer are communicating properly, and it also indicates whether you've selected a compatible printer driver. Click Finish to exit the wizard.

10. The icon for your new printer should now appear in your Printers folder. To check, click the My Computer icon on your desktop, and click the Printers folder to open it.

Installing a Printer under Mac OS 9

Under Mac OS 9, printer drivers are stored within the Extensions folder. Follow these steps to install the driver software for a new printer:

1. Shut down your Macintosh, and unplug it.

2. Next, connect the printer cable to your printer, and connect it to the printer port on the back of your Mac (marked with a printer icon). Connect the AC cord from the wall socket or surge suppressor to your printer, load the feed tray with paper, and turn your printer on.

3. Plug in your Mac, turn it on, and allow Mac OS to boot completely.

Tip

If you're connecting a USB printer to your Mac, you don't need to shut down your computer — simply plug in the USB cable, and proceed to Step 4.

4. Insert the floppy disk or CD-ROM that accompanied your printer, and browse it for the Installer program. Double-click the Installer program icon, and follow any instructions specific to the driver software.

5. Once the installation is complete, you must select your new printer using the Apple Chooser. Click the Apple menu, and select the Chooser menu item. Mac OS displays the Chooser dialog box shown in Figure 6.7.

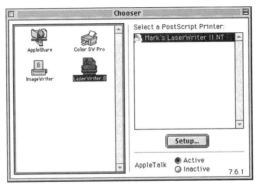

Figure 6.7 You use the Chooser utility to select a system printer under Mac OS.

6. In the left portion of the Chooser dialog box, select the type of printer you installed. In the right-hand portion of the Chooser dialog box, click the correct port icon where you connected your printer cable.

7. Close the dialog box, and Mac OS automatically saves the selections you've made to disk.

Getting the Latest Driver

At some point during the installation and configuration of your new printer, Windows 98 asks you for a printer driver. This driver may already exist on your Windows 98 CD-ROM, or you may load it from a floppy disk or CD-ROM that accompanied your printer. However you install your driver, though, you should know that it probably already needs to be updated.

You may be wondering why a brand-new printer straight out of the box may need a new driver — there are a number of good reasons:

- **Manufacturers constantly update drivers.** Even if your operating system CD-ROM claims to install the latest and greatest version of Windows 98, Windows Me, Windows 2000, or Windows NT, the files on that disc are usually months (or even years) out of date . . . and that includes any printer drivers it installs as well.

- **New drivers may enable new features.** Manufacturers sometimes add enhancements and new features through software drivers and flash BIOS (basic input/output system) updates. These enhancements don't require a hardware upgrade, so they won't cost you anything.

- **New drivers may fix existing driver bugs.** No one's computer code is perfect. A new version of the printer driver likely includes bug fixes for existing errors in the driver (plus, if your printer manufacturer includes technical information along with a driver update, you'll probably find information on what's new with the latest version of the software).

Finding Driver Updates

If you have an Internet connection, Windows 98, Windows Me, and Windows 2000 automate most of the work involved in locating a new driver update, but if you're using Windows 95 or Windows NT, you still have to manually search for a driver. Most manufacturers offer driver updates through at least one of these avenues:

- **A Web site.** Look for the manufacturer's Web site in the printer's documentation; you'll likely find an entire download area dedicated to both driver update files and printer hardware FAQs (*Frequently Asked Questions,* a common name for text files that contain information on a specific topic). Figure 6.8 shows a LaserJet printer driver page from the Hewlett-Packard Company Web site (www.hp.com).

- **A BBS.** If you don't have access to the Internet, you usually can still call your printer manufacturer's BBS (*Bulletin Board System*). If you have a telecommunications program such as Procomm Plus, you can download your driver updates and information files directly from the BBS using the ZMODEM file transfer protocol.

- **The manufacturer's technical support department.** No modem or Internet connection? Never fear, you can usually arrange to have a disk or CD-ROM containing the latest drivers sent to your home. Call the manufacturer's technical support number, and request the latest driver for your printer.

"How do I tell what printer driver version I have?" The easiest way to do this in Windows is to display the Properties dialog box for the printer; the driver version number is usually listed somewhere within this dialog box.

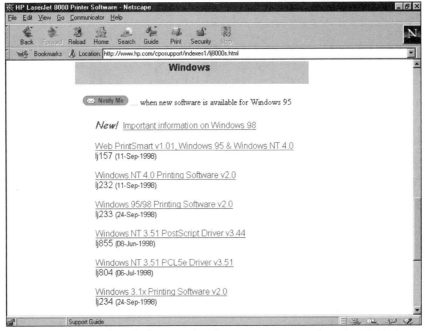

Figure 6.8 Downloading the latest update for a LaserJet printer from the HP Web site

Updating Your Printer Drivers

There are two methods of updating a printer driver under Windows 95/98/Me, Windows NT, and Windows 2000:

- **Programs.** Some manufacturers distribute their printer driver updates as executable program files, which means you can simply run the Setup program and it automatically copies files and makes any necessary configuration changes for you.

- **.INF installer files.** These printer updates are installed using the Add New Hardware wizard within the control panel, so updating your driver software is very similar to adding a new printer. These files are not run as programs.

Note

The Web-based Windows Update system built in to Windows 98 does *not* update your printer drivers! Windows Update only provides updates for your operating system software and Microsoft applications such as Internet Explorer and Outlook Express.

Updates from the manufacturer

Follow these steps to update drivers from the manufacturer:

1. Download the update file into a temporary directory. (If the download file is a compressed Zip archive containing the printer driver, you may have to uncompress it before you can run the program.)

2. Click the program icon, and follow any onscreen instructions. The update process likely requires a reboot of your system, so make sure all other applications are closed as well.

3. Once the update procedure is complete, print a test page to verify that the update was correctly applied.

Updates from .INF installer files

Follow these steps to update drivers from .INF installer files:

1. Click Start, and select Control Panel from the Settings menu. Click the Add New Hardware icon.

2. Click Next in the opening wizard screen.

3 The wizard asks whether you would like Windows 98 to automatically detect your new hardware. However, because we're just updating the driver for an existing printer, click No, and then Next to continue.

4. Select Printer from the Hardware Type list, and click Next to continue.

5. If you're upgrading a printer driver for a printer that's attached directly to your computer, click Local Printer and Next to continue. (I cover network printers in Chapter 7.)

6. The wizard displays a scrolling listbox of all the different printer models in the Windows 98 database, grouped by manufacturer. Click the Have Disk button, and browse for the folder on your hard drive, the floppy disk, or the CD-ROM that contains the driver. Click OK to continue to the next wizard screen.

7. The wizard displays the updated driver name — select it, and click OK. Windows 98 installs the updated driver and announces when it has completed the update.

8. Click Finish to return to the control panel.

Windows 95/98/Me Tips and Tricks

Windows Me, Windows 98, and its older relative Windows 95 are the most popular 32-bit operating systems for the PC, and for good reason: they make your digital life as convenient as possible, including installing and using a printer. Here, I concentrate on providing a number of tips and tricks that can help you improve the performance of your PC and your printer under Windows 98 and Me.

Cross-Reference

I provide step-by-step instructions on installing a printer under Windows 98 in the section "Installing a Printer under Windows 98," earlier in this chapter.

Adjusting the Printer Spooler

Windows 98 can use virtual memory as a *print spooler* (also called a *print buffer*). If you enable this feature, the spooler performs two important functions:

- **Background printing.** With your print job safely stored in a print spooler, Windows 98 is free to return control to your applications, which means that you can continue working in your word processor or spreadsheet program while your printer prints the document. This feature is called *background printing,* and it can be a great timesaver if you print large jobs on your PC.

- **Storage for larger print jobs.** Usually, both laser and inkjet printers have their own onboard memory for storing print jobs, but a large PostScript or PCL print job with many pages and a large number of graphics can easily use up that printer memory. Windows 98 automatically uses virtual memory to store the remainder of the file until your printer can catch up. (There are a few exceptions — some printers use only the computer's memory for processing.)

Unfortunately, your printer driver or printer installation program may not enable print spooling automatically; however, you should be able to enable it manually if necessary. To adjust the spooler, click My Computer to open the window, click the Printers folder, then right-click the desired printer icon, and choose Properties. The location of the print spooler feature differs from one printer manufacturer to another, so you may have to do some searching, but as long as your printer driver supports spooling, you should be able to find it. Figure 6.9 shows the Spool Settings dialog box for a typical printer.

Once you've found the printer spooler settings, enable the spooling feature, and save your changes within the Properties dialog box. If the driver enables you to specify the amount of buffer space, I recommend that you pick the largest available amount.

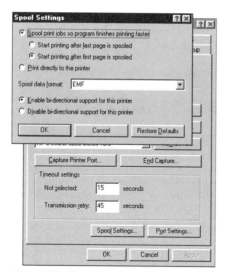

Figure 6.9 The printer spooler controls for a typical printer

Defragmenting Your Hard Drive

While we're discussing virtual memory, I should point out that it actually exists as data stored on your hard drive rather than actual system RAM (hence the name "virtual"). Because your hard drive is far slower than your system memory, it pays to optimize that hard drive. Doing so results in faster virtual memory operation, as well as a faster system overall.

Windows 98 includes a built-in hard drive defragmenter, and it's always a good idea to run this program before you start printing. I use the Windows 98 Task Scheduler to automatically launch the Disk Defragmenter program each morning at 2:00 a.m., so my drive is always working at top efficiency during the day.

To run the Disk Defragmenting program, click the Start button, select the Programs ⇨ Accessories ⇨ System Tools menu, and click Disk Defragmenter.

Turning Off Port Polling

What is *port polling*? It's a procedure that Windows 98 follows each time you boot your computer and each time you send a print job from an application. During polling, Windows 98 automatically checks your parallel port to make sure your printer is ready to receive a print job. This helps prevent errors that can lock up your computer, such as a laptop trying to access a printer that's no longer connected or a printer connected to a network that receives simultaneous print jobs.

Generally, port polling is a good thing if:

- Your printer is available to other users on a network.

- Multiple users share your PC and printer under the control of the Windows 98 User Profile system.

- You use a laptop PC (with or without a docking station).

Unfortunately, printer polling can take seconds to complete each time. Also, it's usually unnecessary if you don't unplug your printer often or share your printer across a network. If none of the previously listed criteria pertain to your computer, you can avoid these polling delays by disabling polling.

First, click My Computer to open the window, click the Printer folder, then right-click the desired printer icon, and choose Properties. Because each printer manufacturer creates a unique type of Properties dialog box, the specific control you must disable varies from one printer manufacturer to another. It may take a little searching, so remember that the control may also be called "Check Port State" or "Port Checking" instead of Port Polling. For example, Figure 6.10 shows a port polling control dialog box for a typical printer.

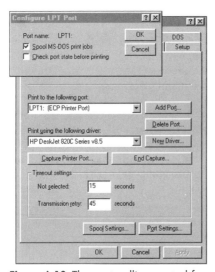

Figure 6.10 The port polling control for a typical printer

Once you've located the polling settings for your specific printer, disable it, and save your changes within the Properties dialog box.

Windows NT Tips and Tricks

If you've never used Windows NT 3.51 or 4.0, you may be fooled into thinking they're similar to Windows 98, and this is true on the surface because NT's user interface closely resembles the look and feel of Windows 98. Underneath the surface, however, NT is a much more complex and powerful beast, and it introduces several multiuser minicomputer concepts to printing that you may not recognize:

- **Security.** First, Windows NT enables the system administrator to assign printing privileges to individual users. Unlike Windows 98, you can choose from a number of different security levels. For example, one user in an office may have no access to the system printer, another may be able to initiate and delete just his or her own print jobs, while another may have control over all print jobs.

- **Pools and queues.** You may be familiar with a personal computer printing queue, but the NT printing queue system offers much more control over page description languages, remote printing around the network, and scheduling of print jobs.

- **Auditing.** Windows NT also enables the system administrator to monitor printing activity for any user or class of users. Naturally, this is more important in an office situation, but even a person with a home office can benefit from a log of what's been printed.

Unfortunately, this book can't even begin to teach you NT user administration; on the other hand, entire books on the subject are common these days. I can, however, suggest features and options that you can use in NT to customize your printing environment. If you need help in changing permissions, controlling a print queue, or other tasks, I recommend the excellent book *Windows NT Networking For Dummies* from IDG Books Worldwide.

Enabling Print Auditing

Are you interested in who is printing on your NT network? The NT print auditing feature records information about each print job to the NT security log file. You can scan the information later onscreen or print it out.

To enable auditing, open your Printers folder, right-click the desired printer, and select Properties; under the Security tab, click on Auditing, add the user IDs you want to monitor, and specify which actions you want logged to disk.

Scheduling Printing for Off Hours

If you need to print a document that is several hundred pages at work, you may have to stand next to the office printer and continuously apologize to everyone that drops by while it's busy with your job. But if you're running Windows NT and you've assigned a queue to your printer (using the LPR port and a static IP address), you can schedule that print job to run at a future time, after everyone has left, and save yourself the trouble.

Open your Printers folder, right-click the desired printer, and select Properties. From the Scheduling tab, you can adjust the times that the selected print queue is active to whatever start time you need. Remember to reschedule the queue *before* initiating your print job.

Configuring Printer Privileges

Windows NT enables you to change the user privileges for a specific printer, so that you can prevent other users from deleting a job or pausing the print queue (two problems that usually seem to crop up in any office). You can also restrict printing so that only one class of users can access a particular printer — for example, a dedicated laser printer for use only by management.

To set privileges, open your Printers folder, right-click the desired printer, and select Properties. From the Security tab, click Permissions to assign users individual rights to the selected printer.

Windows 2000 Tips and Tricks

The latest version of Windows NT, called Windows 2000, comes in multiple forms: Advanced Server, Professional, and Workstation. Each version has different system requirements and is designed for a specific type of user and workload. However, they all share the same security, queuing, and auditing features as their ancestor, the original Windows NT.

So what's new in Windows 2000 Professional? This section includes the latest tips and tricks you can use on your network.

Installing Drivers Automatically

If you've been "drafted" to help maintain an older office network running Windows 95 or Windows NT on the server, you're intimately familiar with trudging around the building, floppy disk in hand, to install driver software on your workstations. Or you saved yourself a step by copying the drivers to a specific network directory, but you *still* had to pay a visit to install those drivers. With Windows 2000 Professional, you can give the "SneakerNet" a rest and enable your server to install that driver for your new network printer on every workstation PC that needs it! The best news is that installing this driver requires no work on your part once you've set it up. When your network user selects a new printer within an application, Windows 2000 automatically checks to see whether the proper printer driver is installed, and if it is not, it performs the installation without any user intervention.

Luckily, most of the printer drivers you need for PCs running Windows 98, Windows Me, and Windows 2000 are shipped as part of Windows 2000 Professional, so they're already ready for installation. But what about older operating systems?

Fortunately, this trick works for all types of Windows-based clients, so that workstations can be running Windows 95, NT 3.5 or 4.0, or Windows 98.

To install drivers for other clients on a printer server running Windows 2000 Professional, click Start, choose Settings and click Printers. Right-click the printer icon that needs the additional drivers for other clients. Click Properties; from the Sharing tab, click Additional Drivers. Enable the additional environments and operating systems you need and click OK to save your changes.

To install a new driver for an existing printer on your server, click Start, choose Settings and click Printers. Right-click the printer icon that needs the updated driver. Click Properties; from the Advanced tab, click New Driver. Windows 2000 automatically runs the Add Printer Driver Wizard, allowing you to specify the location of the new driver. Once you've installed the updated driver on your server, it can be distributed to the client workstations as they use the printer . . . neat!

Browsing a Printer

Now wait, that doesn't sound right . . . how can a Web browser connect to your shared network printer? Well, if you're using Internet Explorer 4.0 or higher and you've installed IIS (*Internet Information Server*) software on your server, you can use this trick to connect and add the printer to your Favorites menu. Then you can use that shared printer just as if it were directly connected to your workstation!

To connect to a shared printer, run Internet Explorer. In the Address bar, enter the printer server in the form:

```
http://ServerName/printers/
```

and press Enter. For example, if the printer server's network name is *netprint1*, you would enter `http://netprint1/printers` to receive a page listing of all the printers you can access through that printer. To select a printer, simply click its icon.

If you already know the specific printer's network name, you can also type its URL and go directly to that printer's page using the form:

```
http://ServerName/PrinterName/
```

For example, the URL `http://netprint1/Rm200HP/` may take you to the page for the HP LaserJet in Room 200.

When viewing the printer's page, click Connect under Printer Actions to connect to that printer. The icon for the printer is added to your Printers folder.

You can also control the queue from the printer's URL page. The functions you can perform include:

■ Canceling documents you've sent

■ Displaying the number of print jobs in the queue

■ Pausing and resuming a document (or, with the right permissions, the queue itself)

Macintosh Tips and Tricks

As you've read in earlier chapters, the Macintosh is a favorite of graphics artists and publishers, so as you can imagine, it has an operating system that enables precise control over your system printer. In this section, I discuss some tips you can follow and tricks you can use to optimize your printing under Mac OS 9.

Enabling Virtual Memory

Like Windows 98, Mac OS offers background printing using virtual memory, but this option may be turned off on your system. Under Mac OS 9, you can adjust the virtual memory settings from the Memory control panel, as shown in Figure 6.11.

I recommend that you configure at least 16–32MB of virtual memory to help speed your printing (as well as your entire system). To do so, select Control Panels from the Apple menu, click Memory, then turn Virtual Memory on, and specify the amount of virtual memory in megabytes.

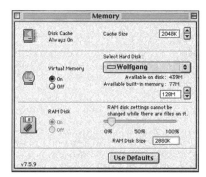

Figure 6.11 Configuring virtual memory under Mac OS 9

Tip

By default, Mac OS does not use a RAM disk; however, if you have enough physical system memory to use one, saving and printing documents from a RAM disk is significantly faster. Remember, though, that any documents you've saved to your RAM disk are lost if your Mac loses power or you turn it off. You can enable your RAM disk and specify its size from the same Memory control panel.

Defragmenting Your Hard Drive

It's a good idea to defragment your Mac's hard drive often, as it has the same beneficial effects on your printing speed as it does in the Windows 98 world. Both systems use virtual memory, so an optimized disk provides the best performance.

Unlike Windows 98, however, Mac OS 9 doesn't come with a built-in hard drive optimization program. There are a number of well-known utility packages for the Macintosh. I use Norton Utilities from Symantec, which includes the defragmenting program Speed Disk, shown in Figure 6.12.

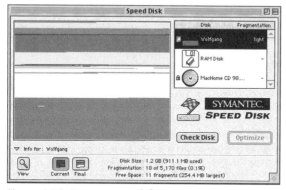

Figure 6.12 Preparing to defragment my Macintosh hard drive with Symantec Speed Disk

Optimizing PostScript Print Options

As you learned in Chapter 4, the Mac uses the PostScript page description language. Most Mac applications enable you to set options within a PostScript printing job that can improve the speed or appearance of your document:

- **Download bit-mapped/PostScript fonts**. When enabled, these settings enable your PostScript printer to download those fonts used in your document that aren't included in your printer's collection of resident fonts. Of course, you want this feature on if you're printing a final copy, but I usually turn it off if I'm printing a quick draft copy, or if I need to examine the layout and placement of graphics on the page. Turning this feature off enables your printer to use one of its onboard resident fonts. Printing without downloaded fonts can often save you half of the normal printing time per page!

- **Include images.** Again, you should certainly have this option enabled when you're printing final copies of your documents. However, turning it off enables you to print pages without any images or graphics, which is perfect for printing a layout test page or a "blank" template that you can use to mock-up drawings or line art. Some Mac applications also call this feature "Proof Print." (Additionally, many Mac and PC applications enable you to print low-resolution images for proof pages and full resolution images for the final print.) All layout applications enable you to print draft versions without graphics.

You can access these PostScript printing controls from the Print dialog box inside most of your Mac applications.

Linux Tips and Tricks

Although it's a relative newcomer to the world of operating systems, Linux has recently come into its own as a powerful, stable server platform for both small business and Internet commerce — in fact, Linux is now seen as a strong competitor to Windows NT and Windows 2000. Unlike the commercial Windows offerings from Microsoft, the source code for the Linux operating system is generally available (in fact, it was largely developed on the Internet).

Note

With all of the variants of Linux available today (and the complexity of configuring a print queue), it would be next to impossible to provide specific step-by-step instructions for printer configuration tips and tricks in this section. However, if you've set up a Linux network at your home or office, grab your Linux reference or contact your favorite Linux newsgroup for more information on how to implement these general suggestions for your specific variant of Linux.

Adding a Raw Print Queue

If you've created a Linux print queue before, you're familiar with the configuration of a /etc/printcap file — this file stores all the information needed to spool a print job to a specific printer. A standard printcap file is fine for sending filtered data, but what if you need to send a print job from another operating system on your network directly to a printer? For example, what if you have a PC running Windows 98 on your Linux network and you want to print to an HP LaserJet 4 across the network using the native Windows print driver?

Unfortunately, you can't send an unfiltered (typically called a *raw*) print job using a normal Linux printer configuration, but you can set up a raw print queue. Unlike a "plain" print queue, a print job sent through a raw print queue is not filtered or processed in any way, so it's perfect for sending jobs to a Samba printer.

Getting Used to Ghostscript

If you have a PostScript printer on your Linux network, you may already be familiar with Ghostscript — if not, run (do not walk) to your Web browser and visit the official Ghostscript site at www.cs.wisc.edu/~ghost/ to download the installation program or the source files. Ghostscript is an indispensable freeware utility that:

■ Displays PostScript files on your screen in a "preview" form (complete with color and graphics), so you can see what information they contain. Take my word for it, you do *not* want to attempt to read a raw PostScript file, which resembles an encrypted code that even James Bond can't decipher.

■ Prints a PostScript file to a non-PostScript printer, which, without Ghostscript, is somewhat akin to the transmutation of lead to gold by a medieval alchemist!

If you'd rather not learn the commands for Ghostscript, I recommend Ghostview — a graphical "front-end" for Ghostscript that works well with the X11 interface standard, which you can also access from the official Ghostscript site.

Testing Printer Communications

The PC parallel port can sometimes be a finicky beast. Windows 95/98/Me and Windows 2000 try to shield you as much as possible from the intricacies of your hardware — in fact, it's practically impossible to pick the wrong printer. Unfortunately, it's easy to "confuse" a parallel port in several other ways:

■ **Installing an external parallel-port device.** Some printer ports don't work reliably if you connect an external parallel-port device such as a Zip drive, parallel-port scanner, or video capture box. This is because these devices don't completely support bidirectional communications.

■ **Using a printer switch.** Automatic and manual printer switches enable more than one computer to use the same printer, but both can cause your parallel port to hang your PC, especially if a switch from one PC to another is attempted in the middle of a print job. Be especially cautious of switches with all-in-one peripherals. Most multifunction device manufacturers either recommend against switches or recommend only specific ones.

■ **Creating a hardware conflict.** If another adapter card inside your PC attempts to use the same hardware IRQ settings as your parallel port, it will likely lock your PC whenever you try to print. This is often the case with older Ethernet network cards, which sometimes default to hardware settings similar to that of a parallel port.

Tip

It's easier to resolve hardware conflicts within Windows 95/98/Me and Windows 2000 than ever before. If you suspect a hardware conflict — they usually show up in the Windows Device Manager — you can display the Device Manager by right-clicking the My Computer icon and choosing Properties from the pop-up menu. Click the Device Manager tab, and look for any hardware items in the Device List that may have yellow exclamation points (or red check marks) next to them. If you find one, select it in the list, click the Properties button, and read what's in the Device Status text area. Go to the Resources tab, and make sure that Use Automatic Settings is turned on. This enables Windows 98 to set resource settings automatically. Then reboot your computer.

■ **Installing an incorrect printer driver.** If you attempt to install a corrupted or incorrect printer driver, either your printer port or your printer will likely refuse to operate.

■ **Using the wrong printer cable.** As I covered in earlier chapters, most of today's advanced inkjet and laser printers require an IEEE-1284 bidirectional cable for proper communications. Without a bidirectional cable, your printer may lock up or only print one side of a duplex page.

■ **Using the wrong BIOS port setting.** Your PC's BIOS may give you a choice of standard, ECP, or bidirectional parallel-port connections. Some printers and devices require the latter two settings; others won't work unless you use the standard setting.

Most of the time, you won't have to worry about these problems when you're installing and configuring your printer; however, a communications problem can occur at any time after you've first plugged your printer in and turned it on, so it pays to keep them in mind in case your printer refuses to work.

If you do encounter a communications error while installing your printer, you can test your printer communications to help you track down the source of the problem. Here's a list of communication tests:

■ **Running your driver software.** Most manufacturers include a communications testing function within their printer utility software or printer drivers. Figure 6.13 shows the bidirectional communications check that runs the first time you install an HP printer. (You can run that same test at any time from within the printer driver's Properties dialog box.)

Figure 6.13 Running a communications test on an HP printer

■ **Printing a document in DOS.** If you think that Windows is the source of your communications problems, restart your PC in DOS mode, and print any plain text ASCII file with this command:

```
TYPE FILE.TXT > LPT1
```

- (Make sure you substitute the filename of your text file for FILE.TXT, and if you're trying to print to your second printer port, substitute "LPT2" instead of "LPT1".) This command copies the contents of your file directly to the printer port, and if it works, your printer and computer are communicating okay. If not, you probably have a software conflict within Windows 98.

- **Printing a self-test page.** A Windows application can also interfere with your printer port, especially if it has terminated abnormally. To check both Windows and your hardware, print a self-test page from the printer driver's Properties page.

Summary

In this chapter we covered how to install and configure your new printer or all-in-one unit. You learned how to recognize the sometimes-elusive printer port in its natural habitat, as well as methods you can use to test your port and cable. You also found a number of tips and tricks for Windows 98 and Me, Windows NT, Windows 2000 Professional, Mac OS, and Linux.

In Chapter 7 I address remote printing for your entire office — it takes only a working network, a single PC, and a fast system printer to save the cost of adding a printer or multifunction device to every desktop system. I also discuss printer sharing.

In Chapter 11, you find step-by-step details for configuring default printer settings, printing a document from a Windows application, performing a printer communications test, and removing a printer and its software.

CHAPTER 7

Network and Shared Printing

IN THIS CHAPTER • Selecting a manual or electronic printer switch

• Using a hardware printer server

• Using a printer buffer

Remember that box of crayons you had in kindergarten? Sooner or later, another kid would ask to borrow your brand-new box, and you'd reluctantly hand it over. An hour later, your fears are confirmed: several crayons are missing, others are broken, and all the colors are hopelessly out of order. The experience taught you a lesson: never let someone else borrow your printing hardware . . . sharing is for the birds!

Well, you're all grown now, and your boss has just told you that you have to share that expensive laser printer on your desk with the others in the room. The first question is obvious: there's only one parallel connector on the printer, yet you have to divide it up among three or four people. And what about your configuration? Will you lose your page setup or end up having to reconfigure Windows 98? Does sharing a printer involve constant unplugging and moving to get the machine from one desktop to another?

In this chapter, you find out how you can avoid these pitfalls. Unfortunately, I can't restore your crayon box from your childhood — sorry about that! — but I *can* help you successfully share a single inkjet or laser printer among several people with as little hassle as possible.

Cross-Reference

Find step-by-step instructions for configuring and installing networked and switched printers in Chapter 11.

Why Add a Network or Shared Printer?

In the early 1980s (the heyday of impact printers) every IBM PC was an island unto itself, and sharing a printer usually involved disconnecting the parallel and power cables and moving the entire printer to the other PC. Because printers were very expensive at the time and most offices only needed one or two IBM PCs, this usually wasn't much of a headache. (The company I worked for in those days was on the cutting edge of technology . . . they bought a wheeled cart for the printer to make this easier on employees!)

In the mid-to-late 1980s, however, PCs were popping up everywhere in the office, and more and more applications offered printed output. Suddenly everyone wanted an expensive printer for their desk. Computer professionals decided that there must be a better method of sharing a printer among more than one computer, and behold: the printer switch and the printer sharing system were born.

The arrival of the PC network provided the ultimate in shared printing because the printer could now be located anywhere on the network, and the network automatically held print jobs in a sequence (or *queue*) until each could be processed.

There's really only one reason why you should add a single printer and share it among more than one computer: the money you save (which is usually reason enough for any office manager or small business owner). This cost savings really adds up when you consider some of the very expensive high-resolution thermal wax printers, mammoth large format printers, or color laser printers. After you've spent several thousand dollars on a state-of-the-art printer for your graphic designer, you're not likely to repeat the experience when you can add some form of printer sharing for others in your office.

Network, Shared, and Switched Printing

As with everything else in computing these days, there's more than one way to handle printing jobs — in fact, there are three methods of connecting multiple PCs to a single printer (or multiple printers to a single PC). Great, I assume that you're in favor of freedom of choice, but that also means that you should understand the advantages and limitations of each method. Many PC users in a small office environment don't need the cost of a full-blown network, while a larger office would never be able to efficiently share a single printer without a complete network.

In this section, I discuss the pros and cons of network printing, printer sharing, and printer switching. Once you've read this material, you'll be able to make decisions about which one of these solutions is right for your needs.

Adding a Network Printer

Okay, so you've decided to link an entire office to a single printer (or perhaps multiple printers). You've also determined that every workstation needs access, and they're spread out over an entire floor of the building. Or perhaps you want to connect several machines to a printer and other hardware devices you want to share, such as an expensive CD recorder or a plotter.

You may already know the solution to this situation (if you're not already using one): an office *local area network* (LAN) can provide all the connectivity you need between your computers and most peripherals, including a printer.

Although this chapter cannot teach you networking, it can certainly help you become familiar with the different types of networks and what's involved with setting up a simple Windows 98/Me network or a LANtastic network for your office printing. LANtastic is my personal favorite networking package, and it's very popular as a LAN for small businesses with anywhere from 3 to 15 computers. However, the built-in networking available in Windows 98 and Windows 2000 is also well suited to network printing.

Tip

Technically, a LAN may include as few as two computers, and many home users create LANs with two or three machines for multiplayer gaming or file sharing. However, we're talking about printers here, and creating a full network for two machines to share a printer is a waste. If you're looking for this kind of functionality, a printer switch or a printer sharing system may be a better choice. I discuss those options later in this chapter. (Before you buy, however, it's a good idea to check on the compatibility of switches or sharing systems with the model of printer or all-in-one you're using.)

Network printer connections

Before I launch into a discussion of networks, I should mention that there are two different methods of connecting a printer to a network:

■ **Network-ready printers.** If you're willing to spend the money, you can buy a printer with built-in network connectivity. In other words, the printer essentially has its own network interface card and can be connected directly to the network's cabling.

■ **A printer server.** With this method, you can hook any printer to your network — however, that printer must be connected to a computer that is a part of the network (using either a USB or the traditional parallel port connection). This computer is called a *printer server*. For the best performance, you can dedicate an entire PC simply to service your printer — it receives the print jobs, handles queuing, and sends the jobs to the printer for you, automatically. If you don't want to dedicate an entire PC to the job, most networking software enables any workstation to act as a printer server, but the person using that computer is likely to experience performance problems whenever someone prints over the network. I'll also discuss a hardware printer server, which is essentially a network connection "black box" that performs the same functions as a dedicated PC printer server.

Why should you network?

A network offers the following advantages over other forms of printer sharing and switching:

■ **No limit on workstations.** Unlike a shared printer or a printer switch, a network can handle several dozen connected computers (or more), so a single fast printer can handle the traffic from an entire small office.

■ **Distance is no problem.** Your printer can be several rooms away, and the network delivers your print job just as if the printer were directly connected to your PC. Naturally, this provides you the flexibility to locate the printer near your workstations, or in a room by itself, or halfway across the office if necessary.

■ **Support for other shared devices.** Why limit yourself to just a printer? You can share hard drives, external peripherals, modems . . . the list of shared network devices goes on. You can also share files with others on the network. (Some printer sharing devices also enable you to share files, but sharing files is not available if you choose a printer switch.)

■ **Support for network software.** Naturally, networking distributes electronic mail throughout an office, but today's network applications can do much more. Office application suites such as Microsoft's Office and SmartSuite from Lotus take advantage of network connectivity to enable groups to work on projects simultaneously.

■ **Automatic routing and queue control.** Today's networks can automatically manage a print queue, so a functioning network really requires very little maintenance and no manual intervention for print jobs.

With benefits such as these, it's obvious why most companies of any significant size have already networked.

Okay, what's wrong with networking?

Networks can't be *that* great, or everyone would be using them! Installing a network can be

■ **Expensive**. A network is typically the most expensive solution for sharing a printer — you have to pay for the network interface cards, cables, and software. (On the positive side, if you're using Windows 98 or 2000, you can take advantage of the built-in network support, so you won't have to buy any extra software.)

■ **A hassle**. Every workstation in your network must be connected to a network cable, and you have to install a *network interface adapter card* (generally shortened to NIC) in each PC. (Although older Macs may need a network interface card to connect to a PC network, the new iMac, G4, and PowerBook computers have built-in network ports.)

■ **Time-consuming.** Although a modern networking system such as the built-in networking in Windows 98/Me, Windows 2000, LANtastic, or NetWare tries its best to reduce the time you spend fine-tuning your network, expect at least several hours of work before everything runs smoothly. (Although the configuration of a network is much more automatic now than ten years ago, it still certainly helps to have someone nearby that knows their networking.)

Selecting a network design

Have you decided that a network is the way to go for your office needs? If so, your next step is to choose from one of the three common network designs or, in network-speak, *topologies* that are generally available today:

■ **Ethernet.** Most small offices use what's called an *Ethernet* network, such as the built-in networking support in Windows 98 and Windows 2000. What does that mean in plain language? Well, an Ethernet network operates by sending packets of data through the network cable, as shown in Figure 7.1. Each data packet has an identifying numeric ID that indicates which computer should process it. When the computer receives a packet with a matching ID, it accepts the data. All other computers on the network ignore that data packet. Ethernet is the cheapest network to set up and the easiest to run and maintain, so I definitely recommend it as the basis for networking a printer. On the downside, Ethernet is the slowest networking topology around because multiple packets can be sent across the network at once, and these packets must often be "sorted out" by your PC's networking software (which can take a second or two).

These speed and efficiency limitations are no big deal for a small office, though, and they won't affect your network printing.

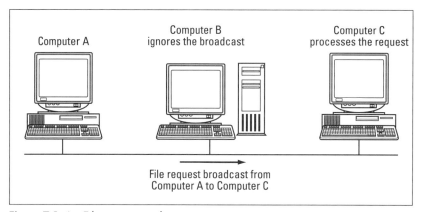

Figure 7.1 An Ethernet network

- **Token-ring.** The next move up in speed, cost, and complexity is the token-ring network, which uses the same system of cabling and numeric IDs for transferring and identifying data packets. Unlike an Ethernet network, however, the cabling is a circular loop (as shown in Figure 7.2), and only one data packet is transferred at once, which is more efficient and results in faster speeds. Unless you need to network an entire floor of a building for high-speed transfers, a token-ring system is unnecessarily expensive and complex for most small businesses.

- **Star.** Finally, we come to the star topology, which offers the fastest networking speeds for the highest price. A star network uses a central switch (as shown in Figure 7.3) that handles all routing of data packets. Each computer is connected directly through the hub, so this design is very efficient. Again, a star network is a solution for an entire building, so it's certainly overkill for most of us (and you had better have someone around to maintain it full time).

What do you need?

Here's a list of what you need for each PC that you connect to a typical Windows 98/Me/2000 Ethernet network:

- **A network interface card.**
- **A licensed copy of Windows.**

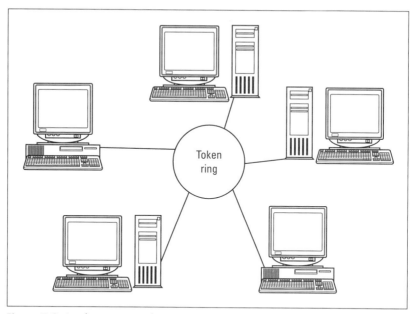

Figure 7.2 A token-ring topology

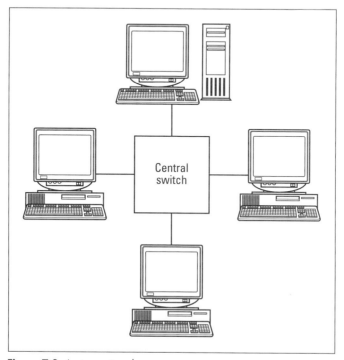

Figure 7.3 A star network

■ **Cabling.** Most inexpensive Ethernet networks use either *twisted-pair* cable, which looks like telephone wire, or *coaxial* cable, which looks like the wiring and connectors used with cable TV. Figure 7.4 illustrates a twisted-pair cable and connector, while Figure 7.5 illustrates a standard coaxial cable with connector.

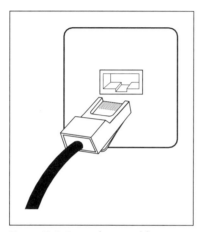

Figure 7.4 Twisted-pair cable is easy to connect.

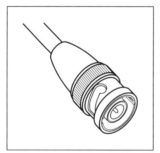

Figure 7.5 Coaxial cable is another popular choice for simple Ethernet networks.

■ **Connectors.** Separate lengths of coaxial cable can be attached to each other with metal T-connectors, which use a twist-on/twist-off connector. Twisted-pair cables can use small plastic connectors with snap connectors.

As I mentioned earlier, the iMac and G4 Macintosh computers have an Ethernet port built in as standard equipment. Older Macs can use a simple peer-to-peer networking system called *LocalTalk* to share a printer connected to one of the computers. The only extra hardware required for a LocalTalk network is the cabling, because this network uses the standard connectors on older Macs.

LAN do's and don'ts

Although I'll leave a complete discussion of local area networking to excellent books such as *Networking For Dummies* and *Windows Networking Basics* from IDG Books Worldwide, I would like to provide you with a few do's and don'ts that may save you headaches while configuring your network:

- **Do** buy a kit or buy extra stuff. If you're not knowledgeable about networking, buy a network kit that contains everything you need; you'll save both time and effort. If you decide to buy individual components and build a network, always buy extra cabling and a few extra connectors. You always seem to need one more to finish the job.

- **Don't** try to make your own cabling. Buy your cables ready-made. I can tell you from personal experience that making coaxial or twisted-pair network cables takes training from a network professional and a lot of practice, and cable components aren't cheap. Also, a faulty cable can cause intermittent network errors that can drive you crazy. Most larger computer stores sell pre-made cables (ask for network "patch cable"), or you can find them in any large online store that carries hardware.

- **Do** use plug-and-play network cards. If you're shopping for network interface cards, make sure they're plug-and-play (easier setup under Windows 98 and 2000) and certified for your network operating system and computer (they've been tested to make sure they're compatible).

- **Do** keep it simple. Full network operating systems such as NetWare offer much more power than Windows 98 networking, but they're also incredibly complex, and they cost many times the price of a simpler system. If you're considering a LAN for sharing a printer and other peripherals, stick with a simple, inexpensive network operating system.

- **Don't** install your network alone. No matter what your level of expertise, you're more likely to make a mistake without someone on your side, and stringing cable always seems easier with more than one set of hands. If you happen to know a network guru with a little spare time, enlist him/her to help with your installation as soon as possible.

- **Do** read all documentation. Read that network administrator user manual from cover to cover — reading the documentation usually helps you solve problems later.

Introducing Home Phoneline and Powerline technology: the other Ethernet networks

I've discussed traditional small business Ethernet networking in this section, but two new neat alternatives to expensive network cards, yards of cabling, and coaxial connections are Home Phoneline and Powerline technology. Either of these networks is perfect for networking two or three computers right in your own home or small office.

Use your telephone wiring Several companies have already developed Ethernet hardware that uses the existing telephone wiring in your home or office to transmit network data packets. For the latest technical information on this network technology, visit the Home Phoneline Networking Alliance (HomePNA for short, at www.homepna.org), a group composed of computer corporations such as Hewlett-Packard, IBM, Rockwell, Intel, and Compaq that is working on standardizing this new home networking technology.

What can home phoneline networking do for you in your home? Naturally, printer sharing comes to mind, but there's also multiplayer gaming and common Internet access — and note also, home phoneline networking provides an Ethernet connection, so it works with just about any network application or operating system. You can also use your telephone for answering and dialing voice calls as usual while you use your home phoneline network (unlike a typical analog modem connection). In addition, connecting a new PC to the network is as easy as finding the nearest telephone jack and plugging in a cable.

The convenience and low cost of a home phoneline network make it the logical choice for those of us with three PCs, a laptop, and an iMac under one roof. Okay, so I'm a computer junkie, but if you have a home office, a home phoneline makes a lot of sense. (And at least in my opinion it won't be long before a second home computer is a necessity for everyone.)

Diamond Multimedia Systems (www.diamondmm.com) offers the HomeFree Phoneline Desktop Pac, which includes everything you need to network two computers. It comes with two home phoneline NICs (PCI bus), Internet-sharing software, demo software, and drivers. You can find the HomeFree Phoneline Desktop Pac for less than $100 in stores, and additional cards for network expansion are about $50 each.

Use your AC wiring Intelogis (www.intelogis.com) offers a networking system that's very similar to home phoneline networking — but it uses your home or office AC wiring instead! The company's PassPort powerline network system uses proprietary adapters that you plug in to a wall socket; in turn, those adapters plug into a cable that leads to your computer's parallel port. The system even offers a printer module that allows your printer to run on the network without a connection to a PC, so you can locate your printer by any convenient AC outlet.

Although powerline networking technology is slower than a home phoneline system, it's still fast enough for simple file sharing and printing. If you are sharing an Internet modem connection, the PassPort system should work well; however, if you are sharing a DSL or cable Internet connection, playing network multiplayer games, or moving huge files across your home network, it's a better idea to go with the faster home phoneline system.

Adding a Shared Printer

A shared printer is the second most complex method of providing access to a single printer from a number of computers. As shown in Figure 7.6, a printer sharing system consists of a central switchbox device connected to the printer by a single parallel cable. All the computers that share the printer connect to this central switchbox using 25-pin parallel cables.

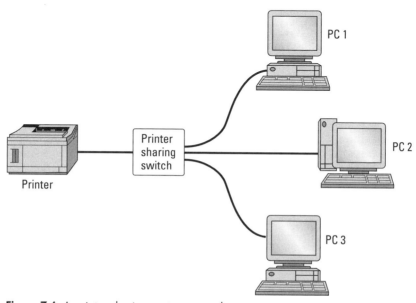

Figure 7.6 A printer sharing system at work

Advantages of printer sharing

I've used a printer sharing system before, and they've been popular since the mid-1980s as an economical way to provide printer access to three or more computers in the same office. This method has several advantages:

- **Accommodates two to ten computers.** When it comes to the number of computers that can be attached to a single printer, the printer sharing method falls in between a full network solution and a simple printer switch. Printer sharing is appropriate for small offices and workgroups.

- **Simultaneous access.** As with a network, print jobs can be sent to the printer from different computers at the same time — no need to wait until the printer is free before submitting a print job. The switch hardware and software store print jobs until they can be processed.

- **Built-in buffer memory.** Because all printer jobs are routed through your printer sharing hardware, most manufacturers include some sort of built-in buffer memory (I discuss the function of this memory in detail later in this chapter).

■ **Simple installation.** Most printer sharing hardware and software can be installed and configured within an hour or less.

Disadvantages of printer sharing

If you're considering printer sharing, it's only fair to warn you about the disadvantages of using this method:

■ **Additional hardware costs.** Although not as expensive as a printing network, expect to pay $100 to $150 for a complete printer sharing system.

■ **Limited by distance.** Because it's important to keep the total length of a standard parallel cable to ten feet or less, your computers can be no farther than ten feet away from the switching device.

■ **Compatibility problems.** A sharing system can be a problem for IEEE-1284 devices; for example, you may lose the scanning capabilities in an all-in-one unit.

Adding a Switched Printer

Looking for the simplest and cheapest possible way to connect both PCs in your home office to the same printer? You're talking about a printer switch such as the one shown in Figure 7.7. A printer switch has three parallel printer ports and two possible configurations: either two computers and one printer, or one computer and two printers. All of the devices are connected to the switch using 25-pin cables.

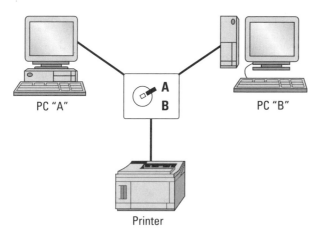

PC "A"   PC "B"

Printer

Figure 7.7 The switched printer is the simplest method of connecting multiple PCs to a printer.

Printer switches are further divided into two different types:

- **Automatic electrical switches.** These switches are more expensive, but they work automatically. When one of the two computers sends a print job, the printer switch senses that data is being sent and completes the connection between the PC and the printer.

- **Manual printer switches.** It just doesn't get any simpler than this. A manual printer switch is a metal box with a knob on the front that you turn to create the connection between computer A or computer B. However, this type of switch may require you to reboot the PC before you can use the printer.

Advantages of printer switching

A basic switched printer system may be just what you need if these advantages sound good to you:

- **Least expensive method.** A switched printer system requires only the switch and the proper cables for your configuration.

- **One computer can control two printers.** If you'd rather have two printers connected to a single PC, the same type of switchbox handles that connection.

- **Perfect for those needing infrequent access.** If one of your PC users needs access to a printer only once or twice a week, why spend all the money involved in adding a network or a printer sharing system? A manual printer switch can provide that access for about $20.

- **Simplest installation and configuration.** Connect your devices through the switch, and you're done. No software to install, either.

Disadvantages of printer switching

The cheapest solution typically has its share of problems, and a printer switch is certainly no exception to the rule:

- **Limited to three devices.** Simple printer switches are limited to three devices, so you are never able to connect more than two computers or two printers. (More expensive printer switches can handle more than three devices, but they're more akin in features and price to a printer sharing device such as those I discussed earlier in the chapter.)

- **Limited by distance.** Like printer sharing devices, printer switching systems are limited to ten feet from each device to the printer switch. (I've known of systems where that ten feet was even too long, and the data signal loss required shorter six-foot cables; for this reason, many electronic switches include a signal boosting feature.)

- **No simultaneous printing.** As you may expect, a printer switch completely severs any connection between one hardware device and another, which means that you can't begin a print job from one computer while the switch is turned to the other computer. (In fact, many printers require that you reboot your PC once the switch has made the connection before you can successfully send a print job.)

- **Manual intervention required.** If you buy an inexpensive manual switchbox, you have to remember to turn the switch to print from the other computer. Electric switches are more expensive, but they automatically detect that a print job has been sent and handle the routing automatically.

- **Compatibility problems.** Switchboxes may not work well with some IEEE-1284 devices; for example, you may lose the scanning function on an all-in-one unit.

Do You Need a Dedicated Printer Server?

If you've decided on a printer sharing system or a printer switch, then there's no reason to read this section because a *printer server* is strictly a network component. A printer server is a PC or a hardware device dedicated completely to a printer: it provides the printer's connection to the network, processes and stores print jobs sent over the network from other workstations. Depending on the configuration, a printer server may also allow you to manipulate the printer queue (a fancy phrase that means you can pause or delete print jobs), display printing errors, or broadcast messages to other network workstations.

Note that a printer server is usually considered different from a printer connected to a regular network workstation. Although both the printer server and the workstation can connect a printer to the network, the workstation can also be used for other applications (such as word processing, Internet communications, or multiplayer gaming), while a dedicated printer server operates only to support the printer.

Because a dedicated printer server is somewhat of a luxury, you may be wondering if you need one. I definitely recommend that you invest in a printer server if your network meets any of these criteria:

- **Heavy multiuser printing.** If your printer is constantly processing jobs from several users throughout the day, a printer server can prove invaluable. It enables you to control the priority of your print jobs, as well as delete specific jobs directly from the server's keyboard.

- **More than one printer to add to the network.** If you have more than one printer that you'd like to use on your network, a printer server with two or more parallel ports is the ideal method of connecting them.

- **Speed is all-important.** Unfortunately, a printer connected to a simple network workstation may slow down because the PC is being used for some other purpose while the print job is being processed. A dedicated printer server puts all of its computing power to work processing print jobs, so you achieve the fastest printing speeds with a server.

- **Uses Windows NT, Windows 2000 Server, UNIX, or Linux.** These operating systems have sophisticated printing and queue controls that work best if you dedicate a PC as a printer server.

If you do decide to build a PC as a printer server, make sure you include:

- **The fastest network interface card that can operate on your network.** Your printer server is not the place to skimp with a cheap NIC.

- **A large-capacity hard drive.** The larger and the faster the hard drive, the better.

- **A multi-IO parallel card.** You can find adapter cards that offer four parallel ports, but your server PC may support two parallel ports with a second connector. Check your system hardware manual to determine the number of parallel ports available on your server PC.

- **System RAM.** As I've discussed elsewhere in the book, the more system RAM you can provide to Windows, the faster your printing will be.

On the positive side, your printer server does not need a fancy monitor (any 14- or 15-inch VGA monitor will do, and even a monochrome monitor will work) or the latest and greatest video card. The same is true of your sound card . . . this computer has better things to do than play games.

The Black Box: Using a Hardware Printer Server

If you'd like to add a printer server to your network but you don't have the space (or the need) for the additional functionality of a PC, you may be ready to start shopping for a *hardware* printer server. These "black box" servers are often no bigger than a paperback book or an external modem (some servers are internal cards that you can install into a slot inside the body of the printer). A printer server can turn your standard parallel printer into a full-fledged network unit, which means you can place that printer in any location with a network connection, and no computer is required. A hardware printer server can save you hundreds of dollars over a dedicated PC printer server.

Figure 7.8 illustrates a very popular hardware printer server from Hewlett-Packard — the HP JetDirect 170X. Designed for home and small office Ethernet networks, it works with almost all PCs with a parallel port, and delivers print jobs up to six times faster than a workstation. With a street price of under $150, the JetDirect 170X is a great choice for a small office with a network and a single printer to share.

Figure 7.8 The HP JetDirect 170X provides the speed and network connectivity of a dedicated PC print server.

What's a Printer Buffer?

As I mentioned in the section, "Advantages of Printer Sharing," most manufacturers of printer sharing hardware include some sort of built-in memory that can temporarily store documents, but you can also buy a stand-alone *printer buffer*. A printer buffer is a small device that contains several megabytes of RAM for storing print jobs and its own simple internal processor; it fits between your printer and your computer. As illustrated in Figure 7.9, the buffer intercepts and stores multiple print jobs until the printer has completed previous printing tasks and can accept the new documents.

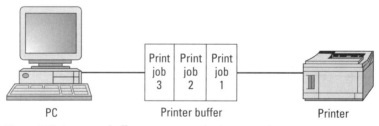

Figure 7.9 A printer buffer can store multiple print jobs.

Although your PC and your printer both have their own built-in memory reserved for storing print jobs, a single large PostScript print job may fill that buffer area.

I recommend a printer buffer for your shared printer if you are using it under these conditions:

- **Simultaneous printing.** If several workstations on your network print documents simultaneously (such as computers used as point-of-sale terminals), a printer buffer can increase the efficiency of your background printing under Windows, and your workstations will perform better.

- **Printing very large documents.** Printing that master's thesis? A printer buffer can "feed" large print jobs to your printer over several seconds to maintain a continuous flow of data.

- **Using an older operating system.** If you're using Windows 3.1, DOS, or a version of Macintosh system before System 7, a buffer may mean the difference between waiting for a print job to finish printing and continuing your work.

- **No printer memory upgrade.** A printer buffer can take the place of a printer memory upgrade if you can't locate the right type of RAM (or if your printer's memory can't be upgraded at all).

Printer buffers are available in a range of storage capacities and prices, and you should be able to find them at your local office supply store or any larger local or Internet-based computer store.

Cross-Reference

In case you don't know where to start looking on the Internet for computer merchandise, take a look at a list of my favorite Internet-based computer stores in the section "Recommended Internet Online Stores" in Chapter 2.

Summary

This chapter discussed shared access to a printer using three methods: a basic Ethernet network, a printer sharing system, and an electronic or manual printer switch. You discovered the advantages and disadvantages of each method, including the requirements for a Windows 98/Me/2000 network suitable for printer sharing. You also received an introduction to the idea of a dedicated PC printer server, a hardware printer server, and a printer buffer.

In Chapter 8, we explore the wild world of fonts. You learn about TrueType, OpenType, and Adobe fonts — how to install them and use them, as well as how you can expand your font collection with hundreds of commercial, freeware, and shareware fonts from many different sources.

In Chapter 11, you can follow the installation projects for networked and switched printers, including installing a network printer under Windows, installing a manual printer switch, and installing an electronic printer switch.

Having Fun with Your Printer

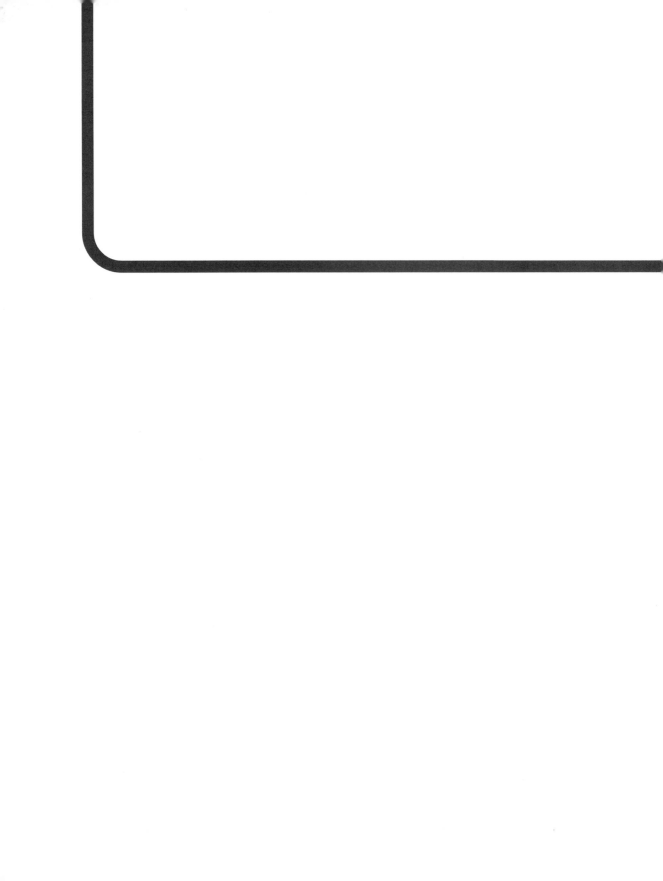

The Wonderful World of Fonts

IN THIS CHAPTER
- Understanding soft fonts
- Comparing Adobe, TrueType, and OpenType fonts
- Locating shareware, freeware, and commercial fonts
- Using a font editor
- Building images with 3-D fonts

Professionals of every type have their tools of the trade — and for a desktop publishing or graphic arts professional, a large collection of alphanumeric and symbol fonts is as necessary as a computer monitor, a mouse, a ruler, and a large cup of coffee. These professionals often spend several hundred dollars to buy some of the more famous and popular font families for their advertising and publishing projects.

That doesn't mean, however, that a family or the owner of a small home office can't invest a few hours in adding to their font collection. Many fonts are available at no charge on the Internet, while others are sold as inexpensive shareware. You can also find fonts on CD-ROMs at your favorite software store or Web site, and font-editing software is available for those of you with an adventuresome spirit. Today's personal inkjet, laser, or all-in-one printer can produce an amazing number of business materials, crafts, and printed items of all kinds. With more fonts to choose from, you can be even more creative and produce better-looking results with your documents and printing projects.

Because fonts aren't quite a common topic of discussion over the dinner table or Internet chat rooms, you may need a little help in expanding your collection. Consider this chapter, then, as your guide to finding, selecting, and creating new fonts on your Windows 95/98 or Mac OS 9 computer.

 Cross-Reference

See Chapter 9 for a guide to the vast array of printing materials, idea sources, and creative techniques that you can use to improve your printing projects. Chapter 12 guides you step-by-step through font installation and display.

Soft Fonts Explained

As you probably know, a *font* is a set of characters used for printing text, typically including all the letters of a specific alphabet, a complete set of numbers, and symbols required by the chosen language (many fonts are also composed of images and symbols instead of alphanumeric characters). A *font family* is a set of fonts of the same typeface that includes an italic version of the basic font, a bold version of the font, and so on.

In the early days of the printing press, each character in a font was an individual piece of type — typically made from tin or lead on a wooden base — and these pieces of type were arranged by hand into special plates that were then used on a simple printing press. This was time consuming, but better than writing everything by hand.

With the arrival of computer printing, fonts took on a new form: *soft fonts*. A soft font produces the same characters on a printed page as the old fonts made of movable type, but a soft font exists only as a software file (hence the name). Soft fonts can be downloaded from your computer to your printer as a part of the print job, so they don't need to be resident (built-in) to the printer's memory.

The two general types of soft fonts are

- **Bitmap.** Bitmap soft fonts are stored as a pattern of dots, in much the same way that an impact printer prints them on the page. This pattern essentially forms a "picture" (or, in programmer-speak, a bitmap) of the font. Bitmap is the older of the technologies, but it still has an advantage: because bitmap fonts don't require any mathematical calculations, they're fast to load. On the other hand, bitmap fonts cannot be resized, so you have to keep a file containing the bitmap images for each different size of the font you wish to use.

- **Outline.** Unlike bitmap fonts, outline fonts are not hard-coded as a series of dots; instead, they're actually stored as a series of mathematical formulas that represent the outline of the font. When you use the font, your computer calculates the outline of the font at the point size you requested and prints it or displays it on your monitor. This feature is called *scaling,* and it means that you can adjust the size of an outline font without losing resolution or detail.

Cross-Reference

See "Adding Fonts" in Chapter 4 to learn about fonts stored in memory cartridges or on memory cards.

Figure 8.1 illustrates the difference between bitmap and outline soft fonts. Although TrueType outline fonts (which I cover in the next section) are the most popular fonts used today for printing, desktop publishing, and other graphics applications, Windows 95/98 and Windows 2000 use bitmap fonts for displaying much of what you see on screen (including messages and icon labels).

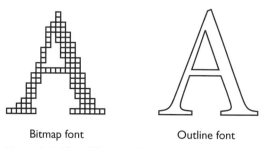

Bitmap font   Outline font

Figure 8.1 The difference between bitmap and outline fonts

Comparisons: TrueType, Adobe, and OpenType

Computer owners will find three common font technologies in use today under Windows 95/98, Windows 2000, and Mac OS 9. Each of these three types of fonts has distinct advantages, so let's review each of them in detail and describe those strengths:

- **TrueType.** The TrueType font standard is the most common font technology used today under Microsoft Windows and Mac OS. As its name implies, the TrueType font produces printed output that looks just like the letters or symbols you see on screen. Apple and Microsoft developed TrueType, but it is an open standard, and anyone can develop their own TrueType fonts. TrueType fonts are scalable outline fonts, so you can resize them without losing resolution, and they can be rotated to any position by your desktop publishing application. All these operations, however, require some of the computer's processing time, so output prints slower than older bitmap fonts. TrueType fonts can be used to display information on your monitor as well as produce documents on your printer. When used for display on your monitor, TrueType fonts can make use of *antialiasing* (meaning that your PC can use mathematical formulas to enhance the detail around the edges of each character, making those edges look "cleaner").

- **Adobe Type 1.** Adobe Type 1 outline fonts are available for PCs running either Windows or Mac OS, but they're probably used most often these days by graphic artists because they usually output their finished work to PostScript (the page definition language I discussed in Chapter 4). Type 1 fonts are actually defined in a special encoded PostScript format, so they're also commonly called "PostScript fonts." Like TrueType fonts, Type 1 fonts require some computational time to process. Adobe offers a program called *Adobe Type Manager* (or ATM) for both the PC and the Mac. It maintains a special memory buffer for preloading Type 1 fonts so that they can be accessed faster by your computer. ATM is required if you use Adobe Type 1 fonts under any version of Windows. Figure 8.2 shows the Macintosh version of the ATM program.

Figure 8.2 The ATM control panel under Mac OS 9

Cross-Reference

In Chapter 12, learn how to get better performance from your PC and your printer by increasing the size of the ATM font cache.

■ **OpenType.** You can consider OpenType fonts to be a new and improved descendent of TrueType font technology. Microsoft and Adobe developed OpenType, and it was released as part of Windows 98 (and further updated in Windows 2000). This standard offers backward compatibility with both TrueType and Adobe Type 1, so as OpenType fonts become more widespread you can continue to use your old font library.

With the gradual acceptance of OpenType, Windows 98, Windows 2000, and Mac OS 9, owners will enjoy a higher degree of cross-platform compatibility in fonts, making it a little easier to display and print documents created on "that *other* computer."

Building a Font Library

As I mentioned at the beginning of this chapter, anyone who creates, displays, or prints documents on a computer can benefit from an expanded collection of fonts. Although Windows 95/98, Windows 2000, and Mac OS 9 install a number of standard font families as a default font library, the selection is pretty mundane. Luckily, some printer manufacturers provide additional fonts. For example, most HP LaserJet models ship with 80 scalable fonts. Hewlett-Packard also includes a font management utility called FontSmart with some LaserJet models.

If your printer didn't come with a library of fonts, you'll have to look elsewhere for creative and unique fonts that you can use with your documents and printing projects. In this section, I share with you my favorite sources for new font families to add to your library.

First, let's cover the best sources for new fonts.

■ **Desktop publishing and word processing programs.** This is the first place to look for fonts to add to your library. If you've ever bought a word processing, desktop publishing, or creative printing application, that program may have come with its own free fonts (which are often not installed unless you specifically indicate that you want them on your hard drive). Check the program's user manual, or run the installation program again to see if additional fonts are offered with the main program.

■ **The Internet.** The Web is literally crawling with fonts — pun somewhat intended — and you can locate either freeware or shareware fonts from a single search engine (you'll learn how a little later in this section). You'll also find many sites dedicated to distributing fonts. My favorite library site is Font Freak at `www.fontfreak.com`. You'll find hundreds of freeware and shareware font families of literally every description at Font Freak, as you can see in Figure 8.3. The best sites display thumbnail examples of each font, but some sites simply provide descriptions and filenames.

Tip

Most TrueType and Adobe fonts for the PC are distributed in .ZIP archive format, whereas most Adobe fonts for the Mac are distributed in .SIT archive format. If your computer can't open files in these formats, pick up a copy of WinZip for .ZIP archives (www.winzip.com) or StuffIt Expander for .SIT archives (www.aladdinsys.com).

Figure 8.3 A typical display page from Font Freak, one of the best font download libraries on the Web

- **Font CD-ROMs.** You'll find discs with literally thousands of fonts for every occasion at your local software store. Make sure that the font CD-ROM you pick has a viewer (for looking at examples of each font without having to install it) and an install utility (for automating the installation of the fonts you want). In Figure 8.4, you see a font-viewing program in action from one of my font CD-ROMs.

- **You!** If you have a font editor — either a popular commercial editor such as Fontographer from Macromedia or a shareware editor — you can create your own TrueType or PostScript fonts (or coax a friend with graphic design talent into doing it for you). Doing the job right requires a few days' worth of precise work, but you'll end up with an original font that exactly matches your needs (which you can later distribute yourself as freeware or shareware)! I delve further into this topic later in this chapter.

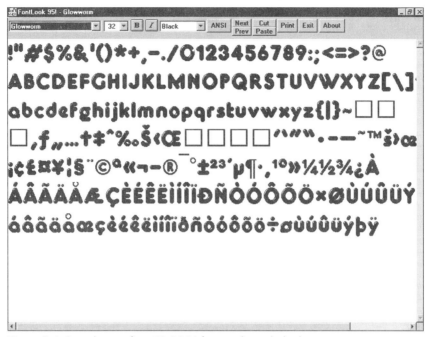

Figure 8.4 Searching a font CD-ROM for just the right look

If you're looking for a site from which to download fonts on the Web, put the power of a Web search engine to work for you. For example, perhaps you may need a unique-looking font for a party invitation, but because you'll only use this font once, you'd rather not buy an entire CD-ROM of TrueType fonts or spend money registering a shareware font. Are you stuck with a mundane font that shipped as part of Windows 98?

Definitely not! Crank up your Web browser, and connect to my favorite search engine, www.yahoo.com. At the Search prompt, enter the search phrase **free fonts**, and click the Search button. Yahoo! displays a page with several dozen sites (I found 41 sites one day), most of which offer free fonts for downloading. Some freeware font families don't include all of the symbols, but virtually every freeware font has a complete set of alphanumeric characters.

Tip

You'll also find other sites if you include the terms shareware and freeware in your searches.

A search engine can also help you locate fonts specific to a certain season or holiday, as well as hobbies, sports, and other special interests. Your search phrase should always include the word *font*, but the possibilities are endless for finding just the specialty font you want.

Creating Your Own Fonts

If you need a special font for a particular project (or you want to create an original font that you can distribute), here are some recommendations you should follow before you crank up your font editor:

- **Map the general look of the font on paper.** Although you can design your font within the editor itself, you may want to draw a visual representation of as many of the characters before you run the editor. These include any characters that feature special angles or complex *glyphs* (a term for a structure within a font, usually a single character). Plus, it's easier to get approval to work on that great font from your boss or client if you can provide some idea of what the font will look like before you start.

- **Determine which characters you need.** If you're really in a hurry and you won't be using every character of an entire font — all alphanumerics and at least the most common punctuation marks — then you can save time by simply designing only those characters that you will actually use.

- **Determine if you need an entire font family.** If a deadline is looming, it's not necessary to include italics and bold characters unless you really need them; however, if you're designing a shareware font that others will want to pay to register, I definitely suggest that you create the entire font family, including all of the standard symbols.

Using a Font Editor

Today's font editors use the same graphical user interface controls as a Windows drawing or graphics application, so they're not hard to use. However, even an old hand at designing fonts will tell you that it does take several hours of time to build an entire font family from scratch . . . it's as if each character is a separate miniature drafting project. However, editing an existing font takes much less time than creating a brand new font. Of course, copyright law applies to fonts as well, so you must have legal permission to modify the original font, and any modified font can be used only for your own documents (you can't sell or distribute it).

Tip

Even if you don't have the time or need to create an entire font, you can still use a font editor to create elegant drop caps, special symbols, or model characters that weren't included in another font you're using. Those special characters can then be used for 3-D modeling, Adobe Photoshop projects, or any other application that can accept TrueType fonts as objects.

For example, Figure 8.5 illustrates the main editing screen from a great shareware font editor called Softy, from D.W. Emmett. You can evaluate Softy free for 30 days, and it's only $25 to register the program. (Connect to http://users. iclway.co.uk/l.emmett/ to download a copy.) Softy can create and edit both

TrueType and bitmap fonts. Softy runs under Windows 3.1, Windows 95/98, and Windows NT.

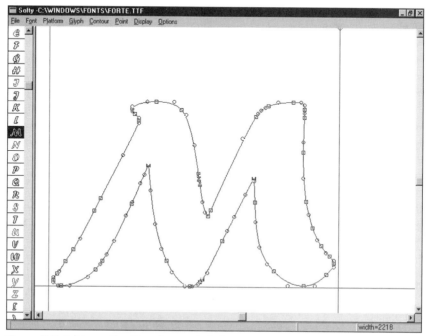

Figure 8.5 Editing a TrueType font with Softy

The boxes surrounding the outline of the glyph (or character) are called *handles* in a font editor; you can grab a handle by clicking it with your cursor and holding down the left button. To move the handle (and the outline edge attached to it), drag the handle to the desired position.

Softy offers a number of features characteristic of a good font editor that make it easier for anyone (even a complete novice) to manipulate a basic glyph:

- You can add new lines, curves, and corners to specific points to add detail to your glyph.

- The entire character can be flipped and rotated.

- You can zoom in to view any portion of the glyph for precise work.

- A character can be designated as *monospaced,* which provides the same uniform spacing produced by a typewriter, or *proportional,* which enables the application using the font to vary both the characters and the spacing in between characters to improve the appearance of the text (as in a published book).

- If you're creating a proportional font, you can designate *kerning* pairs (two characters that require special spacing between them). For instance, the characters *p* and *h* are typical kerning pairs. If they occur side by side in a word, a program that supports kerning automatically adjusts the space between the two characters to make them look tighter and more balanced.

- You can assign any standard attribute — for example, italicizing or bolding, to create a complete font family.

Before you decide to design "the font to end all fonts" and spend several hundred dollars on a commercial font editor such as Macromedia's Fontographer (`www.macromedia.com`), I recommend that you download Softy and try it for a few days. That way, you can see what it's like to use a font editor without paying anything, and you may end up saving that money by registering Softy instead.

Creating 3-D Fonts

Perhaps I shouldn't call this section "Creating 3-D Fonts." That name is actually a little misleading. In fact, the 3-D typography programs currently on the market today don't create bitmap or outline fonts. Instead, they create letters or words in 3-D from existing fonts on your PC or Mac, and their output is an image file instead of a font file. However, practically everyone who uses these 3-D programs calls them "3-D font builders" or "font render programs," so it's a common misnomer.

By the way, *render* means to create a realistic image — usually in 3-D — of something that doesn't actually exist. For example, all of the characters in the classic Disney animated films *Toy Story 2* and *A Bug's Life* were rendered on a computer instead of photographed with a camera. Many of the special effects in science fiction and action movies these days are done with 3-D rendering applications.

I use Xara3D, my favorite 3-D font-rendering program, to build 3-D images for all of my printing projects (as well as my Web sites). Xara3D won't create a realistic 3-D spaceship or a horrible 3-D monster, but it's perfect for designing and rendering logos and 3-D typography. The demonstration version of this program is available for downloading from the Xara Ltd. site at `www.xara.com`.

In Figure 8.6, I've rendered a logo in 3-D that I can use on a T-shirt transfer. I save this image as a .GIF or .JPG image for importing into my transfer printing program. The image can be rotated in any direction, and I can highlight different sections of the type using "virtual" lighting sources to achieve a different mood.

Figure 8.6 Creating an image of 3-D type for a T-shirt

Unlike most computer drafting and drawing applications, a typical 3-D font-rendering program has no drawing tools — instead, you type characters, and those characters are used as the basis for your image. However, you're not limited to just alphanumeric characters; Xara3D enables you to use any TrueType font in your collection, which means that you can also use symbols from a font such as Wingdings or international characters from a foreign language font as a 3-D object.

Other features available in better 3-D font-rendering programs include

- Different colors and textures that you can apply to your font objects, such as marble, wood, chrome, or even water. Figure 8.7 illustrates a 3-D font image I created using marble textures and gold trim.

Figure 8.7 With textures, you can create very realistic surfaces on your fonts.

- Several different types of beveling for the edges of your font that help enhance the 3-D effect of the image.

- Realistic backgrounds, or you can import your own image for use as a background.

- Colored filters to change the virtual lighting and create a mood.

- A lighting *mask*, available in some 3-D font programs, enables you to create a realistic shadow across the face of the type in any one of several different patterns. (I like to use this feature with a lattice mask, which produces a "window shade" shadow on my 3-D text.)

Cross-Reference

Learn how easy it is to build an image with Xara3D in Chapter 12.

Summary

This chapter filled you in on fonts: how to find them, use them, create them, and even make them stand out in three dimensions. I covered the differences between bitmap and outline fonts, and I discussed a number of possible sources for free or inexpensive fonts you can find on the Internet, font CD-ROMs, and your graphics applications. I also included a discussion of font editors and 3-D font-rendering software for creative souls who want to build their own fonts from the ground up.

In Chapter 9 you'll have some *real* fun as you explore the printing projects, special printing materials, and craft supplies that are available for your inkjet printer, laser printer, or all-in-one device. Get ready to create T-shirts, business and greeting cards, banners, and much more.

In Chapter 12, you'll find step-by-step instructions on how to install and manage fonts, including installing a TrueType font in Windows 98, installing fonts in Mac OS 9, displaying TrueType font information in Windows 98, selecting fonts in a Windows application, and creating a logo with 3-D fonts.

CHAPTER 9

Printing with Pizzazz

IN THIS CHAPTER
- Printing personalized items
- Printing images stored on your computer
- Using color in your projects
- Adding clip art to a project
- Printing Web pages
- Using printer suites
- Printing with an image editor
- Printing CD-ROM labels and business cards

Previous chapters of this book focused on installing, configuring, and using an inkjet or laser printer or an all-in-one unit, and it's natural to assume that you'll be printing text on standard paper for most of your documents. Most printers include default settings that reflect this. You generally won't have to change a single setting to print a professional-looking letter or school report on standard 8½×11-inch paper.

That doesn't mean, however, that your printing hardware is suitable *only* for producing print on paper — you can also print images from your scanner or digital camera, capture and print images from the Web, and enhance your documents with clip art! Your printer can produce all sorts of personalized fabric and clothing items, banners, greeting cards for parties, labels for your audio CDs and cassettes, and much more. You and your family may find yourselves having more fun with your printer than with all those expensive games that take up hundreds of megabytes of disk space.

In this chapter (and the corresponding projects in Chapter 12), you learn about the special printing materials you can use for home, hobby, and business projects. You'll also learn how graphics professionals match colors, how to print the entire contents of a Web site (or just a single image), how to acquire images from a scanner or digital camera, where to find clip art images on the Internet, and what printing software is available for your PC. In short, you'll discover how you can add pizzazz to your printing.

Experimenting with Nifty Printing Supplies

In the early years of personal computers —the heyday of the impact printer — the typical PC owner could choose any size, type, or color of paper (as long as it was 8½×11 inches, 20 lb. bond, tractor-fed, and white) and any ink color (as long as it was black). Not much of a choice there, but then again, printers were purely for business and schoolwork, right? Why would a family think of an expensive printer as *fun*?

As you'll see in this section, that perception of the computer printer has all but vanished with the appearance of new materials, such as greeting card stock and glossy photo paper, and the low-cost and high-quality color offered by today's inkjet printers and all-in-one peripherals. Suddenly, the computer printer has become the centerpiece of a whole new hobby industry, producing near-professional results that often compete with expensive commercial printing shops. For example, I like to design and print my own business cards, rather than pay a print shop to produce them. Rather than buy a minimum of 500 or 1,000 business cards from a print shop, I can print a few cards as I need them, and even change the text or image for a specific function.

Most of us use these new printing materials for special occasions (such as a greeting card for a birthday) or to add a custom touch (such as printed labels for those music CDs or cassettes you just recorded). Other computer owners, however, have turned their printing hardware into an important part of a profitable home business, creating personalized T-shirts and novelty items to customers' specifications.

In this section, you'll learn about the latest hobby supplies and materials that are now available for your computer printer — whether you decide to use them for business or pleasure is up to you.

Banners

Banner printing dates back to the days of the high-speed tractor-fed impact printers used with IBM and DEC mainframe computers. The banners that I remember from those days were printed on long, continuous sheets of green-bar computer paper, and they would often stretch the entire length of a hallway. This was the same paper used to print reports and computer code listings, and it was anything but attractive. However, there was one nonbusiness use for the paper; anytime a fellow COBOL programmer left for another job, a birth was announced, or someone got married, one of these huge banners (with letters a foot high) would commemorate the event.

Out of all the hobby applications that I mention in this chapter, banners first appeared on home computers with dot-matrix printers for several reasons:

- **Tractor-fed paper was common.** Almost all early dot-matrix printers made for the home computer market used a tractor-fed system, which made it easy to print long banners without special paper.

- **Color wasn't required.** Sure, banners look better in color, but they do the job just fine in monochrome. In fact, banners could be printed using standard alphanumeric characters, so printers didn't even need the capability to print graphics to print simple banners.

- **No complex software was needed.** Some of the oldest programming books I have for the IBM PC include simple BASIC programs for printing banners; one is no more than about two paragraphs long. Even computers with 16K or less of RAM (such as the Apple II, Atari, or Commodore) could print simple character-based banners.

- **There was universal appeal.** Banners are appropriate and easily to personalize for almost any special event or occasion.

Creating banners on inkjet and laser printers

Although the reasons for using banner paper haven't changed much since the mainframe days, you may remember from earlier chapters that printers using tractor-fed paper have all but disappeared. Only dot-matrix impact printers still use this method of loading paper. How do today's printers create banners?

The answer lies in changes that have been made to the banner paper itself. Today's printers use one of two different types of banner paper:

■ **Specialized continuous banner paper.** Today's inkjet printers can accommodate special continuous-feed paper to create impressive banners, as shown in Figure 9.1. This paper is almost exactly like the traditional tractor-fed paper used by older dot-matrix printers, but it doesn't have the perforated edges with the tractor feed holes — instead, the inkjet printer feeds the paper in the normal fashion, pulling it in with rollers. Naturally, banner paper comes in various colors and designs, so you're not limited to white for a background.

Figure 9.1 Printing on banner paper can yield colorful results.

■ **Standard laser paper.** The bad news: If you own a laser printer, you can't use the continuous banner paper that inkjet printers use. The good news: Most banner-maker programs can create banners on any standard laser paper, so you don't have to buy special paper. There is an extra step involved when printing banners on a laser printer, though. Once the program has printed the pages, you have to match the edges of the design together, and you also need to glue or tape the individual sheets together to form a continuous banner.

Using an inkjet printer with a banner lifter

Many PC owners have discovered that the typical inkjet printer was not designed for feeding in continuous banner paper, so the paper must often be manually fed into the printer to avoid misfeeds and paper jams. Because banner printing has proved so popular, some manufacturers have added a feature to help feed the continuous banner paper through the machine; if you plan on printing many banners for work or school, make sure the inkjet printer you buy can automatically feed banner paper.

The HP DeskJet 695C is one inkjet printer that comes with a specialized banner feed mechanism. With the lifter raised, the printer uses gravity and a higher angle to make certain that the banner paper feeds correctly into the printer. Other printers may use a plastic insert or an extended paper feed tray to help feed banner paper.

Greeting Cards

You've probably noticed a greeting card printing kiosk at your local discount store or department store — these automated machines enable you to print your own personalized greeting cards for birthdays, anniversaries, and such. These coin-operated machines are normally placed near the greeting card and stationery section. When you insert your money, you can select a personal message from a touch-sensitive computer monitor and the specific card design you want to use. Then in a few seconds, the machine spits out a custom greeting card and an envelope. Sounds like a pretty nifty idea, and it seems to be very popular.

There's nothing magical about these greeting card machines, though: that fancy kiosk simply holds a specially designed PC and an inkjet printer. In fact, with the right software and a package of blank greeting card paper, your inkjet printer can turn out greeting cards of exactly the same quality (and probably for significantly less, too).

First, however, you should make sure that your printer or all-in-one unit can handle thicker card stock. The literature that comes with most inkjet printers available these days mentions that they can use greeting card stock, but if you're not sure, you can call the technical support number for your printer manufacturer and ask whether your model can use greeting card paper. You may also be able to find this information on the manufacturer's Web site.

Cross-Reference

See Appendix B for a list of printer manufacturers and their contact information.

Most laser printers can also print card stock, and although you may be limited to monochrome print, the fine quality of laser print (and the fact that it's waterproof) is actually an advantage when you're printing greeting cards. (Personally, I prefer to print greeting cards on my laser printer.) The instructions and tips I mention in this section apply equally to those PC owners with laser printers.

Loading greeting card software

Once you've determined that your printer can use greeting card stock, the next step is to load the software to produce your cards. You have three choices for greeting card software:

- **Specialized greeting card printing software.** Some printing programs are exclusively dedicated to printing greeting cards, complete with suitable clip art, a collection of fonts for setting different moods, and even poetry that you can print on the inside of the card. Greeting card programs can print out different formats of cards (single-fold, double-fold, and more). With these packages, printing a greeting card can be as simple as choosing one of the predesigned cards and changing the recipient's name — the program may even print a matching envelope. You typically receive a sample package of greeting card stock with these programs, so you can try out your new software immediately.

■ **Standard PC printing software.** Most all-purpose printing programs such as PrintMaster and Print Artist can print greeting cards, but they lack the bells and whistles of the specialized greeting card programs. Instead, you'll have to make do with the same clip art and fonts you use to produce signs, banners, and brochures. Also, these packages generally don't include as many predesigned greeting card templates, and they produce fewer card formats.

■ **Word processing or desktop publishing application.** If you'd like to try printing your own greeting cards but you'd rather not spend money on new software, you can produce great results with just your PC's word processor or desktop publishing program. Once again, you're limited to what you have for clip art and fonts, and you may have to create your own template to match the format of the greeting card paper you buy. Luckily, most manufacturers of greeting card paper include instructions on creating templates in popular programs such as Microsoft Word, Corel WordPerfect, and Adobe PageMaker to use their paper.

Once you've determined which software you'll use, make sure it's loaded and working properly before you proceed further — you should be able to successfully print a test page from your software.

Selecting greeting card paper

Now you're ready to select the design and format of the greeting card paper you'll use. When choosing paper, keep these guidelines in mind:

■ **Generic designs are better.** Most manufacturers of greeting card paper don't include titles or interior text in their designs, making it easier for you to use the same paper for birthdays, anniversaries, and even get well cards. For example, if you select a pattern of baby toys and pastel colors for a baby shower, it'll be hard to use that same paper for a quick set of party invitations later. Stick with generic designs that please the eye and can convey more than one message.

■ **Match paper to your printer.** The packaging should indicate whether the greeting card paper is suitable for inkjet, laser, or both types of printers. For the best results, make sure you buy the correct type of greeting card paper for your specific type of printer.

Tip

If you can, use paper and ink produced by the manufacturer of your printer — that way, you can be sure that your printer supplies have been designed for and tested with your printer. For example, if you own an HP inkjet printer or all-in-one, I recommend that you buy the greeting card paper manufactured by Hewlett-Packard.

■ **All card formats are not created equal.** Greeting card paper comes in several formats, from a simple single fold to perforated notecards that must be separated and folded after printing. Make sure you select the right format of greeting card paper for the cards you want to create. Figure 9.2 illustrates a number of different card formats and their uses.

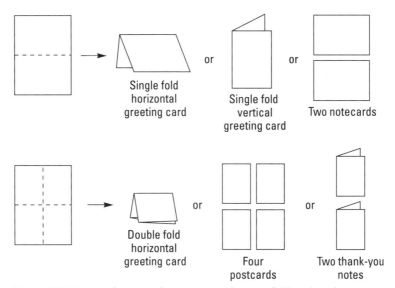

Figure 9.2 Various formats of greeting card paper fold and perforate in different ways.

Greeting card paper is available in packages with a single format and design or in printing kits that include samples of many different designs and formats. If you're just starting out or you'd like to experiment with a wider range of designs and formats, pick a collection of different types of greeting card paper in a single box.

Creating and printing your card

With materials and software at hand, it's time to design and print a card. I show you how to print a birthday card step by step in Chapter 12, so for now I mention a number of guidelines to follow while creating your card:

■ **Deliver a simple message.** It's always a good idea to keep the message of your card as simple as possible, so you should probably avoid the temptation to use one of Shakespeare's sonnets as the interior text for your next Valentine's Day card. (Unless, of course, the target of your affection is a fan of Renaissance literature.)

■ **Personalize your message.** Use the recipient's name, refer to a personal joke or a recent event in the recipient's life, mention family members by name, and otherwise personalize the card whenever possible. After all, that's one of the advantages of a custom printed card over a generic greeting card you can buy off the rack at any local drugstore!

■ **Experiment with different designs.** If you're in a hurry and you're using a program designed for printing projects, select one of the predesigned card designs. Otherwise, take a few minutes to experiment with the placement of clip art, blocks of text, and different colors. Today's printing software makes this much easier by enabling you to preview the results when you move a block of text or a picture — if you don't like the effect, use the program's Undo feature to return the card to its original design. I like to place type along the edge of the card or even eliminate text from the front of the card completely.

Tip

Although using a word processing or desktop publishing program to create greeting cards is more complex than designing cards with a dedicated program, you do have more control over the placement of images and text, including text rotation and special image effects. If you're an expert with a word processing or desktop publishing program, try creating a greeting card layout — you may find another outlet for your creative talent.

■ **Import those photos.** Here's a great idea that really sets a custom card apart from a store-bought card: import a photo or two that you've scanned or taken with your digital camera! (Not even the greeting card kiosks I mentioned earlier can do that.) Just about every printing program can import photos in Windows bitmap (.BMP) or JPEG (.JPG) format, usually through an Add Graphic or Import menu command. If you need help in importing a picture, check the instructions or the online help for the program you're using.

■ **Flex your fonts.** Why stick to plain, run-of-the-mill fonts such as Times New Roman or Arial when you can match your font to your message? If your PC already has a wide variety of fonts (or if you received fonts with your greeting card software), pick a distinctive font that matches the mood of the card. For example, Figure 9.3 shows some fun fonts that I've used before in all sorts of greeting cards.

Photo Paper

Let's suppose you're ready to print the collection of digital photographs that you took on your vacation — you'll send some of the photos to relatives, while you'll keep one set for your own album. You've taken the time to resize and crop these images so they can be arranged nicely on a page, and naturally you've set your inkjet printer to use the highest quality print settings. Yet, when the photos are done, they don't have the "look and feel" of a real photograph; some details don't show up, and they don't have that glossy look. You expected them to look like the sample photos the salesperson showed you at the computer store when you bought your printer. What happened?

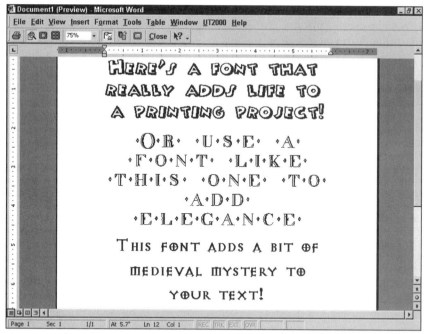

Figure 9.3 These font examples show how you can liven up your custom greeting cards.

I'll tell you the secret to better-looking digital photographs on your inkjet printer: it's the paper itself! Printing those images on regular plain paper may give you acceptable results for a test page, but if you really want photos suitable for framing that resemble those you get back from your film camera, you should spend a little extra and pick up a package of *glossy photo paper*.

Photo paper has three important advantages over regular printer paper:

- **It's thicker.** A sheet of photo paper is thicker than standard printer paper, which helps in mounting and adds durability to the finished photograph. For example, a sheet of HP Premium Plus Photo paper is 9 mils thick (over twice the 4 mil thickness of a standard sheet of printer paper).

- **It has an opaque, glossy surface.** Unlike the porous surface of plain printer paper, the glossy surface of a sheet of photo paper doesn't allow ink to soak into the paper fibers. In plain English, details stand out and the printed surface is raised above the paper, so the finished product looks much more like a traditional film photograph. Your photographs should be dry within 60 seconds or so, too. (Photo paper is also available in a matte surface if you prefer a non-gloss, matte appearance for your photographs — you still get the same results, though.)

- **It carries a printed backing.** Most manufacturers of photo paper add a logo or "brand" to the back of their papers, which further reinforces the illusion of a traditional photograph.

Of course, the better the print quality of your inkjet the better the photos look, but I can tell you that premium photo paper improves the appearance of *any* image, no matter *how much* you've spent on your printer!

T-Shirt Transfers

Most of us have seen T-shirts with designs created on a PC — every mall has at least one booth that can create personalized T-shirts with your picture (taken with a digital camera) or a slogan that you create. Some professional screen printing companies also use computers to create their designs. Whether it's a unique design for a canvas purse, a wall hanging for your office with the company logo, or a design reproduced on shirts for an entire soccer team, these custom-printed items are always popular.

Did you know, however, that you can create custom T-shirts and cloth items at home, on your own inkjet printer? As a matter of fact, you'll be using the same materials as the owner of a T-shirt shop: a PC, an inkjet printer or all-in-one unit, the right software, and a special type of printing paper called a *T-shirt transfer page* (oh, and an iron, too).

Figure 9.4 illustrates the process of printing and applying a transfer; as you can see, the only steps that absolutely have to be performed by an adult are loading the transfer itself and ironing the printed transfer. This means that children as young as seven or eight years old can help create their own clothing designs — one of the reasons why this relatively new advancement in printing materials has proven to be so popular with schools and families.

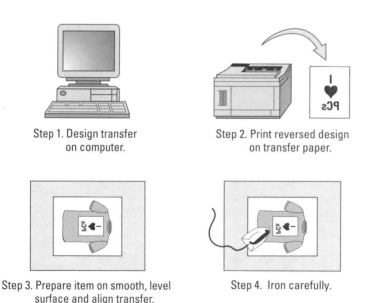

Step 1. Design transfer on computer.

Step 2. Print reversed design on transfer paper.

Step 3. Prepare item on smooth, level surface and align transfer.

Step 4. Iron carefully.

Figure 9.4 The four steps of printing and applying a transfer

Designing a transfer page

Although it is possible to design a T-shirt transfer using a word processing program, it's much easier to use a program written especially for creating these designs. Like greeting card software, these transfer design programs usually include a library of clip art and fonts suitable for T-shirts. We'll cover the printing and transfer process step by step later in Chapter 12, but keep these tips in mind while you're creating your design:

- **Use large fonts.** I always use fonts that are at least 28 point size for two reasons: they're easier to read at a distance, and a larger font carries additional impact. In general, the larger the font, the more effective it is at delivering your message.

- **Keep the message simple.** The more complex your graphics and text become, the harder it is for the reader to discern the message you're trying to convey . . . and remember that a T-shirt design is usually viewed in motion, so the reader may only have five seconds to read a shirt before you walk past.

- **Don't forget to flip.** Most T-shirt transfer design software automatically reverses your design before it's printed, creating a mirror image of the design. Therefore, don't panic because words and graphics are backwards; it is necessary because the transfer is reversed when you apply it to the cloth, so the mirror image transfers in the proper orientation. If your transfer design software doesn't automatically flip the image, your printer driver's Properties page should provide this feature. As you can see in Figure 9.5, the driver for the HP DeskJet 722C inkjet printer includes a Flip Horizontal check box so that you can enable and disable this feature as necessary.

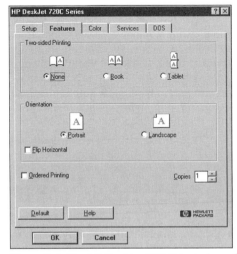

Figure 9.5 The HP DeskJet 722C includes a flip feature for printing T-shirt transfers.

Tips for successful transfers

Unfortunately, it's very easy to print a great T-shirt transfer page and then apply it incorrectly — instead of a professional, screen-printed look, you end up with a design that's patchy, incomplete, or faded. Here are some tips I've learned the hard way. By following them, you can avoid wasting your printer's ink, several transfer pages, and a number of perfectly good white T-shirts.

- **Use the correct temperature setting.** Read the instructions that came with your transfer pages carefully, and make sure you select the same heat setting on your iron that is recommended in the directions. An incorrect heat setting is a primary cause of problems during the transfer of the design.

- **Avoid wrinkles like the plague.** Make sure both the transfer page and the cloth you're using are completely free of wrinkles — it takes only a single wrinkle to destroy your work.

- **Follow those washing instructions.** Did your design transfer successfully? Good! You're not out of the water yet. Every manufacturer of T-shirt transfer paper includes strict instructions on how to wash the finished item after you've applied the transfer. It's critical to follow these instructions to the letter to avoid damaging the design during the first wash.

As you've probably noticed, it's probably more important to follow the manufacturer's instructions precisely when using T-shirt transfer paper than when carrying out any other special printing job. Once you've successfully transferred a page or two, however, you can start concentrating more on the design phase and less on worrying about whether you can properly apply the transfer.

Tip

Are you considering designing custom T-shirts and other items as a small home business? If so, I recommend that you invest in a small laundry pressing iron, which applies transfers faster and more evenly than a simple household iron.

You can also use a monochrome laser printer (color won't work) for transfers. The main difference here is that you have to set the print darkness to the highest setting for the maximum toner amount. Although it sounds useless because few people want or need a black transfer, it is an important technique for those who enjoy embroidery. For example, it's possible to use this procedure to transfer design outlines created in a graphics or drawing program to all kinds of fabrics (even expensive silk).

Stationery, Business Cards, Labels, and Brochures

Do you already run your own business? If so, you've probably admired the matching business cards, envelopes, labels, and company brochures of some larger companies, and if you've researched the prices for creating these professionally printed paper goods, you've probably also decided that you can't afford to offer your customers the same matching materials.

Once again, your PC's printing hardware comes to the rescue — not only can you design your own company stationery, business cards, mailing labels, and product brochures, but you can also save hundreds of dollars. The trick is in buying matching paper supplies, designing your own company logo (if you haven't already), and maintaining a single "look and feel" among all of your printed items.

Selecting matching paper supplies

It's easy to find matching paper supplies — locally, you can find matching blank business cards, stationery, and envelopes at your neighborhood office supply store. If you'd like a larger selection or you'd like to save a little money, a number of printing supply catalog stores offer matching paper supplies via mail order. These same sources may also offer tri-fold brochure paper and business report covers to match the rest of the supplies.

Tip

Do you use a PIM (short for Personal Information Manager) such as Microsoft Outlook or Lotus Organizer? If so, you can print custom pages containing all of your schedule information for your daily calendar or date book from within these programs. I find these schedule sheets are great reminders. Plus, I use the sheets to jot down any notes or information that I pick up during the day, and in the evening I transfer that information back into my PIM software.

When selecting matching paper supplies, keep these guidelines in mind:

■ **Determine the image you want to convey.** Select a paper design that projects the proper image to your customers: for example, a businesslike marble accent for a financial consultant, a stylized art deco for an antique shop, or a colorful design with crayons and toys for a day-care center. Naturally, it's important that your papers carry a distinctive look, but remember, no matter how good your message is, it won't carry the same weight with the reader if it's printed on paper with an inappropriate design.

■ **Don't let a design waste your space.** I've seen paper designs with header and footer graphics that literally occupied a third of a page of stationery. It's a better idea to select a design that takes up no more than a total of two inches or less on each stationery page.

■ **Buy all of your materials at once.** Because most manufacturers of paper supplies package (and restock) their stationery, envelopes, business cards, and brochure papers separately, it's a good habit to make sure you buy all of the paper materials you need at once — that way, you won't be out of luck if the store runs out of your particular paper design. This ensures that you won't end up sending a matching letter and business card in a plain white envelope. (Of course, you can also visit a printing shop and order your own custom paper — more on this later in the chapter.)

Creating a company logo

Corporations spend thousands of dollars (and sometimes much more) to develop their own unique company logo. However, you don't have to run a multi-million-dollar company to reap the benefits of a well-known logo. Any company of any size can enhance its image within its correspondence and its online Web site by developing a unique symbol as a logo.

Here are a number of suggestions for creating your own company logo:

- **Use an initial from your company name.** Believe it or not, many business owners forget to consider one or more letters of their business name as a basis for a logo. If you're thinking about a company logo, sit down with a scratch pad and a pencil, and use the first letter (or letters) of your company name (or the name itself) as the basis for developing a graphic. Combine the letters or stylize them, add an interesting edge design, or whatever floats your boat.

- **Modify an existing piece of clip art.** If you have a bold and easily recognized piece of clip art in your collection, you can simplify it and create an excellent logo. Avoid complex images with too much detail — they won't reduce well for business cards and envelopes. The best pictures to use are simple monochrome line drawings (you can always add color later). Open the image in a graphics editing program, remove any fine detail or delicate edges, and add your company's name in a balanced position somewhere around or inside the logo boundary.

Cross-Reference

Wondering where you can find more clip art than what's included with your current software? See the section "Finding Clip Art" later in this chapter to find out how you can locate free clip art on the Internet.

- **Use a 3-D program to create your logo.** Many shareware and commercial 3-D rendering programs can create impressive, real-looking 3-D images from your company's name. For example, the image in Figure 9.6 illustrates a logo I created in just a few minutes with a 3-D rendering program.

- **Add a shape to your company name.** Probably the simplest company logo is a basic shape — such as a circle, a triangle, or a series of lines — integrated somehow into your company's name, using a bold, stylized type-face. Advanced image editors such as Photoshop can add a 3-D effect to your company name, "wrapping" it around a cylinder or the outside of a circle, for example.

Figure 9.6 You can easily create logos in many shareware and commercial 3-D programs.

Cross-Reference

Chapter 12 contains a section called "Creating a Logo with 3-D Fonts," where you'll find instructions for creating an impressive logo using a 3-D rendering application.

Tip

In fact, Photoshop, Paint Shop Pro, and other such programs can perform all sorts of neat transformations and special effects to both text and graphics, making one of these image editors a great choice for someone who wants to experiment with different looks for a company logo.

Take it from me, creating a logo on your own is a lot more satisfying (and usually much cheaper) than hiring a graphic artist to do it for you — and, of course, you can always hire an artist later if you're not pleased with your results.

Creating a uniform style

Once you've selected a paper design and created your company's logo, you're ready to print professional-looking materials. Creating the same look on all your materials, however, is more than simply using the same logo on everything. Consider these tips:

- **Use fonts consistently.** Use the same fonts and type sizes for all of your printed communications, including your brochures and business cards.

- **Standardize page elements.** Adopt the same page-numbering scheme, the same memo and letter paragraph formats, and the same arrangement of headers and footers on all your documents. For example, if you've decided on a left-justified paragraph format, use that same left justification on all of your brochures, memos, and company letters.

- **Create a company style guide.** If others in your company prepare company documents, create a style sheet or document template for their word processing application as a style guide. The template can automatically help them follow the document design you've developed.

- **Deliver the goods.** Remember, your business cards and brochures can display only a limited amount of your company data, so pick the important points and pieces of information you want to present — don't create a business card design without your e-mail address, or a brochure without your company's address.

With the right appearance, your company's literature and printed materials can project a formidable image — even if you're the only employee.

Labels for Disks, CD-ROMs, and Cassettes

When most PC owners think of printing labels, they think of return address labels — or, if you've organized your address book on your computer, you've printed mailing labels from your address data. Address labels can save you a lot of time and effort — not to mention a sore writing hand — but you may not know about the other types of labels your printer or all-in-one can create. For example:

- **Creating labels for floppy disks.** Do you create shareware programs or distribute software on disk? Disk labels provide a professional, finished look for your disks. Because a standard 3.5-inch floppy disk label has plenty of space, I always include as much information as possible about my shareware programs that I distribute on disk (such as the version number, the operating system, the filenames, my company name, telephone number, and e-mail address).

■ **Printing labels for audio and data CD-ROMs.** Because CD-Recordable and CD-Rewritable (usually abbreviated as CD-R and CD-RW) discs are blank, you can label them on the top surface of the disc with a felt-tip marker. However, if you're going to distribute the data CD-ROMs that you record (or you want to give them a more "finished" appearance), I recommend that you invest in a CD-ROM labeling device. Figure 9.7 illustrates how simple the NEATO CD-ROM labeler (which you can find for about $30 at most office supply stores) actually is. A spindle piece holds the CD-ROM steady, while the base makes it easy to align the label and the top surface of the disc for a perfect fit. Figure 9.8 shows the print preview for a label I created for one of my data discs, using the program DesignExpress from MicroVision Development, which I describe in Chapter 12. (By the way, if you want to learn the details about designing and printing all sorts of labels and jewel box inserts for your collection of recorded CDs, I recommend that you pick up a copy of my book, *Hewlett-Packard Official Recordable CD Handbook,* from IDG Books Worldwide.)

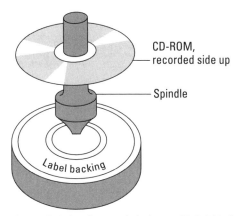

Figure 9.7 Applying a label to a CD-ROM disc

Warning

Never use a mailing label or floppy disk label on a CD-ROM. The label will probably alter the balance of the disc, and your CD-ROM drive may not be able to read it. Also, never try to remove an adhesive label you've stuck on a recorded CD-ROM; it may pull off the layers of lacquer on top of the disc and the thin metal coating within the disc, which will certainly ruin it.

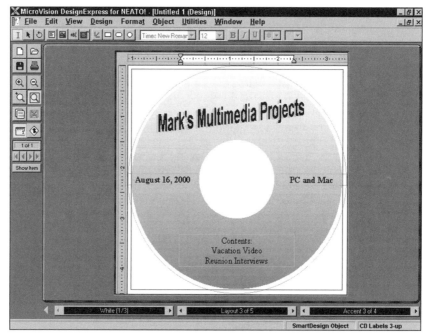

Figure 9.8 This label will soon be printed and applied to a CD-ROM.

- **Printing audio cassette labels.** A number of shareware and commercial programs enable you to print labels for cassettes with a graphic, a title, and an artist name. If your music cataloging program supports a printing feature, you can even add extras such as a song list and total running time.

Where can you get blank labels in these formats? Most office supply stores carry them; on the Internet, you can order them from online paper supply stores like DeskTop Labels (www.desktoplabels.com).

Stickers

Sure, kids love to create their own custom stickers for fun (I show you how in Chapter 12), but there are a lot of other uses for stickers as well — especially if you use the new "reusable" stickers, such as HP Restickables, that can be removed and applied again on fabrics and other surfaces. Reusable stickers can be used for

- **Nametags.** Stickers make great custom nametags for parties, conferences, and meetings. They look much more professional than a handwritten label, and they can carry your company's logo. Plus, they can be reapplied over several days.

- **Product tracking.** If you'd like to keep track of office supplies or store stock, using restickable labels can help keep things organized.

- **Labeling kid stuff.** Summer camp? Sleepover party at a friend's house? Stickers can identify your children's belongings (and they also look cool).

- **Last-minute labeling.** Stickers are perfect for drawing attention to a product box — take a walk though a software store and you'll see what I mean! You can use them to promote important features, remind a customer of discounts, and even add warning labels.

Today's sticker stock comes in a number of different sizes, shapes, and colors, so you can match the dimensions and color of the sticker to your needs. For example, you can buy a red sticker stock instead of wasting ink by "painting" a white sticker solid red.

Custom Papers

So far, we've been discussing paper materials that you buy as blanks — they may have a design, but they won't carry your logo, address, or other contact information. Generally, those who use these papers add such finery as a part of their document design.

However, if you're buying forms, or if you're buying paper materials for a larger company or for direct mailings, you may find that it's more cost-effective to visit your local printing shop and order custom papers. In general, custom papers offer the following advantages:

- **Custom papers save time.** Saving time is especially important for those using forms, or for those who print the same document often. It simply takes less time to pull a preprinted form from a box than it does to print a new copy of the same document.

- **Custom papers save ink.** If you send a large number of letters and each piece of stationery you send has the same header or footer, it makes sense to order that stationery in bulk from a printing shop (especially if your design incorporates large areas of a single color, which tends to use large amounts of ink or toner after several dozen copies). Inkjet ink can smear, which is not a desirable trait for printed business correspondence. If you use an inkjet device, a custom paper with a semi-gloss surface can help reduce the possibility of a smeared business or e-mail address.

- **Custom papers save on maintenance.** By using custom paper with company letterhead, headers, or footers, you greatly reduce the wear and tear on your printer. Using custom paper saves you the money and time you would otherwise spend on printer maintenance (and your printer will have a longer operational life as well).

Custom papers can also carry fancy borders or edge designs — but unlike preprinted materials, you can specify the exact placement and color of the design.

Printing Digital Images

Digital images are created in one of four ways:

- **Freehand.** Believe it or not, some computer artists and graphics professionals still like to create digital images the old-fashioned way: they draw them. Many drawing and painting applications available today enable you to use your mouse or a drawing tablet to "paint" onscreen. These programs can closely simulate the appearance of watercolor and charcoal drawings, and oil paint surfaces.

- **Scanned.** If you have a scanner connected to your PC, you're ready to open the door to a world of images. Scanners can capture an image from just about any printed material, usually at a color depth of 16 million colors, and they can also "read" text into your word processor using a process called OCR (*Optical Character Recognition*). Scanners are available as SCSI devices (faster, but more expensive, and they require that you install a SCSI adapter if you don't already have one), USB devices, and parallel port devices (slower than SCSI or USB, but these scanners connect right to your printer port, so you don't have to install another card just to get the right type of port).

Tip

Are you shopping for a scanner for your computer? I recommend a flatbed scanner (or all-in-one unit) — they're the most versatile breed of scanner, operating very much like a copy machine. Unlike sheetfed scanners, which operate more like a fax machine, you don't have to tear pages out of books or worry about odd-shaped items getting stuck with a flatbed scanner.

- **Photographed.** Prices for digital cameras are rapidly dropping — a camera that once cost $750 can now be had for under $300. Even the lower-cost cameras under $200 can capture photographs at 800×600 resolution with a color depth of 16 million colors. The more you spend on a digital camera, the higher the resolution and the closer your electronic image is to the quality of a true 35mm film photograph. Higher-priced cameras also offer features such as zoom, built-in LCD viewfinders, and removable RAM cards that enable you to "reload" your digital camera for another round of pictures.

- **Rendered.** Many computer owners are creating realistic 3-D images with rendering software. Some images are purely for business, such as a company logo or Web site graphic; other images are more akin to works of art, featuring animals, machines, structures, and the human form. Rendering software can deliver images directly to your printer, or you can save an image as a file on disk for future modification.

Most of the digital images produced with a scanner are quite big (on the order of 30 or 40MB, depending on the size and color depth of the image), so your PC prints slower than usual. Also, the size of these images makes them harder to transfer from computer to computer. (If you're not on a network, I recommend a Zip drive or other removable media drive that can hold at least 100MB.) By the way, all of this is covered in more detail in the *Hewlett-Packard Official Scanner Handbook,* from IDG Books Worldwide.

Unless you have a monitor larger than 17 inches, a larger scanned image with a resolution of 2048×1536 will probably have to be resized to a more manageable 1024×768 or 800×600 in order for you to view the entire image on your monitor. The shareware program Paint Shop Pro is perfect for this task; it can resize images to whatever size you like, and you can choose to maintain the *aspect ratio* (a fancy term for the relative dimensions of the image) so that the image doesn't end up stretched or distorted.

Paint Shop Pro is also great for quick editing jobs. For example, did Uncle Milton's head get caught in that picture you just took of your Christmas tree? With a film camera, you'll have to explain that disembodied head every time you show the picture to others; with a digital camera, however, you can simply edit the image, and remove Uncle Milton before you print a hard copy. Paint Shop Pro can also print a border for your digital images or sharpen the edges in the image to provide a better-printed copy.

Warning

Before you save an image to disk from a drawing, scanning, or rendering package, make sure you're not saving it in a proprietary format. If you do, you'll have to open the image in that program in the future, and if you transfer the image to another computer, it may not have the same program. To make sure your image can be opened on most computers without requiring any third-party program, use the Save As menu item, and select Bitmap or JPEG as the image format. Macintosh owners should use either TIFF or JPEG format.

Working with Clip Art Images

Luckily, you no longer have to be talented with a pencil or brush (or even with a mouse or drawing tablet) to add just the right image to your printed documents — like me, you can peruse a huge collection of *clip art* from any one of a number of sources, and simply cut and paste.

Finding Clip Art

If you don't already have an extensive collection of clip art, here are a number of sources (some are free, some may cost you a little cash):

- **The Web.** Hundreds of sites on the Internet offer free clip art files for downloading; some are collections from many artists, with all different styles and subjects, while other sites showcase a range of clip art with the same style from a single artist (usually the artist also maintains the Web site).

Cross-Reference

You can search for clip art and download these images to disk files by using the technique I describe in Chapter 12.

■ **CD-ROM.** You'll find clip art collections on CD-ROM at any computer software store, including specialized collections such as religious or business clip art. These CD-ROM collections usually include some sort of viewing program that displays thumbnails of the clip art — it's very hard to select just the right image when all you have is a filename to judge the content. Figure 9.9 shows a typical clip art browsing program; any image can be viewed full size, copied to the clipboard, or saved individually to any location on your hard drive.

Figure 9.9 This CD-ROM-based clip art collection contains hundreds of images ready for use in your printed documents.

■ **Printing and word processing applications.** Almost all the software applications that center around printing, word processing, or desktop publishing now ship on CD-ROM, which means that they usually include their own collection of clip art for use in your documents. For example, Microsoft's Office 2000 business application suite includes an excellent clip art collection.

- **Paper clip art books.** Before the widespread use of scanners and the popularity of CD-ROMs, clip art was physically pasted into an artist's layout, and then the entire layout was used to produce a document. With the popularity of electronic clip art, the books of paper clip art that I used to use in high school and college are slowly disappearing in the world of graphic design and publishing, but you can still find a number of these books at bookstores and your local library.

- **Your artist friends.** If you have a friend who has artistic talent and can create clip art images for you, make sure that you have the artist's written permission to use those images in your documents. Many businesses also commission an artist to create an entire series of clip art images in the same style for a flat fee, so the company owns the images after they're finished. In the same manner, many Webmasters commission a site's worth of images at one time.

Selecting the Right Clip Art

If you're somewhat familiar with graphic design, you know that the right image can add visual impact to a document or Web page. It can also help explain a complex process or help highlight a point you're trying to make. The right clip art can transform a boring block of text into something pleasing to the eye.

On the other hand, the wrong piece of clip art can do a good deal of damage to your document: it can confuse the reader, draw the eye away from important points, add a humorous tone to a serious subject, or, at the very worst, actually offend the reader. You've probably encountered this unfortunate effect if you've ever picked up a newsletter or brochure and said to yourself, "Certainly they didn't mean to use *that* image!"

The fact is that the same exact piece of clip art can have either effect — it depends upon a number of factors. When selecting clip art and using it in your documents, keep these tips in mind:

- **Match the context of your document.** Determine whether your document has a light, neutral, or serious tone, and choose clip art according to that tone. For example, look at the three pieces of clip art I've selected in Figure 9.10 — each has a specific mood that matches it to a specific context.

Tip

As a rule, I use clip art with a light tone only for humorous documents — and the entire document must be humorous, not just a section. This helps make sure that a light piece of clip art doesn't diminish the impact of a serious portion of the document that may appear on the same page. The classic example is a happy clown cavorting at the top of a newsletter page with an obituary beginning an inch or two down the page.

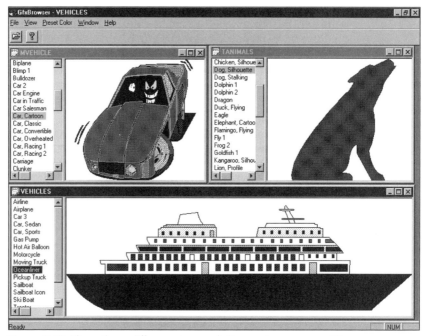

Figure 9.10 These three different pieces of clip art demonstrate different tones.

■ **Avoid complex images.** The most effective clip art is simple and dramatic. This explains why most of the line art and incidental artwork you see in professionally produced magazines, company newsletters, and brochures tend to be silhouettes, simple cartoons, and freehand drawings. Of course, complex artwork such as cutaway drawings, photographs, and flowcharts have their place in a document, but they're tied directly to the text, and they don't really count as clip art. Clip art images usually aren't tied directly to a specific section of the text, and they don't detract from the text content of the document, so they can be placed freely as part of the overall design of the page.

■ **Use images from one artist.** A document that contains clip art from the same artist throughout the document has a continuity of graphic design — this is especially important for a longer document, such as the book you're reading. For this reason, the same icon symbols are used throughout the book. Mixing clip art from two artists or two sources with different styles can be disastrous.

■ **Don't overuse your clip art.** It's easy to fall into the trap of overusing clip art, but clip art doesn't take the place of text in your documents — if you're using more than two or three clip art images per page, you're probably adding too much artwork to your document design. (Note that this limit I'm recommending doesn't include complex artwork.)

Tip

Today's word processing and desktop publishing applications can "wrap" text around the edges of an image — this is a perfect feature to use in a document crowded with images. I find it adds an interesting visual effect to a document that a straight columnar treatment can't match.

Clip Art Legal Issues

Because electronic clip art is so popular today, it pays to know which images can be legally used in your documents — not every image advertised as clip art is suitable for use in your company's yearly business report or a newspaper advertisement. How can you tell which clip art images are legal for you to use, and which images can lead to trouble if you include them in a distributed document?

The most important guideline that can help you steer clear of questionable clip art sources is a simple phrase: *royalty-free*. Before you download a clip art image from a Web page, check the page's text content to see whether the artist has declared that the image is "royalty-free" clip art (or some variation of the phrase). If it is, the artist has released you from any fee. For example, visit www. royaltyfreeart.com and www.absolutelyfreebies.com/clipart.html on the Web.

Tip

If you're unsure about whether you can legally use a particular image, visit a Web site that discusses copyright law. Two interesting ones are Copyright Resources at www.copyright-resources.com and Copyright on the Internet at weber.u. washington.edu/~daryn/copyright. If you need expert help, consult a lawyer.

Adding Colors

In earlier chapters, you learned why the capability to print colors has led to the immense popularity of the inkjet printer. I also discussed why graphics professionals dig deeper into their pockets to afford a high-end, photo-quality dye-sublimation printer. Color adds visual impact that a monochrome document simply can't match, and it helps draw the eye to the important points in your document text.

At this point you know *why* color is so important, and in this section you get some tips on *how* to use color to add pizzazz to your documents and printed items.

Spot Color versus Process Color

If you're a home PC owner creating a document bound for your inkjet printer, adding color to your text takes only a keystroke or two — the printer drivers used by Windows and the Mac OS provide approximately the same colors displayed by your monitor. The blue may not look exactly like the blue displayed on your monitor, but it's close enough.

On the other hand, if you're creating a document for distribution and it will be printed at a print shop on an offset printer, you'll want more control over the saturation and hue of your colors. I describe how publishing professionals match colors in the next section; for now, I cover how colors are handled at a professional offset printing shop. You'll find this information helpful if you have to produce artwork for a print shop, and it provides a general background in the use of color for your own projects.

Professional printers have two options for applying color to paper:

■ **Spot color.** The name is highly descriptive here: spot color adds solid color highlights to printed material, and each color is printed with its own unique ink. Spot color is used mostly for adding color to text, creating blocks of color for sidebars, and printing symbols, such as icons, in a single color. Figure 9.11 illustrates how spot color is applied to paper.

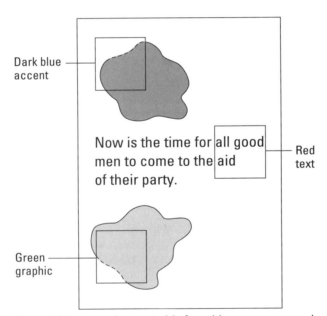

Figure 9.11 Spot color is suitable for adding one or two colors during offset printing. Each color is applied individually.

■ **Color separation.** Color separation (also called process color) is a much more complex color printing method than spot color — instead of actually applying the unique color to the paper, a standard set of colors is separately applied in layers, and the combination of these layers creates the different colors. Most process color printing uses four colors: cyan, magenta, yellow, and black (usually abbreviated as CMYK by people in printing and publishing). If your publication includes any four-color photographs or images, they must be produced with color separation. Most desktop publishing programs and graphic design programs can create these individual color separation layers in electronic format, so an image can be printed using color separation directly from a disk file — this technology has all but eliminated the film camera in modern publishing. Figure 9.12 illustrates the color separation process.

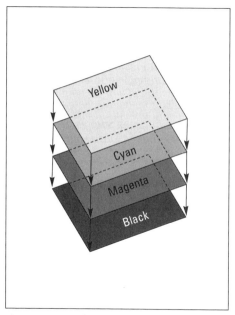

Figure 9.12 Color separation is used to print complex graphics and four-color photographs and images during offset printing. Process colors are applied in layers.

What Is Color Matching?

"Okay, so now I know how color is applied to the printed page by an offset printer, but how does a graphic artist or a desktop publisher ensure that those colors are accurate?" These professionals use a *color matching system* to guarantee that the purple you see in a printed magazine advertisement is the purple they intended. Color matching is especially important when printing using the color separation technique.

For example, let's consider my favorite color, emerald green, as displayed by a typical monitor or printed by an expensive thermal wax printer. As you can imagine, those colors differ significantly when printed on a standard inkjet printer. All three devices produce a noticeably different version of emerald green.

A color matching system helps calibrate all the individual elements of your desktop publishing system — both hardware and software — to ensure the colors displayed on your monitor during the layout process match as closely as possible with those produced as output (whether that output is printed directly or sent elsewhere as an electronic file).

For example, the Apple Mac OS, the operating system used on today's Macintosh computers, includes a built-in feature called *ColorSync* that handles color matching between the computer, monitor, and color printer. ColorSync actually defines each color that can be produced by each piece of hardware in your Macintosh system according to an international color palette called the *CIE XYZ standard*. If you buy a monitor or printer for your Macintosh, it should include a ColorSync profile on disk or CD-ROM that you can use to calibrate the color output to match the ColorSync model. In order for ColorSync to work correctly, it must know the exact characteristics of the hardware you're using.

Windows 98 offers a feature similar to ColorSync called *ICM/ICC profiles* that help ensure correct calibration across devices. Such profiles now ship with many printers, scanners, and monitors, and can be obtained for older models at the manufacturer's Web site.

Cross-Reference

See Appendix B for a list of printer manufacturers and their contact information.

Using Standard Color Palettes

There are also standard ink color palettes produced by ink manufacturers. The most popular standard ink palette by far (and the best-supported) is the PANTONE Matching System (PMS) developed by PANTONE, Inc., which is used only for spot color output. Other standard ink palettes include Toyo and TruMatch.

In its simplest form, PANTONE palette matching can be performed with a simple *color wheel* (also called a *color catalog*). The color wheel consists of a number of cards, each of which carries a different color; the cards are arranged by color, so the cross-section of the color wheel resembles a rainbow. Besides carrying an example of a specific color, each card in the wheel also bears a PANTONE ink color name and number. These PANTONE identifiers are recognized by just about every advanced desktop publishing and graphics program available for your computer, as well as by the folks at any print shop.

For example, if you specify PANTONE 320 in your desktop publishing program as a border color, the electronic document created by that program specifies that particular color during printing. If your printer uses PANTONE inks, this should guarantee that your final printed piece has the border color that you specified.

Polishing Your Documents with Color

Color matching systems such as ColorSync and the PANTONE ink color palette help underline just how important colors are to a graphics professional. The use of color in a printed document is a science unto itself, and entire books have been written on the influence of different colors on human emotion — devoting many more pages than I could hope to include in this book.

However, I *can* provide you with a number of proven guidelines that can help you make the best use of color in your work:

- **Avoid using too many colors.** Select two or three colors to use when adding highlighted blocks of color to a document, and stick with those colors throughout — too many colors can distract the eye from your text content. The same rule holds if you add color clip art or borders to the pages of your document.

- **Use color sparingly.** In the same vein as the preceding tip, color is most effective when it's used to highlight important portions of your text, or to draw the eye toward a specific spot on the page. Unless you're designing materials for a circus, avoid using more than two color items per page (not counting complex graphics such as photographs and charts, of course).

- **Use contrasting colors.** Make sure your text and background colors contrast effectively so that your document is easy to read. (Black text on a white page hasn't been the standard all these centuries for nothing.) I also use dark blue or dark green text on a white background; on a dark or black background, use white or yellow lettering for the best effect.

- **Bold any text printed in color.** Adding a block of colored text to a document? No matter what color you use for your background, it's always a good idea to use the bold attribute on colored text to make sure that it provides more visual impact in your document.

- **Match color to the tone of your document.** Colors such as dark blue, dark green, brown, and gray are better suited for highlighting within a document with a serious tone — such as a business brochure or a software user guide. On the other hand, flashier colors such as red, neon green, orange, pink, purple, and yellow are perfect for light-hearted work such as greeting cards, banners for birthdays and special events, and documents with a holiday message.

As a general rule, I try to include some use of color in every document that I create for public distribution. Even a simple letter or memo looks much more polished and professional with a simple rectangle of color at the top and bottom, or as a highlight under my return address. It takes only a second to add that finishing touch.

Printing Web Pages

If you've been surfing around the globe on the World Wide Web, you've probably encountered pages that have made you laugh and pages that have made you angry — but occasionally you'll jump to a page that takes your breath away with the beauty of its images. You may be looking at the Louvre in Paris, or the Metropolitan Museum of Art, or the National Geographic Web site — or you may be entranced by the NASCAR Hall of Fame or a page devoted to your favorite movie star.

Whatever your tastes, most of us have wanted at one time or another to capture images, text, or the content of an entire Web page on our printers. Some browsers make the printing process harder than others, and some of the proprietary programs and plug-ins used on the Web to provide animation, fancy buttons, and nifty controls can also wreak havoc on your browser when you try to print the page. I demonstrate how to print individual images, blocks of text, and an entire page of text in a separate project in Chapter 12. For now, though, I provide you with some guidelines for printing material from the Web:

- **Avoid printing animated GIF images.** Animated images are all over the Web now, and some of them are very well done. However, it's almost impossible to print a specific frame of an animated GIF with just your Web browser because these programs were not meant to provide instant screen captures. To print an individual frame of an animated GIF (or to print each of the frames in sequence), you need a program such as GIF Construction Set from Alchemy Mindworks (www.mindworkshop.com). As shown in Figure 9.13, this shareware program can display and save each frame as an individual file for printing later with a program such as Paint Shop Pro.

- **Be aware that older Web browsers may not print Java controls.** I always recommend that my consulting customers upgrade to the latest version of their favorite Web browser. Believe it or not, HTML and multimedia technology on the Web is advancing so fast that you'll likely miss out on displaying and printing the contents of many pages if you're using a browser you installed as little as a year ago. Here's an example: if you're using Netscape Navigator 3.0 or Internet Explorer 3 on either the PC or the Macintosh, many Java and JavaScript controls won't load, and you won't be able to access those links; plus, you often won't be able to print a page that contains these controls.

- **Download the proprietary plug-ins.** "Do I *really* have to download that 13MB proprietary animation plug-in file just to print this page?" Sorry, but I think you probably already know the answer to that question. You may be able to cut and paste text to Notepad and print text from there, but if you want to view, capture, or print the entire contents of the page as intended by the page's author, you'll have to take the time to download the plug-in required by your browser.

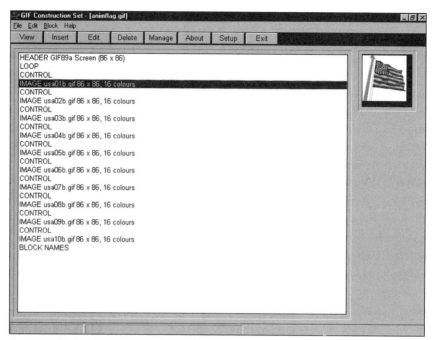

Figure 9.13 Displaying an individual frame of an animated GIF with GIF Construction Set.

Tip

From time-to-time, you may run across a plug-in with animation that can't be printed through your browser's regular Print Window function. If you have to capture the data on that screen and your browser steadfastly refuses to do so, then pull out a screen capture program such as Paint Shop Pro (available for shareware download at www.jasc.com), and capture it to a GIF or JPEG image. Then you can print the image to achieve the same result as if you had printed it from your browser.

■ **Watch those colors!** Unfortunately, not everyone that places a new site on the Web has the same taste in color—and you're likely to encounter pages with dark red text on black, or yellow text on a white background. If you want to print the text from one of these pages, set your printer to monochrome or grayscale mode if possible (avoid printing one of these pages in color because you're likely to waste ink on a page that's practically unreadable). If you print in monochrome or grayscale, the text should at least be clear enough to read; also, check to see if your browser has a setting that prints all text (regardless of its color onscreen) as black text.

Tip

If you're looking for a quick copy of a Web page, use your printer driver's Print in Grayscale option to produce a simple black-and-white document — you won't have to wait longer for color that you don't need!

■ **Use landscape mode when printing Web images.** Many browsers can automatically resize an image to fit the dimensions of the paper you've loaded, so if you select landscape mode, your printer can produce a much bigger image. This tip is especially useful if you're printing a huge, high-resolution JPEG image from the Web; in portrait mode, that image will likely lose detail.

■ **Add a header or footer to your Web page printouts.** If your browser enables you to print information such as the Web URL address, the page name, and the date and time, make sure you have this feature enabled (it's already turned on in Internet Explorer and Netscape Navigator by default). I've found that this printed information is very convenient if you need to return to that page in the future, and you haven't added it to your Favorites or Bookmark file.

If you're printing high-quality color images from a Web page, I assume that you want that hard copy image to look as good as possible. If so, make sure that you use premium glossy paper for your inkjet device so that you get the best color reproduction.

Tip

Does your browser enable you to control the size of your display and printing fonts? If so, you can adjust this value to view (and subsequently print) text from Web pages at larger or smaller sizes. For example, in Internet Explorer, click View, click Text Size, and choose the Largest setting.

Checking out Popular Printing Software

Most of the printing projects I've discussed in this chapter are much easier and much more enjoyable if you have software especially written for that printing application. For example, you can print basic business cards with your word processing program (or even with a basic text editor such as Microsoft's Notepad), but a program written for designing business cards automatically formats your text and graphics to fit in the dimensions of a business card. It also automatically replicates your design so that you can print an entire sheet of identical cards at one time. Plus, the business card printing program probably includes a number of predesigned cards that you can use or modify.

Dozens of specialized printing programs covering all of the business and hobby applications discussed in this chapter have come onto the market as a result of the inkjet printer's popularity. To give you some idea of what's out there, in this section I review some of the best-known printing software packages.

Your Printing Suite

What's the easiest way to design the printed materials I've discussed in this chapter? As I said earlier, you can use a simple word processor to print most of these items, but you save both time and trouble by using an application especially designed for printing. You can buy separate specialized printing applications — each of which can create one type of item — and run each as necessary. Using a specialized printing application makes sense if you're interested in printing only a specific item, such as greeting cards, T-shirts, or business cards.

On the other hand, many software companies offer printing *suites* that can produce *all* of the printed items mentioned in this chapter, and the prices on these suites are now as low as the price for one of those specialized printing programs. Printing suites are good choices for families, an entire office, or any person who might print many different items on many different materials. Some of the most popular printing suites date back to the days of dot-matrix printers, when they produced only simple folded cards, signs, and banners.

Printing suites are popular with PC owners these days for several reasons:

- **Uniform interface.** Although you may be printing several different materials and items with a single program, the user interface and all of the commands remain the same. Once you've learned how to print, or resize text, or include a clip art image, that process is the same whether you're creating Christmas cards or business cards, banners, or CD-ROM labels.

- **One purchase, one installation, one configuration.** You can install four or five applications that, taken together, perform all the functions of a printing suite (and some of them may offer more features than the suite can offer), but be prepared to install four or five separate applications. If you have to reconfigure your printer or — heaven forbid — you change your printer's options, you won't find yourself reconfiguring each one of your programs.

- **More extras.** Many suites, such as Print Artist Platinum, come packed with literally thousands of clip art images, borders, photographs, and fonts that enable you to create just about anything printed that you can imagine. Individual programs simply don't include such a broad range of resources — in fact, Print Artist Platinum even includes bundled applications such as an image editor and a photo manipulation program.

A printing suite for adults

When you're evaluating a printing suite for office or family use, I recommend that you check to make sure that the following features are included. I use my favorite printing suite, Print Artist Platinum from Sierra (www.sierra.com), as an example.

- **Sample clip art and fonts.** Most of us don't have a huge library of clip art or a large number of fonts loaded — and these are the "building blocks" of good printed materials. Therefore, the more clip art and the more fonts included with your printing suite, the better. Print Artist Platinum includes a whopping 32,000 clip art graphics: 7,000 photos, and 300 fonts. With a selection such as that, an all-in-one printing package such as Print Artist Platinum can even fulfill the needs of an entire school or large office.

- **Predesigned layouts.** You'll find it's much easier to use an existing layout as a foundation for a new document. The layout includes default fonts, colors, and graphics that are already arranged, so all you generally have to do is change a few words to personalize your printing. With one of the 2,500 predesigned layouts that ship with Print Artist Platinum (which cover every type of printed item you can create with the program), you are ready to print within two or three minutes of running the program.

- **Special text effects.** The better printing suites enable you to apply special visual effects to the fonts you use on your printed materials. These effects are usually found only in graphics editors and desktop publishing programs, but they come in handy when you're creating a design to print. Print Artist Platinum includes common text effects such as font warping, text rotation, and 3-D shadows, as shown in Figure 9.14.

- **Calendar generator and event tracker.** If your printing suite offers the capability to print calendars and daybook pages, it should be able to automatically generate weekly, monthly, and yearly calendars. I also appreciate an event tracker, which not only adds holidays to calendar and daybook pages but also enables you to enter your own special days that appear when you print these pages.

- **Quotes and verses for greeting cards.** Let's face it, "Roses are red" doesn't cut it anymore. Print Artist Platinum includes more than 1,000 verses that you can add to your greeting cards . . . and, if you like, you can always change a word or two to customize the verse you've selected.

Another example of a popular printing suite that has stood the test of time is PrintMaster Deluxe, from Mindscape (www.mindscape.com). Like Print Artist, PrintMaster Deluxe prints most of the items I mention in this chapter, along with fax coversheets, simple Web pages, and newsletters. Kids can create masks, hand puppets, and bookmarks. PrintMaster Deluxe features stock photographs from National Geographic among more than 10,000 images and more than 2,000 pieces of clip art. The suite also offers a unique voice help feature — a human voice guides you through simple tasks and provides tips and tricks on using the interface. Figure 9.15 illustrates PrintMaster (Gold) in action.

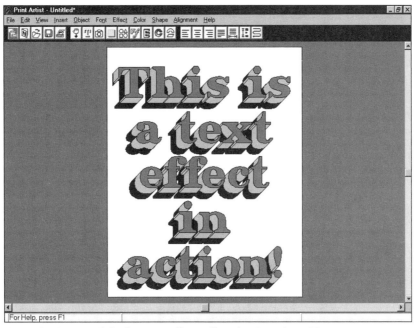

Figure 9.14 One of the font text effects offered in Print Artist Platinum

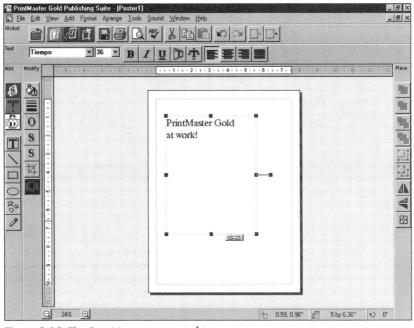

Figure 9.15 The PrintMaster user interface

A printing suite for kids

If your children like to use your printing suite to create their own items, you may want to consider buying a printing suite especially designed for kids. A great example of a kid's printing suite is the Disney Print Studio, which is distributed by Hewlett-Packard with many of its printers. These child-oriented printing suites usually include:

■ **Clip art for kids.** Naturally, the Disney Print Studio includes clip art with very recognizable faces: Mickey Mouse, Donald Duck, and their friends appearing both separately and together. Other printing suites from Disney have featured characters from popular Disney movies, such as *The Little Mermaid*, *101 Dalmatians*, and *The Lion King*. Figure 9.16 shows a small example of the clip art from the Disney Print Studio.

Figure 9.16 Kid-oriented clip art from the Disney Print Studio

■ **School-oriented projects.** The projects in a kid's print studio usually concentrate on items that can be used at school or around the house: bookmarks, book covers, diary pages, and placemats, for instance. Not much here for the business owner, so you won't be using one of these programs to print business cards.

■ **Easy-to-use interface.** These applications are designed to be easy to use, so they typically offer less control over fonts and clip art options, and little or no special effects. Because fewer advanced features also mean fewer requirements for help and adult supervision, this is probably a good thing.

Your Image Editor

Today's image-editing program is much like a graphical Swiss Army knife — it takes care of a wide range of tasks. For example, take a close look at Paint Shop Pro from Jasc Software, which has always been my favorite image-editing program. The program first appeared in the days before the Internet, when practically every online *bulletin board system* (popularly called a BBS) offered it as downloadable shareware. Like any graphics editor, it provided the basic functions that everyone wanted in those early days, such as image cropping and resizing, format conversion, the capability to add text to an image, and the capability to change the brightness and contrast of any picture.

However, Paint Shop Pro has grown along with the popularity of high-resolution graphics on the PC, and now it includes a host of other impressive features that set it apart. The program can acquire images from a scanner or digital camera, and it can capture screen images produced by Windows programs. The Browse function makes it easy to build a catalog of image thumbnails from any folder on your hard drive. You can reduce or increase the number of colors in an image, add a border, reverse the colors, or even change a color image into a grayscale image. Naturally, Paint Shop Pro enables you to edit the individual pixels in an image with a large range of brush shapes (including airbrush and fill tools), so you can touch up a defect or remove something from the background. The latest version of Paint Shop Pro also supports Photoshop-compatible plug-ins, so you can use all sorts of third-party commercial graphics filters for spectacular special effects. Figure 9.17 shows Paint Shop Pro at work.

Paint Shop Pro is also no slouch when it comes to printing images. Besides the standard print preview function, this program can perform many neat tricks on your hard copy. For example, I really like the automatic sizing feature, where the program can automatically expand an image to fit the full dimensions of the paper you're using. With Paint Shop Pro you can print an entire folder of images in thumbnail format, including the filename along with each image. You can add alignment marks for color separations, rotate the printed image, and even create a negative print with all the colors reversed.

The free evaluation version of Paint Shop Pro is available from Jasc Software's Web site at `www.jasc.com`; you can use it for 30 days, and I bet you'll find it valuable enough to register. I use it whenever I need to print a single image, or whenever I need to create a hard copy catalog of thumbnails for a collection of images.

Figure 9.17 Paint Shop Pro can apply mind-boggling special effects to any image.

Your CD-ROM Label Printer

As I mentioned earlier in the chapter, if you record your own CD-R discs for distribution, or you just want your finished discs to look more professional, you can use a CD-ROM label applicator such as the NEATO machine to add an adhesive paper label. These labels can be printed on any inkjet or laser printer, so you can create CD-R labels with full-color high-resolution graphics. A standard CD-R label sheet carries three disc labels and a number of smaller labels for the outside of the CD jewel case.

I use Design Express from MicroVision Development (www.mvd.com) to create CD-R labels. It offers many of the powerful features you'd normally associate with a desktop publishing program or a computer drawing package. You can twist and turn text into all sorts of interesting shapes, and you can select the size, color, and shading for any font. For example, one of my favorite tricks is to run the title of a disc in a circular shape around the outside of the label and then add shadow effects to provide a 3-D effect. Of course, you can also import clip art and place it anywhere on the page. Figure 9.18 shows the Design Express interface, complete with an array of drawing tools.

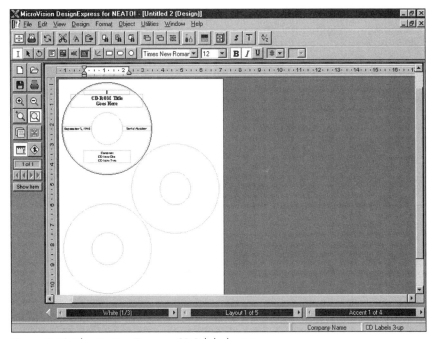

Figure 9.18 The Design Express CD-R label-printing program

Because most CD-R labels come in three colors — white, gold, and silver — the program provides several different predefined label designs for each color, but you can build your own design from scratch in a few minutes. Naturally, it also pays to invest in a large number of fonts and clip art with musical themes to match every mood of your audio CDs.

Most CD label-printing programs can also print the front and back inserts for your CD-ROM jewel case — if you're recording your own audio CD, why not add a colorful cover for the front and a music track list on the back? You print these inserts on regular paper (or high-gloss inkjet paper) and cut them to fit.

For the ultimate in CD printing, however, you can invest in a CD screen printer. These specialized inkjet printers actually use screen printing techniques to "paint" a permanent label on the top side of your recorded CDs. Be prepared to pay a considerable amount for one of these printers, though.

Summary

This chapter introduced a number of fun and rewarding projects you can create using your printer and one of several printing applications. You learned tips and tricks that you can apply when printing items in color and designing paper materials for your company. We covered the features of several different programs you may use for printing, as well as how to capture and print text and images from a Web page. You found out how to use clip art in your document. You also discovered how you can use digital images in your printing projects.

In the next chapter, I provide you with several step-by-step projects to help you upgrade and maintain inkjet printers, laser printers, and all-in-one units.

Printer Projects

CHAPTER 10

Inkjet, Laser, and All-in-One Unit Projects

IN THIS CHAPTER • Using the typical features found on inkjet printers, laser printers, and all-in-ones

• Maintaining your printer

• Upgrading your printer

In this chapter, you find step-by-step projects that show how to use typical features found on most inkjet printers, laser printers, and all-in-one peripherals. You also perform common maintenance tasks for these devices, as well as learn hardware upgrade procedures.

Although I list a specific HP model in the list of materials for each set of projects, you should be able to substitute whatever similar printer or unit you use.

Before you begin any procedure, make sure you read your printer's documentation for warnings or specific instructions that may apply to your specific model.

Inkjet Projects

In this section, I discuss some features of typical inkjet printers. Then I describe a number of step-by-step projects that illustrate how to perform simple maintenance tasks to keep your inkjet printer running like the day you bought it.

MATERIALS

HP DeskJet 722C

Paper suitable for an inkjet printer

Inkjet cartridge

Note

If you have another model or brand of printer, don't skip these projects. Although your printer's driver and utility software may use different names for dialog boxes, buttons, and commands, you should still be able to follow along and perform the same tasks.

Adjusting Print Quality

The HP DeskJet 722C has three different levels of print quality, and you can adjust them for each document that you print.

Follow these steps to select a print quality before printing from a Windows 98 application:

1. From within your Windows 98 application — let's use Microsoft Word as an example — select File ⇨ Print to display the Print dialog box shown in Figure 10.1. If your printer does not automatically appear as the default, click the Name drop-down listbox and click the desired printer name.

2. Click the Properties button to display the Properties dialog box for your printer. Although Figure 10.2 illustrates the Properties dialog box for the HP DeskJet 722C, your printer should have a similar dialog box (it may take some searching to locate it, but you should find print quality controls).

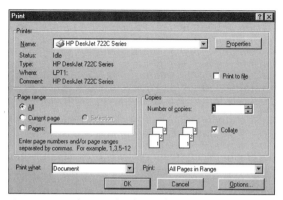

Figure 10.1 The standard Windows 98 Print dialog box

3. The three print quality settings are Best, Normal, and EconoFast. If you want the best possible monochrome text and color graphics print quality for a document, click Best. Most final draft documents use Normal print quality. If you're producing a fast hard copy or a first draft, click EconoFast for the fastest possible print speed and the most economical use of ink. To change all values on this dialog box to their default settings, click the Default button.

4. Click OK to return to the Print dialog box. Remember, any changes you've made to your printer's print quality affect only the document you are printing. The print quality setting reverts to the default quality setting after you print the document.

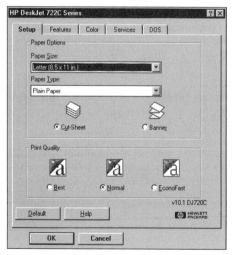

Figure 10.2 The Windows 98 Properties dialog box for the HP DeskJet 722C printer

Adjusting Paper Size and Type

Follow these steps to select the proper paper size and type before printing from a Windows 98 application:

1. Select File ➪ Print from within your Windows 98 application to display the Print dialog box. If your printer does not automatically appear as the default, click the Name drop-down listbox and click the desired printer name.

2. Click the Properties button to display the Properties dialog box.

3. Click the Paper Size drop-down listbox and click the paper size for the document; the default paper size is standard letter size, 8½×11 inches.

4. Next, click the Paper Type drop-down listbox to select the type of paper to use for the document. The default paper type is plain paper.

5. Click OK to return to the Print dialog box. If you made any changes to the paper size or type, remember that the values you chose affect only the document you are printing; the paper size and type settings revert to the default quality settings after you print it.

Using Duplex Mode

If you're using a new printer that provides automatic two-sided printing, like the HP DeskJet 970 or the HP PhotoSmart 1218, you won't have to follow these steps. Check your printer's manual to see if your printer has an automatic duplex mode.

If you need to set duplex mode manually, follow these steps to print a two-sided document from within your Windows 98 application:

1. Select File ➪ Print from within your Windows 98 application to display the Print dialog box. If your printer does not automatically appear as the default, click the Name drop-down listbox and click the desired printer name.

2. Click the Properties button to display the Properties dialog box.

3. If you're using an HP DeskJet 722C, click the Features tab to display the dialog box shown in Figure 10.3.

4. Click the desired duplex mode: click None to select single-sided pages, click Book to print pages facing at the sides, or click Tablet to print pages facing at the top and bottom. The default duplex mode is None.

5. Click OK to return to the Print dialog box. The duplex mode you choose affects only this document.

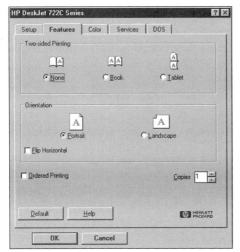

Figure 10.3 The Features tab of the Properties dialog box displayed by the HP DeskJet 722C printer driver

Choosing Landscape or Portrait Orientation

If you need to set a specific document to print in landscape orientation, follow these steps:

1. Select File ⇨ Page Setup from within your Windows 98 application to display the Page Setup dialog box.

2. Click the Paper Size tab.

3. The default orientation is Portrait. (When you click a radio button, the icon to the left and the preview to the right demonstrate each page orientation.) To print the open document in landscape mode, click Landscape.

4. Click OK to return to the application. The orientation you choose affects only this document.

Printing Multiple Copies

Follow these steps to print multiple copies of a document within your Windows 98 application:

1. Select File ⇨ Print from within your Windows 98 application to display the Print dialog box. If your printer does not automatically appear as the default, click the Name drop-down listbox and click the desired printer name.

2. Click the Number of Copies field and select the number of copies to print.

3. Click OK to begin printing. The number of copies you choose to print affects only this document.

Collating Copies

Follow these steps to collate one or more copies of a document within your Windows 98 application:

1. Select File ⇨ Print from within your Windows 98 application to display the Print dialog box. If your printer does not automatically appear as the default, click the Name drop-down listbox and click the desired printer name.

2. Click the Collate check box to enable it.

3. Click OK to begin printing. The collation mode you choose affects only this document.

If you have an HP DeskJet 722C, you can also enable the Ordered Printing check box from the Features tab on the printer's Properties dialog box. With both Ordered Printing and Collation toggled on, you can print multiple copies of a multiple-page document in collated order.

Cleaning Your Inkjet Print Head

Does cleaning the nozzles on your inkjet printer's print head sound like a complex and messy process? I'm happy to report that there's no hassle involved for most inkjet printers — you don't even need to take the cartridges out of your printer, and everything is handled through software.

Follow these steps to clean the print head on the HP DeskJet 722C from Windows 98:

1. Click the HP DeskJet 722C Toolbox icon on your desktop (or click the Start menu and select Programs ⇨ HP DeskJet 722C ⇨ Toolbox). The Toolbox dialog box appears.

2. Click the Printer Services tab, as shown in Figure 10.4.

3. Click the Clean the Print Cartridges button, or click Cancel to return to the Toolbox dialog box.

4. The Toolbox program performs an initial cleaning, which is usually enough to restore your ink cartridges to their best performance. The cleaning process produces a test page, which you should examine.

Figure 10.4 The Printer Services tab from the HP DeskJet 722C Toolbox

5. If the initial cleaning did the trick, click Done. If you feel the initial cleaning was not thorough enough, the next step is to perform an intermediate cleaning (see Figure 10.5). Click the Intermediate Clean button. The cleaning process produces another page for you to examine.

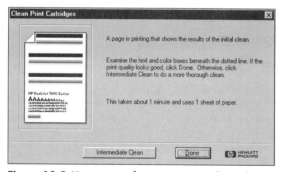

Figure 10.5 You can perform an intermediate cleaning of your inkjet print heads from this dialog box.

6. If you feel the intermediate cleaning was sufficient, click Done. Otherwise, you can choose to prime the inkjet cartridges, which is effective if one of the nozzles is nearly or completely clogged. Click Prime to start the process. Priming takes a significant amount of ink, so prime your cartridges as a last resort.

7. Click Done to return to the Toolbox dialog box.

Aligning Cartridges

You should align your cartridges whenever you insert a new one (even if you think your printed documents look okay). Some all-in-one units prompt you when a new cartridge is inserted, and you start the process by pressing a button on the front panel.

Tip

Some new printers — for example, the HP DeskJet 932 — align the cartridge automatically when you install it, so they don't require this process. Check your printer's manual to see if you need to align the cartridges manually.

1. Click the HP DeskJet 722C Toolbox icon on your desktop (or click the Start menu and select Programs ➪ HP DeskJet 722C ➪ Toolbox). The Toolbox dialog box appears.

2. Click the Printer Services tab.

3. Click the Align the Printer Cartridges button.

   The Toolbox program produces a test page with two rows of double parallel lines. Select the two pairs of lines that align the best on the test page, and click the corresponding values on the screen.

4. The Toolbox program prints a test page with a number of graphic and font examples; you should examine this page to verify that the alignment you set was correct.

5. Click Done to return to the Toolbox dialog box.

Testing Printer Communications

As I mentioned earlier in the book, most printers sold today require an IEEE-1284 bidirectional printer cable. With an older cable that doesn't support this standard, your printer is unable to send messages back to your PC, and many of your printer's advanced features do not work correctly.

Cross-Reference

See the section "Printer Cables" in Chapter 1 to learn more about the various types of printer cables.

The HP DeskJet 722C Toolbox program includes a nifty feature: a function to test your printer port and cable to make sure bidirectional communication is working properly. To test your PC-printer communications, follow these steps:

1. Click the HP DeskJet 722C Toolbox icon on your desktop (or click the Start menu and select Programs ➪ HP DeskJet 722C ➪ Toolbox). The Toolbox dialog box appears.

2. Click the Printer Services tab.

3. Click the Test Printer Communications button.

   The Toolbox program displays the dialog box shown in Figure 10.6, and an animated status bar is updated to indicate the progress of the test.

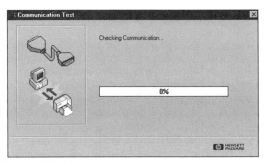

Figure 10.6 The Toolbox program can test communications between the HP DeskJet 722C and your computer.

4. The Toolbox program reports the status of the PC-printer communications link. If an error message displays, consult Appendix A at the end of this book.

5. Click Done to return to the Toolbox dialog box.

Changing Inkjet Cartridges

All inkjet printers share one process with almost exactly the same steps: changing inkjet cartridges. Follow these steps to change the cartridge on your HP DeskJet 722C printer:

1. Turn your printer on and open the top cover — on most HP inkjet printers, opening the top cover centers the print heads for easier access.

2. Lift the latches to remove the old cartridges. Pull the cartridges up and forward to remove them, leaving the latches in the upright position.

3. Remove the new cartridges from their packages and peel off the vinyl tape that protects the ink nozzles and print head. *Do not touch the print head* — it's extremely easy to damage!

4. Push each cartridge into the correct slot — note that the color and black-and-white cartridges carry different symbols — and push the latches down to secure the new cartridges.

5. Close the top cover and check the print cartridge light — it should turn off after a few seconds, indicating that the cartridges have been properly installed. If the light doesn't go out or blinks, reinstall both cartridges.

6. Follow the instructions in the previous section, "Aligning Cartridges," to complete the installation process.

Printing from a Digital Memory Card

MATERIALS

HP PhotoSmart 1100 or 1100xi

Paper suitable for an inkjet printer (glossy high-resolution photo paper, such as HP Premium Plus Photo Paper)

Inkjet cartridge

The latest generation of photo-quality inkjet printers include a number of features designed specifically for those of us with digital cameras. As I mentioned earlier in the book, the HP PhotoSmart 1100 inkjet printer allows you to print photographs directly from the standard memory cards used by digital cameras (even without a connection to your PC)!

Follow these steps to print directly from a CompactFlash (CFA) or SmartMedia memory card using the HP PhotoSmart 1100 printer:

1. Turn your printer on and load it with the desired paper — naturally, you want to use glossy high-resolution photo paper for the best results. Because the HP PhotoSmart 1100 has a built-in 4×6 paper tray, you can also use specialized 4×6 postcard stock. Remember, printers like the HP PhotoSmart 1100 don't have to be connected to your computer to print directly from a memory card.

2. Plug the memory card into the correct slot on your printer; SmartMedia cards go in the top slot, whereas CompactFlash cards go in the bottom slot. *Remember to always insert the memory card with the pin-holes (or the edge with the connectors) first!*

3. Once the printer has finished reading the contents of the card and displays the completion message, press the No button on the printer's front panel until the display reads **ALL PHOTOS – 1 copy – Index.** Make sure that the 4×6 paper tray is not engaged, and that you have plain paper loaded. Press the Print button to print an index page.

4. Use the thumbnail images on the index page to determine which digital photographs you'd like to print.

5. Press the Choose Photos button until the index number of the first photo that you want to print appears. (Alternately, if you want to print all of the pictures, simply choose the All option.) Press the OK button sto mark the photo.

6. If you're printing only selected images, repeat Step 5 until you've marked all of the images you want to print.

7. Once you've marked all your photos for printing, press OK.

8. Choose the desired size for your photographs by pressing the Photo Size button until the proper size appears on the display — note that this is not necessarily the same as your paper size!

9. Specify the number of copies by pressing the Copies button until the proper number appears on the display.

10. Press the Print button.

LaserJet Projects

Most laser printers are actually very similar under the skin, and you should be able to perform these projects on just about any model from any manufacturer (with one exception — you may not be able to add resident fonts through cartridges).

MATERIALS

HP LaserJet 1100

Paper towels

Q-tips

Alcohol or a cleaner recommended by the printer manufacturer

Toner cartridge

Laser printer cleaning sheet

Adding Printer Memory

If you have an older printer, an external module that you plug in may provide additional printer memory. Today's models usually require you to open your laser printer's case to add more RAM in the same fashion that you add it to your PC's motherboard.

Installing an external RAM module

If your laser printer accepts additional RAM in the form of a plug-in external module, follow these general steps to upgrade your printer's memory:

1. Turn your laser printer off.

2. Locate the memory upgrade slot on your printer (you'll usually find it on the back of the machine). Check your printer's manual for the proper orientation and push the RAM cartridge into the slot. Remember, if the cartridge doesn't seem to fit, don't force it — check your manual again to make sure you're installing it properly.

3. Turn on your laser printer and check to see if it makes use of the new RAM. One way to do so is to check your printer's information page, which is usually printed once by default each time you turn on your laser printer (it typically includes the amount of on-board memory). Alternately, run your printer's setup utility, or check the Property panel within the printer's Properties dialog box. If your printer does not seem to recognize the additional RAM, turn your printer off and remove the module. Then consult your printer's manual for something you may have missed during the installation, and try again.

Installing internal RAM

If your laser printer must be upgraded with standard internal RAM modules, follow these general steps to add memory to your printer:

1. Turn your laser printer off and unplug it from the wall.

2. Follow the instructions in your printer's manual to open your printer's case and locate the memory upgrade slot. If your printer uses standard SIMM (*Single Inline Memory Module*) memory, face the front of the slot and position the SIMM in the slot as shown in Figure 10.7, with the notch aligned to your left and the metal contacts on the bottom of the module aligned with the contacts in the slot. If your printer uses proprietary RAM with a different size or shape, check your manual for instructions on how to position it.

3. If your printer uses standard SIMM memory, push the module back toward the back of the slot until it clicks into place, as illustrated in Figure 10.8.

4. Next, turn on your laser printer and check to see if it recognizes the new RAM. Check your printer's information page, run your printer's setup utility, or check the Property panel within the printer's Properties dialog box. If your printer does not seem to recognize the RAM upgrade, turn your printer off, consult your printer's manual for something you may have missed during the installation, and try again.

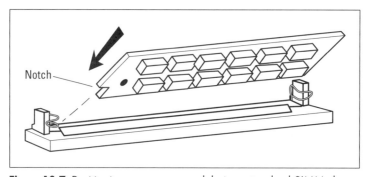

Figure 10.7 Positioning a memory module in a standard SIMM slot

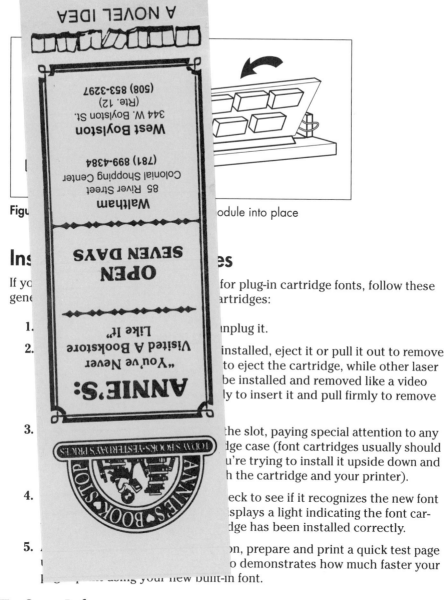

Figu... ...odule into place

Ins... ...es

If yo... ...for plug-in cartridge fonts, follow these
gene... ...artridges:

1. ... ...nplug it.

2. ... ...installed, eject it or pull it out to remove
   ... ...to eject the cartridge, while other laser
   ... ...be installed and removed like a video
   ... ...ly to insert it and pull firmly to remove

3. ... ...he slot, paying special attention to any
   ... ...dge case (font cartridges usually should
   ... ...u're trying to install it upside down and
   ... ...h the cartridge and your printer).

4. ... ...eck to see if it recognizes the new font
   ... ...splays a light indicating the font car-
   ... ...dge has been installed correctly.

5. ... ...on, prepare and print a quick test page
   ... ...o demonstrates how much faster your
   ... ...using your new built-in font.

Cross-Reference

This book devotes an entire chapter all to fonts. Learn everything you ever wanted
to know about fonts and discover the possibilities they hold for accommodating
your creative side in Chapter 8, "The Wonderful World of Fonts."

Changing Toner Cartridges

Although the shape and size of your laser printer's toner cartridge may differ from the HP LaserJet's 1100, the general procedure you use to change toner cartridges should be similar to the steps I outline here.

1. Turn your laser printer off and unplug it. Open the cartridge door.

2. Turn or lift any latches to remove the old cartridge; pull the cartridge backward. Remember, some older printers use cartridges that can spill toner if you tilt the cartridge too far up or down.

3. Remove the new cartridge from its packaging. Some cartridges require you to pull a tape strip to allow toner to escape, others require you to move a lever, while others open automatically when they're correctly installed. Check your laser printer's user manual or the documentation that accompanied the toner cartridge for the specific steps for your model. It's a good idea to gently rock the cartridge forward and backward, which spreads the toner across the transfer roller and helps extend the life of the cartridge.

4. Push the new cartridge into the empty slot and push any retaining latches down to secure the new cartridge.

5. Close the cartridge cover, plug the printer back into the AC socket, turn on your laser printer, and check the toner level or cartridge light. It should register full, indicating the cartridge has been installed correctly. If the cartridge light still indicates that toner is low, reinstall the toner cartridge and make sure that it has snapped completely into place.

6. If you have a laser printer cleaning sheet, this is a good time to run it through your laser printer to trap any spilled toner.

Cleaning Corona Wires

Most older laser printers have exposed corona wires, and they must be cleaned periodically to provide the best possible printing. Unfortunately, these wires are usually buried deep within the innards of your printer, and they are extremely easy to break or damage. Here is a general set of steps for cleaning the corona wires on most laser printers — first, of course, you should check your printer's documentation for any warnings or specific do's and don'ts concerning these wires.

Follow these steps:

1. Turn your laser printer off and unplug it. (If you're working in a brightly lit room, turn down your room lights to prevent damaging the photosensitive cartridge.) Open the cartridge door for ventilation and allow it to sit for about 15 minutes before proceeding, which cools down your printer somewhat.

2   Turn or lift any latches to remove the cartridge and pull the cartridge backward. (Remember, older laser printers have cartridges that can spill toner if you tilt the cartridge too far up or down.) Place the cartridge on a clean paper towel and cover it with another paper towel. Once the cartridge is removed, you can open the cartridge door as far as possible.

3.   Locate the corona wires inside the body of your laser printer — they generally look like five or six short lengths of fine fishing line strung between two rods, as shown in Figure 10.9.

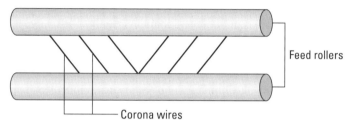

Figure 10.9 A set of corona wires from a typical laser printer

4   Using a clean, dry cotton swab, gently dust each wire. Don't forget the underside of the wire, and *do not* use any alcohol or chemicals (these can damage the wires or leave residue that can interfere with their function).

5.   Reload the toner cartridge, close the cartridge cover, plug your machine back in, and turn on your laser printer.

6.   If you have a laser printer cleaning sheet, this is a good time to run it through your laser printer to trap any spilled toner.

Tip

Naturally, it's a good idea to perform the next project, cleaning the paper feed rollers on your laser printer, at the same time that you're doing this task. If you're like me, you prefer to take care of as many maintenance tasks on your computer hardware at one time as possible. So plan ahead and take care of everything that needs maintenance at once.

Cleaning Paper Feed Rollers

If your printer's manual mentions that you can clean the paper feed rollers inside your laser printer, you can follow these general steps for cleaning them. As always,

I recommend that you consult your printer manual for any specific instructions about cleaning the paper feed rollers on your printer before you begin.

1. Turn your laser printer off, unplug it, and turn down any bright room lights to prevent damage to the photosensitive cartridge. Open the cartridge door for ventilation and allow it to sit for about 15 minutes before continuing, which cools down your printer somewhat.

2. Turn or lift any latches to remove the cartridge and pull the cartridge backward, making sure that you don't tilt the cartridge, which may spill toner. Place the cartridge on a clean paper towel and cover it with another paper towel. Now, open the cartridge door as far as possible.

3. Locate the exposed paper feed rollers inside the body of your laser printer — once again, your laser printer manual may identify the rollers you can safely clean and provide suggestions on which cleaning solvents you may use.

4. Using a cotton swab dipped in alcohol or other approved solvent, gently rub the exposed surface of each roller, as shown in Figure 10.10. Take care not to turn the rollers by hand, as this can cause alignment problems and may damage the mechanism.

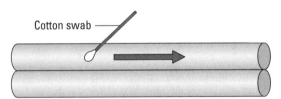

Cotton swab

Figure 10.10 Cleaning the paper feed rollers on a typical laser printer

5. Reload the toner cartridge, close the cartridge cover, plug the machine back in, and turn on your laser printer.

6. If you have a laser printer cleaning sheet, this is a good time to run it through your laser printer to trap any spilled toner.

All-in-One Unit Projects

In this section, I provide step-by-step instructions for common all-in-one tasks, using a laser printer as an example. Because all-in-ones use both laser and inkjet technology, I've also included references to common inkjet procedures described earlier in this chapter.

MATERIALS

HP LaserJet 3100

Paper suitable for your all-in-one

Document to scan

Toner cartridge

Laser printer cleaning sheet

Note

Even if you don't have an all-in-one from Hewlett-Packard, you'll find these same general procedures apply to just about any brand and model of sheetfed all-in-one unit. Refer to your manual for more detailed information on performing these tasks.

Sending and Receiving Faxes

Follow these steps to send a fax under software control with the HP LaserJet 3100:

1. Load the document into the paper feed tray.

2. The machine detects that you've loaded paper, and the JetSuite software Document Assistant automatically runs.

3. Click the Document Assistant dialog box to select it and click Fax.

4 The JetSuite software displays the Send Fax dialog box shown in Figure 10.11, where you can enter the information identifying the recipient of the fax. (Remember that it is considered common courtesy to include a cover sheet.)

5. Click Send Fax to start dialing.

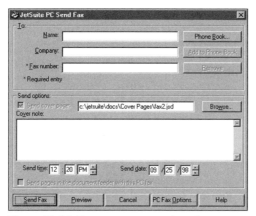

Figure 10.11 Entering recipient data for an outgoing fax

Follow these steps to receive an incoming fax:

1. Load paper into the paper input bin.

2. If you answer the telephone and hear the connection tones of a fax machine, hit the Start button on the unit's front panel to manually begin receiving the document.

3. If you've set the HP LaserJet 3100 to automatically answer after a specified number of rings, it picks up the call during the next ring after the specified value and handles any incoming fax (by default, the machine is set to take the incoming call after the fifth ring).

Scanning a Document

Need to scan a document? Follow these steps to scan text or graphics under software control with the HP LaserJet 3100:

1. Load the document you wish to scan into the paper feed tray.

2. The unit detects that you've loaded paper, and the JetSuite software Document Assistant automatically runs.

3. Click the Document Assistant dialog box to select it and click Scan.

4. The JetSuite software displays the Scan dialog box, where you can select the scan resolution.

5. Click Scan to start the scan process.

Using the Copy Function

To copy a document under software control, follow these steps:

1. Load the document into the paper feed tray.

2. The unit detects that you've loaded paper, and the JetSuite software Document Assistant automatically runs.

3. Click the Document Assistant dialog box to select it and click Copy.

4. The JetSuite software displays the Copy Settings dialog box shown in Figure 10.12, enabling you to set various copier options for this specific document.

5. Click Copy to start the copy process.

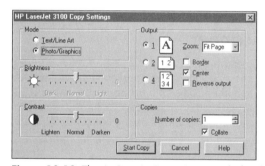

Figure 10.12 The JetSuite's Copy Settings dialog box

Changing the Toner Cartridge

If your all-in-one uses a laser printing engine, follow these steps to change the toner cartridge:

1. Turn your all-in-one off or unplug it, open the cartridge door an inch or so, and allow it to sit for about 15 minutes before proceeding; this delay cools the heated components inside.

2. Turn or lift any latches to remove the old cartridge; pull the cartridge backward. Remember, some older laser printing engines use cartridges that can spill toner if you tilt the cartridge.

3. Remove the new cartridge from its packaging. Some cartridges require you to pull a tape strip to give toner access to the rollers, whereas others open

automatically when they're correctly installed — check your documenta-tion or the documentation that accompanied the cartridge for the specific steps used with your model. It's a good idea to gently tilt the cartridge, which spreads the toner across the transfer roller and helps extend the life of the cartridge.

4. Push the new cartridge into the empty slot and push any retaining latches down to secure the new cartridge.

5. Close the cartridge cover, turn on your all-in-one unit, and check the toner level or cartridge light. It should register full, indicating the car-tridge is installed correctly. If the cartridge light still indicates that toner is low, reinstall the toner cartridge and make sure that it has snapped completely into place.

6. If you have a laser printer cleaning sheet, this is a good time to run it through your all-in-one to trap any spilled toner.

Recalibrating the Scanner

From time to time, the scanning engine in your all-in-one unit may require recalibra-tion to adjust the alignment of the scanning sensor and the feed rollers. I generally recommend that you recalibrate a sheetfed scanner once every three months. Luckily, the software that accompanies the HP LaserJet 3100 makes recalibration easy (you don't even have to open the machine's case). Follow these steps to recalibrate the scanner:

1. Select the recalibration function using the control keypad on the front panel (the unit does not have to be attached to your computer).

   The HP LaserJet 3100 automatically prints a test page to use for the calibration procedure.

2. When prompted by the software, load the test page into the document feed tray. The machine automatically loads the test page and uses the pattern printed on it to calibrate the scanning sensor.

3. Once the test page has been ejected, it can be discarded.

Summary

In this chapter, you found a number of general projects that demonstrated typical features, upgrade procedures, and maintenance tasks that apply to most inkjet printers, laser printers, and all-in-one units.

In the next chapter, you'll find a number of printer installation and networking projects.

CHAPTER 11

Printer Installation and Network Projects

IN THIS CHAPTER • Configuring a printer under Windows 98/Me (Millennium Edition)

• Printing in a Windows application

• Selecting a shared "peer-to-peer" network printer

• Removing a printer and its software

• Installing an HP JetDirect printer server

• Installing and using printer sharing and switching hardware

This chapter includes step-by-step projects that demonstrate the configuration of a printer under Windows 98 and Windows Me, the printing process within a Windows application, selecting a shared "peer-to-peer" network printer, installing an HP JetDirect printer server, removing a printer and its software, and installing and using printer sharing and switching hardware.

Your hardware installation may require additional steps. Before you begin any procedure, make sure that you read your printer and hardware documentation for any warnings or specific instructions.

Printer Installation Projects

In this section, I cover the step-by-step details on how to install a printer under Windows 98 and Windows Me. If your printer came with its own installation software to automate this process, I recommend that you run the installation program. However, the procedures here should work with just about any printer, so you can refer to them if you need to manually add a printer to your system.

MATERIALS

HP DeskJet 970C

Paper suitable for your printer

Configuring Default Printer Settings

If you need to make global changes for your printer that affect all applications under Windows 98 and Windows Me, you can modify the default settings for your printer from the Printer Properties dialog box.

Unlike the Windows 98/Me Print dialog box (which is standard for every Windows application), the Properties dialog box for a printer is displayed by the printer driver and therefore is different for each manufacturer. If you don't use an HP printer, you should be able to find most or all of the same fields and controls within just about any Printer Properties dialog box from any printer manufacturer. (Note, however, that these fields may not be named the same within the Printer Properties dialog box on your system.)

To display and/or change the global default settings for your printer under Windows 98 and Windows Me, follow these steps:

1. Click the My Computer icon to display the resources on your PC, and click the Printer folder to open it.

2. Right-click the printer icon for the printer you want to configure, and select Properties from the pop-up menu.

Windows displays the Properties dialog box for the selected printer; Figure 11.1 illustrates the Printer Properties dialog box for a typical HP DeskJet printer.

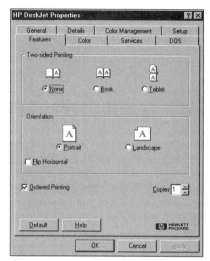

Figure 11.1 Configuring default settings for an HP DeskJet printer

The following settings are typically available for most printers under Windows 98 and Windows Me:

- **Default port.** If you reconnect your printer to another port on your PC, make sure you change this value to reflect the change and yes, laptop owners, you can have multiple ports in the drop-down listbox. You can use Add Port or Delete Port to change the available entries in this field.

- **Timeout settings.** This controls the number of seconds that your PC waits for your printer to acknowledge and process a printed page. If Windows sometimes displays a dialog box telling you that your printer has timed out, you can raise the values to give an older printer the additional processing time it needs.

- **Spool settings.** Most printer drivers enable you to turn *spooling* on and off, as well as specify the size of the spool. (Think of spooling as a "temporary memory bank" that holds your document: Windows returns you to your application as it prints the document in the background.)

- **Paper dimensions.** Typically you can specify the size and margins for a default page.

- **Paper orientation.** You can determine whether documents print in landscape or portrait mode by default.

- **Print quality.** As I discussed in earlier chapters, there's a tradeoff with most inkjet and laser printers between the best image quality and the fastest, most economical printing.

- **DOS settings.** Your printer driver may enable you to choose the font used to print output from a DOS program running in Windows within a DOS box.

3. Once you've made any desired changes, click OK to save them and exit the Printer Properties dialog box.

Printing a Document from a Windows Application

One of the attractions of Windows 98/Me is the consistency of certain menu items, including commands that control printing. Follow these steps to view and print a document from within any Windows 98 or Windows Me application:

1. Before you print, you may want to see how your document looks on the page, and many Windows applications provide a Print Preview function you can use to do that. You can scroll through your document, page by page, and get a general idea of how it looks as it's currently formatted, which can help you spot formatting errors before you print the page. Figure 11.2 illustrates the Print Preview function available within Microsoft Word — to switch to this mode, click File and click Print Preview.

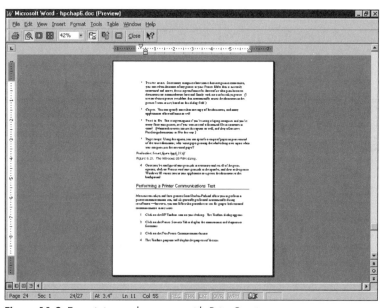

Figure 11.2 Examining a document with Print Preview

2. If everything looks okay from the Print Preview screen, click the application's File menu, and select Print.

3. The application displays the standard Windows Print dialog box (the Windows 98 dialog box is shown in Figure 11.3). The application you're using may add extra options and features to this dialog box, but all Print dialog boxes have these basic controls:

   - **Printer name.** Because many computers have more than one printer connection, you can select the name of any printer in your Printer folder that is currently connected and active. This feature is great for those of us who print business documents on a monochrome laser and family work on a color inkjet printer. (I use an electric printer switchbox that automatically routes the document to the printer I want to use, based on this dialog box field.)

Cross-Reference

If you'd like to learn more about printer switching, see the section "Adding a Switched Printer" in Chapter 7.

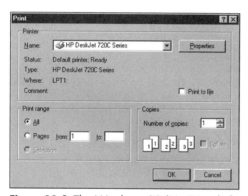

Figure 11.3 The Windows 98/Me Print dialog box

   - **Copies.** You can specify more than one copy of the document, and many applications enable collation as well.

   - **Print to file.** This option is great if you're using a laptop computer and you're away from your printer (more on this in the next section). *Print to file* is also a great way to e-mail a formatted file that is ready to print. (Macintosh owners can use this option as well, and they often save PostScript documents as files this way — as do graphics designers working on PCs.)

- Page range. Using this option, you can specify a range of pages to print instead of printing the entire document; why waste paper printing the whole thing when you can print just the pages you need?

4. Once you've configured your print job and set all the print options, click Print to send your job to the spooler and then to the printer.

Printing from a Formatted File

You can print a document to a file from most Windows 98 and Windows Me applications instead of sending it to a printer. While you're on the road with your laptop, this is a great way of preparing documents for printing later. You simply save the document to your laptop's hard drive as a print file. Once you return to your home or office, you can print the document without even opening up the application that created it! Remember that the document must be printed using the printer driver you selected from the Print dialog box; for example, you can't print a document to a file using the HP DeskJet 970C printer driver and print that document later on an HP DeskJet 2000C. (This typically isn't a problem for most of us because most PC owners have only one printer, but it is something to watch for if you have different printers at your office.)

Before you begin, reconnect your printer, turn it on, and reboot your PC (which enables Windows 98/Me to recognize that your printer has been reconnected). Then, follow this procedure to print a document that was printed to a file:

1. Locate the formatted file on your system, and note the name of the file. (Most Windows applications add an extension of .PRN to a print file, which may not be shown in Windows Explorer.)

2. Select Start ⇨ Run.

3. Enter the following command, and click OK:

```
command /c copy /b filename.prn lpt1:
```

You must substitute the name of your print file, including the full DOS path, for *filename.prn*. For example, if your file is in the C:\WORK folder and it's named *myfile.prn*, you should type

```
command /c copy /b c:\work\myfile.prn lpt1:
```

Also, note that you should use the proper port ID for the parallel port that's connected to your printer; for most of us, that's LPT1, but if you're using LPT2, you should substitute that in the command as well.

You'll probably notice a DOS box pop up briefly as Windows processes your command, and then your printer prints the document as if it had just been sent from your Windows application.

Performing a Printer Communications Test

Most current inkjet and laser printers and all-in-one units from Hewlett-Packard enable you to perform a communications test, and it's generally performed automatically during installation. However, you can follow this procedure to test for proper bidirectional communications at any time:

1. Click the HP Toolbox icon on your desktop. The Toolbox dialog box appears.

2. Click the Printer Services tab to display the maintenance and diagnostics functions.

3. Click the Test Printer Communications button.

   The Toolbox program displays the progress of the test.

4. After the test is completed, the Toolbox program reports whether everything is working correctly or if there are any printer-PC communications problems; if an error message appears, consult Appendix A at the end of this book.

5. Click Done to return to the Toolbox dialog box, and click OK to exit.

Removing a Printer and Its Software

Need to remove a printer and its associated software from your Windows 98 or Windows Me system? Follow these steps:

1. Click Start, and select Printers from the Settings menu, which displays the Printers folder.

2. Click the icon for the printer you want to delete, and select Delete from the File menu (or just press the Delete key).

3. Close the Printers folder — you've deleted the printer from your system.

4. To delete any related software, click Start, select Control Panel from the Settings menu, and then click the Add/Remove Software icon. Windows 98/Me displays the Add/Remove Programs dialog box, as shown in Figure 11.4.

5. Scroll through the list, and locate any software installed by the printer's manufacturer. Highlight the entry for the software, and click the Add/Remove button.

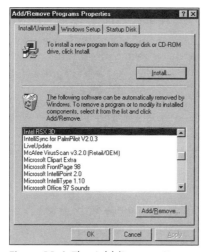

Figure 11.4 The Add/Remove Programs Properties dialog box

6. Windows 98 and Windows Me typically ask for confirmation before removing software; click Yes to confirm.

7. Once the software is removed, the Add/ Remove Programs dialog box reappears; click OK to return to the control panel.

Network Printer Projects

These projects help you install printer server and sharing hardware.

Cross-Reference

Chapter 7 analyzes and explains network, switched, and shared printing.

MATERIALS

HP DeskJet 970C

Paper suitable for your printer

HP JetDirect print server

Manual or electronic printer switch

Cable from switch to printer

Cable for each PC connecting to the switch

Label maker (Dymo or similar product)

Phillips screwdriver

Tip

A "reversible head" screwdriver, which has a reversible barrel with both Phillips and standard heads on each end, is the most practical tool to use.

Connecting to an Existing Network Printer under Windows

Follow these steps to install a shared printer that's already connected to another PC somewhere else on your Microsoft Windows 98/Me network:

1. Click Start, and select Printers from the Settings menu, which displays the Printers folder.

2. Click the Add Printer dialog box, which runs the Add Printer Wizard, and click Next on the opening wizard screen.

3. The wizard prompts you to specify whether the new printer is attached to your PC locally or via a network; select Network Printer, and click Next.

4. Identify the printer's network path (as shown in Figure 11.5); if you don't know the path by heart, the simplest way to do this is to click Browse, and browse the list of PCs with attached network printers. To display the PC's network printer, click the plus sign next to it. Once you've located the desired printer, click it to highlight it, and click OK to accept it.

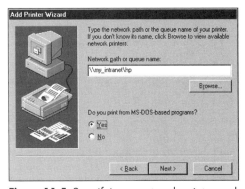

Figure 11.5 Specifying a network printer under Windows 98

5. If you need to print from legacy DOS applications, click Yes to indicate that you do need to print from MS-DOS applications, and click Next.

6. The wizard displays a scrolling listbox of all the different printer models in the Windows 98 database, grouped by manufacturer. If you have a driver disk, click the Have Disk button, and browse for the floppy disk or CD-ROM that contains the driver. If you don't have a driver disk for the printer you're installing, find the manufacturer, and choose the closest model to yours. Click Next to continue to the next wizard screen.

7. Before closing, the wizard asks if you would like to print a test page to check things out. Click Finish to exit the wizard.

8. The icon for your new printer should now appear in your Printers folder (click the My Computer icon on your desktop, and click the Printer folder to open it).

Installing an HP JetDirect Printer Server

The specific instructions for installing a printer with a HP JetDirect connection under TCP/IP vary somewhat according to the type of network and the topology — for example, the steps differ if you're using a traditional cabled Ethernet system, a Token ring system, or a home phone line network. However, the basic procedure remains the same when adding an external HP JetDirect server:

1. Turn the printer off.

2. Connect the parallel port cable from the HP JetDirect printer port to the parallel port on your printer. (Other JetDirect units use USB or Firewire connections to your printer instead.)

3. Connect the network cable to the corresponding Ethernet connector on your HP JetDirect unit (or, if you're adding an HP JetDirect unit to your home phone line network, connect the telephone cable from the wall jack to the Line jack on your HP JetDirect).

4. Connect the HP JetDirect power supply to the wall outlet and plug it into the power jack on the back of the unit.

5. Turn the printer on.

6. Turn on your HP JetDirect unit and check the status indicators to make sure that it is operating properly (your manual shows you how to read the status display on your model).

7. Press the Test button (or check your manual to determine how to print a configuration page) and check to see if the printer is receiving data properly from the HP JetDirect unit.

8. Run the HP JetDirect Setup program to configure and initialize the HP JetDirect unit.

Tip

By default, most HP JetDirect servers use a factory default TCP/IP address of 192.0.0.192, which shouldn't require a change on non-TCP/IP networks. However, this figure can be set to another address within the HP JetDirect Setup program.

To reset your HP JetDirect server to factory default settings, unplug the power cord from the unit and plug it back in while pressing and holding the Test button for five seconds. Wait about five minutes for the unit to initialize.

Installing a Manual Printer Switch

To install a manual printer switch, follow these steps:

1. Shut down Windows, and turn off your PC and printer.

2. Attach the printer cable to your printer, and connect it to the printer port on the back of your printer switch (probably labeled "I/O" or "Printer") — and use a screwdriver to secure the connection.

3. Connect the parallel cable from your PC — note that it is a straight-through parallel cable, not a printer cable, so it should have the same type of connector on both ends — to either the A or B port on the back of the printer switch, using a screwdriver to secure the connection.

4. Repeat Step 3 for each PC that uses the printer switch.

Tip

You'll probably label the front of a manual switch with the name of the user of each PC, but it's also generally a good idea to label your cables with the port letter on the back of the switch. Doing so enables you to quickly reattach everything in case you ever have to move your equipment.

5. Turn the switch to the correct PC, and turn on your printer. (Remember, the printer must be on for Windows 98/Me to successfully poll it. It should always be switched to the correct PC and turned on before you boot so that Windows can access it.)

Installing an Electronic Printer Switch

To add an automatic electronic printer switch to your system, follow these steps:

1. Shut down Windows 98, and turn off your PC and printer.

2. Connect the printer cable to your printer, and connect the other end to the printer port on your printer switch, using a screwdriver to secure the connection (refer to the user manual to determine which port).

3. Connect the parallel cable from one of your PCs; it is a straight-through parallel cable, so it should have the same type of connector on both ends to the proper port on the printer switch, using a screwdriver to secure the connection. (The manual for your printer switch indicates the ports for connecting PCs.)

4. Repeat Step 3 for each PC that uses the printer switch.

5. Set the miniature switch bank (also called DIP switches) on the printer switch unit to configure it as indicated by your manual. Because your electronic printer switch doesn't use software, the pattern of DIP switches indicates which devices are printers and which are PCs.

6. Turn on your PC and printer. (Remember, the printer must be on for Windows 98 to poll it successfully.)

Summary

In this chapter, you learned how to generally configure printers, select network printers, and install printer servers, printer switches, and printer sharing devices under Windows 98 and Windows Me. You also learned how to print from within a Windows application.

Font and Fun Projects

IN THIS CHAPTER
- Installing and displaying fonts
- Creating a 3-D logo with Xara3D
- Printing custom greeting cards
- Fashioning custom T-shirts
- Making your own business cards
- Designing and printing CD-ROM labels
- Creating custom stickers
- Printing Web pages
- Finding and printing clip art

In this chapter you find step-by-step projects that offer both fun and functionality. They include:

■ Installation of new printer fonts under Windows 98 and Mac OS 9

■ Instructions for printing Web pages and finding clip art on the Web

■ Instructions for creating wonderful custom printed items such as greeting cards, T-shirts, business cards, and more

Note

No matter what printing software or materials you use, be sure that you read all accompanying documentation for any warnings or specific instructions.

Font Projects

In this section, I provide step-by-step instructions on how to install fonts in Windows 98 and Mac OS 9, and how to load them in applications.

MATERIALS

Adobe Type Manager

Xara3D version 3 or 4 (Xara Ltd.)

Fonts on a disk or in a folder

Cross-Reference

Chapter 8, "The Wonderful World of Fonts," covers fonts from every angle — learn exactly what they are, how to get more of them, how to edit them, and how to "three-dimensionalize" them.

Installing a TrueType Font in Windows 98

There are two methods of manually installing a new TrueType font under Windows 98: "dragging and dropping" the font, or installing it from the Fonts dialog box. (If you prefer to use a font management program, visit www.fontsmart.com, and download a free "lite" version of HP's FontSmart program.)

Installing fonts using drag and drop

To install one or more new TrueType fonts using drag and drop, follow these steps:

1. Click the Start button, and choose Control Panel from the Settings menu.

2. From the Control Panel folder, click the Fonts icon to display the contents of your Fonts folder. Each icon you see with the stamp "TT" represents a specific TrueType font that's available to your Windows 98 applications.

3. From the Windows Explorer or your My Computer folder, browse to the location of the font files that you wish to install, as shown in Figure 12.1.

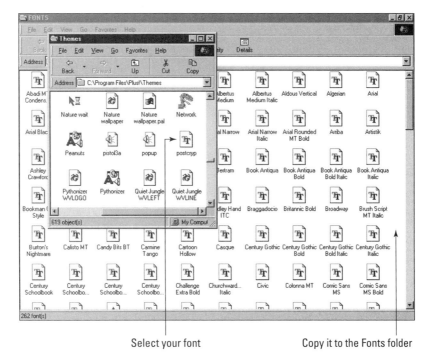

Select your font   Copy it to the Fonts folder

Figure 12.1 Preparing to drag and drop new fonts under Windows 98

4. Use your cursor to highlight the fonts you'd like to copy, and drag them to the Fonts folder by clicking and holding the left mouse button.

5. Once the new font files are in position above the Fonts folder, release the left mouse button, and Windows 98 copies the files to the folder.

6. Select Close from the File menu in the Fonts folder to close the folder. The new fonts are available immediately to all of your Windows applications.

Installing fonts through the fonts folder

To install one or more new TrueType fonts from the Fonts folder, follow these steps:

1. Click the Start button, and choose Control Panel from the Settings menu.

2. From the Control Panel folder, click the Fonts icon to open the Fonts folder.

3. Select Install New Font from the File menu to display the Add Fonts dialog box (Figure 12.2).

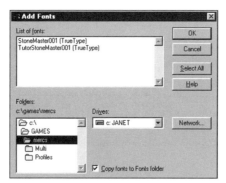

Figure 12.2 Installing fonts through the Add Fonts dialog box

4. Browse and locate the new fonts you want to add to your system.

5. Click one or more font names to highlight them, and click OK to begin the installation. Windows 98 returns to the Fonts folder display once the installation is complete.

6. Select Close from the File menu in the Fonts folder to close the folder. The new fonts are available immediately to all of your Windows applications.

Tip

Once you've installed a new font, it can also be used within the Windows 98 interface, including many of the dialog box and menu items displayed by the system. You can select a font for use within Windows 98 from the Appearance tab of the Display Properties dialog box.

Installing Fonts in Mac OS 9

To install one or more fonts on a Mac OS 9 system, follow these steps:

1. Double-click the icon representing your startup disk (usually your hard drive). Mac OS 9 displays the contents of your startup disk.

2. Browse and locate the new fonts you want to add to your system.

3. Use your cursor to highlight the fonts you'd like to copy, and drag them to the closed System Folder icon in the directory window by clicking and holding the left mouse button. (Don't open the System Folder — the file icons for your new fonts must be dropped onto the *closed* System Folder icon.)

4. Once the new font files are in position on top of the closed System Folder icon, release the left mouse button.

5. Click OK to confirm that you do wish to install the fonts, and Mac OS 9 takes care of the rest.

The fonts are available the next time you run a Mac application. You must quit and reopen applications that were open during the installation before the fonts can appear.

Displaying TrueType Font Information in Windows 98

Have you forgotten what a particular font looks like? You can display all of the characters in a particular TrueType font and see them in a complete range of point sizes by following these steps:

1. Click the Start button, and choose Control Panel from the Settings menu.

2. From the Control Panel folder, click the Fonts icon to open the Fonts folder; each icon with the label "TT" is a TrueType font.

3. Double-click any TrueType font icon to display the Font dialog box shown in Figure 12.3.

You can also print the contents of this Font dialog box by clicking the Print button; sometimes it's more convenient to have a hard copy of a font to show others.

Tip

Does your laser printer or all-in-one unit offer its own on-board resident fonts? Unfortunately, those font families may not show up within your Fonts folder. Some models provide matching screen or TrueType fonts for the resident fonts. If yours doesn't, check the utility programs that came with your model, and see if one of them enables you to print resident fonts.

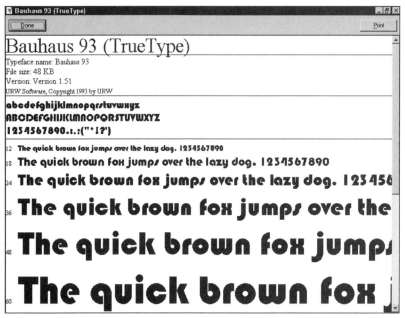

Figure 12.3 Displaying the characteristics of a TrueType font under Windows 98

Adjusting the ATM Font Cache

If you use the Adobe Type Manager for displaying or printing Adobe Type 1 fonts on your Windows or Macintosh system, I suggest that you raise the amount of system memory you dedicate to the font cache to provide the best performance. Your system's graphics card and your printing jobs will process PostScript fonts more efficiently.

If you have 32MB or more of RAM in your PC, follow these steps to expand the font cache:

1. Click the Start button, and choose Programs ⇨ Adobe ⇨ Adobe Type Manager to run the program.

2. Select the Settings tab in the Adobe Type Manager dialog box.

3. Click the up arrow next to the Font Cache field until the value reads at least 512K.

4. Close the Adobe Type Manager dialog box to save your changes, and reboot.

If you have 32MB or more of system RAM in your Macintosh, follow these steps to expand the cache:

1. Click the Apple menu, and select Control Panels.

2. From the Control Panels menu, click ATM to display the ATM dialog box.

3. Click the up arrow next to the Font Cache field until the value reads 512K. (If you have over 64MB of system RAM, you can use 640K.)

4. Close the ATM Control Panel dialog box to save your changes.

Creating a Logo with 3-D Fonts

Think it's hard for graphic designers to dream up corporate logos? They're not the only ones that can have fun: you can create an impressive 3-D logo yourself in seconds using Xara3D Versions 3 or 4 (Xara3D for short) from Xara Ltd. (www.xara.com). You can then export that logo for use in all your business printing. Run Xara3D, and follow these steps:

1.. Choose Text from the Window menu. Xara3D displays the Text Options dialog box, where you can select a font and its attributes to use in your logo. Choose a font from the scrolling listbox; you can also select a text alignment and add any desired attributes (such as bold or italics) by clicking the corresponding button on the toolbar.

2. Enter the text you want rendered in the Text field. I'll use my initials for this example and click the OK button to create the 3-D image of the text you specified.

3. Once the image has been created, I usually select a new texture instead of the default of "natural wood veneer." To select a new surface, choose Texture from the Window menu. Xara3D displays the Texture Options dialog box. You can use the sliders on this dialog box to zoom in or out on the size of the texture, position a specific part of the texture on the letters — a technique that's good for textures that are actually pho-tographs — and rotate the texture on the 3-D surface of the text. For now, though, let's load a new texture; click Load Texture.

4. The program displays the Load Text Texture dialog box shown in Figure 12.4. Browse through your system, and locate an image on your hard drive that you'd like to use as a texture; the program can load files in .GIF, .JPG, .BMP, and .PNG image formats. (Your Windows directory is a great place to find .BMP files that work well as textures.) The preview window displays a thumbnail view of the selected file. Once you've found the right texture, click Open to apply it, and click Close to exit the Texture Options dialog box.

Figure 12.4 The Xara3D Load Text Texture dialog box

5. Choose a bevel size and shape by selecting Bevels from the Windows menu. You can make a big difference in the appearance of the finished image by experimenting with bevel settings, but I usually get good results with the default values of a 30-degree miter bevel.

6. Xara3D offers several different levels of rendering quality, each of which produces different results at a different rendering speed. You can set these values by selecting Quality Settings from the Window menu. If you're using an older 486-based PC or older Pentium, select the Medium value for the Export quality and Animation quality fields; your rendering takes less time and produces satisfactory results. If you have a Pentium II or III, pick Highest for both of these fields, and enable both Anti-aliased check boxes for the absolute best results, with the most realistic appearance and shading.

7. Once rendering is done, you have a realistic 3-D text logo similar to the one in Figure 12.5 that you can export as an image for use in all of your printing projects. It looks as if you spent hours, but a fast Pentium III PC can do the job for you in seconds.

Fun Projects

Here's the most fun part of this book — the part where you get step-by-step instructions on how to create some of the great printed materials discussed in Chapter 9.

Cross-Reference

Adding clip art enhances several of the projects outlined here. If you feel your supply of clip art is limited, check out the last section of this chapter, "Searching for Clip Art on the Web."

Figure 12.5 A completed 3-D text logo built with Xara3D

Printing a Birthday Card

Why spend 15 minutes (or even half an hour) rummaging through the greeting cards at the store, trying to find the card that says exactly what you want — when you can create precisely the greeting card you want, complete with a personalized message and your own photographs, in minutes on your inkjet printer? Today's greeting card programs make it easy to achieve professional-looking results, even if you're like me and you can't draw anything other than a stick figure.

Tip

Does your printing software create "picture frames" that you can use to matte a photograph? This is a neat feature . . . but it's a recent idea, and you probably won't find a picture frame design within your printing software if it's more than a couple of years old. If your printing software can't create a picture frame directly, you can still print one by designing it as a greeting card or sign. Follow the steps in this section, but create a design that only takes up the outside edge of the page. Once you've printed the page, you can cut the exact area for your photograph with a hobby knife and ruler!

MATERIALS

Blank greeting card paper

Inkjet or laser printer

Several sheets of regular printer paper

Greeting card printing software

Designing your card

In this section, I use Print Artist Platinum and HP Greeting Card paper to create a custom birthday card on my HP inkjet printer. Although you may be using another greeting card program, as long as it can create single-fold cards, you should be able to follow the same general steps:

1. Run your greeting card program (or if you're using a printing suite, choose the greeting card function). I've run Print Artist, selected Greeting Card as my document type, and clicked New to create a new card design.

2. Although you can create double-fold cards, most greeting card paper that's available is single-fold — therefore, choose ½ Fold-Vertical, and click OK to print a standard format card (see Figure 12.6).

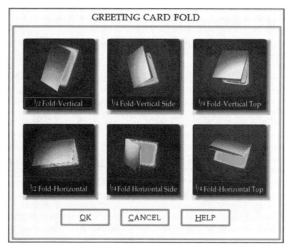

Figure 12.6 Selecting the dimensions and number of folds for your new greeting card

3. Print Artist prompts you to select a category and a layout to use as a starting point for your card. Your layout usually automatically sets up a font and color scheme, and your program may even include an appropriate piece of clip art. (Of course, you don't have to settle for these default fonts, colors, and artwork, but if you're in a hurry or you like the design, you can simply personalize the card and print it.) We'll choose Occasion as the category and — as usual — I'll take it for granted that I'm late and pick the Belated Birthday card layout. To continue, click OK. Figure 12.7 illustrates the Print Artist Select New Greeting Card dialog box.

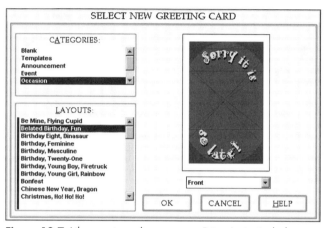

Figure 12.7 Like most card programs, Print Artist includes a variety of predesigned cards.

Tip

Naturally, you're not limited to simple clip art or drawings . . . if you have a digital camera or you've scanned a photograph into your computer as a digital image, you can import that photo as the graphic for your greeting card. Nothing adds a personal touch to your printing projects like your own photographs.

4. Print Artist loads the card design and displays it full size on your screen. At this point you can make any necessary changes to the font, choose another clip art image or photograph, or change the wording on the front of the card. For example, let's add an elephant to the front of our card — after all, elephants never forget, so it makes a good illustration for a belated birthday card. Click the camera icon in the toolbar, select Animals as the clip art category, and choose Elephant. Print Artist automatically places the new image in the center of the card. Figure 12.8 shows the new look for the front of our greeting card.

Figure 12.8 Adding clip art gives interest and humor to our birthday card.

5. The front of the card is finished, but we still need to personalize the inside. After all, what's a custom card without the personal touch? Select the Inside Right item from the View menu to display the text inside the card, and click the text to select it. Next, click Edit Text from the Edit menu to display the Change Text dialog box. Click the mouse insertion cursor at the end of the word "Birthday," and type the recipient's name; Print Artist automatically matches the font and centers the text when you click OK.

6. Now that you've finished personalizing your card, it's always a good idea to save a new card design to disk before you try printing it. If you save it first, you can reload it later in case you need to make a change (instead of redesigning the card from scratch). A saved copy is also a great backup in case your printer runs out of paper or that game you're playing as you print suddenly locks up your PC. To save your work in Print Artist Platinum, choose Save from the File menu, enter a short description of this card design, and choose a filename. Print Artist automatically adds the .GC extension to the end of the name to identify the file as a Print Artist greeting card design. You're now ready to print your custom card.

Printing a test card

Before you use a piece of greeting card paper — which is much more expensive per sheet than standard printer paper — it's always a good idea to print a test page. Follow these steps to print a test page:

1. Run your greeting card program (or if you're using a printing suite, choose the greeting card function), and load the design you created in the last section.

2. Take a single sheet of your regular printer paper and mark one end of the paper with a large arrow pointing toward the 8½-inch edge. Empty your printer's paper feed tray and insert the marked sheet of paper with the arrow face down and pointing away from the printer, as shown in Figure 12.9.

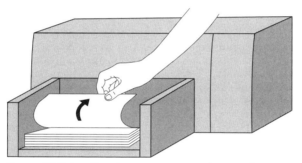

Figure 12.9 Loading the paper to print the outside greeting

Tip

The alignment I'm using in this step-by-step procedure corresponds to the proper alignment for most HP inkjet printers. If you're using another brand of printer, it may take some experimentation to figure out which direction the paper should point and which side should be facing up. Until you know for sure, use plain paper; once you've printed a test card successfully, keep that card (with the arrow markings) to help you remember the proper alignment in the future, and write down in the margin any changes to the steps I provide here.

3. Print the outside greeting for your card. If everything is aligned correctly, the greeting should print over or somewhere near the arrow mark you made. If not, repeat Steps 1 through 3 with the test page face down and the arrow pointing toward the printer.

4. Now print the inside greeting by inserting your test page into the paper feed tray again, this time with the arrow facing up and pointing toward the printer. Once the page has printed, fold it in half, and check to make sure that the interior of the card is oriented in the proper way. If not, repeat Step 4 with another test page, this time inserting the paper with the arrow facing up and pointing away from the printer.

As if all these different directions and faces weren't enough, I'm assuming that your greeting card printing program prints the outside of the card first, but some programs print the *inside* of a greeting card first. If you're using one of these programs, reverse the order of Steps 2 and 4.

Speaking from experience, I can tell you that determining the proper alignment of a piece of greeting card paper can be a real pain if your test page doesn't print correctly the first time — take heart, however, because you only have to perform these contortions for your first card. Remember, take a moment to write down any changes to the steps in this section, and keep a working example of your test page for future reference.

Printing a greeting card

Now that you've determined how to load paper so that the design prints correctly with your printer and software, it's time to actually print a card using your greeting card paper. Follow these general steps:

1. Run your greeting card program, and create or load a design.

2. Load a single sheet of greeting card paper into your printer using the alignment you determined in the last section.

3. Select the printer options within your greeting card program, and set your printer for its best print quality (refer to the instructions that accompanied your greeting card software for instructions on how to access your printer's options dialog box). Also, if your printer enables you to set the paper type, choose "glossy" or "greeting card paper" for the best results.

4. Print the outside greeting (or the inside greeting, depending upon your greeting card printing software). To ensure that this first printing has plenty of time to dry, *wait at least five or six minutes before printing the other portion of the card!* If you try to print the other greeting too quickly, you may smear the image — remember, greeting card paper takes a little longer to dry than plain paper.

5. Once the first printing has dried, turn the page, and print the reverse side. Again, use the alignment you determined for the second pass of printing in the previous section.

6. Print the remaining greeting, and wait at least five or six minutes for the card to dry.

Congratulations, you've printed your first custom greeting card! If you are going to mail this card, you may want to configure your favorite word processor to print the envelope.

Tip

If you think that a greeting card design works only for greeting cards — time to change your mind! Once you've printed a card for a party or a special gathering, you can reproduce the same design for other paper projects . . . including place-mats, party invitations, banners, and even a wine label or two. Just make sure that you save the graphic that you've created (as we did in the previous section, "Designing your card"). Most applications like Print Artist Platinum allow you to import an existing graphic or design into a new project. A consistent graphic design throughout your decorations adds a professional touch.

Printing a T-Shirt Transfer

Whether you're printing a single transfer for yourself or creating several copies of a T-shirt transfer for an entire soccer team, you should follow the same general process for each transfer you create.

MATERIALS

T-shirt transfer paper

Prewashed, cotton or cotton/polyester T-shirt or cloth item

T-shirt printing software

Scissors

Inkjet printer

Several sheets of regular inkjet paper

Sturdy table or countertop

Sheet or pillowcase

Clothes iron

Tip

You achieve the best results if your T-shirt or fabric item is made of pure cotton, a mixture of cotton and polyester, or canvas. Fine fabrics such as silk and velvet are not suitable for transfers.

Preparing the fabric

Before you apply a transfer to a T-shirt or other fabric, you should prepare the item for the best possible results. Follow these general steps:

1. Do *not* apply a transfer to a brand-new item that has never been washed — in order for a transfer to adhere correctly, the item must be prewashed in cold water.

2. Machine-dry the item at normal temperature, but do not use any fabric softener or other additives during the drying cycle.

3. Once it has been prewashed, the item may be ironed *without starch or steam* to help keep it wrinkle-free during the transfer. Allow the item to cool to room temperature before applying the transfer.

Printing the design

Warning

Unless your T-shirt transfer paper is specifically made for a laser printer, never print a T-shirt transfer on a laser printer. Most transfer paper is not designed for laser printers, and you may damage your hardware.

Follow these general steps to print a transfer on your inkjet printer:

1. Complete the design you wish to transfer and save it to disk. You can use any application that prints in color to prepare your design, but remember that the design *must be reversed* to appear correctly after the transfer has been applied. If you're using a program especially designed for printing transfers, it should perform this "mirror image" processing automatically. However, if you're using a program such as Microsoft Word to create your design, check to see if your printer has a "mirror image" or "flip horizontal" option that you can enable to reverse the image. (If your machine can handle an "Iron-On," or "Transfer Paper" paper type, it may flip the image automatically.)

2. Print a test page using regular paper to make sure that your design fits on the fabric in the desired orientation. I generally leave at least two inches of border all around the design to ensure that it fits and, in the case of a T-shirt, does not "wrap around" out of sight. If you need to resize your design, do so, save it to disk, and print another test page; repeat this until your image has the right dimensions.

3. Place a single sheet of transfer paper on top of a few sheets of regular paper, and load it into the printer. Make sure you load the paper according to the instructions that accompanied your transfer paper. Most transfer paper has some sort of design on the back of each page, while the front side of the page is blank.

4. If necessary, select the option to reverse the image within the Print dialog box. Also, select Transfer Paper or Iron-On as the paper type (if your printer enables you to set the paper type), and choose the best possible print quality.

5. Select the Print command from the File menu in your application to send the design to the printer.

6. Once the design has printed, trim closely around the edges of the design with scissors — for the most professional appearance, maintain a consistent distance from the border of your design. (It's also a good idea to leave a small "flap" of extra border at one corner so you can easily remove the transfer.)

Applying the transfer

Warning

Keep in mind that different brands of T-shirt transfers may require different iron settings or they may require more or less heating time. The settings and application times that I mention in this section apply only to HP Iron-On T-shirt Transfers, so read the instructions for your specific brand of transfer, and follow those instructions when they differ from the directions I give here.

Follow these steps to apply a transfer to a cloth item:

1. Select a table or countertop in your home wide enough to provide a hard, smooth backing for the entire item — a Formica countertop is an ideal surface. Do *not* use an ironing board, which usually isn't stable enough and can leave wrinkles. Cover this surface with a sheet or pillowcase, and smooth all wrinkles from the fabric to provide the smoothest backing possible.

2. Fire up your iron on the highest setting it provides for at least 10 minutes. Do not use a steam setting, as steam can damage the transfer.

3. Arrange the item in the middle of the backing, with the surface that receives the transfer facing up.

4. Align the transfer on top of the item, printed side down, facing in the correct direction. At this point, you're ready to begin ironing, as shown in Figure 12.10.

5. Move the iron slowly from the top of the design toward the bottom along one edge of the transfer, applying constant pressure and keeping the iron in motion. Make sure that the iron overlaps the transfer so that the edge of the transfer bonds to the fabric. The iron should be in contact with the transfer for at least 30 seconds, but to avoid scorching the fabric or the transfer, do not rest the iron in one place.

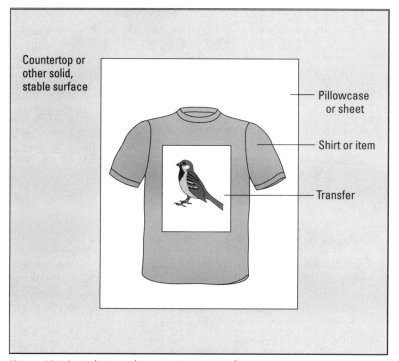

Figure 12.10 A shirt ready to receive a transfer

Tip

If you're applying the transfer to a cloth with a heavy weave (such as canvas or rough cotton), you should press harder to make sure the transfer bonds properly to the cloth.

6. Repeat Step 5 with the other three edges of the design, making sure you have completely sealed the edges of the transfer. If you've left a small flap of border at one corner, leave it unsealed to use for removing the transfer when you're done.

7. Once you have sealed all four edges of the design, move the iron slowly in a circular motion around the middle of the design, applying constant pressure and keeping the iron in motion.

8. Turn your iron off and set it down in a safe position, and then immediately begin pulling the transfer backing from the fabric with a slow, steady motion, beginning at the unsealed corner. Do not allow the transfer to cool before you have removed the paper backing.

9. Once you have removed the backing completely, hang the finished item and let it cool.

Printing Business Cards

Whether you use specially perforated card stock or a cutting board to make your own business cards, your laser printer can produce a high-quality personalized product for your company — including color highlighting, which usually costs a pretty penny if you buy your cards at a print shop. In this section, I use the program Visual Business Cards, distributed by RKS Software (www.rks-software. com), to design and print my cards.

MATERIALS

Blank business card stock

Inkjet or laser printer

Several sheets of regular printer paper

Business card printing software

Paper cutting board, ruler, and pencil (for card stock without perforations)

Designing a business card

Although you can use a word processing program to create your cards, designing a business card is much easier with a program such as Visual Business Cards. If you're using a business card printing program, follow these general steps:

1. Run your business card printing program (or if you're using a printing suite, choose the business card function). Figure 12.11 shows the blank template I used to design my card.

2. From the Edit menu, click Set or Change Background Art to select a background for your card.

3. Next, select Personal Information from the Edit menu, and add your data, as shown in Figure 12.12. Storing your personal information within the program's data enables you to easily experiment by placing the same text elements in different places, without having to retype the same data over and over.

4. Using the Text tool, add your personal information to your card design; optionally, you can also include clip art, so you can add your company logo to one of the predesigned backgrounds. The program enables you to select different font styles and sizes, and position text anywhere on your design that you wish using the standard Windows drag-and-drop method.

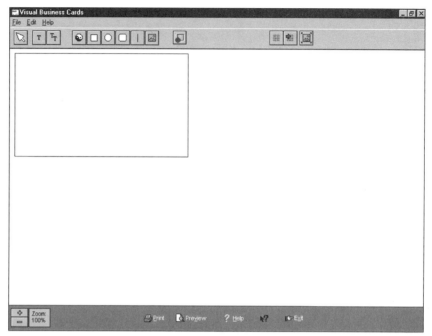

Figure 12.11 Opening a new design file within Visual Business Cards

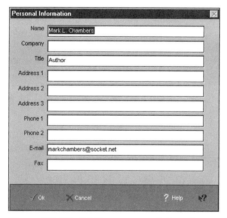

Figure 12.12 Adding personal data for my business card design

5. Once you've finished your card design, save it to disk before you print it. To save your work in Visual Business Cards, choose Save As from the File menu, and choose a filename; the program automatically adds the .VBC extension to the end of the name.

Checking alignment with a test page

Printing business cards requires a little less experimentation than printing greeting cards before you get it right, especially if you're using a standard card format (such as an Avery business card format) recognized by your business card printing software. However, you should still use plain paper to print a test sheet of cards before you try using that expensive perforated business card stock.

Tip

If you're using regular card stock and you plan on cutting your cards by hand later, alignment is less important, and you don't need to follow these steps.

Perform these steps to print a test page:

1. Run your business card printing program (or if you're using a printing suite, choose the business card function), and load the design you created in the last section.

2. Take a single sheet of plain paper, and mark one end of the paper with a large arrow pointing toward the 8½-inch edge. Empty your printer's paper feed tray, and insert the marked sheet of paper with the arrow face up and pointing toward the printer. The correct orientation varies with the specific printer being used.

3. Print a sheet of cards, and place the printed sheet over the perforated card stock. If everything is aligned correctly, your design should be aligned within the perforations. (If you're having problems determining where the perforations are, do what I do, and hold both sheets up to a strong lamp or the ceiling light to illuminate the sheets from the back.) If the alignment isn't correct, repeat Steps 2 and 3 with the arrow pointing away from the printer.

Remember to keep a working example of your business card test page for future reference.

Printing business cards

This procedure shows you how to print business cards from your design:

1. Run your business card printing program, and create or open a design.

2. Load a single sheet of business card stock into your printer using the alignment you determined in the last section.

3. Open the printer options dialog box within your business card printing program — it's usually available from the File menu or from the Print dialog box — and set your printer for its best print quality. If your printer includes a "card stock" paper type, pick that as well.

4. Print the sheet of cards.

5. If you're using perforated business card stock, carefully separate each card by tearing along the perforations. If you're using plain card stock, use a pencil and ruler to mark the edges of the cards. I recommend that you cut your business cards with a paper cutter to ensure a straight edge.

Tip

If you're using an inkjet printer, wait at least five or six minutes before removing the sheet from the printer to allow your sheet of business cards to dry.

Printing your own business cards gives you the flexibility to print only as many as you need, and you can change your business card design quickly to update information or add a new logo or a new piece of clip art.

Printing a CD-ROM Label

Printing suites usually don't offer a function to print CD-ROM labels, so you probably have to use a separate program. In this project, I use the program DesignExpress from MicroVision Development to create a CD-ROM label. You need a label applicator such as the NEATO system to apply your label after it has been printed.

MATERIALS

One or more recorded CDs

Blank CD-ROM labels

Inkjet or laser printer

Several sheets of regular printer paper

Disc label-printing software

Label application system

Designing the label

To design the CD-ROM label, follow these steps:

1. Run the CD-ROM label-printing program. DesignExpress includes a number of predesigned templates, one of which is shown in Figure 12.13.

2. At the bottom of the screen, choose white, gold, or silver for the color of your labels. DesignExpress has predesigned layouts for each background color, each of which uses different fonts and text colors.

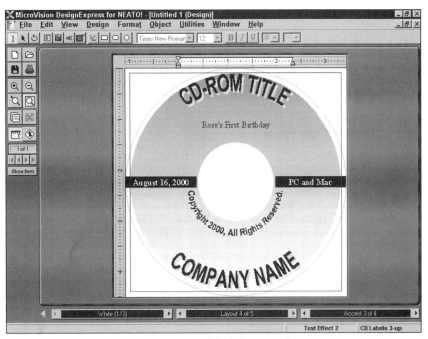

Figure 12.13 Creating a new CD-ROM label design with DesignExpress

3. Select one of the layouts from the layout control at the bottom of the screen; these layouts control font size, text placement, and text effects. You can also control these properties for each text box in your design.

4. Once you've chosen a layout, click in the text field, and make any changes to the layout text. Of course, you'll want to include a title to indicate the contents and your name (or that of your company), but I also recommend adding the date. If the material you're recording is orig-inal and suitable for copyright, you can add a copyright line. Also, if you're recording an audio disc, you may want to add the total time and number of tracks in the recording. You can also add clip art such as your company's logo.

5. Once you've completed all the necessary changes to your label layout, save it to disk before you print it. In DesignExpress, choose Save As from the File menu, and choose a filename; the program automatically adds the .DSN extension to the end of the name.

Once you've determined which side of the label sheet should be facing up, it's very easy to align a sheet of CD-ROM labels, so you really don't need to print a test page. However, I usually print one anyway simply to check how my design looks printed in color. If I catch something on the test page, I can still update the CD-ROM layout before I actually print a label. Use plain paper to print your test page.

Tip

Alignment is easier with CD-ROM labels than it is with greeting cards or business cards, but remember to select a label still on the sheet. Most programs print to the first label on the sheet by default, but if you've already printed and removed that label, you have to manually choose one of the other two labels to print. This is generally done from the Print dialog box within your label printing software.

Printing the label

These steps show you how to print your CD-ROM labels:

1. Run your CD-ROM label-printing program, and create or open a design.

2. Load a single sheet of CD-ROM labels into your printer. Insert the paper with the arrow pointing toward the printer, but note that the side facing up depends on the paper path used in your particular printer.

3. Locate the printer options dialog box within your program — it's usually available from the File menu or from the Print dialog box — and set your printer for its best print quality.

4. Print the label — in DesignExpress, you can either select Print from the File menu or click on the Printer icon on the toolbar. If you're using an inkjet printer or all-in-one, wait at least five or six minutes before removing the sheet from the printer to allow your new label to dry.

Never try to apply a CD-ROM label by hand. The slightest misalignment can affect the rotation of the disc inside your CD-ROM drive. Instead, use one of the commercial CD-ROM label application systems, such as the NEATO label system, which guarantees that the label is positioned correctly.

Printing Stickers

Recent arrivals to the world of printing projects, custom-made stickers are a big hit with kids and organizations. You can use them for decorating magnets or creating ID tags for everything from baked goods to sewing projects (and even people, too). I use Disney's Pooh Holiday Print Studio, which is a very fun and easy program for kids to use. Let's create a set of stickers for the Christmas holidays!

MATERIALS

Blank inkjet sticker stock (with or without magnetic backing)

Inkjet printer

Several sheets of regular printer paper

Sticker printing software

Designing stickers

Your sticker design must match the size and shape of your stock — for example, I use large square and large round Hewlett-Packard Restickables, but circular and rectangular sticker stock is also available from companies such as Avery. (As the name implies, HP Restickables can be removed from most surfaces and reapplied several times.) Your printer software should allow you to modify the size and shape of your design to match your stock.

Follow these general steps:

1. Run your sticker-printing program (or if you're using a printing suite, choose the sticker function).

2. Click the Stickers icon to display the three different shapes you can design; I picked the square shape.

3. Select the stock you're using — HP large square Restickable stock uses the same dimensions as Avery #3111, so I chose that size.

4. Next, choose the graphic for the first sticker from the clip art collection.

Tip

If you're creating a new sticker or adding text to an existing design, it's a good idea to keep the text short and use a larger font, so that the message can be read at a glance. (It's no accident that everyone remembers the slogan, "I Like Ike" or "Just Do It" — four or five words is usually the maximum length for a phrase on a sticker.)

5. Click the Display Next Item button to create the second sticker (naturally, you can also repeat the existing design from the first sticker for the rest of the sheet).

6. Repeat Steps 4 and 5 until you've created each sticker on the sheet.

7. Save your project to disk by clicking on the Save Current Project icon. Choose a filename; the program automatically adds the .HPS extension to the end of the name.

Printing a test page

Like any other printing project that uses special stock, you should use one or two sheets of plain paper to check your alignment before attempting to print your stickers.

Follow these steps to print a test page for your stickers:

1. Run your printing program and load the design you created in the last section.

2. Take a single sheet of plain paper, and mark one end of the paper with a large arrow pointing toward the 8½-inch edge. Empty your printer's paper feed tray, and insert the marked sheet of paper with the arrow facing up and pointing toward the printer. The correct orientation varies with the specific printer being used.

3. Print a sheet of stickers, and place the printed sheet over the perforated sticker stock. If everything is aligned correctly, your design should be aligned within the edge of the stickers. (If you're having problems determining where the perforations are, do what I do, and hold both sheets up to a strong lamp or the ceiling light to illuminate the sheets from the back.) If the alignment isn't correct, repeat Steps 2 and 3 with the arrow pointing away from the printer.

Hang on to the test page once you've determined the proper direction. I keep a test page with markings to indicate the alignment for my sticker stock.

Printing stickers

Ready to print your stickers? Follow these general steps:

1. Run your sticker-printing program, and create or open a design.

2. Load one or more sheets of sticker stock into your printer using the alignment you determined in the last section.

3. Click the Print Current Project icon or select Print from the menu. (Don't forget to set your printer for multiple copies if you're printing more than one sheet of stickers.)

4. Print the stickers and allow each sheet to dry for at least two minutes.

5. Peel, stick, and enjoy!

Printing Web Pages

You're probably familiar with this situation: you've got five minutes before you have to leave for work or class, and you've just located the Web page that holds the secret to life itself. Do you laboriously copy down the secret by hand, which will likely take more time than you have? Of course, you can bookmark the page for later, but you really want to share this information with others right now . . . and there's even a neat illustration that you'd like to use to explain the secret.

Sounds like a tall order to get all that information down so you don't forget anything — unless, of course, you have a printer hooked up to your system. In this section, I describe how you can print text, images, and the contents of entire Web pages, using both the PC and the Macintosh.

MATERIALS

Web browser

Any printer

Printing a Web page

To print the contents of an entire Web page from within your browser, complete with graphics, follow these steps:

1. Load the page from disk, or connect to the desired page. Make sure the entire page has loaded before continuing.

2. Select Print from the File menu.

3. If you're printing a rough draft of the page for future reference on your inkjet printer, make sure you've turned your print quality to draft (or in the case of an HP inkjet printer, EconoFast). This speeds up the printing of the page and uses the least amount of ink.

Capturing and printing text from a Web page

Follow these general steps to print selected text from a Web page in Windows 98 using Microsoft's Internet Explorer:

1. Holding down the right mouse button, select the desired text by highlighting it with the mouse.

2. Release the mouse to display the pop-up menu, and select Print.

3. Click Selection under the Print Range option (otherwise you'll print the entire page), and then click OK.

Tip

To save the selected text to a disk file on the PC, right-click the selected text, select Copy from the pop-up menu, paste the text you copied into Notepad or your favorite text editor, and save it to disk. Under Mac OS, select Copy from the Edit menu, paste the text you copied into your favorite text editor or word processor, and then save it to disk.

Capturing and printing images from a Web page

Follow these general steps to print an image from a Web page:

1. On the PC, move your cursor on top of the image you want to print, and right-click to display the pop-up menu. On the Mac, move your cursor on top of the image you want to print, and hold the button down until the pop-up menu appears.

2. Select Save Picture As to display a standard file save dialog box; if the image is in GIF, JPEG, or bitmap format, the browser saves it in the correct format.

To print the image, simply double-click it in Windows Explorer — Windows 95 and Windows 98 can open most of the image formats you find on the Internet. Macintosh owners can do the same with Mac OS 9.

Tip

If you need an image editor to display a certain picture on the PC, consider downloading the evaluation version of Paint Shop Pro, which I discuss in detail in Chapter 9.

Searching for Clip Art on the Web

If you're looking for a single piece of clip art on a specific topic across the entire World Wide Web, it may feel as if you're looking for a needle in a haystack. But thanks to the excellent search engines provided by sites such as Yahoo! and Infoseek, you can actually pinpoint single image files, or locate collections of royalty-free artwork with just a few minutes of searching.

Note

It's easy to nab cool pictures from the Web — but don't forget the responsibility that comes with them. If you're going to sell or publicly distribute any item that uses an image — or text for that matter — taken from a Web site, you must gain permission from both the site's Webmaster and the holder of the original copyright.

To search the Web for clip art on a specific subject, follow these general steps:

1. Open your Web browser, and go to `www.yahoo.com`.

2. Click the text input field next to the Search button, and type **clipart** followed by the subject of your search; for example, "**clipart horse**." Click the Search button to start the search engine.

3. In a few seconds, Yahoo! returns the results of your search. To jump directly to the site that Yahoo! located, click the name link — it's underlined in your browser.

Tip

You can use other keywords for searching — for example, keywords such as *picture*, *graphic*, or *image* work well. If I need more than one piece of clip art — for example, a series of images for a newsletter — I use the keywords *clipart collection*. Also try *clip art* as two words in your search.

4. Once you've found the image you want to download, follow the instructions in the earlier project "Printing Web Pages."

Summary

In this final chapter, you added fonts to your Windows 98 or Mac OS 9 system and created all sorts of printed items. You also learned more about printing Web pages and finding clip art on the Web.

You're now ready to tackle just about any printer task. I showed you how to buy the right printer, how to install and maintain it, and how to use it. We also discussed topics such as installing and displaying fonts, finding and printing clip art, home networking, and optimizing your computer for the fastest possible printing speeds.

However, we're not done yet! You'll find helpful technical support information for Hewlett-Packard printers and a list of contact information for popular printer manufacturers in the appendixes, as well as a glossary for important terms that we covered in the book.

Hewlett-Packard Technical Support's Frequently Asked Questions

IN THIS APPENDIX
- Inkjet printer solutions
- Laser printer solutions
- All-in-one unit solutions

The material in this appendix has been collected over several years as a "knowledge base" resource by the Hewlett-Packard technical support staff at Customer Care Centers around the world. This appendix includes the most common questions asked by owners of HP inkjet printers, laser printers, and all-in-one units, as well as the solutions to those questions.

If you own HP printing hardware I would highly recommend that you read the appropriate sections of this appendix (even if you're not currently experiencing problems with your unit) — you'll find tips and tricks that may help you maintain your printer or improve its performance.

Note

If you don't own an HP printer, you'll still find this appendix a valuable resource. Although the solutions and procedures in this appendix address specific printer models manufactured by Hewlett-Packard, much of this material applies to any printer used on a PC under Windows 95, Windows 98, Windows Me (Millennium Edition), Windows 2000, or Windows NT, and you can easily adapt the solutions to fit your printer.

Inkjet Printer Questions

References to specific printer names are applicable to any inkjet product unless noted otherwise.

Some of my applications (Adobe Photoshop, WordPerfect, CorelDRAW, Microsoft Access, Microsoft Publisher, and so on) always report that my HP DeskJet printer is using a Print Quality selection of 300 dpi. Is there any way to change the resolution?

No. Even though the Print Quality selection appears as 300 dpi, the HP print driver software takes over the print quality and adjusts it automatically. The print quality and paper type settings selected in the print driver determine the dpi based on the printer's specifications.

In order to speed printing, your DeskJet driver is designed to be as fast and efficient as possible; therefore, HP prefers that the application send the image to the printer driver at 300 dpi. Once the image is transferred to the driver, it is changed so that it is the higher resolution advertised with the printer. The driver does not want to rely on the application making this adjustment because it is much faster for the print driver to do this.

For example, if the driver reported 600 dpi to the application, the application would send a 600 dpi image to the driver — in other words, the application would send eight times as much data to the driver than it would if the driver had reported 300 dpi. Instead, the process that is used is much more efficient. The application sends the driver a 300 dpi image and the driver changes it to 600 dpi, or whatever is supported for the printer. This process results in faster printing and the same print quality as if the application had "done all the work."

I want to share my HP printer on my network under Windows 95/ Windows 98, using Microsoft Networking. How do I share a printer?

Install the HP Printer product as a dedicated device on your desktop using the instructions in the printer user's guide or the Quick Setup Guide. Then, make sure the printer is working fine before you proceed.

First, ensure that Print Sharing is enabled in the Control Panel on the computer that's connected to your HP printer by performing the following steps:

1. Select Start ⇨ Settings ⇨ Control Panel.

2. Double-click the Network icon.

3. Select the File and Print Sharing button.

4. Verify that a check mark is next to "I want to be able to allow others to print to my printer(s)" in the File and Print Sharing dialog box.

5. Click OK in the File and Print Sharing dialog box.

6. Click OK in the Network dialog box. (You may be prompted to restart Windows. If you receive this prompt, choose Yes to restart, then proceed to the next step.)

7. Close the Control Panel.

Now you can share the printer by following these steps:

8. Select Start ⇨ Settings ⇨ Printers.

9. Click the HP Printer icon in the Printers window with the right mouse button.

10. Select Properties from the Menu.

11. Choose the Sharing tab in the HP Printer Properties.

12. Select Shared As.

13. Type a name for the printer in the Share Name box (for example, "Control Room Printer").

14. Click OK and close the Printers window.

My inkjet printer seems to be printing text "tilted" on the page. What can I do?

You have a *skewing* problem. Skew occurs when the movement of paper in the mechanism is not square to the printhead movement. The result is inconsistent print margins along the paper's edge (printing appears tilted on the page).

Here are some tips to avoid skewing:

- Properly handle and load the paper to minimize skew. Make sure that the paper is loaded evenly against the right wall of the tray and the paper guides are against the paper stack.
- Maintain a stack of paper in the trays.
- Load only one type of media in the trays.
- Check your paper supply; some types of paper and preprinted forms can impact print skew.
- Load a stack of paper into an empty tray rather than add paper to an existing paper stack in the tray.

I'm using a tractor-feed system for labels and continuous paper, and I'm having problems with paper jams and misfeeds. Why?

Tractor feed materials are prone to paper jams unless they've been properly loaded. Here are some guidelines for avoiding misfeeds and paper jams. Make sure that

- Pin holes are aligned over the pins on the tractor feed.
- Tractor gates are closed over the paper.
- Paper bail is closed.
- Paper is not dog-eared or wrinkled.
- Paper is loaded evenly in tractors.
- Pinch rollers are spaced one-half inch from each edge of the paper.
- Paper-release lever has been moved to the proper position.
- Paper path is clear, with no bits of paper stuck in the tractors or under the pinch rollers.
- Paper is not feeding back into the rear of the printer.

How do I clean my HP DeskJet 600 series printer to prevent black ink streaks?

Small quantities of dust, hair, fibers, and other debris can build up inside your HP DeskJet or DeskWriter printer to produce streaks or smears on your output. Occasional cleaning of the printer prevents this from happening.

The following is a quick and simple process that cleans debris and fibers from your printer to guarantee clear, sharp output every time. HP recommends that you perform this process at least every three months.

Before you start, make sure you have the following:

■ About 10 cotton swabs or any clean pieces of soft, lint-free material that does not come apart when wet or leave fibers behind.

■ Enough distilled, filtered, or bottled water to moisten the swabs. Tap water should be avoided since it can contain contaminants that may damage the print cartridges.

■ Sheets of paper or paper towels to rest the print cartridges on while you are working.

Warning

Keep the print cartridges out of reach of children.

Step 1. Remove the print cartridges. To remove print cartridges, follow these steps and refer to Figure A.1:

1. Turn the printer on and lift the top cover; wait while the print cartridges move to the center of the printer.

2. After the print cartridges have moved to the center of the printer, unplug the black power cord from the back of the printer.

3. Remove both print cartridges and place them on their sides on a sheet of paper.

Note

Do not leave the print cartridges outside the printer for longer than 30 minutes. If a cartridge is left uncapped for too long, the ink dries out and the cartridge becomes unusable. Be careful not to get any ink on your hands or clothes.

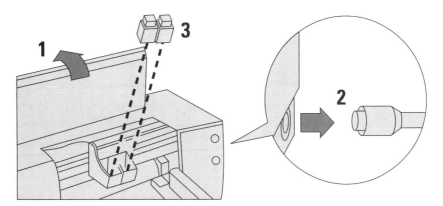

Figure A.1 Removing print cartridges

Step 2. Clean the print cartridges. Here's how you clean the print cartridges:

1. Dip a clean cotton swab in water and squeeze out any excess.

2. Hold the black print cartridge by the colored cap.

3. Use the swab to wipe clean the face and edges of the print cartridge as shown by the arrows in Figure A.2. *Do not* wipe the nozzle plate.

4. Inspect the cartridge to see if any debris has been left behind. To do this, hold up the cartridge to the light and tilt it at an angle. If you see any traces of dust, dirt, or fibers, repeat Steps 2 and 3 to remove them.

5. Now repeat Steps 1–4 to clean the color print cartridge. Always use a fresh cotton swab for each cartridge to avoid transferring debris from one cartridge to another.

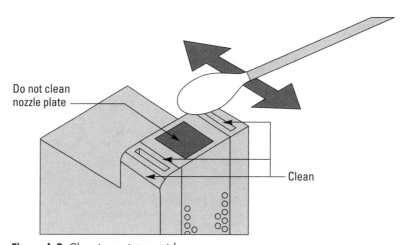

Do not clean nozzle plate

Clean

Figure A.2 Cleaning print cartridges

Step 3. Clean the print cartridge cradle. Here's how you clean the print cartridge cradle:

1. Locate the cradle that holds the print cartridges.

2. Locate the three black, hook-shaped arms on the base of the cradle. If you lift the front of the printer slightly, you will see these more easily. Lower the printer before proceeding to step 3.

3. Using clean, moistened swabs, wipe the flat surfaces (the shaded areas shown in Figure A.3) underneath each arm, from back to front.

4. Repeat the process until no ink is left on a clean swab.

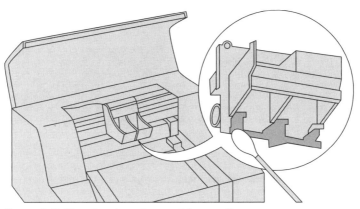

Figure A.3 Cleaning the print cartridge cradle

Step 4. Clean the service station. To clean the service station, follow these steps and refer to Figure A.4:

1. The service station is located behind the on/off switch on the right side of your printer (see Figure A.4). You need to reach back behind the casing to clean it.

2. Using a clean, moistened swab, wipe the rim of the sponge holder (shown in black).

3. Remove any built-up ink and fibers from the top of the sponge. If the sponge is higher than the rim, use the cotton swab to push it down below the rim.

4. Using a clean, moistened swab, clean Wiper 1 and the top surface of Cap 1. Always use a light touch when cleaning the print cartridge caps. Rubbing may unseat the caps which can eventually damage the print cartridges.

5. Take another clean, moistened swab and clean Wiper 2 and the top surface of Cap 2.

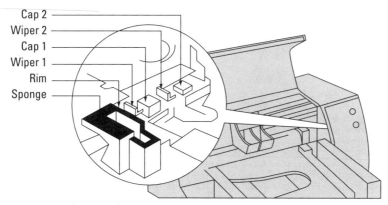

Figure A.4 Cleaning the service station

Step 5. Reinstall the print cartridges. Now you put the print cartridges back:

1. Reinstall the print cartridges and close the printer's top cover.

2. Reinsert the black power cord into the back of the printer.

Step 6. Check your output. Run paper through your printer to see if it worked:

1. Open your HP DeskJet or DeskWriter 600 Series Toolbox.

2. Select the Printer Services tab in the Toolbox.

3. Click the Print a Self-Test Page button.

4. Check the output for streaks.

Note

One careful cleaning is usually enough to remove any streaks. However, it is possible that fibers or debris may have been missed, which may interfere with print quality. To remove them, repeat the cleaning procedure until the test printout is totally clear and sharp.

For trouble-free printing with your HP DeskJet or DeskWriter printer, remember to clean the cartridge, cradle, and service station every three months. You can find other useful tips about how to maintain an HP DeskJet printer at the HP DeskJet Customer Self-Service Center site at www.deskjet-support.com.

I have an HP DeskJet 710C/720C/880C/895C-series printer and Windows is suddenly displaying the printer status message "Incompatible Color Cartridge." What's going on?

The printer driver has detected that the wrong print cartridge is in the color (left) cartridge slot of the print carriage. This may be true, or it may be a false message caused by something interfering with the electrical contact points on the cartridge.

Check to see if the installed cartridge is the correct one for the printer. The correct color ink cartridge part numbers are HP C1823A, C1823D, and C1823G for most of the printers in this product series. For the HP DeskJet 840C/842C printers the part number for the color cartridge is C6625 series.

If the cartridge is the proper part number, remove the ink cartridge and make sure that all packaging tape has been removed from the copper circuitry strip on the back side of the cartridge. Reinsert the cartridge and try printing again.

If the error continues, remove the cartridge again. Clean the copper circuitry strip on the back side of the cartridge, and the contacts inside the printer, by following the instructions listed:

1. Use a clean, dry, soft, lint-free cloth. Locate the copper-colored circuitry strip on the back of the cartridge.

2. Wipe the copper-colored strip with the dry cloth. Use an upward motion, from the nozzle end to the top of the cartridge. Do not wipe the nozzle end of the cartridge or touch the nozzle plate. Wipe the contacts only once.

3. To clean the printer contacts, carefully look for fibers or contamination on the electrical contacts inside the carriage assembly, but do not wipe the printer contacts with any object. The contacts in the printer can be damaged if too much pressure is applied during a wiping process. Try to remove any visibly attached debris within the carriage assembly by gently pulling the debris off with your fingers. If the carriage contacts show noticeable damage, contact the HP Customer Care Center listed in the printer user's guide.

Reinsert the cartridge and try printing again. If the error continues, the cartridge may need to be replaced.

Why do my HP DeskJet print cartridges sometimes print wrong colors? For example, red looks like brown.

Incorrect configuration settings in the software program that you're using to print or accidental mixing of colors inside the print cartridge can cause this condition.

■ **Configuration settings.** Configuration settings in the program that you are using can affect the way that colors print. Suspect this cause if the colors print correctly in another software program. If all of the software programs print wrong colors, configuration settings are not the cause.

- **Accidental mixing of colors.** You can print a self-test page to determine if the colors in the cartridge have mixed (see the instructions in this book or your owner's manual for step-by-step instructions). If the self-test page does not print with the proper colors, call Hewlett-Packard for help in resolving the problem.

  The print cartridge has three separate chambers — one for each of its three ink colors (cyan, yellow, and magenta). The colors become mixed when ink from one chamber finds its way to another chamber. This color mixing can happen in several ways:

  - Any nonporous material placed in contact with the nozzle area can cause the inks to mix through a phenomenon known as *capillary action*. Generally, color mixing results after reapplying tape to the nozzle area of the cartridge in an attempt to prolong its life. The tape is not designed to be reapplied once you remove it from a new print cartridge, and reapplying the tape can cause color mixing.

  - Color mixing also occurs when you place the entire print cartridge in a resealable plastic bag to keep the print cartridge from drying out. If the nozzle area comes into contact with the plastic bag, color mixing can result.

  If color mixing is the problem, the print cartridge is probably permanently damaged. However, if the mixing did not occur over a long period of time, the output may improve with use. When the color mixing occurs only in the print-head portion of the cartridge and does not contaminate the ink in the reservoir itself, the print quality may improve as you use the printer.

  If the print cartridge is new or if the color mixing has occurred even though nothing was allowed to come into contact with the nozzles, the tape placed on the nozzles during manufacture may have caused the problem. The tape over the nozzles occasionally lifts slightly during shipment, thereby providing a path for the inks to mix.

Are there any limitations to using USB with my HP DeskJet 810C, 830C, 880C, or 895 series printer?

At the time of this writing, Hewlett-Packard's drivers for these printers do not support bidirectional communication when using USB. Although the printer will work, it is not able to send error messages back to the computer if a problem exists. As a result, any driver feature that depends upon bidirectional communication (such as two-sided printing) will not function using USB. Printing from DOS is also not supported with USB, because DOS does not recognize a USB-connected printer.

Why won't my USB printer work after I've moved it from one USB hub to another?

If you shut down the computer and move USB devices from one hub to another, the USB devices become "confused" and may not work when you bring the system back up again. To fix the problem, unplug and then replug the USB devices, starting with the one closest to the root hub. In general, you should move USB devices only when the computer system is turned on. If the HP printer is having trouble with certain hubs when they are chained together, move the printer to Tier 1, the hub directly connected to the computer's USB port.

Why is my HP DeskJet printing in black and white when the file is displayed in color on my monitor?

There are several reasons why the printer may not print in color. Some software packages have options to print only in grayscale or black and white. Check the options or preferences of your software package.

Follow these steps to check your printer:

1. Run a self-test to ensure that the color cartridge is functioning properly; the self-test page should print with color ink as well as black ink. With the Power light on, press and hold the Resume button until the printer picks up a piece of paper. (If you have an HP DeskJet 710C, 720C, 820C, or 1000C series printer, hold the Power button, press the Resume button four times, and then release the Power button. If you have an HP OfficeJet, select Self Test from the Print Reports menu. If you have an HP OfficeJet Pro, press the menu button until Self Test displays and press Copy.)

2. If the self-test does not print in color, there may be a problem with the color print cartridge. Make sure the tape is removed from the nozzles of the cartridge. Try a different color print cartridge if the problem persists.

3. Make sure you've selected the appropriate printer driver. A monochrome (black-only) driver, like the LaserJet or the generic HP DeskJet driver, causes the printer to print all files without color ink. Visit the HP Web site at www.hp.com to download the proper printer driver for your printer.

Checking drivers in Windows 95, Windows 98, and Windows Me Follow these steps to check your driver for color operation under Windows 95/98/Me:

1. Exit the software program.

2. Choose Start ➩ Settings ➩ Printers.

3. Highlight the appropriate printer (for example, HP DeskJet 670C Series Printer).

4. Choose File ⇨ Set As Default.

5. Choose File ⇨ Properties.

6. Choose the Details tab.

7. Verify that the listing in the box titled "Print using the following driver" matches the HP printer that is being used.

8. Choose OK and close the Printers window.

9. Run the software program and try printing again.

Checking drivers in Windows NT 4.0 and Windows 2000 Follow these steps to check your driver for color operation under Windows NT 4.0 and Windows 2000:

1. Exit the software program.

2. Choose Start ⇨ Settings ⇨ Printers.

3. Highlight the appropriate printer (for example, HP DeskJet 670C Series Printer).

4. Choose File ⇨ Set As Default.

5. Choose File ⇨ Properties.

6. Verify that the listing in the box titled "Driver" matches the HP printer that is being used.

7. Choose OK and close the Printers window.

8. Run the software program and try printing again.

9. Check the software settings for sending color to the printer.

Checking printer settings in Windows 95, Windows 98, and Windows Me Follow these steps to check your printer's settings for color operation under Windows 95/98/Me:

1. Exit the software program.

2. Choose Start ⇨ Settings ⇨ Printers.

3. Highlight the appropriate printer.

4. Select File ⇨ Properties.

5. Choose the Setup or Color tab and remove the check from the "Print in Grayscale" box.

6. Choose OK and close the Printers window.

7. Run the software program and try printing again.

Checking printer settings in Windows NT 4.0 and Windows 2000 Follow these steps to check your printer's settings for color operation under Windows NT 4.0 and Windows 2000:

1. Exit the software program.

2. Choose Start ⇨ Settings ⇨ Printers.

3. Highlight the appropriate printer.

4. Select File ⇨ Document Defaults.

5. Choose the Setup or Color tab and remove the check from the "Print in Grayscale" box.

6. Choose OK and close the Printers window.

7. Run the software program and try printing again.

One of the following error messages appears when I attempt to load the HP DeskJet 500, 600, 700, 800, 1000, or 1100 series printer driver in Windows — or when I try to print. What should I do?

- HPVSETUP caused a General Protection Fault (GPF) in module FX-Comm.drv or PBComm.drv at XXXX:XXXX.

- The program has performed an illegal operation. The details of the illegal operation reveal HPVSETUP caused a GPF in COMM95.DRV.

- There was an error writing to LPT1 for the printer. The parameter is incorrect.

- There was an error writing to LPT1 for the printer due to an unknown system error.

Contact your computer manufacturer or FaxWorks/Phone Center technical support to update to the latest release of its software.

If the printer is needed immediately, modify the SYSTEM.INI file as follows, so that the driver may be loaded and the printer prints properly:

Warning

The following workaround may disable portions of the FaxWorks or the Phone Center software.

1. In Windows 95, select Start ⇨ Run.

2. On the Open line or the Command Line, type **SYSEDIT** and choose OK. Double-click the title bar that reads C:\WINDOWS\SYSTEM.INI to bring that window to the front and maximize it.

3. Under the [boot] section, locate the line `comm.drv=fx-comm.drv` (or locate the lines `comm.drv=pbcomm.drv` and `pbcomm.drv=comm.drv`). The lines are normally 6 to 10 lines down from the top of the [boot] section.

4. Move the cursor to the beginning of each appropriate line and insert a semicolon (;), which disables that particular line. The lines should now read as follows:

   ```
   ;comm.drv=fx-comm.drv
   ;comm.drv=pbcomm.drv
   ;pbcomm.drv=commdrv
   ```

5. Place the cursor at the beginning of the `;comm.drv=fx-comm.drv` or `;comm.drv=pbcomm.drv` line and press Enter. This creates a blank line above the respective line.

6. Place the cursor at the beginning of the blank line and type

   ```
   comm.drv=comm.drv
   ```

7. Save the file by choosing File ⇨ Save. When the SYSTEM.INI file is saved, SYSEDIT automatically creates a backup copy of the SYSTEM.INI file that is named SYSTEM.SYD.

8. Close the SYSTEM.INI by choosing File ⇨ Exit.

9. Restart Windows for the changes to take effect. Once Windows has restarted, the printer driver can be installed. If the driver is already installed, the system is ready to print.

If an ink cartridge is not properly inserted and identified by the HP DeskJet 600 series printer, one of the following symptoms occurs. What can I do?

- The yellow Resume light blinks.

- The ink cartridge carriage remains stalled in the center position of the carriage guide.

- Documents display poor print quality, are missing colors, or have blank pages.

As your printer gets older, changing the ink cartridges more often increases the chance that an ink cartridge does not seat perfectly in the ink cartridge carriage. If this occurs, sufficient electrical contact between the ink cartridge and the printer may not be established, and the printer may not correctly identify the ink cartridge. Dust, dirt, lint, or foreign residue on the ink cartridge, carriage, or contact points and worn or damaged contact points can cause improper ink cartridge seating.

When changing the ink cartridges, use the following procedure to properly install them, as well as extend the life of the ink cartridges:

1. With the power on, lift the top cover so that the carriage moves to the center position.

2. Remove the currently installed ink cartridge (if the ink cartridge is to be used again, place the ink cartridge in the storage container).

3. Place a new or alternate ink cartridge into the carriage (if the ink cartridge is new, carefully remove the protective tape that covers the ink nozzles).

4. Snap the ink cartridge into position. You should hear a click when the ink cartridge snaps snugly in the carriage.

5. Close the top cover. The Resume light should flash for a few seconds before going off. The carriage should return to the home position on the right side of the printer.

If the Resume light (top yellow light) continues to flash, the ink cartridge has not established sufficient contact and has not been properly identified by the printer. In this case, use the following procedure:

1. Do not turn the power off.

2. Open the top cover so that the carriage moves to the center position.

3. Remove the ink cartridge.

4. Unplug the power to the printer.

5. Check to see if the ink cartridge contacts are clean (the contacts are located on the back of the ink cartridge). If the contacts are not clean, clean the contacts with a foam rubber swab or lint-free cloth slightly dampened with water (do not touch the contacts or nozzle plate).

6. Inspect the contacts located on the back wall of the carriage for cleanliness and damage. If dirt or dust is present, clean the carriage contacts with a foam rubber swab or lint-free cloth slightly dampened with water. If the carriage contacts show noticeable damage, contact the HP Customer Support Center listed in the printer's user guide.

7. Use a dry foam rubber swab or lint-free cloth to remove the moisture from the contacts.

8. Plug in the printer. Turn the printer on.

9. Place the ink cartridge into the carriage.

10. Snap the ink cartridge into position. You'll hear a click when the ink cartridge snaps snugly in the carriage.

11. Close the top cover. The Resume light should flash for a few seconds before going off. The carriage should return to the home position on the right side of the printer.

12. If a good connection is still not established, try the procedure with a new ink cartridge.

13. If a new ink cartridge is not establishing a good connection, the printer may need to be serviced. Contact the HP Customer Support Center listed in the printer user's guide.

What can I do if my HP DeskJet 600 series printer is not printing and exhibits one or more of the following symptoms?

- Drive rollers rotate but do not pick up paper.

- Printer makes grinding noises.

- Printer lights blink.

- The carriage assembly, which holds the ink cartridges, stalls at the left side of the printer.

The cause of the problem may be that the printer's clutch actuator is disengaged. Follow these instructions to re-engage the clutch actuator:

1. Open the printer lid.

2. Unplug the power cord from the back of the printer.

3. Remove the upper (Out) paper tray.

4. Slide the carriage assembly, which holds the ink cartridges, away from the left side of the printer. If the carriage assembly moves away from the left side, go to Step 6. If the carriage assembly is stuck on the left side, go to Step 5.

5. If the carriage assembly is stuck at the left side, push down on the large black bar directly above the three large rollers and release it so it springs back up. Gently lift the carriage assembly and try moving it to the right again.

6. Locate the metal gear assembly at the left side of the printer. Directly above the metal gear is the clutch actuator (also known as the slider arm) — a small plastic arm that is approximately 50 mm (2 inches). On the right edge of the clutch actuator is an "arrow" or "tooth" that points down. The arrow on the clutch actuator should be in the space to the right of the metal gear and plastic half-gear just below the clutch actuator.

7. If the arrow on the clutch actuator is stuck between the metal gear and plastic half-gear, lift the clutch actuator and move the arrow to the right of the plastic half-gear. Once the arrow on the clutch actuator is to the right of the gears, the clutch actuator should move freely right and left about 12.7 mm (0.5 inches).

8. Replace the upper (Out) paper tray.

9. Close the printer lid.

10. Plug in the power cord to the back of the printer.

11. Turn the printer on.

12. Print a self-test by pressing and holding the Resume button (upper button) for five seconds and releasing it.

13. If the same problem still exists, verify that both ink cartridges are snapped into the carriage tightly and are not loose. See the procedure listed in this book, the printer's User Guide, or the HP Toolbox in Windows for instructions on installing the ink cartridges.

14. Try printing a self-test again.

15. If the same problem still exists, contact the HP Customer Care Center listed in the printer user's guide.

Carriage stalls caused by the clutch actuator being out of position can result from

■ Clearing paper jams by pulling the paper out of the printer without first turning the printer off.

■ Improper ink cartridge installation, causing the cartridge to bump the clutch actuator and push it out of position.

To prevent this problem from occurring in the future

■ Always turn off the printer before trying to clear a paper jam. See the printer user's guide or the HP Toolbox in Windows for instructions on clearing paper jams.

■ Ensure that the ink cartridges are installed correctly. See the printer user's guide or the HP Toolbox in Windows for instructions on installing the ink cartridges.

I'm trying to install the printer software for my HP DeskJet 880C/895C printer through the Add Printer Wizard, and Windows displays the error message "This printer cannot be installed because its driver (You_must_ use_the_supplied_setup_program_to_install_this_printer!) could not be loaded. The driver or the INF file may be damaged. Restart Windows and then try again." What's wrong?

This message appears because the correct method for installing the HP Desk-Jet 880C/895C printer software is through Start and Run, not through the Add Printer Wizard. Click Start and Run, and then click Browse and select SETUP.EXE from the HP CD. The Start and Run method runs the INF file from the root directory of the CD.

The printer software can only be installed through the Add Printer Wizard using the INF file located in the \ENU\9XINF directory on the CD. To do this, go through the Add Printer Wizard until prompted to select "Have Disk." Select Browse and go to the \ENU\9XINF directory on the CD and use this INF file. The printer software will now load without errors.

What should I do for a paper-feed problem on my HP DeskJet 600 Series printer?

Paper feed problems on the HP DeskJet 600 series printer typically fall into one of these categories:

- Problem 1: Paper-pick problem
- Problem 2: Paper does not advance to the Out tray
- Problem 3: The printer feeds multiple pages
- Problem 4: Envelopes do not advance into the printer
- Problem 5: Cards do not advance into the printer
- Problem 6: Banner paper does not advance into the printer

Problem 1: Paper-pick problem If the Resume light blinks, the HP DeskJet printer may be detecting a *paper-pick* (feed) problem. A paper-pick problem occurs if the printer tries to pull paper from the In tray to the platen (paper-feed mechanism) but does not detect paper at the Out Of Paper Sensor (OOPS) flag. Always verify that the paper you use meets the specifications for HP DeskJet 600 series printers. Table A.1 lists possible causes for and solutions to Problem 1.

Table A.1 Solutions to Problem 1	
Possible Cause	**Solution**
The In tray is out of media.	Load media in the In tray and press the Resume button.
Media is not properly loaded.	Remove media, re-square the stack, and reload the media in the In tray. Press the Resume button.
The media-width adjuster or media-length adjuster is not properly set.	Ensure that the media-width adjuster is against the left side of the stack, but is not blocking the stack. Push in on the media-length adjuster to ensure that the media are fully seated in the printer. Do not push too hard or else you'll buckle the media.
The In tray is too full.	Load no more than 100 sheets of 20-lb. paper in the In tray.
Media is outside of specifications.	Verify that the media meets media specifications. If it is outside of specifications, replace the media in the In tray.
The drive rollers need cleaning.	Clean the drive rollers with a soft cotton cloth slightly dampened with water.
The Out tray assembly is not properly installed on the HP DeskJet printer.	Remove and reinstall the Out tray assembly.
Different media types, sizes, or weights are loaded at the same time.	Reload the stack with media of only one type, size, and weight.
Media is improperly loaded.	Remove the media stack from the In tray. Ensure that the stack is even and does not contain wrinkled, curled, or damaged media. Reload the media stack.
The HP DeskJet printer is faulty.	Return the printer for repair.

Problem 2: Paper does not advance to the Out tray Table A.2 lists possible causes for and solutions to Problem 2.

Table A.2 Solutions to Problem 2	
Possible Cause	*Solution*
If printing on a transparency or special paper, the HP DeskJet printer may be waiting for the automatic dry timer to complete its cycle.	Wait a few minutes for the page to drop.
The computer was turned off while the HP DeskJet printer was printing.	Turn on the computer and printer to eject the page. Resend the file to the printer if it is not complete.
The Out tray is not properly attached to the HP DeskJet printer.	Remove and reinstall the Out tray.
Media is not properly loaded or is buckled.	Remove and reinstall media in the In tray.
The media feed rollers need cleaning.	Clean the drive rollers with a soft cotton cloth slightly dampened with water.
The HP DeskJet printer is faulty.	Return the printer for repair.

Problem 3: The printer feeds multiple pages Table A.3 lists possible causes for and solutions to Problem 3.

Table A.3 Solutions to Problem 3	
Possible Cause	*Solution*
Media is stuck together.	Remove media from the In tray, bend or flex the stack, and reload it into the In tray.
The In tray is too full.	Load no more than 100 sheets of 20-lb. paper in the In tray.
The In tray contains different types of paper.	For best results, load only one type, size, and weight of media in the In tray at a time.

Possible Cause	Solution
Media was added to an existing stack in the In tray.	Remove the stack from the In tray, re-square the stack, and reload it in the In tray.
Media does not meet the media specifications	Remove the media and reload with media that meet the media specifications.
Media is damaged, such as torn, bent, or curled.	Replace the media in the In tray.
The HP DeskJet printer is faulty.	Return the printer for repair.

Problem 4: Envelopes do not advance into the printer Table A.4 lists possible causes for and solutions to Problem 4.

Table A.4 Solutions to Problem 4	
Possible Cause	**Solution**
Envelopes do not meet the media specifications.	Replace the envelopes.
Envelopes are improperly loaded.	Slide the media-width adjuster to the appropriate envelope setting. For A2 and C6 size envelopes, release and lower the media-length adjuster; then push it toward the envelopes until it stops. Do not bend the envelopes.
Envelopes are bent or damaged.	Replaced the damaged envelopes.
Too many or too few envelopes are in the In tray.	Adjust the number of envelopes in the In tray.
More than one envelope was loaded through the envelope-feed slot.	Load only one envelope at a time through the envelope-feed slot.
The envelope is not fully pushed into the HP DeskJet printer.	Push the envelope into the printer as far as it will go without buckling.
Paper in the In tray is interfering with an envelope from the envelope-feed slot.	Reload the paper in the In tray.

Problem 5: Cards do not advance into the printer There are various causes for this problem; refer to Table A.4, in this case applying its possible causes and solutions to cards, and ensure that the card guide is flipped up in the In tray (rather than use the right wall of the In tray as a guide).

Problem 6: Banner paper does not advance into the printer Table A.5 lists possible causes for and solutions to Problem 6. (This problem applies to HP DeskJet/DeskWriter 680 and DeskJet 690 series printers only.)

Table A.5 Solutions to Problem 6	
Possible Cause	**Solution**
Media is not properly loaded or is buckled.	Cancel the print job, turn the HP DeskJet or DeskWriter printer off, and pull out the jammed media.
Media is outside of specifications.	For best results, print banners on HP Banner Paper. Avoid coated paper.

How do I cancel a print job for my HP DeskJet 600, 700, or 800 series printer?

To cancel a print job, follow these steps:

1. Open the printer's top cover when it is printing.

2. A message appears on the screen stating "Printer Top Cover is open." Choose Cancel Print on this message to cancel the print job.

3. Close the printer's top cover.

The HP DeskJet 700 series printer is not printing from a DOS program, even though the program is accessed through a Windows icon or the MS-DOS shell. The computer generates no error messages and no lights blink on the printer. Printing from Windows 95 works well. What can I do?

DOS printing is not supported within Windows NT 4.0. However, if you're printing within Windows 95 or Windows 98, follow this procedure.

Step 1. Check settings. First check your settings:

1. Select Start ➩ Settings ➩ Printers.

2. Ensure that there are no duplicate icons for the HP DeskJet 700 Series printer. If more than one icon for the printer exists, remove all the duplicates by highlighting the extra icon and choosing File and Delete.

3. The HP DeskJet 700 Series printer icon must not be renamed in the Printers window. If the icon has been renamed, change the name back to "HP DeskJet 710C Series" or "HP DeskJet 720C Series." To do this, highlight the icon for the printer, select File and Rename. Then, type the correct name of the printer and press Enter.

4. Highlight the HP DeskJet 700 Series printer icon. Open the File menu and look for a check mark beside Set As Default. If there is no check mark, highlight the Set As Default line and click once. If the check is already there, close the File menu by clicking once on any blank space.

5. Highlight the HP DeskJet 700 Series printer icon. Open the File menu and ensure that no check mark is beside Pause Printing. If there is a check mark, highlight the Pause Printing line and click once. If the check is already there, close the File menu by clicking once on any blank space.

6. Select File ➪ Properties. Select the Details tab. Ensure that the correct port and printer driver are selected.

7. (If you're using the version 10.3 printer driver, skip this step.) In the Properties window, select Port Settings under the Details tab. Ensure that "Spool MS-DOS print jobs" is selected and "Check port state before printing" is not selected. Select OK.

8. In the Properties window, select Spool Settings under the Details tab. Ensure that "Enable bidirectional support for this printer" is selected. Select OK. If this selection is grayed out, delete and reinstall the printer driver software.

9. Under the Details tab of the Properties window, select OK.

Step 2. Access the program from the MS-DOS prompt. Now run the program in DOS:

1. Select Start ➪ Programs ➪ MS-DOS Prompt.

2. At the C:\ prompt, type the path to the DOS program and press Enter.

3. Print from the DOS application. Within the DOS application, select an HP DeskJet printer driver such as an HP DeskJet 660C, 550C, or 500 printer. If an HP DeskJet printer selection is not available in the DOS application, a LaserJet or a LaserJet II selection may work. If these selections are not available, contact the DOS application vendor for an appropriate driver. If printing does not occur from the DOS box or a partial page is printed, follow these steps.

Step 3. Verify that the problem is not program-specific. Sometimes the problem depends on the program:

1. Select Start ➪ Programs ➪ MS-DOS Prompt.
2. At the C:\WINDOWS prompt, type **CD** and press Enter.
3. At the C:\ prompt, type **DIR>LPT1** and press Enter.
4. Press the printer's Resume button to complete the directory print.
5. If the directory prints, print from the DOS application again. If the directory does not print, continue with the following steps.

Step 4. Check the port mode. Sometimes you have to determine the proper port:

1. At the C:\ prompt, type **MODE LPT1:,,P** and press Enter. If the printer is connected to another port such as LPT2, replace LPT1 with LPT2 in the command. Print the DOS directory again.
2. If the directory prints, print from the DOS application again. If the directory does not print, continue with the following steps.

Step 5. Delete and reinstall the printer driver. If the directory prints, print from the DOS application again. If the directory does not print, continue with the following steps.

Step 6. Run the DOS program in a partial window. Try running the program in its own window:

1. Right-click the Start button and select Open.
2. Open the Programs folder.
3. Right-click the MS-DOS Prompt and select Properties.
4. Select the Screen tab.
5. Change the Usage option to "Window" instead of "Full-screen" and select OK.
6. Close the Start Menu window.
7. Open the MS-DOS Prompt and run the DOS-based application.
8. Try printing again.

Tip

Pressing Alt-Enter toggles the DOS application from a full screen to a window or from a window to a full screen and can be used in place of the previously mentioned procedures.

Step 7. Determine whether the Windows 98 spooler is receiving the DOS print job. It's possible that the spooler is not receiving the print job:

1. Select Start ⇨ Settings ⇨ Printers.

2. Highlight the HP DeskJet 700 Series printer icon and select File ⇨ Pause Printing.

3. Print a DOS directory again by following the instructions in the previous "Step 3. Verify that the problem is not program-specific" section.

4. When the DOS prompt returns, type **EXIT** and press Enter.

5. In the Printers window, double-click the HP DeskJet 700 Series printer icon to view the print spooler. If a print job appears, select Printer ⇨ Pause Printing. The print job should begin printing at the printer. Print from the DOS application again. If the print job does not appear in the print spooler, contact the computer manufacturer's technical support or Windows 95 technical support and ensure that the Windows 95 print spooler is set up to spool DOS print jobs. Also, verify that the LPT.VXD file in Windows 95 is the latest version.

Step 8. Disable bidirectional communications/launch toolbox when printing. Disabling these options may do the trick:

1. Select Start ⇨ Run. Type **HPFCFG06**, **HPFCFG13**, or **HPFCFG14** and select OK.

2. In the HP DeskJet Configuration dialog box select Continue.

3. Deselect Bidirectional Communication and Launch Toolbox When Printing and select OK.

4. Select Return to Windows.

5. Select Start ⇨ Run. Type **HPFDJC06.INI**, **HPFDJC13.INI**, or **HPFDJC14.INI** and choose OK.

6. In the HP DeskJet 700 series printer initialization file, locate the section [LPT1,HPDeskJet 7x0C Series]. In this section, find the line 2DSMEnable=0200 and change the line to read 2DSMEnable=0000.

7. Select File ⇨ Save.

8. Exit and restart Windows 95.

9. Print the directory from the DOS shell. If successful, print from the DOS application.

Step 9. Change the form feed timeout settings. Altering the timeout settings can help:

1. Select Start ⇨ Settings ⇨ Printers.

2. Highlight the HP DeskJet 700 Series icon, and select File ⇨ Properties.

3. Select the DOS tab and deselect Form Feed Timeout.

4. Select OK and close the Printers window.

5. Print the directory from the DOS shell. If successful, print from the DOS application. If unsuccessful, restart the computer.

Note

The printer does not receive the form feed signal if you remove the check from the Form Feed Timeout line. If the Resume light on the printer flashes, press the Resume button to provide a manual feed command to the printer.

Step 10. Delete any temporary files from the hard drive.

Warning

Deleting temporary files should be done carefully so necessary files are not deleted. All temporary files use the extension .TMP. If you are unsure about the proper procedures for identifying, locating, or selecting temporary files for deletion, contact the computer manufacturer's technical support or Windows 98/Me technical support for assistance.

Deleting temporary files may solve the problem:

1. At the Windows 98/Me main desktop, select Start ⇨ Find ⇨ Files or Folders.

2. On the Named line, type ***.tmp** and on the Look In line, type **C:**. Ensure that Include Subfolders is selected. Click the Find Now button.

3. Highlight the files in the Search Results list by selecting Edit ⇨ Select All.

4. Select File ⇨ Delete. (Windows does not allow Windows files that are currently being used to be deleted.)

5. Print the DOS directory again. If the directory prints, print from the DOS application again.

Step 11. Run the Windows ScanDisk and Disk Defragmenter utilities.

Step 12. Install the printer driver software on another computer and print from a DOS application or print a DOS directory.

My HP ScanJet 6300 scanner has a "Scan to Print" button in the HP ScanJet Copy Utility. When I'm printing to my HP DeskJet 900 series printer through a USB connection, the "Scan to Print" button can be used once without a problem. But when used a second time, the printer's power light flashes and/or the print job never prints. What's going on?

Press the "Printer Setup" button on the HP ScanJet Copy Utility before using the "scan to print" button. All "scan to print" jobs will then print correctly without problems. This needs to be done each time you open the program. The other option is to switch to a parallel connection.

When the Power light is on and the Resume light is flashing, my HP DeskJet 710C, 712C, and 720C series printer indicates a paper jam — but that doesn't seem to be the problem. What can I do?

If the Power light is on and the Resume light is flashing, the printer may be detecting a paper jam, but it can also mean you have other paper problems. Check these other possible causes and solutions:

Is paper buckled in the In drawer? If so, then

- Make sure the media length adjuster is snug against the end of the paper stack, but doesn't push the paper enough to cause buckling.
- Make sure the adjustable left wall is against the left side of the stack, but doesn't push the paper enough to cause buckling.

Is the paper loaded correctly in the In drawer? If you're not sure, then

- Remove the paper from the In drawer, and tap the paper stack on a flat surface to square the stack. Reload the paper in the In drawer.
- Make sure the Left Wall is against the left side of the paper stack.
- Make sure the media length adjuster is snug against the end of the stack.

Is the In drawer too full? If so, then remove any excess paper. The In drawer can only hold up to 100 sheets of 20-lb paper (about a half-inch stack).

Is the Out tray too full? If so, then remove any excess paper. The Out tray can only hold up to 50 sheets.

Is the paper the proper size and type? If not, then

- Select different paper. The printer does not work properly if the paper is longer than 14 inches.

- When printing banners, make sure the banner switch is in the up position and the banner light is on.

- Use paper that meets the media handling specifications listed in your printer user's guide.

Are mixed paper types in the In drawer? For best paper handling, load only one type of paper at a time in the In drawer.

Was paper added to an existing stack in the In drawer? Follow this procedure to add paper to your printer:

1. Remove all paper from the In drawer.

2. Add more paper to the stack while it is not in the printer.

3. Tap the paper stack on a flat surface to square the stack, and load the paper into the In drawer as one stack.

Is something blocking the paper path? If so, then look for obstructions that may block the paper path. Follow this procedure to clear a paper jam on the HP DeskJet 710C, 712C, and 720C series of printers:

1. Turn the printer off and then on to let the printer clear the paper jam. If the paper is still jammed, turn the printer off and follow the remaining steps.

2. Turn the Clean-out Assembly handle counter-clockwise to the unlocked position, and remove it from the rear panel of the printer.

3. Grab the jammed paper in the middle. Slowly and firmly pull the jammed paper out of the back of the printer. Remove all torn pieces from the paper path.

4. Remove any wrinkled or torn paper from the In drawer.

5. Reload the paper in the In drawer.

6. Replace the Clean-out Assembly handle.

7. Turn the printer on.

The HP DeskJet 500, 600, 660C, or 850C series v 5.0x or 6.1x printer driver has been loaded into Windows 95. These drivers were written for Windows 3.1x and do not work in Windows 95. How can I use my printer in Windows 95 and Windows 98?

Loading these drivers in Windows 95 corrupts the printing system and the driver. Remove the Windows 3.1*x* printer driver and install the Windows 95 printer driver by following these steps:

1. Verify that the Windows 95 Installation CD-ROM is available for use when installing the Windows 95 printer driver.

2. Start or restart Windows 95.

3. Select Start ⇨ Settings ⇨ Printers.

4. Right-click the HP DeskJet 500, 600, 660C, or 850C series printer icon to display the drop-down menu and select Delete. If the message "There are now unused files on the system" appears, select Yes to remove these files. (If the icon cannot be deleted, right-click the icon to display the drop-down menu and select Purge Print Jobs — then repeat this step.)

5. Close the Printers window after deleting all the HP DeskJet 500, 600, 660C, or 850C series printer icons.

6. Select Start and Shut Down.

7. Select "Restart the computer in MS-DOS mode" and click Yes.

8. If your computer doesn't restart in the \WINDOWS directory, type **cd \windows** at the DOS prompt and press Enter.

9. At the C:\WINDOWS prompt, type **del hpv*.*** and press Enter.

10. At the C:\WINDOWS prompt, type **del deskjetc.*** and press Enter.

11. At the C:\WINDOWS prompt, type **cd system** and press Enter.

12. At the C:\WINDOWS\SYSTEM prompt, type **del hpv*.*** and press Enter.

13. At the C:\WINDOWS\SYSTEM prompt, type **del deskjetc.*** and press Enter.

14. At the C:\WINDOWS\SYSTEM prompt, type **cd** and press Enter.

15. At the C:\ prompt, type **deltree DeskJet** and press Enter. When asked to confirm the removal of this directory, click Yes.

16. At the C:\ prompt, type **Exit** and press Enter to restart Windows 95.

17. Select Start ⇨ Settings ⇨ Printers.

18. Double-click the Add Printer icon and select Next.

19. Under Manufacturers, highlight Hewlett-Packard.

20. Select the printer model as follows:

- For the HP DeskJet 500 series printers, highlight the printer name under Printers and select Next.

- For the HP DeskJet 600, 660C, or 850C series printers, insert the HP Printing System for Windows disk 1 (v 7.0 or greater) into the computer's floppy drive, select Have Disk, and select OK. Highlight the printer name and select Next.

Note

If the HP Printing System for Windows (v 7.0 or greater) disks are not available for the HP DeskJet 600, 660, or 850 series printer, the HP DeskJet 550C Printer can be selected under Printers. The latest printer drivers may also be downloaded from HP's home page on the Internet at www.hp.com.

21. Select the desired port (usually LPT1:) and select Next.

22. Verify the printer name, then do the following:

- For the HP DeskJet 500 series printers, select Yes to make this the default Windows printer, and select Next. Choose Yes to print a test page and select Finish.

- For the HP Printing System for Windows v 7.0 or greater, choose Yes to make this the default Windows printer, and select Finish.

23. Follow the screen prompts to complete the installation.

What steps should I follow for loading envelopes or executive-size paper in the HP DeskJet 510, 520, 550C, or 560C series printer?

The following steps describe the procedure for loading envelopes or executive-size paper in the HP DeskJet printer.

Loading envelopes To minimize print skew, use envelopes with a rectangle-shaped flap as opposed to a triangle-shaped flap:

1. Open the Out tray cover.

2. Pull the In tray drawer outward until it stops.

3. Slide the paper width adjustment lever to the appropriate envelope setting.

4. Take out a stack of up to 20 envelopes and tap the short edge of the stack on a flat surface to even the stack.

5. Slide the stack squarely into the In tray, address side down (flap side up), past the green envelope stop.

6. Raise the green envelope stop.

7. Push the In tray into the printer until it stops. The In tray drawer does not close completely when loading envelopes.

8. Close the Out tray cover.

Loading executive-size paper Using executive-size paper can be tricky:

1. Open the Out tray cover.

2. Pull the In tray drawer outward until it stops, and remove all remaining media from the In tray.

3. Slide the paper width adjustment lever to the executive-paper size setting.

4. Remove a half-inch (1 cm) stack of media from its packaging and tap the short edge of the stack on a flat surface to even the stack.

5. Insert the paper into the In tray past the green envelope stop. Align the right edge of the paper stack with the right side of the printer.

6. Raise the green envelope stop.

7. Push the In tray into the printer until it stops. Make sure the paper does not bend in the In tray.

8. Close the Out tray cover.

Executive-size paper must be supported in the software application or the printer driver, because there is no switch setting on the printer for such paper.

What do I do if the carriage stalls on my HP DeskJet, DeskJet Plus, or 500 series printer?

The Control Panel light indications for a carriage stall differ among the HP DeskJet family of printers. They are as follows:

- The HP DeskJet printer has alternating blinking lights on the Control Panel.

- The HP DeskJet Plus and HP DeskJet 500 printers have the COUR 10/20 and Online lights blinking alternately with the other lights on the Control Panel.

- The HP DeskJet 500C, 510, 520, 550C, and 560C printers have the Portrait and Ready lights blinking alternately with the other lights on the Control Panel.

- The HP DeskJet 540 printer has the Power light blinking alternately with the Resume light.

Follow the steps under the appropriate section to solve the carriage stall.

Fixing carriage stalls on the HP DeskJet, DeskJet Plus, 500, and 500C printers

Here's how to fix stalls on these printers:

1. Turn the HP DeskJet printer off; then unplug the power to the printer.

2. Remove the Out tray cover. (A common cause of carriage stalls is the Out tray cover installed backward on the Out tray.)

3. Remove any visible obstructions to the carriage path.

4. With the HP DeskJet printer still off, manually slide the carriage across the slide bar mechanism. If the carriage does not slide across the full length of the mechanism, find and eliminate possible causes such as binding or obstructions.

5. Test to determine if the carriage stall is solved. Plug in the power and turn the HP DeskJet printer on. The carriage should move to the "home" position on the right side of the printer.

6. Reinstall the Out tray cover. Ensure that the tallest portion of the cover is against the HP DeskJet printer's lid.

7. Print a self-test page. Turn the HP DeskJet printer off and hold the Font button down on the Control Panel; then turn the printer on and release the Font button after the printer picks up paper.

If the self-test page prints properly, the carriage stall has been solved. If the carriage stall recurs, call HP Support.

Fixing carriage stalls on HP DeskJet 510, 520, 550C, and 560C printers

Warning

Do not attempt to move the carriage if it is in the home position on the right side of the HP DeskJet printer. The printer locks the carriage from moving when it is in the home position. Attempting to slide the carriage from the locked position may damage the printer.

Here's how to fix stalls on these printers:

1. Turn the HP DeskJet printer off.

2. Remove and reinsert the power module connector into the HP DeskJet printer. A power module that is not fully seated can cause a carriage stall problem.

3. Print a self-test page to determine if a loose power module connector was causing the carriage stall. To print a self-test page, hold the Font button down on the Control Panel; then turn the HP DeskJet printer on and release the Font button after the printer picks up paper. If the printer continues to experience carriage stalls, continue to the next step.

4. Press the Install Print Cartridge button to move the carriage away from the home position. Then unplug the power to the HP DeskJet printer while the carriage is out of the "home" position on the right end of the printer. If the carriage is stuck in the home position and the HP DeskJet printer cannot be turned off without the carriage in the home position, contact the HP Customer Support Center.

5. Remove any visible obstructions to the carriage path.

6. With the HP DeskJet printer still off, manually slide the carriage across the slide bar mechanism. If the carriage does not slide across the full length of the mechanism, find and eliminate possible causes such as binding or obstructions.

7. Test to determine if the carriage stall is solved. Plug in the power and turn the HP DeskJet printer on. The carriage should move along the mechanism path and return to the "home" position.

8. Print a self-test page. Turn the HP DeskJet printer off and hold the Font button down on the Control Panel; then turn the printer on and release the Font button after the printer picks up paper. If the self-test page prints properly, the carriage stall has been solved. If the carriage stall recurs, call Hewlett-Packard Support.

What can I do if the Update Device Wizard appears with the HP license agreement when installing an HP DeskJet printer driver, or the Update Device Wizard appears every time Windows is started and prompts me to install my printer?

To complete the Update Device Wizard, do the following:

1. Click Next when the Update Device window appears.

2. Click Finish to the message indicating a new driver could not be found. The Update Device window will not appear again for this printer.

3. If the HP DeskJet printer driver is being installed, click Agree To License to continue with the HP printer driver installation.

What should I do if my computer does not have a bidirectional parallel port and I am trying to print with my HP DeskJet Printer?

Printing problems may occur and you may receive error messages when the HP DeskJet printer driver is installed on a computer that does not have a bidirectional port or a bidirectional printer cable. Printing problems specific to bidirectional communication can be fixed permanently by upgrading your computer's hardware so that it does have a bidirectional port or a bidirectional printer cable, or by turning off the bidirectional function in your printer driver software.

If you turn off the bidirectional communication in your printer driver, the print quality is not affected. However, some of the advanced features of the Status Monitor or HP Toolbox are disabled:

■ You will no longer receive reminders to align the print cartridges after a new print cartridge is installed.

■ You will no longer receive error messages associated with the print cartridges.

■ You will no longer receive error messages associated with the banner lever on HP DeskJet 680C, 690C, and 720C series printers.

■ The Printer Status tab in the HP 2000C Toolbox will not show ink cartridge levels.

■ You will be unable to scan or fax using any HP all-in-one unit.

Here's how you disable bidirectional communication:

1. For Windows 95, Windows 98, or Windows NT 4.0, click Start and then click Run.

2. On the Command line, type the appropriate filename and click OK. Refer to Tables A.6 through A.9 to find your printer and its appropriate filename.

3. Click Continue in the message window.

4. Remove the X next to Print Cartridge Query and Bidirectional Communication. (There is no Print Cartridge Query line for the HP DeskJet 1120C series printer.)

5. Click OK.

6. Click Restart Windows. The bidirectional communication is disabled after Windows is restarted.

Table A.6
HP DeskJet 600 Series Printers

Printer Model	Driver Version	Operating System	Filename
DJ600/660C	6.1–6xx	Windows 3.1	HPVCNFIG.EXE
DJ660Cse	6.3–660Cse	Windows 3.1	HPFCFG01.EXE
DJ600/660C	7.0–6xx	Windows 3.1/95	HPFCFG02.EXE
DJ660Cse	7.0–660Cse	Windows 3.1/95	HPFCFG03.EXE
DJ660C/660Cse	8.0–660C/Cse	Windows 3.1/95	HPFCFG04.EXE
DJ660C/660Cse	9.01–660C/Cse	Windows 3.1/95	HPFCFG05.EXE

Printer Model	Driver Version	Operating System	Filename
DJ660C/660Cse	9.02–66x/68x/69x	Windows 3.1/95	HPFCFG07.EXE
DJ660C/660Cse	11.0–660C/Cse	Windows 3.1/95/98/ NT 4.0	HPFCFG19.EXE
DJ670C/672C	9.03–670C	Windows 3.1/95	HPFCFG08.EXE
DJ670C/672C	11.0–670C	Windows 3.1/95/98/ NT 4.0	HPFCFG18.EXE
DJ680C/682C	8.0–68x	Windows 3.1/95	HPFCFG04.EXE
DJ680C/682C	9.01–68x	Windows 3.1/95	HPFCFG05.EXE
DJ680C/682C	9.02–66x/68x/69x	Windows 3.1/95	HPFCFG07.EXE
DJ680C/682C	11.0–68x	Windows 3.1/95/98/ NT 4.0	HPFCFG17.EXE
DJ690C/693C	9.0/9.01–69x	Windows 3.1/95	HPFCFG05.EXE
DJ690C/692C/ 693C/694C	9.02–66x/68x/69x	Windows 3.1/95	HPFCFG07.EXE
DJ690C/692C/693C/ 694C/695C/697C	11.0–69x NT 4.0	Windows 3.1/95/98/	HPFCFG16.EXE

Table A.7			
HP DeskJet 700 Series Printers			
Printer Model	Driver Version	Operating System	Filename
DJ710C/712C	10.3–71x	Windows 3.1/95/98/NT 4.0	HPFCFG13.EXE
DJ720C/722C	10.0/10.1–72x	Windows 3.1/95/98/NT 4.0	HPFCFG06.EXE
DJ720C/722C	10.3–72x	Windows 3.1/95/98/NT 4.0	HPFCFG14.EXE

Table A.8			
HP DeskJet 800 Series Printers			
Printer Model	Driver Version	Operating System	Filename
DJ820C	8.0/8.2–820C	Windows 3.1/95	HPFCFG04.EXE
DJ820C	8.5–820C	Windows 3.1/95/98/NT 4.0	HPFCFG09.EXE
DJ850C	6.1–6xx	Windows 3.1	HPVCNFIG.EXE

Continued

	Table A.8 (continued)		
Printer Model	**Driver Version**	**Operating System**	**Filename**
DJ850C/855C	7.0/7.01–85x	Windows 3.1/95	HPRCFG01.EXE
DJ850C/855C	8.0–85x	Windows 3.1/95	HPRCFG02.EXE
DJ850C/855C	9.0/9.2–85x	Windows 3.1/95	HPRCFG03.EXE
DJ870C	9.0/9.2–870x	Windows 3.1/95	HPRCFG03.EXE
DJ890C	11.0–890x	Windows 3.1/95	HPRCFG06.EXE

	Table A.9 HP DeskJet 1000, 1100, and 2000 Series Printers		
Printer Model	**Driver Version**	**Operating System**	**Filename**
DJ1000C	9.0–1000	Windows 3.1/95	HPW3CFG.EXE
DJ1100C	10.0–1100	Windows 3.1/95	HPW4CFG.EXE
DJ1120C	11.0/11.1–1120x	Windows 3.1/95	HPW5CFG.EXE
HP2000C	1.0–2000	Windows 3.1/95/NT 4.0	HPRCFG07.EXE

How can I change the default settings in the HP DeskJet Printer Driver?

Changing the default settings is not hard. It depends on your operating system.

Windows 95/98/Me Follow the steps listed:

1. Select Start ➪ Settings ➪ Printers.
2. Highlight the appropriate HP DeskJet printer.
3. Select File ➪ Properties.
4. Click the Setup, Features, or Color tab and make any desired changes. (Some printer drivers may require clicking the Details tab and then the Setup button to change the printer settings.) Do not select the Default button. This button returns the printer settings to the original factory settings.
5. Click OK to save the new default settings and close the Printers window. Because some programs may overwrite the default settings set in the Printers window, it's a good idea to check the printer settings before printing.

Windows NT 4.0 Follow these steps:

1. Select Start ⇨ Settings ⇨ Printers.

2. Choose the appropriate HP DeskJet printer.

3. Select File ⇨ Document Defaults.

4. Make any desired changes. Do not select the Default button if one is available. This button returns the printer settings to the original factory settings.

5. Click OK to save the new default settings and close the Printers window. Since some programs may overwrite the default settings set in the Printers window, it's a good idea to check the printer settings before printing.

How do I clear a paper jam on my HP DeskJet 800 series printer?

Use the following procedures to clear the paper jam on your HP DeskJet 800 Series printer.

Warning

Do not attempt to turn the paper feed rollers manually. Doing so can damage your printer.

If the Power and Resume lights are alternately flashing, the printer may be detecting a paper jam error. The paper jam error occurs if the printer detects paper at the platen after attempting to eject paper to the Out tray.

Clearing a paper jam Here's how:

1. Remove paper from the In tray and Out tray.

2. Open the top cover.

3. While pulling on the jammed media, press the Resume button to turn the paper feed rollers. If necessary, release and press again on the Resume button to change direction of the paper feed rollers.

4. If Step 3 does not work, try removing as many sheets of paper as possible from the center portion of the jammed paper:

   a. Grasp one or more sheets of paper from the center of the jammed paper and pull on the sheet of paper.

   b. Continue pulling paper from the center of the paper jam until as many sheets as possible have been removed from the paper jam.

   c. Use the Resume button to turn the paper feed rollers.

5. If the paper is still jammed, turn the printer off or remove the power cord from the printer and then turn the printer back on or plug the power cord in. The printer runs through a reset cycle, which may clear the paper jam.

6. After the paper jam is cleared, remove all scraps of paper and any other obstructions from the printer's paper path.

7. With the paper path cleared, cycle the power on the printer. If only the Power light is on without other lights flashing, try printing to verify that the problem is resolved.

8. If the paper path is clear but problems continue, follow the steps listed next to check for a carriage stall.

Checking and clearing a carriage stall The carriage assembly, which holds the ink cartridges, sometimes stalls on the left side of the printer after a paper jam. You may hear a grinding noise as the printer attempts to operate, and the lights may flash alternately or in unison. This is caused from the actuator arm being positioned incorrectly (the actuator arm is also known as the clutch actuator or slider arm). Follow these steps to check and clear a carriage stall:

1. Open the top cover of the printer.

2. Unplug the power cord from the back of the printer or from the power outlet.

3. Remove the paper tray by squeezing together the two levers found under the center of the paper tray and pulling the tray out.

4. Slide the carriage assembly, by hand, away from the left side of the printer. If the carriage assembly is stuck at the left side, try these steps to free it:

    a. Push down the large black bar (directly above the three large rollers) and release it so that it springs back up. Gently lift the carriage assembly and try moving it to the right again. If it still fails to move, continue to Step b.

    b. At the base of the printer, in the paper tray's compartment (directly below the three large rollers), is a flat black plastic piece. This piece should lay flat, parallel with the base of the printer rather than pointing upward. Try moving both black pieces (above and below the three large rollers) at the same time to free the mechanism. The carriage assembly must be moved away from the left side before continuing.

5. Locate the white (or gray and white) gear assembly at the left side of the printer. Lift the actuator arm found directly above the gear assembly. This should release the paper pickup assembly into its proper position. If it does not release easily, try pulling the actuator arm slightly to the right and allow it to re-seat in its proper position.

Note

The proper positioning of the actuator arm is for the right end of the arm (the downward pointing "arrow") to be resting in the space just to the right of the gear assembly, not on top of it. Also make sure it is able to move freely left and right approximately 6.4 mm (0.25 inches) and is not locked too far to the right of the space.

6. Replace the paper tray.

7. With the top cover of the printer still open, plug the power cord into the back of the printer or to the power outlet and turn the printer on. The carriage assembly should move to the center once the printer is on.

8. Press and hold the Resume button (upper button) to move the paper pick rollers. If needed, release the Resume button, then press and hold it again to move the paper pick rollers in the opposite direction.

9. Close the top cover of the printer.

10. Print a self-test, as follows:

    • For HP DeskJet 820C series printers, press and hold the Power button (lower button), press the Resume button (upper button) four times, and then release the Power button.

    • For HP DeskJet 850C, 870C, and 890C series printers, press and hold the Resume button (upper button) for five seconds and release it.

11. If the alternately flashing lights or grinding noises still continue, as a last resort before servicing the printer, try gently cleaning the carriage encoder strip with a lint-free cloth moistened with water. (The encoder strip is the thin, quarter-inch wide clear plastic strip that passes through the back of the ink cartridge carriage and extends across the back of the printer.)

If these steps do not clear the error state, the printer may require repair.

Possible causes of paper jams and common solutions Table A.10 lists some possible causes for and solutions to your paper jam.

Table A.10 Paper Jam Causes and Common Solutions	
Possible Cause	*Solution*
The paper is not properly loaded in the In tray	Remove the paper from the In tray. Re-square the stack and reload it into the In tray. Make sure the paper width adjuster is against the left side of the paper stack. Make sure the paper length adjuster is against the end of the stack of paper but not bending it.
The In tray is too full	The In tray can hold up to a three-quarter-inch stack of media. This is approximately 150 sheets of 20-lb. paper.
The Out tray is too full	The Out tray capacity is 50 sheets of 20-lb. paper.
The paper is too long	The printer does not operate properly with paper longer than 14 inches.
The paper is outside of printer specifications	Verify that the paper meets the paper handling specifications.
Mixed sizes or types of paper or media are in the In tray	For best paper handling, load only one size and type of paper or media in the In tray at one time.
An obstruction is blocking the paper path	Look for and remove obstructions that may block the paper path.
The paper tray assembly is improperly installed	Remove and reinstall the paper tray assembly.
The printer is defective	Call Hewlett-Packard Customer Care

How do I engage the clutch on my HP DeskJet 1000C, 1100C, or 1120C series printer so that paper is lifted under the rollers and is loaded into the printer?

There are two different ways to engage the clutch.

Method 1

1. Turn the printer off and open the top cover on the printer.

2. On the left side of the printer below the carriage rod are two sets of white gears. The clutch is located in the "rightmost" set of gears and is the smooth, white piece to the right of the first gear. Tap the clutch with your finger to engage the clutch.

3. Close the top cover on the printer, turn the printer back on, and run the self-test to verify that the printer will load paper.

Method 2

1. Remove all paper from the paper trays.

2. Remove the output tray from the printer as follows:

   a. Raise the output tray to the fully upright position.

   b. Ensure that the pins on the output tray line up with the slots on the tray sides.

   c. Lift the output tray up from one side.

   d. Remove the tray from the printer.

3. Place your hand through the opening where the paper is inserted and press down on the pressure plate two or three times.

4. Reload the paper, reinstall the output tray, and run the self-test to verify that the printer will load paper.

The printer clutch needs to engage so that the pressure plate can lift the paper under the rollers.

How can I correct print skew on my HP DeskJet 1120C?

Skew occurs when the movement of paper in the mechanism is not square to the cartridge movement. The result is inconsistent print margins along the paper's edge, so printing appears tilted on the page. Several factors must be understood when dealing with skew:

■ The total measured skew is the sum of the printer skew and the paper skew.

■ Properly handle and load the paper to minimize skew. Make sure the paper is loaded evenly against the right wall of the main bottom media tray or the alternative top media feed.

- Make sure the paper width and length adjusters fit snugly against the left and bottom edges of the paper stack so the paper is being fed "squarely" into the printer.

- Use envelopes with rectangular flaps rather than triangular flaps.

- Maintain a stack of paper in the main bottom media tray.

- Load only one type of media (paper or transparency) in the main bottom media tray or alternative top media feed.

- Some types of paper and preprinted forms can impact print skew.

- Understand how to measure and correct print skew.

Always load a stack of paper into an empty main bottom media tray rather than placing paper on top of paper already in the main bottom media tray.

Measuring paper squareness Skew may be impacted by the squareness of the paper. The industry standard for paper squareness is 0.003 inch per inch. This measurement must be added to the print skew specification to obtain a true overall skew specification. Test the paper squareness by printing on one side of the paper, flipping the paper over, then printing on the other side. If the print slopes down on one side and up on the other side, the squareness of the paper may be impacting the print skew. In this case, try a different, higher-quality paper to improve the printer's skew.

Here's how you measure paper skew:

1. Perform the diagnostic test. The diagnostic test has the skew information built into the test printout:

   a. Starting with the printer power on, press and hold the Power button.

   b. While holding down the Power button, press the Resume button four times.

   c. Release the Power button. The diagnostic page now prints A, B, C, or D on each corner of the page. A and B should be in the upper-left and upper-right corners, respectively. C and D should be in the lower-left and lower-right corners, respectively.

2. Without creasing the paper, fold the diagnostic test in half vertically until A meets B and then align the top edge of the paper.

3. Is the printer top skew out of specification? Hold the folded diagnostic test in front of a light source to examine it:

   a. If the equal sign (=) by A overlaps or touches the equal sign by B, then the printer top skew is within the product specification. Continue with Step 4 to test the printer side skew.

    b. If the equal sign by A does not overlap or touch the equal sign by B, then the printer top skew is not within the product specification. Repeat the procedure on a second printout. If the printer top skew is out of specification on the second printout, check the following possible solutions.

4. Without creasing the paper, fold the diagnostic test in half horizontally until A meets C and then align the left edge of the paper.

5. Is the printer side skew out of specification? Hold the folded diagnostic test in front of a light source to examine it:

    a. If the vertical line left of the A falls on or between the two vertical lines left of the C, then the skew is within the product specification. No further testing is required.

    b. If the vertical line left of the A does not fall on or between the two vertical lines left of the C, then the skew is out of specification. Repeat the procedure on a second printout. If the skew is out of specification on the second printout, check the following possible solutions.

Possible solutions Here's how you fix paper skew:

■ Remove the paper and then reload it.

■ Make sure the paper width and length adjusters fit snugly against the left and bottom edges of the paper stack so the paper is being fed "squarely" into the printer.

■ Check that there are no more than 100 sheets of paper loaded in the main bottom media tray or 10 sheets of paper in the alternative top media feed.

■ Check to make sure that only one type of paper is loaded in the main bottom media tray or alternative top media feed.

■ Make sure the paper weight is between 16- and 36-lb. bond.

■ Try a different type of paper.

    If the problem persists, contact the HP Customer Support Center listed in your printer user's guide.

LaserJet Printer Questions

References to specific printer names are applicable to any laser printer unless noted otherwise.

How do I prevent the error message "System Error -1027" from displaying when printing either with a serial connection or with AppleTalk from a Macintosh to any HP printer?

Follow this procedure:

1. Check how the Chooser is set up:

   a. If the connection is serial, then AppleTalk must be Inactive in Chooser, and the DW or DJ serial driver icon must be selected.

   b. If the connection is AppleTalk, then AppleTalk must be Active in Chooser, and the DJ or DW AppleTalk (AT) driver icon must be chosen.

2. If AppleTalk connectors are used, check for missing or extra terminators on the daisy chain.

3. Restart the Macintosh with Extensions disabled and try printing again.

4. If using a serial cable, check for failure on the Macintosh port by moving the cable to the other port. For example, if the cable is currently attached to the Printer port, move it to the Modem port. Be sure to reselect the driver and port in Chooser before printing again.

5. Replace the cable.

This error is defined by Apple as an AppleTalk NBP (Network Binding Protocol) error. Generally, the cause of the error is a mismatch between the type of connection used and the driver selection in Chooser. In addition to seeing a System Error -1027 message, the user may also see messages such as "Printer Not Responding" or "Serial Port Already Open or In Use"; and the computer may simply hang or freeze, requiring the user to restart the Macintosh.

I am getting no output or garbage output from my LaserJet printer. The printer reacts the same way in any software application. The printer is also connected to the PC by an electrical or mechanical "A/B" switchbox. What should I do?

No output or garbage output from a LaserJet printer is often caused by the electrical or mechanical "A/B" switchbox. To ensure that the switching device is not causing the problem, connect the LaserJet printer directly to the PC. If the normal print quality resumes, contact the manufacturer of the switching device for additional help.

If the issue still exists in a direct connect situation, try another parallel cable. HP recommends an IEEE-1284 compliant parallel cable with a maximum length of 10 feet. (The maximum length of a parallel cable for use with the LaserJet 5P/5MP and 6P/6MP printers is 30 feet.)

What are Hewlett-Packard's guidelines for connecting networks and switchboxes to LaserJet printers?

Most devices connected between the printer and the host computer prevent the printer from sending data back to the computer. Therefore, the Remote Control Panel, Status Monitor, and Status Window may not work with networks, most hardware print spoolers, some software print spoolers, and some switchboxes. Newer sharing devices are available that fully support status feedback. Check with your supplier for hardware that supports bidirectional communication.

If you use a mechanical switchbox, follow these guidelines:

1. Do not switch while the printer is spooling or receiving data.

2. Do not switch to a host computer that is turned off and then switch the computer on. The computer that is turned off can appear to be sending data. If a communication error occurs, reset the printer.

3. Use a surge protector.

4. Install LaserJet printer driver software only. Do not install any Status Window, Status Monitor, Remote Control Panel, or other bidirectional software included with the printer.

Damage to the printer's parallel port caused by a switching device is not covered under the printer's warranty.

When printing from my Hewlett-Packard LaserJet Printer, what are the alternatives to using switchboxes?

Alternatives to switchboxes include the following:

1. On printers with more than one port, use the alternate port(s) on the printer. This is helpful in cases where two PCs currently share one printer.

2. Install another parallel port to the PC. This is helpful in cases where two printers are shared by one PC.

LaserJet printers (with more than one port) provide automatic I/O switching between all installed I/O ports. This allows more than one PC to be connected to the printer. The printer switches between ports automatically as jobs are received.

Why does my computer running Windows 95/98/Me lock up, display GPF errors, or display printer communications errors when a Zip drive is installed?

Other devices attached to the same port as the printer can interfere with bidirectional communication. To fix this situation

1. Disconnect the tape or disk type backup drive and connect the printer directly to the parallel port.

2. Reload the printer driver.

An additional parallel port should be added for the tape or disk type backup drive, or contact the manufacturer of the tape backup drive for other suggestions.

When starting Microsoft Windows 95, the printer picks up a piece of paper, stops, and then the power light blinks. How do I stop this?

Remove Iomega icons from the StartUp group using one of the following methods listed:

Method 1 This method is easy, but is only a temporary fix:

1. Restart Windows 95 by selecting Start ➪ Shut Down ➪ Restart the Computer. Choose Yes.

2. Press and hold the Ctrl key when the Windows 95 logo appears and continue to hold it down until Windows 95 has fully booted. This prevents any items in the StartUp group from loading.

3. If the password screen appears, type in the password; press and hold the Ctrl key on the keyboard, and press Enter.

If you use this method, you need to follow Steps 1 and 2 each time the computer is rebooted to prevent the items in the StartUp group from loading.

Method 2 This method is a more permanent fix:

1. Right-click the Start button and choose Open.

2. Double-click the Programs folder and then the StartUp folder.

3. Drag and drop all of the Iomega icons onto your Windows Desktop:

   a. Press and hold the left mouse button over each Iomega icon.

b. Drag the icon from the StartUp group to an empty area on the Windows Desktop and release the left mouse button. The selected Iomega icon should now appear on the Desktop and should no longer appear in the StartUp window.

c. Repeat this procedure until all Iomega icons have been removed from the StartUp group.

4. Close all the open folders and select Start ⇨ Shut Down ⇨ Restart the Computer.

When the printer is installed on a computer that also has a Zip drive installed, the printer is unable to communicate with the computer. What should I do?

If the Printer Services tab is selected in the HP Toolbox, a *General Protection Fault* (GPF) error message occurs stating that "HP?TBX0? caused a General Protection Fault in module mmsystem.dll." The filenames listed in the error vary depending on the printer and driver being used.

For example, HPFTBX08 would be the filename for the HP DeskJet 670C and 690C series printer driver v 9.03. HPRTBX03 would be the filename for the HP DeskJet 850C and 870C series printer driver v 9.0 or 9.2, and HPW3PAL would be the filename for the HP DeskJet 1000C series printer driver v 9.0.

When the Zip drive is installed on the computer, a line in the SYSTEM.INI file is modified. Changing the line back to the default setting should stop the GPF from occurring, but it may disable some functionality of the Zip drive:

1. In Windows 95/98/Me, select Start ⇨ Run. (In Windows 3.1*x*, select File ⇨ Run in Program Manager.)

2. On the Open line or Command Line type **SYSEDIT** and then click OK.

3. Double-click the title bar that reads C:WINDOWS\SYSTEM.INI to bring that window to the front and maximize it.

4. Under the [boot] section, locate the line

   ```
   DRIVERS=MMSYSTEM.DLL POWER.DRV PRINT PRO
   ```

5. Move the cursor in front of the PRINT PRO reference and insert a semi-colon (;). The line should now read as follows:

   ```
   DRIVERS=MMSYSTEM.DLL POWER.DRV ;PRINT PRO
   ```

   The semicolon disables the information to the right of the semicolon in the SYSTEM.INI file.

6. Select File ⇨ Save.

7. Select File ⇨ Exit.

8. Restart Windows for the changes to take effect.

What are some basic troubleshooting guidelines for my LaserJet printer?

These general symptoms help you to track down the source of a problem with your LaserJet printer.

Prove printer functionality Can you turn on the power and print a self-test on the LaserJet printer? If not, check these possible solutions:

- If there is no power, is it plugged in?
- Remove the LaserJet printer from the surge protector, if applicable.
- Plug the LaserJet printer into a different outlet.
- Remove any extra devices that are added, like RAM chips or HP JetDirect cards. Accessories that have been improperly installed may cause any printer to exhibit symptoms of hardware problems such as no power, blank display, or printer control panel error messages.
- Unplug the communication cable from the LaserJet printer and firmly reconnect it.
- Resolve and clear any paper jams or misfeed errors.
- Cold reset the LaserJet printer (check your manual for instructions on how to do this).

Establish communication Try verifying correct communications between the PC and the LaserJet printer by these methods:

- Print a directory from the DOS prompt with the following command (if applicable, replace "lpt1" with the appropriate port):

  ```
  dir > lpt1
  ```
- Plug the LaserJet printer directly into the PC with no external devices (for example, a printer switchbox, a printer sharing system, or tape backup).
- Use a different parallel cable. The cable should be IEEE-1284 compliant.
- Verify that the proper driver is installed. Print from the driver to the LaserJet printer (under Windows 95, Windows 98, Windows Me, Windows NT 4.0, or Windows 2000) by printing a test page from the HP driver setup page.
- Test from WordPad in Windows 95/98/Me (or Write in Windows 3.1x). Bring up the application, type **This is a test**, then select File ⇨ Print. Make sure that the correct driver is selected and click OK. If it prints okay from Write or WordPad, the driver is functioning from within Windows.

Why is my LaserJet printer not producing good-quality print?

To help you narrow down the problem with your print quality, follow this general checklist:

- Try printing the printer self-test or demo page. If the defect cannot be reproduced on the printer's self-test or demo page, verify the integrity of your hard drive by running SCANDISK.

- Try to isolate the problem to one particular document, one particular application, one particular software driver, one particular platform (for example, Windows 98, Windows NT, or DOS), or one particular PC workstation (in a networked environment).

- Redistribute the toner in the toner cartridge. Follow these steps:

  1. Open the printer cover and remove the toner cartridge.

  2. Rotate the toner cartridge back and forth to redistribute toner.

  3. Reinsert the toner cartridge and close the top cover.

  4. Print a self-test or demo page.

- Clean the inside of the printer as described in the manual.

- Adjust the print density from the printer's control panel or the printer driver.

- Check the paper type to make sure it meets the printer's specifications, and that the paper was loaded properly.

- Replace the toner cartridge, then check the print quality again.

- If the print is too faint, check to make sure EconoMode is disabled from the printer's control panel and from the printer driver.

I'm having problems printing directly from an Internet site to my LaserJet printer. What's wrong?

Internet printing difficulties may include the following:

- The printer does not respond.

- The printer ejects a blank page.

- The printout does not match the screen.

- The printing process is very slow.

- Problems may occur when attempting to print either text or graphics.

Note

For Windows 95, Windows 98, and Windows NT 4.0 users, HP Web PrintSmart software optimizes Web content specifically for printing. PrintSmart software is available for most of the HP DeskJet and LaserJet product line; it can be downloaded from the HP Web site.

Verify that the most current version of the Internet browser (for example, Netscape Navigator or Microsoft Internet Explorer) is being used. Check the browser company's home page to download the most current version.

Try downloading the file and saving the information on the hard drive or on a diskette, then open and print the file from within a Windows application. Follow these steps:

1. In the Internet browser program (for example, Navigator or Internet Explorer), choose File ⇨ Save As.

2. When prompted, enter the location where the file is to be saved.

3. Name the file and then select Save to save the file to the specified location.

4. Open the file and print from within a Windows application.

Next, install a universal Microsoft printer driver that is compatible with the LaserJet printer and select the universal Microsoft driver to print with the Internet. The original Windows 95 and Windows 98 installation disks or CD-ROMs may be required to install a universal driver.

To install a universal printer driver under Windows 95 or Windows 98, follow these steps:

1. From the Windows Desktop, select Start ⇨ Settings ⇨ Printers.

2. Double-click Add Printer.

3. Select Next, until the Manufacturer/Printer screen appears.

4. Under the Manufacturers list, select HP; under the Printers list, select the appropriate universal driver. For early LaserJet printers, select the matching universal Microsoft driver. For LaserJet printers that are not listed, select an earlier version of the model (for example, select a 4SI universal driver for the LaserJet 5Si printer).

5. Select LPT1 and select Next.

6. Under the Printer Name box, select No so that the universal driver is not set as the default. Select Next.

7. When asked to print a test page, select No and then select Finish.

The same procedure may solve problems in Windows 3.1x as well. The Windows 3.1x installation disks may be required to install a universal driver.

To install a universal printer driver under Windows 3.1*x*, follow these steps:

1. From Program Manager, open the Main program group and then double-click Control Panel and choose Printers.

2. Select the Add button.

3. Under the list of Printers, select the appropriate universal Microsoft Windows 3.1*x* driver and choose Install. For early LaserJet printers, select the matching universal driver. For LaserJet printers that are not listed, select the most recent driver.

4. Click OK.

What should I know when printing from DOS to my LaserJet printer?

These guidelines provide you with hints and tips for printing from DOS.

Printing from DOS   The LaserJet printer composes a page of information before it prints it. The default for most LaserJet printers is 60 lines of text per page.

When a print command is issued from DOS, DOS sends ASCII text characters to the printer. DOS does not send any other printer setup information such as font type, orientation, or page eject commands. Because no form feed/page eject commands are sent from DOS, the printer waits until one of two things happens:

■ The 60-line text buffer in the LaserJet printer is filled.

■ A form feed or page eject command is issued to the LaserJet printer.

In the case of Print Screen, Print, or Copy commands from DOS, the LaserJet printer's buffer may not fill to the 60 line maximum. To eject a page in these cases, do one of the following:

■ Manually eject the page from the LaserJet printer.

■ For LaserJet printers that do not have front menu panels, press and release the front panel button or the Go button.

For LaserJet printers with front menu panels, do the following:

1. Verify that the Form Feed light is on.

2. If the Form Feed light is on, take the printer offline by pressing the On Line key.

3. Press the Form Feed key.

4. Put the printer back online by pressing the On Line key.

Send a page eject printer setup command to the LaserJet printer. You can find this command in the PCL Printer Command section in the LaserJet printer user's manual.

Line-draw characters from DOS In some instances, printouts may have characters printing where lines should be. This occurs because the LaserJet printer's default symbol set is Roman-8. This symbol set does not contain line-draw characters. To change the symbol set to PC-8 to accommodate line-draw characters, do the following:

1. For LaserJet printers that do not have front menu panels, use the Remote Control Panel in the Explorer system to change this setting.

2. For LaserJet printers with front menu panels, change the front panel of the printer to the PC-8 /IBM US Symbol Set. See your user's manual for instructions pertaining to your particular printer.

3. Send the printer command for the PC-8 Symbols set prior to printing your print screen. You can find this command in the PCL Printer Command section in the LaserJet printer user's manual.

Why won't my LaserJet printer print correctly in Windows 95 or Windows 98?

Several troubleshooting options are available in Microsoft Windows. Try these procedures.

Verify that the LaserJet printer works This is the simplest thing to overlook:

1. Unplug the parallel cable from the back of the LaserJet printer, so the printer is not receiving information from the PC.

2. Ensure that the LaserJet printer is turned on and is in the ready state (no errors).

3. Print a self-test from the LaserJet printer. The method for printing a self-test is different for different printers, so check the printer manual for instructions. If the self-test prints a blank page, check to make sure that the tape has been removed from the toner cartridge. If nothing prints, try plugging the LaserJet printer into another wall outlet. The power cable may be faulty; if so, try using the power cable from the monitor to plug into the LaserJet printer and the wall outlet. If the LaserJet printer still does not print, it may need to be serviced.

Reset and restart Starting all over can sometimes do the trick:

1. Reset the printer by turning it off and back on again.

2. Restart Windows. When the system has finished rebooting, it should display a message that you have one or more documents to print. Click No to cancel the printing jobs. Run the application from which you were trying to print and try printing again.

Print from an MS-DOS prompt This procedure bypasses Windows entirely:

1. Verify that the LaserJet printer is turned on and ready.

2. Attach the LaserJet printer directly to the PC. Verify that no printer sharing devices or daisy-chained devices are between the computer and the PC.

3. Restart your computer. Press the F8 key when you see "Starting Windows 95 or 98" appear on your screen. Select "command prompt only."

4. At the C:\ prompt, type **DIR>LPT1** and press Enter. (LPT1 is generally the parallel port to which you are printing. If your port is different, insert the correct path to the port.)

This command copies your root directory to the LaserJet printer. If nothing prints, press the form-feed button or the Go button on the LaserJet printer to enable the printer to print the page. If you get the message "Write Fault Error" when you try to print, you can have a bad parallel cable connection. Try reseating the cables at both the LaserJet printer end and the PC end (make sure that you have the correct length of cable; see your printer manual for specifications).

If this does not work, try another cable. If another cable does not work, try attaching the LaserJet printer to another PC. If you have another port on the PC, attach it to the other port to see if it will print. If your LaserJet printer has another port, try attaching a cable to this port. If it does not print, there may be a problem with the LaserJet printer, and it may need to be serviced.

Try an alternate LPT.VXD file (Windows 95 only) An alternate LPT.VXD file resolves the following problems:

■ You cannot print, or you receive a timeout error message when you print to a bidirectional printer.

■ You experience problems printing to any bidirectional printer. Symptoms include an extra page being printed and "garbage" commands appearing on the printout.

The alternate LPT.VXD file is located in the Drivers\PrinterLPT folder on the Windows 95 CD-ROM, and it can be downloaded from the Microsoft Software Library. To install the alternate LPT.VXD file from the Windows 95 CD-ROM, follow these steps:

1. Using Windows Explorer, rename the LPT.VXD file in the Windows\System folder to LPT.OLD.

2. Copy the LPT.VXD file from the Drivers\PrinterLPT folder on the Windows 95 CD-ROM to the Windows\System folder on the hard disk.

3. Restart Windows.

Print from WordPad This is a simple printing method direct from Windows:

1. With the LaserJet printer directly connected, restart your computer.

2. Select Start ➪ Programs ➪ Accessories ➪ WordPad.

3. Type **This is a test** and print the page.

If you cannot print from WordPad, verify that the port is set up correctly in Device Manager (for example, make sure that there are no port conflicts and the port's resources are set correctly).
To open the Device Manager

1. Use the right mouse button to click My Computer and then select Properties in the drop-down menu.

2. Click the Device Manager tab, double-click Ports (COM & LPT), and then double-click the appropriate port for your LaserJet printer, for example, Printer Port (LPT1).

3. Click the Resources tab and verify that the settings are correct for your printer port. For example, the input/output range for a standard LPT1 port is 0378-037A (a physical LPT2 port typically uses I/O 278). Also, verify that the conflicting devices list reads "No conflicts."

Change the ECP port mode Try changing the ECP port mode to any of the port settings (start with ECP or Bidirectional) to determine if you can print. Contact your PC vendor for help.

DOS printing works, but Windows 98 applications cannot print If you can print from DOS but not any Windows applications, there may be a problem with the spool settings or with bidirectional communication.

1. Select Start ➪ Settings ➪ Printers.

2. Right-click the name of the printer to which you are trying to print. Left-click Properties.

3. Click the Details tab and click Spool Settings. Select *Print directly to the printer* (you will lose the ability to spool print jobs, so it will take longer for you to access your application).

4. If your LaserJet printer supports bidirectional communication, click "Disable bidirectional support for this printer."

5. Click OK and try printing from WordPad. If that does not work, you can try different combinations of spool settings and bidirectional support until you find a combination that works. For example, try disabling bidirectional support with RAW and EMF spool data format settings. Also, try bidirectional support with the RAW spool data format. If you're using a PostScript printer, remember that RAW is the only spool data format supported for PostScript.

Change the printer driver Most LaserJet printers are backward-compatible, so they can use drivers from earlier printers. If you have trouble printing with your current printer driver, try installing a LaserJet II, LaserJet III, or LaserJet IV printer driver from Windows:

1. Select Start ⇨ Settings ⇨ Printers.

2. Double-click the Add Printer icon and follow the instructions in the Add Printer Wizard to install the alternate older driver.

3. Try printing with this driver.

Remove and reinstall the printer driver If your LaserJet printer has an uninstall (or de-install) option in its program group, uninstall and reinstall it. If the printer driver is a Windows 95/98/Me driver, do the following:

1. Select Start ⇨ Settings ⇨ Printers.

2. Right-click the name of the printer that you want to remove and click Delete on the menu that appears.

3. If you are prompted to remove all the files associated with the LaserJet printer, click Yes.

4. Select Start ⇨ Settings ⇨ Printers.

5. Double-click the Add Printer icon and follow the instructions in the Add Printer Wizard to reinstall the Windows 95/98/Me printer driver.

Verify printer properties Incorrect printer property settings can cause poor or incomplete output, or can cause your LaserJet printer not to print at all. Follow these steps to check the printer property settings:

1. Select Start ⇨ Settings ⇨ Printers.

2. Right-click the name of the printer that you want to check and click Properties on the menu that appears.

3. Verify that the printer properties are correct. Look at the page size, orientation, and paper source or paper tray.

4. Look at the Graphics tab or Print Quality tab. Try different variations in the graphics mode. Try Raster, Vector, or HP/GL-2 (depending on your choices). Change the Text Mode (if available) to TrueType as Graphics or TrueType as Bitmaps (if allowed). Depending on the printer driver, you can change to Print TrueType as Graphics in the Fonts tab. If you have a LaserJet 4 printer, change the graphics mode from Vector to Raster. This takes less memory and is useful if the printer displays the message Error 21 on the control panel.

5. Lower the resolution; for example, change 600 dpi to 300 dpi.

6. Simplify the document. If you cannot print a complex document, try removing some of the graphic elements in the document or convert all the fonts in the document to a printer-resident font such as Courier.

Print to LPT1.DOS to correct local printing problems If you have problems printing to a local printer, try the LPT1.DOS port. This method is similar to printing to a file and then copying the file to the printer port. To enable the LPT1.DOS port, follow these steps:

1. Select Start ➪ Settings ➪ Printers.

2. Right-click the name of the printer that you want to use and click Properties on the drop-down menu.

3. Click the Details tab.

4. Click Add Port in the Details tab.

5. In the Add Port dialog box, click Other, then Local Port and OK. Type **LPT1.DOS** in the *Enter a Port Name* box. Click OK.

Printing to the LPT1.DOS port may be slower than printing to the LPT1 port.

A Spool 32 error occurs when I print to my LaserJet printer in Windows 95. The error usually reads: "Spool 32 Caused a General Protection Fault in Module GDI.EXE." How do I fix this?

Typically, the computer has preinstalled fax or answering machine software that interferes with the printer spooler. To correct the Spool 32 error, try one of the following solutions.

Configure the Windows 95 spooler This is the preferred solution, because it provides full-time use of the program and full printer functionality:

1. Restart Windows 95.

2. Select Start ➪ Settings ➪ Printers.

3. In the Printers window, right-click the LaserJet or DeskJet icon.

4. Click Properties.

5. Select the Details tab.

6. Click the Spool Settings button.

7. Click the Spool data format list box and change the setting from EMF to RAW, and then click OK to close the Spool Settings window.

8. Click OK to close the Properties window.

9. Close the Printers window.

10. Restart Windows 95 and try to print again. If you are still unsuccessful, restart Windows 95 again and go on to the following procedure.

Disable the spooler   Disabling the spooler in Windows 95 limits the computer's capability to multitask, which makes it run slower than normal while printing. This option does not work with a host-based driver. Follow these steps to disable the spooler:

1. Select Start ⇨ Settings ⇨ Printers.

2. In the Printers window, right-click the LaserJet or DeskJet icon.

3. Click Properties.

4. Select the Details tab.

5. Click Port Settings.

6. Click *Spool MS-DOS print jobs* and *Check port state before printing* to clear both options, and then click OK.

7. Click Spool Settings.

8. Select *Print directly to the printer*. The Spool data format defaults to RAW.

9. Click OK, click Apply, and then click OK.

10. Close the Printers window.

11. Restart Windows 95 and try to print again. If you are still unsuccessful, restart Windows 95 again and proceed to the following solution.

Temporarily close the interfering program while printing   Sometimes another program can be the culprit:

1. Press Ctrl-Alt-Delete to open the Task window.

2. Highlight any fax/answering machine program listed and select End Task. Repeat this process for each program listed that may interfere with the printing process.

3. Try printing again. If printing is successful, the program(s) closed were interfering with the printing process. Repeat the preceding two steps each time you print.

Remove the interfering program from your PC Permanently remove any interfering programs from the computer by uninstalling the software. For assistance, contact the manufacturer of the software or the computer manufacturer.

Remove unnecessary *.TMP files Check the C:\TEMP and C:\WINDOWS\TEMP directories for any unnecessary ".TMP" files. Delete any unnecessary .tmp files and then run DEFRAG and SCANDISK to check out and clean up your hard drive.

All-in-One Unit Questions

References to specific all-in-one names are applicable to any multifunction unit unless noted otherwise.

I have a portable phone on the same phone line as my HP LaserJet 3100/3150 all-in-one unit, and the telephone is always disconnected by the all-in-one picking up the line. What's wrong?

The HP LaserJet unit detects static on the phone line as fax tones. This causes the HP LaserJet 3100/3150 to pick up the line, which disconnects the extension phone.

Turn off the Extension Phone setting in the hardware of the HP LaserJet 3100 or 3150 unit by following these steps:

1. Press the Enter/Menu key on the control panel of the HP LaserJet product.
2. Use the < or > arrow keys to select Fax Settings.
3. Press the Enter/Menu key.
4. Use the < or > arrow keys to select Incoming Faxes.
5. Press the Enter/Menu key.
6. Use the < or > arrow keys to select Extension Phone.
7. Press the Enter/Menu key.
8. Use the < or > arrow keys to select No.
9. Press the Enter/Menu key.
10. Press the Stop/Clear to return to the main screen.

I installed Windows 98/Me and now I can't print from a Windows application from my HP OfficeJet 300, 500, 600, 700, OfficeJet Pro 1170, and 1175 Series.

If you're unable to print from Windows-based programs but you can print from MS-DOS-based programs (such as Edit.com), or if you receive the error message

```
"The printer could not be found."
```

when you attempt to print from WordPad, your WIN.INI file may be set as "read-only."

To resolve this behavior, remove the read-only attribute from the WIN.INI file and then install the printer driver again to update the WIN.INI file.

Follow these steps:

1. Select Start ➪ Find ➪ Files or Folders.

2. In the Named box, type **win.ini** and click Find Now.

3. In the list of files, right-click the WIN.INI file and click Properties.

4. Click the Read-Only check box to clear it and then click OK.

5. Quit the Find tool and then restart your computer.

6. Install the printer driver by following the installation steps in your printer user's guide.

Are switch boxes and sharing devices supported with the HP OfficeJet?

When using the HP OfficeJet with a switch box, Zip drive, or other parallel port-sharing device, you may encounter problems with your HP OfficeJet. These devices need bidirectional communication to provide full print, copy, scanner, and fax capability. Consequently, using a switch box or other port sharing device often interrupts communication with the HP OfficeJet. If you need to install multiple devices on a single parallel port, Hewlett-Packard recommends installing a second parallel port that supports ECP (Extended Capabilities Port).

My HP all-in-one is scanning very slowly. What can I do?

There are several things you can do:

■ Always use the lowest resolution (dpi setting) or image type possible that still gives good image quality. Setting text to Photo or Enhanced Text may increase the scanning time.

■ The more complex the image, the longer it takes to process the document.

■ Your PC's processor speed, amount of memory available, and amount of available hard disk space all affect scanning speed.

Setting your PC's parallel printer port to ECP mode can help increase scanning speed. ECP is a system-level setting. To change it, you need to access your system's BIOS (basic input/output system). (Typically, you do this by pressing a key to display Setup when your system is starting up.) If you do not know how to do this, contact your computer manufacturer for more information. Note that not all computers have this option available.

Here's how you can check to see whether your printer port is set for ECP mode:

1. Select Start ⇨ Settings ⇨ Control Panel.

2. In the Control Panel window, double-click System.

3. In the System Properties dialog box, click the Device Manager tab and check your ports by clicking on the plus (+) sign to expand the list. If your printer port is set to ECP mode, the port is listed as an ECP Printer Port.

My fax transmissions are slow. Why is that?

Complex faxes take longer to send than simple ones because more data has to transfer over the phone line. If your fax has a lot of graphics, it takes longer to send than a simple fax.

The error "JetSuite Fax has detected that the LaserJet 3100 is either switched off or is not connected to your computer" appears when the LaserJet 3100 printer cannot establish bidirectional communication with the PC. What should I do?

This error message may be caused by many things, such as the parallel port mode, other printing software, device conflicts, a bad or disconnected cable, and other devices connected between the LaserJet 3100 printer and your PC (such as a docking station, switchbox, internal or external tape backup).

Follow these steps to determine the problem:

■ Check to make sure that the parallel cable is securely connected and working properly. If you have another C-type connector cable available, try using it.

■ Ensure that the LaserJet 3100 printer is directly connected to the parallel port and that there are no switchboxes, Zip drives, security keys, or other parallel devices connected to the same parallel port.

■ Reset the LaserJet 3100 printer, or unplug the power cable from the back of the LaserJet 3100 and plug it in again.

■ Shut down the PC. Unplug the power cord from the back of the LaserJet 3100. Disconnect the parallel cable from the back of the LaserJet 3100 and from the back of the PC. Reconnect the parallel cable to the LaserJet 3100 and the PC. Plug the power cable back into the LaserJet product and turn on the computer again.

- Close down any open applications. In Windows 95/98/Me, simultaneously press Ctrl-Alt-Del. Examine any running applications and background tasks to determine possible conflicts.

- Check for conflicts in the Device Manager, which are indicated by an exclamation point. Conflicting devices on the system need to be taken care of before troubleshooting on the LaserJet 3100 can proceed.

- Change the COM ports (also called serial ports) in JetSuite Pro by holding down the Ctrl and Shift keys simultaneously while clicking the Configure icon. Select Modify Port Settings for the LaserJet 3100 printer and change the COM ports. (This setting is not available in Windows NT.)

Warning

Do not use the following workaround if you have a tape backup device connected to a parallel port. This file is installed to detect tape backup devices on a parallel port.

- In Windows 95 and Windows 98, search for the file named "drvwppqt.vxd" and rename it "drvwppqt.old" using the following steps:

  1. Select Start ⇨ Find ⇨ Files or Folders.

  2. In the Named section, type **drvwppqt.vxd** and make sure the Look in section has the correct drive selected. Then click Find Now.

  3. If the filename appears in the list, highlight it. Choose File ⇨ Rename.

  4. Type **drvwppqt.old** as the new name for the file and press Enter.

  5. Restart the computer.

- Check for other devices loading:

  1. Check the load and run lines in the WIN.INI file.

  2. Check the SYSTEM.INI file for device conflicts (see other documents related to device conflicts). Add a semicolon in front of the line `device=turbovcd.vxd` if it is there, or in front of any other conflicting devices.

- Check the parallel port mode, and change it to either *ECP* or *Bidirectional*. If neither of these modes work, try any other available mode.

- As a last resort, reboot the computer into Safe Mode and check the Device Manager for *ghost* ports — duplicate ports that may show up in the Device Manager in Safe Mode, but not in Normal Mode. Delete the port that does not show up in the BIOS. For instance, if the parallel port mode is set to ECP in the BIOS and you see both "ECP Printer Port, LPT1" and "Printer Port, LPT1," delete "Printer Port, LPT1."

Windows displays this error message when I'm trying to use my all-in-one unit: "Low Level I/O Error." Other error messages sometimes accompany this. How can I fix it?

This error is normally caused by a lack of bidirectional communication with your all-in-one unit. Check the following:

Power Check the power by following these steps:

1. Turn the power off. Unplug the power cord. Wait ten seconds. Plug the power cord back into the power outlet or all-in-one unit.

2. Turn the power back on. Perform a copy and look for any error messages in the display or for any blinking lights.

3. If an error exists, then communication may not be able to be established and the "Low-Level I/O Error" occurs.

Hardware and connections Check the hardware and connections with the following procedure:

1. Turn off the all-in-one unit and close its software (if it is installed and running).

2. Unplug the parallel cable from the port on the back of the PC and from the port on the back of the all-in-one unit.

3. For the HP OfficeJet 500, 600, 700 series devices, reseat the line interface unit (the cartridge in the back). Gently pull on the line interface unit while sliding an old, unused credit card between its underside and the product's case. When the cartridge comes out, inspect all of the pins inside the product. If any of the pins are broken or bent, then the unit needs service. Carefully insert the line interface unit back into the all-in-one unit.

4. Connect the parallel cable back onto the parallel port of the PC. There should be nothing else connected to the port, only the cable.

5. Connect the parallel cable to the port on the back of the all-in-one unit. There should be no other devices connected between the product and the PC. If the all-in-one's port has a fastening device, then make sure that the device can attach fully.

6. Turn the power back on to the all-in-one unit and check to see if the error still occurs.

Communications Any of the following can cause communication problems between the computer and any HP all-in-one unit:

■ Loose or faulty parallel cables

■ Improper PC parallel port configuration

■ Lockout device installed on the parallel port or cable

■ *Dongle* (a passthru software key) installed on the parallel port or cable

■ Gender changer installed on the parallel port or cable

■ Switch box installed on the parallel port

■ External drive connected to the parallel port

Try the following steps to correct the problem. Test functionality after completing each step.

1. Reboot the computer and then try printing again.

2. Shut down the computer and HP all-in-one unit. Disconnect the printer cable at both ends and then reconnect it securely. Restart the HP all-in-one unit and then the computer. Try printing again.

3. Windows 95 and 98 users can try a DOS print test. Do the following:

    a. Click Start and then Shut Down.

    b. Select Restart in MS-DOS (R) mode and then click OK or Yes.

    c. When a DOS prompt is on the screen type in **dir > lptx** where *x* is the parallel port that the HP all-in-one unit is connected to.

    d. Press ENTER.

    e. If a directory of drive C prints, the hardware is OK and there may be a software conflict. If an error occurs (for example, "Write Fault") or nothing prints, disconnect and reconnect the cable, try a different cable, perform the following Step 7, or connect to another PC's port. Try entering the line again. This helps you determine if the problem is with the PC's port, the cable, or the printer's port. Until you are able to print a directory from MS-DOS, the unit is not able to pass the communication test in Windows.

4. Windows NT 4.0 and Windows 2000 users should check the printer properties to make sure that "Enable bidirectional support" on the Ports tab is selected (if not grayed out).

5. Remove any other hardware that connects to a parallel port and uninstall the software. Also, uninstall any other printer or scanner drivers

loaded on the system. Try printing again. See the following "Contact HP?" section for more information.

6. Uninstall the HP all-in-one software and then install an alternative print driver. If the unit prints with the alternative driver but not from the HP all-in-one software, the problem is that the parallel cable that is not IEEE-1284 compliant, a hardware conflict exists, a software conflict exists, or the port configuration is incorrect.

7. Change the parallel port mode. Enter the computer's BIOS Setup and change the parallel port mode. This is done during the computer boot cycle. Because computer BIOS setups are different from computer to computer and detailed instructions are not possible here, please contact your computer's vendor for assistance. As the computer starts up, watch for a message that says Press (*key*) to enter setup. Press the key indicated. Locate the Input/Output section or tab. Locate the parallel port settings. Do one of the following:

   a. If the parallel port mode is set to anything other than ECP, change the setting to ECP mode if that setting is an option. If ECP is not an option, choose Standard Bidirectional or SPP mode.

   b. If the setting is already ECP, switch the setting to Standard Bidirectional or SPP. Some computers do not work correctly in enhanced capabilities or ECP mode.

I can no longer print to my HP all-in-one after upgrading my operating system to Windows 98 or Windows Me. Windows displays the error messages "There is a problem with the printer driver . . . " and "There was a problem printing to LPT port."

The references in the WIN.INI file were not updated or were altered when the upgrade took place. Try the following steps to fix the problem:

1. Select Find ⇨ Files or Folders from the Start menu.

2. In the Named field type in **WIN.INI**.

3. Make sure the Include subfolders has a check mark and the root hard drive is selected (usually C:\).

4. Select Find Now. The icon for the WIN.INI file should appear.

5. Right-click the WIN.INI icon and select Properties from the menu that appears. If more than one WIN.INI file is shown then select the WIN.INI file found in the Windows directory.

6. If there is a check mark next to Read Only then remove the check mark, select OK, then uninstall and reinstall the HP all-in-one software. If there is no check mark then select Cancel and proceed to the next step.

7. Make a backup of the WIN.INI file by right-clicking the icon and selecting Copy from the menu that appears. Find a blank area on the open desktop and click the right-mouse button. Select Paste from the menu that appears.

8. Open the file in a text editor (probably Notepad) by either double-clicking the WIN.INI icon or right-selecting it and choosing Open.

9. Scroll up or down in the text editor and find the text "[Devices]." There should be one or two lines of text that start with "HP OFFICEJET" or the name of the HP all-in-one product below "[Devices]."

   a. If there is a semicolon at the beginning of the line of text, then remove the semicolon and select SAVE from the FILE menu.

   b. If there is no reference to the HP All-in-One unit, then try uninstalling and then reinstalling the product's software.

   c. If there is a semicolon in front of every line of items or if there is an abundance of unreadable text, then the WIN.INI has been corrupted during the upgrade. The operating system's support avenues should be used to find out how to fix or replace the WIN.INI file.

My HP LaserJet 3100 always answers on the first ring, regardless of the Rings to Answer setting, so it's picking up my voice calls. What can I do to stop this?

You can try these options:

■ Check the firmware version. If the unit has v.1.10 or v.1.12 firmware then visit the HP LaserJet 3100 product Web site at `www.hp.com/support/lj3100` for the HP LaserJet 3100 firmware/BIOS upgrade.

■ Isolate the HP LaserJet 3100 product from the PC and all other devices.

■ Verify that the phone line is working properly.

■ Make sure you're using the phone cord that shipped with the HP LaserJet 3100.

■ Reset the HP LaserJet 3100.

■ Clear memory using the softkeys. (You'll have to set up the time, date, and header.)

The HP LaserJet 3100 unit needs service if the preceding troubleshooting steps fail to resolve the issue.

 # List of Manufacturers

This appendix provides the customer contact telephone numbers and Web sites for all major manufacturers of personal computer printers, as well as a number of manufacturers of printer accessories. Although most of these manufacturers are not named directly in the book, this list can help you contact these companies and locate information about your printer.

Alps Electric
Phone: (800) 825-ALPS
Fax: (408) 432-6035
www.alpsusa.com

Apollo Consumer Products
Phone: (877) 692-7655
www.myapollo.com

Apple Computer, Inc.
Phone: (800) 538-9696
Fax: (800) 505-0171
www.apple.com

Brother Industries
Phone: (800) 276-7746
Fax: (800) 521-2846
www.brother.com

Canon Computer Systems, Inc.
Phone: (800) OK-CANON
www.ccsi.canon.com

Citizen America Corporation
Phone: (310) 643-9825
Fax: (310) 725-0969
www.citizen-america.com

Compaq
Phone: (800) 888-0220
www.compaq.com

Epson America, Inc.
Phone: (800) GO-EPSON
Fax: (310) 782-2600
www.epson.com

Genicom
Phone: (800) 436-4266
www.genicom.com

Hewlett-Packard Company
Phone: (800) 222-5547
Fax: (650) 857-5518
www.hp.com

IBM
Phone: (888) SHOPIBM
www.ibm.com

Kensington Technology Group
Phone: (800) 280-8318
Fax: (650) 572-9675
www.kensington.com

Lexmark International, Inc.
Phone: (800) 539-6275
www.lexmark.com

Minolta Corporation
Phone: (888) 264-6658
Fax: (800) 528-4767
www.minoltaprinters.com

NEC USA
Phone: (800) 632-4636
Fax: (800) 366-0476
www.nec.com

Okidata Corporation
Phone: (800) 654-3282
Fax: (800) 654-6651
www.okidata.com

Panasonic (Matsushita Electric Corporation of America)
Phone: (800) 742-8086
www.panasonic.com

QMS Corporation
Phone: (800) 523-2696
www.qms.com

Ricoh Corporation
Phone: (800) 63-RICOH
www.ricoh-usa.com

Tektronix Inc.
Phone: (800) 835-9433
Fax: (503) 682-2980
www.tek.com

Xerox Corporation
Phone: (800) ASK-XEROX
www.xerox.com

Glossary

A

all-in-one

A multifunction peripheral that can perform more than simple printing tasks. Most all-in-ones can print, copy, and scan, and many can also fax. Some of these products are based on sheetfed scanners, and some are based on flatbed scanners.

anti-aliasing

The use of mathematical formulas to enhance the detail around the edges of each character in the text displayed on your monitor. Windows and Mac OS use anti-aliasing to make the character edges look "cleaner."

auditing

A Windows NT feature that enables the system administrator to monitor printing activities for any user or class of users.

autoanswer

A setting available for most fax machines, faxmodems, and multifunction devices with fax capability. With autoanswer, your all-in-one automatically picks up incoming fax calls after a specified number of rings.

B

banner lifter

An attachment to help smoothly feed continuous banner paper through your inkjet.

banner paper

Designed especially for printing banners, this inkjet paper is manufactured in one continuous length. The printed banner can be torn off at perforations.

bidirectional

A term for a parallel printer connection where data flows regularly in both directions between computer and printer (or an external parallel peripheral). Many models no longer work correctly (or at all) without a bidirectional computer cable; both the port and the cable should conform to the IEEE-1284 specification.

bitmap file

Usually carries the file extension .BMP. The standard graphics format for Windows images.

broadcast faxing

A fax machine feature that sends the same fax document to multiple recipients. Most faxing all-in-ones enable you to send broadcast faxes.

C

CD-recordable

Usually abbreviated CD-R. A technology that enables you to record your own data and audio CD-ROMs, which can then be read on any computer CD-ROM drive.

CD-rewritable

Usually abbreviated CD-RW. Like CD-R, CD-RW allows you to record your own data CD-ROMs; however, unlike a CD-R disc (which can be recorded only once),
a CD-RW disc can be erased and recorded again.

Centronics

Another name for the standard PC printer cable design (also called a *parallel printer cable*).

charging roller

One of the complex system of rollers inside a typical laser printer or all-in-one. The charging roller transfers an electrical charge to the photoconductor, which repels particles of toner.

coaxial cable

The cable typically used in Ethernet networks; also used to provide cable TV
service.

collation

A feature offered on some inkjet printers, laser printers, and all-in-ones; with
collation turned on, multiple copies of a document are printed as separate
documents. Many of these products have a box labeled "ordered printing."
With ordered printing turned on, the pages in a multiple page document are
printed
in the correct order. Collation is often included under ordered printing.

color matching system

A system of computer software, display hardware, cardboard color wheels,
and color filters. Used together, these elements help guarantee that the colors used on a computer monitor or a physical layout page are the same colors that will
be printed on the final document.

color separation

A color printing technique used to print full-color photographs and multi-
color images and text. A standard set of colors (usually cyan, magenta, yellow, and black) is applied in separate layers, and the combination of these
layers creates the different colors.

color wheel

A number of cardboard or plastic cards held together by a wire or a bolt;
each card carries a different color and an identifier for that color in a particular color matching system. A color wheel is useful for comparing the actual
color represented within the color matching system with the color displayed
on a monitor or on a physical layout page. This color wheel is different from
the standard one found in art supply stores, which describes the relationships
of colors to each other.

compressed air

Sold in cans for cleaning computer hardware. Unlike a brush or cloth, compressed air removes accumulated dust from circuit boards and components without damage or static electricity.

corona wires

A set of thin wires inside the body of a laser printer that transfer a static charge to each sheet of paper; this charge in turn attracts the toner to the paper.

cost per page

An estimate of how much an individual page produced from a specific printer or all-in-one costs when you factor in the price of the toner (or ink) and the cost of the paper (and sometimes the electricity) used to create that page. Cost per page is often used as a comparison value for those shopping for fast network printers that are designed to handle a large number of pages.

D

daisywheel

An early letter-quality impact printer that used a typewriter-style daisywheel or rotating ball; the printer wheel or ball was usually interchangeable. You could use different fonts in your document by replacing the wheel or ball with another.

defragmenting

The process of optimizing a computer's hard drive by rearranging files to make them contiguous. Defragmenting helps speed up your computer's operation because all tasks related to your hard drive run faster on a defragmented drive.

device independent

A print job saved as a file is device independent when it can be printed or displayed on any compatible hardware platform and achieve the same results. PostScript files are device independent because the same PostScript file produces the same results whether printed on a computer printer, a professional typesetting machine, a laser etching system, or even when it's shown on a computer monitor.

dictionary

As a PostScript term, a file containing font descriptions. Each description specifies how every character in a font family is constructed, including derivatives such as bold and italic versions.

digital camera

A camera that saves an image as a computer data file (or in, as it's commonly known, *digital* format) instead of using traditional film.

distinctive ring

A service available through some telephone companies that provides up to three individual telephone numbers for one incoming physical telephone line. Each number uses a unique, distinctive ring sequence; if your multifunction unit supports distinctive ring, it can detect that unique pattern and answers only those calls made to that number.

dot matrix

A popular early impact printer that uses a grid of tiny pins to transfer ink from a ribbon to the page. Dot-matrix printers can produce basic graphics, but they are inferior compared to an inkjet printer. They're loud and slow and produce only one color. These printers are still used where multiple carbon copy forms are required.

dots per inch

Usually abbreviated as dpi. A measurement of print resolution, dpi indicates how many individual dots a device can create on a page per a square inch of area. Dpi is typically listed as horizontal resolution by vertical resolution; the higher the dpi, the better the resolution.

driver software

The software that enables your operating system to properly build and format commands and data bound for your printer; in effect, a print driver tells your operating system all that it needs to know to successfully operate your printer. Driver software for all-in-one units usually also includes support for scanning and copying (and faxing in fax-capable products).

dual-cartridge inkjet

An inkjet printer that can accommodate two ink cartridges at the same time: one black and one color cartridge. Dual-cartridge printers are more expensive than single-cartridge systems, but they are faster and can automatically switch between monochrome and color.

duplex

Printing both sides of a two-sided document. Unlike a copy machine, most lower-end printers and multifunction devices with duplex capability still require you to manually feed the printed pages back into the machine in order for the second side to be printed. More expensive office printing products may have duplexing accessories that enable them to print both sides automatically.

E

encapsulated PostScript file

Usually abbreviated EPS. An EPS file is a stand-alone, self-contained PostScript file that describes the contents of a printed page, which may hold vector illustrations, images, and type. EPS files can be scaled to any size, and they are commonly exchanged by desktop publishing and graphics professionals, publishers, and printing houses. Many clip art libraries on CD-ROM and the Web offer graphics in EPS format.

enhanced capability port

Usually abbreviated as ECP. An international specification describing bidirectional communications using your PC's parallel port. ECP focuses on printers and scanners.

enhanced parallel port

Usually abbreviated as EPP. An international standard documenting bidirectional communications using your PC's parallel port. EPP focuses on peripherals other than printers and scanners.

Ethernet network

The simplest, slowest, and least expensive network design, usually well suited for a home or small office. An Ethernet network broadcasts data packets to all computers in the network simultaneously.

F

family

In the world of typesetting, a font family is a specific font and all of its derivatives: italic, bold, bold italic, small caps, strikethrough, and such. A simple font might include Times Roman, but a font family includes Times Roman, Times Roman italic, Times Roman bold, and so on.

fax forwarding

A fax machine feature that enables your machine to automatically forward any documents it receives to another fax machine. Most fax-capable multifunction units offer fax forwarding.

fax header

An informational line of text printed at the top of every page by a fax machine; it includes your full name, your station ID (the abbreviated name displayed on the fax machine during a fax transmission), and your fax number. Depending on your product, it may also include your company name and voice telephone number.

fax polling

A fax machine feature that enables your machine to automatically distribute the documents you specify to other fax machines that connect to it. Many fax-capable all-in-ones enable you to set faxes for automatic polling.

fax remote retrieval

A fax machine feature that enables you to retrieve faxes from your machine remotely. Remote retrieval works much like the remote retrieval of answering machine messages; you use the keypad to send tone commands to your fax machine. Remote retrieval is a relatively new fax feature, but it is available on some of the latest multifunction peripherals.

flatbed scanner

A scanner that uses a stationary glass bed, just like a copy machine. The document to be scanned is placed flat on the glass bed, and the scanner's optical pickup moves across the stationary document. Flatbed scanners usually provide the best scanning results, and they can scan pages from a book or magazine without tearing out the pages. Some high-end all-in-one units are based on the flatbed scanner.

font

A set of printing characters that share the same distinctive appearance. Fonts are used on your computer to display text on your monitor and print documents on your printer. A font typically includes all the alphanumeric and symbol characters for a specific language.

font cartridge

A cartridge (or, in newer printers, an internal memory card) that is plugged into a laser printer to add one or more "built-in" resident fonts; these resident fonts print much faster than fonts which must be downloaded to your printer, and they don't use any printer memory.

freeware

A program distributed free of charge by the author. Freeware is usually offered "as-is," with little or no support, but many great freeware programs, fonts, and original clip art files are offered on the Internet and computer bulletin boards. You can't beat the price!

fuser roller

One of the system of rollers inside a laser printer. The fuser roller heats the page after the toner is applied, so the toner partially melts and sticks to the page for a permanent bond.

G

GIF image

Usually carries the file extension .GIF, short for Graphics Interchange Format. The first truly universal standard format for image files, originally developed by CompuServe. Widely used on the Web, GIF files are best used for small images with limited colors. JPEG, another file format for Web publishing, is better suited for photographic images with many colors.

glyph

A structure within a font — typically, a single character or symbol. You can edit the glyphs in an existing font or create your own glyphs with a font editor.

H

hardware conflict

A situation where two adapter cards inside your PC attempt to use the same hardware IRQ settings. If one of these cards is your I/O adapter and the conflict involves your parallel port, it will likely lock your PC whenever you try to print.

Home Phoneline Networking Alliance

Usually abbreviated as HomePNA. A group of computer hardware and software manufacturers working to create a standard for home networks that use existing home telephone lines instead of network cables.

I

IEEE-1284 standard

The international design specification for a bidirectional parallel printer cable. Most late-model inkjet and laser printers do not work properly unless your printer cable meets this specification.

image editor

A program that enables you to display and edit image files from several popular formats; for example, you may resize a JPEG image from the Web or rotate a Windows BMP image. With an image editor, you can also add text to a picture, change the colors in the image, or add special effects. Paint Shop Pro, PhotoDeluxe, and Photoshop are popular image editing programs.

impact printer

A printer that uses the force of an impact through an ink ribbon to create a printed character on a page. This impact is delivered by a rotating ball or wheel (as in a daisywheel printer) or through a grid of pins (as in a dot-matrix printer). Impact printers are noisy and slow and have mostly been relegated to duties where multiple carbon forms are required.

inkjet printer

A printer or all-in-one unit that shoots fast-drying ink through tiny nozzles onto a page to form characters. The inkjet is currently the standard for personal computer printing: it's fast, cheap, relatively quiet, provides high-quality graphics, and can print in color.

input/output card

Usually abbreviated I/O card. A standard PC adapter card that typically provides two serial ports for your modem and two parallel printer ports.

interface

A connection standard for transferring data that's recognized by all PCs or Macintosh computers. For example, a parallel printer port is a common interface found on virtually all PCs for transferring data from the computer to a printer.

interrupt request

Usually abbreviated IRQ. A signal generated by an adapter card in your PC that alerts your CPU to handle incoming data from the keyboard, mouse, serial port, or parallel port. Each IRQ requires a unique channel; channels are represented by numbers. If two hardware devices try to send data to your PC using the same IRQ number, it results in a hardware conflict, and your PC may malfunction or lock up entirely.

J
JPEG file

Usually carries the file extension .JPG. The current favorite image format among Web surfers and many graphics professionals, JPEG images are highly compressed to save more space than a BMP or GIF file — at the same time, they also deliver 24-bit color (which provides over 16 million colors in an image).

L

label stock

A thick paper sheet carrying peel-off or perforated labels arranged in a regular pattern.

landscape printing

Printing where the longer length of the page runs from side to side rather than top to bottom; landscape mode is often used to print spreadsheets and larger photographs.

LANtastic

A popular network operating system used with Windows 98, Windows 3.1, and DOS and is typically sold as a complete package with cable and network interface cards.

large-format printer

An inkjet printer that's designed to handle paper sizes of 11×17 inches or larger sheets. Some large-format printers also use continuous rolls of paper 24, 36, or 54 inches across. These printers are especially designed to produce photo-quality posters, blueprints, maps, and signs.

laser printer

A printer or all-in-one unit that uses static electricity and heat to bond particles of toner to a page to create characters, the same technology used by a copy machine. Laser printers are the current standard for business correspondence, and they deliver the best black text print quality.

letter quality

An old term for a printer that produces text that looks as if it was created with a typewriter.

line connector

The jack on the back of a telephony device that is usually connected to the telephone wall jack.

local area network

Usually abbreviated as LAN. A group of computers in an office or building connected to each other by cable. A network computer can access files on other computers in the network or enable others to open and use its files. Printers, modems, and CD-ROM drives are also typically shared peripherals on a network.

M
Mac OS

The operating system used on Apple's Macintosh computers.

modular ink delivery system

Usually abbreviated as MIDS. A next-generation ink, cartridge, and print head design from Hewlett-Packard that separates the ink supply from the print heads. In an MIDS printer, the ink is stored in single-color, stationary tanks inside the body of the printer, and four print heads are used instead of one — this improves the speed and quality of the output and prolongs the life of the print heads.

MIDS also adds a special read/write memory chip and sensor to each print head, allowing these printers to alert you when the ink or print head needs changing.

monochrome printer

A printer that prints in only one color (usually black, of course). Some monochrome printers can also produce text and graphics in shades of gray as well as strict black and white.

multifunction device

Another name for an all-in-one device. Multifunction units can perform more than simple printing tasks; for example, most models can copy, and scan as well, and many can also fax. Some of these products are based on sheetfed scanners, and some are based on flatbed scanners.

N
near–letter quality

A description of advanced 9-pin and 24-pin dot-matrix printers, where the text produced by the printer was hard to distinguish from a letter-quality daisywheel printer or a typewriter.

network interface card

Usually abbreviated as NIC. An adapter card installed in a computer that enables it to connect to a network; most NICs support several different types of networks and network cabling.

network printer

A printer available for use by workstations on a network. A network printer either has its own built-in network interface card, or it's connected to a printer on the network.

O

optical character recognition

Usually abbreviated OCR. A feature found in most fax and scanning software that enables you to scan words directly off a printed page or a faxed image into your word processor.

P

page description language

A language recognized by computers and printers that defines the physical characteristics of a page, including fonts, graphics, margins, spacing, and colors. Hewlett-Packard's PCL and Adobe's PostScript are the two most common page description languages used today.

pages per minute

Usually abbreviated as PPM. A measurement of printer speed, indicating how many finished pages a printer can produce in 60 seconds. PPM speeds are typically listed for both monochrome-only and color documents.

PANTONE

A spot color matching system supported by most computer desktop publishing and graphics design software.

paper guides

Adjustable plastic dividers that help hold paper in the proper alignment in a printer's paper feed tray. These guides can be moved to fit different dimensions, such as international sizes, envelopes, or custom-sized paper.

parallel communications

A method of sending data from one computer to another over several wires simultaneously, which results in faster transfer rates. Almost all printers available today use parallel data communications.

parallel port

The common name for the printer connector on the back of a typical PC. I/O adapter cards are available that can provide your PC with up to four separate parallel ports, but most computers come with one as standard equipment.

peer-to-peer network

A simple network design that uses no file or printer servers. All workstations on the network are connected by cabling, enabling users to share files and hardware, such as printers.

peripheral

A computer term for any external hardware device you can connect or attach to your computer system (for example, a printer or an external CD-ROM drive).

personal information manager

Usually abbreviated PIM. A general information database program for personal contacts, task reminders, and scheduling, such as Microsoft Outlook or Sidekick 98 from Starfish Software.

phone chain

A line of devices all connected to the same telephone wall socket; each device
is linked using the line and phone jacks. These devices may include an internal computer faxmodem, an external computer faxmodem, a multifunction unit, an answering machine, and a standard telephone.

phone connector

The jack on the back of a telephony device that is usually connected to a standard telephone.

photo printing

Printing high-resolution images with continuous tones and at least 16 million colors. Most modern inkjet printers can print photo-quality images; older printers may require special photo cartridges in conjunction with special glossy paper.

photoconductor

A cylinder that applies toner to each page of a document inside a laser printer. Areas of the photoconductor that are struck by the printer's laser beam attract toner, which is then transferred to the paper to form text and graphics.

PhotoREt II

A technology from Hewlett-Packard that improves the appearance of high-resolution color images printed on an inkjet at any resolution, using any type of paper. The system uses an enhanced microprocessor and an ink cartridge with smaller nozzles, which enables finer control over ink application. A PhotoREt II cartridge can apply more dots and smaller ones to paper with more precision, resulting in a high-quality, high-definition image.

PhotoREt III

The latest advancement in PhotoREt technology, incorporating even smaller dots, a wider range of colors, and twice as many ink nozzles per cartridge for faster printing than PhotoREt II.

port polling

A procedure performed by Windows 98 each time you boot your computer, and each time you send a print job from an application. The operating system automatically checks your parallel port to make sure your printer is ready to receive a print job. You can turn port polling off in many cases to improve your printing speed.

print buffer

A separate, stand-alone print spooler with its own built-in memory that connects your computer and your printing hardware. The print buffer can spool print jobs, freeing up all your computer's resources for your applications.

print driver

The software that enables your operating system to properly build and format commands and data bound for your printer; in effect, a print driver tells your operating system all that it needs to know to successfully operate your printer.

print head

The component in an impact or inkjet printer that moves back and forth across the length of the printer to transfer ink to the page. In an impact printer, the print head contains a typewriter-style wheel or ball, or it may be a dot-matrix print head that uses a series of pins to transfer ink from a ribbon. In an inkjet device, the print head contains the printer's ink cartridges and the nozzles that control the flow of ink.

print quality

Today's printing hardware enables you to adjust the quality of the print; the lower the quality, the faster the print speed, and the less ink or toner you use. The higher the quality, the slower the print speed, and the better the finished results.

printer booth

A box made of fiberglass or plexiglass that encloses a printer. A printer booth is insulated to reduce noise; you open the door on the top of the booth to add paper or retrieve your printed documents.

printer command language

Usually abbreviated as PCL. The page description language developed by Hewlett-Packard for use in its laser and inkjet printers.

printer emulation

A printer emulation enables a newer printer to "act like" an older, widely used printer so it can recognize and print documents formatted for that older model.

printer server

A computer completely dedicated to supporting a network printer. The server's system RAM and hard drive are used to store print jobs in the queue, and print jobs can be reordered, paused, or deleted from the server's keyboard. Stand-alone devices (which don't require a computer) like the JetDirect line of peripherals from Hewlett-Packard can also act as printer servers.

privileges

A Windows NT feature that enables the system administrator to change the user privileges for a specific printer. Privilege settings can prevent other users from using a printer, deleting a job, or pausing the print queue.

process color

See color separation.

properties

Under Windows 95 and Windows 98, you can display the properties for most printers by right-clicking the unit's icon in the Printers folder; doing so enables you to change the configuration or default settings.

Q

queue

A sequence of documents sent to a printer to be processed sequentially (usually in the order in which they were sent by the computer). Some multiuser operating systems such as Linux and Windows NT enable you to set privileges and delete print jobs from a network queue.

R

RAM cartridge

A cartridge that can be plugged into a laser printer to add more RAM; the more RAM a laser printer has, the faster it can print larger (and more complex) documents.

random access memory

Usually abbreviated RAM. RAM built into your printer can store data from a print job temporarily until the printer is ready to print that data.

Index

Continued

Continued

hpshopping**.com**

find complete hp solutions:

- printers, scanners, & all-in-ones
- desktops, notebooks, & handheld PCs
- customized PCs
- digital cameras & printing supplies
- calculators and much more!

order online or call
1 - 8 8 8 - 9 9 9 - h p h p

- 24-hour shopping
- FedEx® shipping including
  optional next day and saturday delivery
- online order tracking
- instant online eFinancing
- rebates, coupons, and product bundles

hp

®

i n v e n t

$15 **off any hp scanjet**

After supplying shipping and billing information, go to the Checkout page and look for the "Redeem Coupon" icon. Insert coupon code **SJ4955**. Coupon expires 03/31/01. Valid while supplies last. Valid for online purchases only. Not valid for Customized PC orders or eFinance orders.

FedEx® used by permission

my2cents.idgbooks.com

Register This Book — And Win!

Visit **http://my2cents.idgbooks.com** to register this book and we'll automatically enter you in our fantastic monthly prize giveaway. It's also your opportunity to give us feedback: let us know what you thought of this book and how you would like to see other topics covered.

Discover IDG Books Online!

The IDG Books Online Web site is your online resource for tackling technology — at home and at the office. Frequently updated, the IDG Books Online Web site features exclusive software, insider information, online books, and live events!

10 Productive & Career-Enhancing Things You Can Do at www.idgbooks.com

- Nab source code for your own programming projects.

- Download software.

- Read Web exclusives: special articles and book excerpts by IDG Books Worldwide authors.

- Take advantage of resources to help you advance your career as a Novell or Microsoft professional.

- Buy IDG Books Worldwide titles or find a convenient bookstore that carries them.

- Register your book and win a prize.

- Chat live online with authors.

- Sign up for regular e-mail updates about our latest books.

- Suggest a book you'd like to read or write.

- Give us your 2¢ about our books and about our Web site.

You say you're not on the Web yet? It's easy to get started with IDG Books' *Discover the Internet*, available at local retailers everywhere.